A
LAWYER'S CASE
FOR
NETWORK MARKETING

PAMELA BARNUM

TYCHE

Tyche Publishing
www.tychepublishing.com

Ordering Information:
Quantity sales. Special discounts are available on quantity purchases by corporations, associations, and others. For details, contact the publisher at the address above.
Orders by U.S. trade bookstores and wholesalers. Please visit www.alawyerscasefornetworkmarketing.com for details.

Printed in the United States of America

Library of Congress Cataloging-in-Publication Data
Pamela Barnum

A Lawyer's Case for Network Marketing / Pamela Barnum.
p. cm.
ISBN: 978-1-54391-666-9
1. Network Marketing. 2. Quality of Work Life. 3. Entrepreneurship (Business). I. Barnum, Pamela. II. A Lawyer's Case for Network Marketing.

First Edition

14 13 12 11 10 / 10 9 8 7 6 5 4 3 2 1

ISBN: 978-1-54391-666-9

ISBN: 978-1-54391-667-6 (ebook)

For Kevin and Kaleb: My reasons why. Thank you for loving and supporting me. Without you, none of this would be possible.

CONTENTS

INTRODUCTION

"There has to be an easier way to make a living!"

T his very thought might have passed through my mind that day in 2001—had I not been busy jumping out of a speeding car driven by a drug dealer. What *did* pass through my mind was that I was making a horrible mistake, and it only took me seconds to realize this. My right shoulder, elbow, and thigh told me very clearly within an instant that jumping out of a fast-moving car onto a paved road was not one of my better ideas.

It was the middle of May and the undercover project I was working on was wrapping up. The next day was "takedown day"— the day our undercover unit rounded up and arrested all the drug dealers we'd been buying from. It was my job to coordinate one of the "rips" we had planned. A rip is pretty much what it sounds like: you rip off the drug dealer by ordering up a large quantity of drugs and then taking it without paying. On this particular day, I was going to rip a couple of drug dealers off for $250,000 worth of Ecstasy.

For the previous eight months, I had cultivated a relationship with a drug dealer named Joe. He'd sold cocaine to my partner, Kevin Barnum, and me on several occasions. (Yes. Barnum. As you can probably tell, I ended up marrying my partner when the project ended. That's a story that deserves it's own book!)

The plan was supposed to play out like this: Joe and his 'backend' (the dealer's dealer) were both supposed to get into my undercover Jeep Wrangler. Then, I was supposed to drive them and the drugs to meet *my* 'backend': another undercover police officer at a local hotel. There would be a half dozen cover officers in the area ready to arrest all of us when the deal went down. The police would get the drugs, the drug dealers would be arrested and I would be crowned a superhero. OK, not really a superhero, but I would get to continue ripping off drug dealers for another twenty-four hours until everyone was rounded up.

Notice that jumping out of a moving car was not in the plan. Trust me, when you fall, jump, roll, or whatever from a moving car, it looks nothing like it does on TV; at least, not from the perspective of the person jumping. My uncontrollable skidding along the pavement turned out to be a metaphor for so much more than the undercover project I was working on. My jumping was symbolic of what my professional life had become: micro-management, politics, assumptions, and power struggles. As I'm sure you know, these are all things we deal with in every part of our lives, both personally and professionally. Perhaps you're skidding along life's road and you don't like the direction you're headed in ... but you're also not too keen on the idea of jumping out.

Maybe the road you're on leads to a cubicle for fifty or sixty hours a week. You don't really remember which off-ramp you took that led to your current situation; but here you are, stuck in traffic listening to the Top 40 to pass the time. It's not so bad, you have air conditioning and a cup holder, what more could you ask for? You're so used to the path you're on that the very idea of change terrifies you. Better to stay on cruise control for forty years rather than risk making another wrong turn.

Maybe you are just starting on your journey. You've just finished college and you're excited about the opportunities ahead. The problem is you're looking around and you can't see any exit ramps, no fun stops, just a long straight road that never seems to end. On top of all of that, you have student loans to pay. You can't think of anything else right now.

Or maybe your road is exciting! It already has lots of turns and interesting scenery. I hope it is. I'm doubtful though, because if you were on a joy ride with two tickets to paradise you likely wouldn't be reading this book looking for an alternate route to your goals.

It's more likely that your vehicle is pretty comfortable. It may not be the vehicle of your dreams but it gets you from A to B. It's the same one most of your friends are driving. It's probably the same one you're all complaining about. You've settled for a safe vehicle that gets you to your destination safely every day. Your adrenaline rarely, if ever, pumps, and you're terrified to admit that this is not the vehicle you want to keep for forty years. You're driving a minivan but you fantasize that, "one day" you'll be sporting a Lamborghini.

Every once in awhile you head over to the Lamborghini showroom and you slide in behind the wheel, you take a selfie and fantasize about "one day." And then you get out and you settle. You settle for less than you want, less than I deserved. You settle for average.

I know a bit about settling. Not only from living in a drug culture for so many years, but also from my own mistakes. The fact is that even though I was a successful undercover investigator, and later a respected prosecutor, I settled for less than I wanted, less than what I deserved. Until recently, I thought success was a good career that ended with a lifetime benefits package and a good pension. Instead of building an income around the lifestyle I wanted, I made a lifestyle around my income and the fragments of time not eaten up by my career.

Experience tells me I'm not alone. Ask yourself the following question: "Is the life I'm living worth the price I'm paying?" In 2009 my resounding answer was no. At the time, I was working more than sixty hours a week as a prosecutor in Canada, specializing in prosecuting drug dealers. I had given up my life as an undercover officer to get married and start a family. Apparently buying drugs for a living is not a family-friendly/mom kind of job. I thought going to work in an office as a prosecutor for sixty-plus hours a week was. Turns out I was wrong about that, too. Working twelve hour days doesn't leave a lot of time for family, or anything else for that matter. I went from Breaking Bad to Breaking Busy.

Don't get me wrong, having a career is great. This isn't a book about leaving your job behind so you can become a network marketer. Becoming a network marketer has its share of challenges, too. This book is about looking at options and weighing them against what works best for you, based on the facts, not hype.

Here's the thing; it wasn't what I was doing that made the cost outweigh the benefit. It was what I had to give up in exchange for my career that eventually cost more than I was willing to pay. I gave up the best hours of the best days of my life for my job. Every day I would argue why another drug dealer should go to prison. But I felt like I was the one in prison. I was serving a life-sentence, twelve hours a day, five days a week, and sometimes on weekends. And my sentence had no end in sight. The average North American spends forty of their adult years working. People convicted of murder often serve less time than that.

The truth is, I choose my sentence. I made a conscious decision to work as hard as I did. My husband Kevin and I both chose demanding careers. We both consciously put our careers ahead of our family life. Of course, these armchair quarterback reflections are much easier to reflect on as I write this overlooking the Rocky Mountains from my comfortable home office. Reality was much too painful for us to admit at the time.

It's only been since we traded in our fill-time jobs for full-time lives that we've been able to admit the sorts of things that once seemed normal to us now seem crazy, like hiring a nanny to raise our son, or to accept paying almost half of our income in tax. We were willing to put our lives on hold for forty years until retirement, because that's what everyone else was doing. I'm not saying this is wrong, I'm just saying it wasn't for us. It's not what *we* wanted.

Even worse, we have had to admit that we'd embraced a life of mediocrity. We had always seen ourselves as risk-taking mavericks who blazed a trail. We jumped out of cars and hung out with drug dealers. Kevin still had a pretty cool job as a canine handler for the police and my job had it's moments, but we'd still settled for less than we wanted. We punched a clock, kept track of overtime hours, and had to wait our turn in the seniority line for summer holidays. We'd become what we had once mocked: people who were at the mercy of decisions made by others. Control was in the hands of our bosses, colleagues, and the system we were a part of. We decided it was time to take back control and that's how we ended up as network marketers.

When Kevin and I entered the world of network marketing, completely by chance, we saw the veil of mediocrity begin to lift. We started to meet people who wanted more, not only for themselves, but for everyone around them. Network marketing may or may not be for you—it's certainly not for everyone. I wrote this book to help you make an informed decision about it. In my eight years as a professional network marketer I have spoken to thousands of people who charted a course based on misinformation, hype, and lies. I want to help change that with the facts. No Johnny Cochran spin-doctor stuff here, just the facts. By the end of this book you'll know if the glove fits or not.

As a lawyer I learned that getting to the truth isn't about asking for answers, it's about asking the right questions. *A Lawyer's Case for Network Marketing* will take you on a journey that puts common misbeliefs about network marketing on trial. You get to be the judge *and* jury. I invite you to weigh the facts against opinion and come to a verdict that serves you.

Ladies and gentlemen of the jury, let's get started.

CHAPTER 1

OPENING ARGUMENTS

There are no secrets to success. It is the result of preparation, hard work, and learning from failure.

— Colin Powell (Former United States
National Security Advisor)

"Pyramid Pam, you're wanted in courtroom six," Mark said, snickering as he walked past me in the hallway. Mark was a shining example of the stereotypical defense lawyer: slick, opinionated, and poorly dressed. Most of his shine came from his suit and his gel-shellacked hair.

"Good one." I replied in my most dignified lawyer voice. I'd always tolerated good-natured jibes from defense counsel. That's what you do as a prosecutor, it's practically in the job description. As a police officer and lawyer; defending myself was not a new experience: police headlines and lawyer jokes. Of course, before I was Pyramid Pam I had a few other nicknames: "Narc" (undercover drug officer), Whammer (my driving technique while working undercover), Blondie (you've seen the cover of the book), and a plethora of other nicknames not appropriate for print. In the courtroom, I was referred to as "Madam Federal Crown". Today, I'm simply Pamela, Pam, or mom. I'll admit, the nickname Pyramid Pam really irritated me at first. It gave me that feeling you have when you walk out of the restroom with toilet paper stuck to your shoe, not that that's ever happened to me. Over time, however, the nickname grew on me. Honestly, as my income increased, my concern over what others thought lessened. Funny how that works.

• • •

Network marketing, put simply, is a legitimate business model that pays distributors a percentage of their organization's sales; the sales organization is known as a distributor's downline. Some people confuse network marketing with pyramid schemes, but you will soon see they have nothing of importance in common. The first time I remember hearing the term "network marketing" was on a Sunday afternoon in my driveway. Kevin and I were working outside, trying to fit a months' worth of maintenance into a few hours. Our neighbors rode by on their bikes and stopped to say hi. I noticed that my neighbor Janey was looking amazing. As a woman in my forties, I was starting to notice women who looked like they weren't ageing, and Janey was becoming one of those women. "Wow, you look great. What have you been up to?" I asked her. She told me about some products she was using and looking at her results it made me want to give them a try.

The words "I'd like to give them a try" were hardly out of my mouth when she leaned into me and said: "By the way, it's network marketing." She said it was like she was offering bootleg liquor or some other contraband. Very much on the down low. I didn't want to ask her what network marketing was because I didn't want to look like an idiot, and frankly I wasn't sure I wanted to know. After all, I had a Master's degree and a law degree; I should know what this "network marketing" thing was all about.

As we were walking up the driveway I asked Kevin as nonchalantly as I could, "What's network marketing?"

"Oh it's one of *those* things. We don't want anything to do with it. They bring flip charts into your house, fill your garage with stuff, and we'll lose all our friends. It's like a pyramid scheme." I didn't know what a pyramid scheme was but I knew it was bad because he reacted like I had just asked him to streak naked through the neighborhood on Easter Sunday.

"Wow. Janey didn't mention any of that," I said. I decided to order the products anyway, because Janey looked great. I vowed to myself not to fill the garage or join a pyramid scheme.

Fast forward and Kevin decides he wants to try some too; maybe he was considering streaking after all. Of course, I wouldn't be writing this book if we hadn't had great results from using the products Janey recommended. People started to notice that we looked and felt better, just like we had noticed that about Janey. Because of that people started to ask what we were doing, just like I asked Janey. Thousands of people and thousands of stories later and here I am presenting you with the case for network marketing.

So, is it one of "those" things that fills your garage, puts flip charts in your living room, and eliminates your friends? No. Okay, no need to read any further. Case closed. I wish it were that simple. The very term "network marketing" provokes a strong response from people on both sides of the fence. Some network marketers are almost evangelical in their praise for the business model. Shouting from the rooftops, living rooms, and social media pages that network marketing is the only answer to financial freedom. You know, the kind of hype that scares the hell out of people — constant "lifestyle" posts featuring big checks, expensive cars, and designer handbags. It can be kind of creepy.

Then there are the people on the other side of the fence, the critics. Most have little or no experience with network marketing yet they toss out labels like *pyramid*, *scam*, and *cult*. One network marketing critic who has a blog (and allegedly a PhD), reports that network marketing is responsible for many suicides, divorces, and natural disasters in the United States. No folks, I'm not making this stuff up. Others simply use the word "pyramid" as a catchall term for their ignorance.

Clearly there are crazies on both sides of the fence. But just because you feel strongly about something doesn't make you right. A belief that is not based on facts, experience, common sense, and the law is just an unfounded opinion. I like to base my beliefs on the truth, not hype. As a result, I've found that network marketing is a business model that requires skills, work, and commitment. Network marketing is not like winning the lottery, nor is it a scam. It's not the only way to achieve financial freedom, and for the majority of people it won't be.

I can also state from a legal point of view that network marketing is a legitimate and respected business model, not a pyramid scheme. For ease of reference I will be citing Canadian and American laws because that is my frame of reference. Network marketing exists in over one hundred countries on every continent, except Antarctica, and not much exists in Antarctica. Network marketing is governed by local laws and customs. If you are reading this outside of North America, many of the principles still apply, but for specific legislation regarding your country, please refer to your government's website for direction and guidance.

My experience tells me that network marketing is the perfect environment in which to see the potential greatness in people actually expressed. That is why I want to present the case for network marketing to you.

You may end up finding that network marketing is exactly what you've been looking for, like I did. Or, you may decide that it's not for you but you totally support people who decide to go for it. I believe that once you have all the facts you, like me, will be convinced that keeping your mind open to opportunities is one of the things that makes life a juicy adventure.

I am not going to present network marketing as the be-all-end-all financial freedom vehicle because it isn't. It isn't for everyone and not everyone can do it. Network marketing can be difficult. It requires a certain degree of competence and confidence. It may require shifting your belief system. It requires a thorough self-evaluation, which can sting. And it also requires you to finish something you started; not an easy task for everyone.

But, if you're determined and willing to work and follow systems, network marketing can provide a level of financial and time freedom unparalleled by most careers or small businesses.

My goal in this book is to teach you how to be a success on your own terms by keeping your mind open to possibilities. I'm going to explore many of the popular misconceptions we have about network marketing. I'm going to provide you with facts, not just opinion, about how network marketing can work for <u>almost</u> anyone.

Case Notes

- Network marketing is a legitimate business model that requires skills, commitment, and work.

- Network marketing allows people to realize their potential. However, it is not for everyone and not everyone will succeed.

- You owe it to yourself to investigate the truth before deciding whether it will work for you.

CHAPTER 2

THE INVESTIGATION

It is by doubting that we come to investigate, and
by investigating that we recognize the truth.

— Peter Abelard (French Philosopher)

"In the end we only regret the chances we didn't take. If not now, when?"

The woman at the front of the room looked around at her audience. I was sitting in the back row as far away from these people as I could get, but it felt like she was looking right at me. I turned and looked behind me but no one was there.

What had I signed up for? A night of name tags, clichés, and clapping. And don't forget about the hugging. Oh, the hugging. Complete strangers hugging me as I came into the room. I was going to kill Kevin. What had he gotten me into?

• • •

Initially, we had no intention of doing anything more than using the products my neighbor recommended. But Kevin sniffed a business opportunity and decided to look into it. He flew to Phoenix to check out the network marketing company that Janey was working with.

After a few days in Phoenix, he came home and announced: "Pamela we could make money at this!"

Kevin has always been entrepreneurial. Let's just say he's had more than one idea that didn't work out for us. So, when he got excited about this network marketing thing I began to worry. A lot.

He talked about "residual income," helping more people than we ever thought possible, and on and on. I hadn't seen him this excited since the day he lined up a ten-ounce cocaine deal during our undercover project.

"What are you on?" I asked him. I'd been afraid he'd drink the Kool-Aid on his trip, but I didn't think he'd inhale it too! My antennae were up. Anytime Kevin came home excited about an "opportunity" it usually meant risk, loss of money, and, on my part, loss of sleep. One of the many things I love about Kevin is his open mind and his "think *way* outside the box" attitude. Heck, he usually just kicks the box over and then lights it on fire. I liked this about him when we worked undercover buying drugs. That was a great place to think outside the box and take risks. It was fun, we got paid, and we were only risking life and limb, not our retirement fund. Now that we were investing our personal time and money, his "outside the box" thinking needed to be put back in the box and duct taped shut.

I did what any good and loving wife would do. I cross-examined him. As usual, Kevin didn't seem to mind. His answer was always, "check it out for yourself." To be completely transparent here, Kev was right about half the time, which by default meant I was wrong half the time. And when he was right, he was bang on and I would jump on the glory train and enjoy the results. When he was wrong ... well, let's just say being wrong was occasionally painful for him.

So "check it out" is exactly what I did. He told me about a business meeting happening in Toronto and that's where I experienced the name-tagged, stranger-hugging, clapping, loud music "business meeting". With arms and legs crossed, I sat at the back of the room to endure the two-hour meeting. But here's what happened: by the end of the two hours I had uncrossed my legs and arms and I started to listen. I listened to people who shared their product and business experiences. These were professional people, working people, stay-at-home parents, retired people, young people, every kind of people. What I found was that they all had one thing in common: a burning desire to go after their dreams instead of pretending that they couldn't have any, or didn't deserve them. These people were brave enough to stand up and declare that they wanted more and that they had decided to change their life.

Who was I to sit in judgment? Me? The fearless woman who sat in judgment of others every day as a lawyer? The woman who judged herself harshly because she worked so many hours she rarely had time for her family? Screw it. I guzzled the Kool-Aid and started high-fiving people. Because none of things I had already tried could offer me so much freedom with so little risk.

Of course, my journey consisted of more than a single network marketing meeting. Slamming back the Kool-Aid was a process. A process of personal growth, learning the skills necessary to build a business, and frankly developing the mindset that I could be a success at network marketing. I will be sharing that journey with you throughout the book.

* * *

Kevin and I had been hungry for change long before we were introduced to network marketing. We both liked our jobs and we felt a sense of accomplishment and pride around our careers. Kevin had served over twenty years as a police officer and I had almost twenty years combined policing and prosecuting. We liked our work, but we liked our family life a lot more and we weren't getting nearly enough of that time together. Our lives were becoming a game of catch-up. We spent most weekends that we weren't working getting to overdue household chores, errands, and appointments. It never felt like we had time to just relax. We missed the fun, spontaneous people we once were. Every plan we made revolved around our professional schedules. What happened to those risk-taking spontaneous crazies that loved to live life to the fullest?

The idea of getting more financial freedom, and therefore more time together, had motivated us for a long time, and before we discovered network marketing, we tried a lot of things. We went to seminars on franchising, real estate, small business ownership, and on how to invest in the markets. We attended trade shows and took courses online and in person. We read a lot of books and started connecting with people who were successful investors, business people, and entrepreneurs. Of course, all those things took time and money but we were serious about changing our future. We knew we could only work so many hours in a day and our salaries were capped because of that. We believed that there were opportunities that weren't tied to time for money. Other people were making it happen. Why not us?

Before I go deeper into network marketing, I want to save you some time and money by outlining our experiences in these areas. Maybe one of them will work for you. Perhaps you can learn from our mistakes and I won't make you high-five, hug, or dance. Unless you want to.

Real Estate

We started our quest for financial freedom with real estate. We didn't have a lot of extra money to invest but what we had was a great credit rating and jobs that made the bank feel very secure about lending us money. We purchased a small fixer-upper and put a lot of sweat equity into it. We found some tenants and thought we were pros. So, we bought another property, and then another, and then a duplex and finally a four-plex. We thought we were on our way to Real Estate Mogul heaven. It was only a matter of time before we had our own show on HGTV.

However, we quickly found out that owning investment properties is not always easy or profitable. In fact, sometimes it's downright excruciating and costly. Of course, you must do your own due diligence, and we ran into some real snags as real estate investors.

Ask any landlord: tenants are the number one problem. I could fill volumes with horror stories of vandalism, unpaid rent, and criminal activity by tenants. And it is more common than you think; just Google 'landlord horror stories' and you will have over three-million hits. I can't tell you how many times Kevin and I fantasized about breaking into one of our rental properties wearing a balaclava, carrying a baseball bat, and evicting people. This usually popped into our minds after driving by one of our properties in February with the snow driving down, minus forty weather, and the smell of pot wafting out the open windows. I could literally see the utilities I was paying for drifting out the window in plumes of pot smoke.

If you're looking for a fast turnaround on your investment, real estate may not be for you. Unlike the real estate late-night infomercials, there aren't many people buying and flipping properties from their yachts surrounded by a bevy of bikinied babes. No camera crew follows you around as you pick out tiles and paint colors that turn a dump into a palace. Even if you bought a property and had a buyer lined up for it the next day, closing the deal would still take about a month on average. Darn lawyers, they always slow things down, and they can be expensive. And how are you going to afford that yacht? When you "flip" a property you will likely pay a costly capital gains tax. Unfortunately, those late-night infomercials and real estate investment seminars in hotel ballrooms rarely tell you about the downside of real estate investing.

Given this, Kevin and I still own rental properties and for some people it works out. I've found that buying real estate and holding on to it for the long term (so temporary market setbacks do not affect you), is the best strategy. Done correctly, investing in real estate can be profitable and offers long-term residual income, if you have the skills, knowledge, finances, and can tolerate the risk.

The Stock Market

Okay, maybe based on the tenant horror stories detailed above you may be questioning my "investigative abilities." I'm going to blame those on inexperience and move on to the stock market. Like real estate, Kevin and I learned some valuable lessons about the market the hard way. We made some mistakes that hurt more than the utility and renovation bills we faced as landlords. When we started investing on our own we lost more than $50,000 overnight because we didn't educate ourselves. We've since learned and have enjoyed a small amount of growth over the past ten years. We view our investments as long-term assets not short-term investments.

Regardless of your financial IQ, investing in the market is something we recommend looking at. Like the other strategies outlined in this chapter, it is important to review the pros and cons and do your own due diligence before making major financial commitments. You don't have to talk to many people to learn that the markets can be very risky. Every day you can find news about people losing it all on Wall Street. Again, don't get me wrong, I'm not telling you avoid investing in the stock market. I invest; but with the help of a trusted financial planner. When it involves your hard-earned money, it's important to work with a professional. My portfolio has had some losses and some gains. I'm in it for the long haul and expect to see moderate gains over a long period. I like to follow Warren Buffett's advice: "Don't buy something unless you would be willing to hold on to it if the market were shut down for ten years." For a very small number of people the markets make them very wealthy. For the rest of us it's simply part of an overall financial planning strategy.

Successful investing, like successful property management, takes hard work and effort. A partially informed investor is about as effective as a partially informed surgeon; he or she will only hurt themselves and those around them.

Franchising

Over time, our investigation into financial freedom strategies naturally gravitated to going into business. We didn't know anything about starting or running our own, though, so we looked at franchising. Franchising was attractive because we were looking at businesses that already had brand recognition, training systems, and tested products or services. Wait a second, sounds a bit like network marketing, because it too offers brand recognition, training systems, and tested products or services. More on that in a bit.

Franchising emerged as a new business model in the early 1900s with Henry Ford franchising dealers for his Model T, and Rexall franchising drug stores. A franchise is a business in which the owners, or franchisors, sell the rights to their business logo, name, and model to independent operators called franchisees. This idea was so revolutionary that many criticized it, and in the 1940s and 1950s franchisors operated in a legal quicksand, unsure of whether their actions constituted violations of federal anti-trust laws. [1]

Imagine a world without your favorite franchise. Where would you get that delicious burger with the special sauce or that drive-thru latte on your morning commute? Funny how something so common today was once thought of as a scheme. From perceived scheme to financial dominator, franchising is responsible for more than three-percent of American retail sales and is thriving around the world. Keep that resistance to franchising in your mind as you read on.

We were drawn to the idea of owning a franchise and applied to purchase the mecca of all Canadian franchises: Tim Horton's. Kevin and I started fantasizing about all the money rolling in from those faithful coffee and donut addicts. Seriously, what could be more natural than a couple of cops owning a donut shop? So, we headed out on the investigative supernova highway and put our application in. We interviewed current franchisees and communicated with Tim Horton's corporate on a regular basis. We discovered that we needed $500,000 with $150,000 of that liquid cash and ready to go. Okay, that was a bit of a hiccup but we managed to scrounge and come up with the cash. Here's where things started to get stickier than a frosted chocolate dip donut; they also required a full seven-day per week 24 hours per day commitment. Wait a second, we were in this for the freedom, and the money of course. So far it looked like zero freedom and a whole lotta money tied up. But, we'd seen other people succeed with franchising so we continued with the process.

We were initially offered a location in Ohio. We were both still working full-time in Ontario, Canada and we were not ready to quit our jobs and relocate to the US to serve coffee and donuts. Don't get me wrong, I love coffee and donuts and I think Ohio is a lovely place. I just wasn't ready to completely uproot my family and give up my profession for a polyester uniform, name tag, and a deep concern over how many creams you want in your coffee.

As with anything there are no guarantees. And with franchising the location is often at the discretion of the franchisor and in the case of large chains like McDonalds and Tim Horton's the corporation owns the land and the building, you simply own the rights to that franchise. If you want to see a really cool movie about this very thing, watch *The Founder* starring Michael Keaton. It's about Ray Kroc, who turned McDonald's into the first franchise success story in America.

I don't want to dampen your franchising sprit because I still believe that franchising is a great opportunity for people who fit the model. You must be comfortable being responsible for everything that happens in your day-to-day business, and paying royalties even if you're not profiting. Franchising may work for you if you have the cash, the time, and the enthusiasm to eat, live, and breathe someone else's business vision regardless of personal risk.

Small Business Ownership

We decided to take a pass on franchising. There were too many unknowns coupled with a huge financial investment and risk. Onward and upward to a traditional business; something that was completely and utterly ours. With a start-up, you control everything, you can exercise your inner-creative genius. But controlling everything means you must also do everything.

Michael Gerber's book *The E-Myth: Why Most Businesses Don't Work and What to Do About It* is a great resource if you are determined to start your own business. When Kevin and I were first looking at it, a friend recommended this book and I'm so grateful they did. If you're not up to reading the book here's the Cliff Notes: The E-Myth (entrepreneurial myth) is the mistaken belief that most businesses are started by people with tangible business kills, when in fact most are started by "technicians" who know nothing about running a business. Hence, most businesses fail. He tells a great story about a woman who makes amazing pies and decided so start a pie shop. Long story short, she's great at making pies but knows nothing about running a business. So, Kevin and I started considering businesses that we already knew something about. We had used storage units in between moves, and we had experience with real estate so we thought storage units might fit the bill.

We jumped on a plane and flew to Vegas with our then eighteen-month old son Kaleb to attend a storage unit convention. This was long before the popular "Storage Wars" TV show hit the airwaves, which frankly may have discouraged us from this idea. Once we arrived, we started chatting with people at the convention, finding out what worked for them and what didn't work. By the end of the three-day convention, our enthusiasm had waned considerably. The upfront land and construction costs, coupled with employees, technology, and unpaid fees was more than we were willing to commit to. I think it was the stories about the storage-unit meth labs that really shut the dream down for us. As police officers, we'd seen this on more than one occasion and without much discussion we walked away from the opportunity.

We thought maybe we should look a little closer to home. Lots of people ran businesses from their homes. Even some of the lawyers I knew were running their practices from home. During the last twenty-years, large numbers of people have chosen to market their skills and talents from home. Experts predict the number of micro-businesses will continue to grow in direct response to the shrinking of traditional employment. Recent census bureau statistics show that fifty per cent of new small business enterprises are operated out of the home, and this trend is growing. Many of them are started on a part-time basis and then expand into full-time businesses as the market for their product or service develops and grows.

It's not surprising that owning your own business has a lot of appeal for people. The businesses you can start and run from your home are limited only by your imagination. Low overhead costs and minimal risk is certainly appealing; as are the tax benefits that aren't available when you're an employee building someone else's business.

However, once you start your own company you become everything to everyone. In the beginning, you're the CEO, COO, and CFO. You're the marketing department, shipping department, customer service, research and development, and all the other roles that must be filled. Your fantasy of freedom can crash down around you when you realize that you must do it all in the beginning.

On top of all of that, it's unlikely you'll receive a regular income when you first start out. For many small business owners, even making a profit in the first year can be a challenge. The thrill of the entrepreneurial roller coaster may seem exciting until you find yourself trying to hold onto your cookies to survive the ride.

Although Kevin and I didn't start a traditional business, we haven't ruled it out. We love creating and launching new ideas. Now that we have the cash flow, business experience, and time freedom from our network marketing business, starting a new business seems much more doable than it did when we were both working sixty-plus hour work weeks at our jobs. If you're considering starting your own business I would strongly encourage you to reach out and interview at least ten people who have had success in the area you are thinking about and ask them for their tips and advice. Trust me, you'll be happy you spent a little time investigating before you invest your time and money.

Staying Where You Are

Even with so many options available (real estate, investing, franchising, and small business), many people continue on the path they've always taken because it's comfortable. They already know how to do the job they're doing and putting in some extra time results in making extra money; problem solved. Staying where we are is comforting because we already know how to do our job. Maybe you've dedicated a lot of hours, or invested a lot of money gaining the experience and expertise to perform your current job and for that I congratulate you. I also dedicated a lot of time and money to becoming a lawyer, and I enjoyed my job. The problem was I was running out of hours each day and days each week to get all the things done that I wanted to do. I physically couldn't work all twenty-four hours of every day. And extra hours resulted in extra taxes and fewer hours to do the things I was really passionate about, like spending time with my family.

On top of that, I was spending more money. I had to pay for childcare, travel, and clothing that were all related to my job. It seemed like the more money I earned, the more I spent just to keep up. So many people have become comfortable living on the cliff between comfort and collapse that they don't know any other way to exist. Living pay check to pay check has become the norm for too many people, and many rely on their next pay check to cover the last month's expenses. An estimated 38 million households in the U.S. live hand-to-mouth, meaning they spend every penny of their income. The number of Americans who have no cash to fall back on is staggering: Approximately twenty-six per cent of adults have no savings set aside for emergencies, while another thirty-six per cent have yet to start saving for retirement. North of the border isn't any better: Three in ten Canadians are living pay check to pay check or spending more than they earn. One in five has less than $1000 in savings. And apparently, Canadians like to get out of the cold. The most common savings goal for Canadians[2] is to pay for a vacation, not retirement. Screw tomorrow, let's go on a sunny holiday!

The debt-to-ratio in Canada clocks in at 1.67, meaning that for every $1 earned, Canadians owe banks, credit-card companies, auto dealerships, and other lenders $1.67 in debt. In 2016, borrowing grew faster than incomes in Canada. Americans are slightly better at $1.40. Clearly the recession was too short because it didn't change our behaviors. We've all become increasingly comfortable with debt. People are spending more than they make chasing a desire to have the latest and greatest of everything. You don't have to look any further than your own neighborhood. Check out all the new cars that your neighbors are financing. Or the latest and greatest iWhatever, that you "need". You will find lineups of people waiting to finance what they can't afford and what they don't need everywhere you look. Credit is available to almost anyone anytime. We have become a generation of spenders, not savers.

However, baby boomers tend to do better when it comes to hanging on to their extra money. Adults aged fifty-five and older have a positive personal savings rate of about thirteen per cent, but that still won't be enough for almost half of them to retire with the lifestyle they had while they were working. Millennials, on the other hand, meaning adults who are thirty-five and under, have a personal savings rate of negative two per cent. Between high student loan debt and stagnating wages, saving anything at all seems impossible to many of them.

You may be thinking, "OK, I read the paper. I get it. Enough with the doom and gloom. I still don't want to be a network marketer. I have job security." I get what you're saying. Kevin and I worked for the government. We were part of the JFL club - Job for Life club. That meant we had a guaranteed income with a pension and benefits. Or so we thought. At the time of writing this, government cutbacks were affecting the public servants Kevin and I once worked alongside of.

Most people will agree that gone are the days of guaranteed pensions and benefits. Experts predict that more changes are in store for us and that increasing the age of retirement and cutting government benefits is just the beginning. Don't take my word for it, research it yourself. A great place to begin your search is on your country's census website. Or look around your workplace, neighborhood, community, and country. Are you seeing exponential growth, or cutbacks? The times they are a changin'. Here's the thing, "job for life" has another name and that's Unicorn; if you actually find one, throw a saddle on it and ride to the end of the rainbow to collect your pot of gold.

Sadly, people are working longer and retiring with less money than their parents did. Today we should rely on our financial knowledge and ourselves if we want real security. There is a greater risk in being an employee than in minding your own business and investments. We need to take our thinking from the industrial age mentality of time for money, and exchange it for a new way of thinking, one that gives us one hundred per cent control ... *and* responsibility. Because job security is a myth. Governments and corporations are laying off employees in the thousands. The average employee tenure is under five years and for millennials it's under three years. [3] Long gone are the days of starting and finishing your career with the same company. For many of you reading this, your financial future is directly linked to the success of your employer. You do not have any control. You may have comfort, but you do not have control.

The truth is, when it comes to employment there are no guarantees. In most cases, an employer will pay employees just enough so they don't quit. Consequently, employees will work just hard enough to make sure they don't get fired. Think about your own situation. Are you passionate about your current career? Would you show up to work for less money? Let's suppose you love your job and you'd keep working at it no matter what. But what about the stress that comes from multitasking and trying to manage it all? For many, it traps them in endless burnout.

That burnout means we're tired, impatient, unable to lose fat, get sick more often, and have a lack of energy that makes even basic tasks impossible. We don't recognize ourselves anymore. What happened to that happy, fun, spontaneous person you once saw in the mirror? Perhaps they've disappeared because the time left over after commuting, answering emails, running errands, and completing chores leaves little left for rest, recovery, and fun. Unless you count the time spent on the sofa in a Netflix-induced coma sipping soda and munching on salt and sugar to forget about it all.

But we deserve those Netflix binges. We work hard. The average professional works more than fifty hours per week. A recent article in the *Wall Street Journal* stated that many professionals see a forty-hour workweek as part-time and "career suicide". I know I did. I looked down on the people who just put in their 9 to 5 hours and actually took lunch and breaks. What?! Where was the dedication? Like many people, I prided myself on working extra hours to show my commitment to the cause. Or maybe it was to prove something. I convinced myself that spending less time working meant I was a slacker. I've since worked through those issues.

Maybe you are spending some time thinking about this too. You have the time because you're spending an hour commuting to work, each way. That gives you approximately four-hundred-eighty hours a year commuting (based on working forty-eight weeks per year). That's twelve forty-hour workweeks spent in the car, on top of the forty to fifty hours you spend at work. You really love your job. And why wouldn't you? In today's economy just having a job is viewed as a luxury. Getting a raise or getting a promotion is like winning the lottery. Have you ever dreamt about winning the lottery? Maybe you fantasize about dream vacations, or having the time and money to travel wherever, whenever you want. You deserve it, so why shouldn't you think about it? But traditional businesses and government employers do not encourage us to have big dreams. They operate better if we have modest dreams: a brief summer vacation or a hobby to enjoy, that kind of thing.

As an employee, you must work for around forty years until you can retire if you start working in your early twenties and retire in your six-ties. As a result, we've morphed into the forty-forty-forty plan. It works something like this: you work forty hours per week for forty years and then retire with forty-percent of your income (the average pension plan). Sounds good, right? Just imagine what you could accomplish living on for-ty-percent of your current income.

Let's not worry about that right now, it's a long time away. Let's look at the here and now. Do you feel stressed on Sunday nights as you prepare for your upcoming work week? Do you look forward to Fridays and find your-self posting TGIF posts on your social media sites? Do you look at long weekends like they are gifts from the gods? Even though I liked my job, I suffered from the effects of stress, and I found that as the days grew longer, my patience grew shorter. I had chronic headaches, high blood pressure, and I found sleeping through the night almost impossible. It would take all of Friday night and most of Saturday to start to relax. Then I'd start stress-ing again Sunday night thinking about all the things that were waiting on my desk Monday morning.

Remaining in your current profession without change allows for pre-dictability and routine, which is a great fit for people who desire a sense of security (either real or perceived). But here's where things get tricky. Even if you're not at risk to lose your job, because you're one of the few lucky ones working for a unicorn company that will never downsize or outsource, you may still be at risk of stress-related diseases and illnesses.

Every week, 95 million Americans suffer some kind of stress-related symptom for which they take medication. In 2010, twenty-five per cent of adult Canadians surveyed by Statistics Canada reported that most days are 'extremely stressful' at work. According to the American Psychological Association, in 2011, thirty-six per cent of employees reported that during a typical workday they felt very stressed. Stress carries several negative health consequences, including heart disease, stroke, high blood pressure, as well as immune and circulatory complications. Boil down the findings and the message is clear: even if you love your job, you are likely to have stress; chronic stress that interferes with your ability to function normally over an extended period. It's becoming a public health crisis.

If you take an honest look at how you're feeling, right now, how would you describe yourself? Vibrant, energized, ready to take on the world? Or are you tired, impatient, prone to headaches, weight gain, and a list of other stress-related symptoms? Sixty-seven per cent of North Americans think about quitting their job on a daily basis.[4] On a daily basis! Can you imagine that? Every day you go to work and every day you think "If only I could just quit this job." Maybe that's why songs like Johnny Paycheck's "Take This Job and Shove It" are so iconic. *Take this job and shove it. I ain't workin here no more.* Thank me later when you can't get this song out of your head.

More people than ever before are realizing that there is something better. Seventy-two per cent of Americans would rather work for themselves than someone else. By 2020, more than forty per cent of the American workforce—or sixty-million people—will be freelancers, contractors and temp workers according to a study conducted by Intuit, a business software company. The entrepreneur business model will play a major role in the future workplace. The report also says that the number of small and personal businesses in the U.S. alone will increase by more than seven-million, and that full-time benefit jobs will be harder to find by 2020. Most of these businesses will be web or mobile-based and will work closely with a global workforce.[5] It's a good thing that so many are embracing the entrepreneurial spirit because nearly half of all jobs are at risk of being automated within the next two decades.[6] Specifically, the average-wage, middle-skill routine worker. Jobs in the manufacturing industry are being hit particularly hard.

If the time away from home, job uncertainty, and stress weren't enough; think of the dreaded three-letter word: T-A-X. Employees pay higher taxes than self-employed or business owners because they do not have the same deductions available to them. Take a look at your last T4 (Canada) or W2 (United States). Kevin and I paid 46.8% in income tax the last year we worked for the government. We both earned over $100,000 in income and were taxed at the highest personal rate. I don't want to stress you out about taxes, but they're like death, a certainty.

I realize that you may be one of the many people who are content with being an employee and have no desire to change that. A steady paycheck is very comforting because it allows you to base your financial choices, holidays, housing, and the education of your kids on your weekly take-home pay. Some people love their job and wouldn't give it up for any amount of money. If that's you: congratulations! However, now would be a good time to gift this book to someone who is looking for more. But I'm guessing that if you've made it this far, you're open to checking out some other options. So, let's get started on the details.

The strategies I've told you about can create the opportunity to receive a great ROI (return on investment). Investing in real estate, the market, your own business, and even working overtime, all create some sort of return on investment. However, the rest of this book is dedicated to increasing your ROI and your ROE (return on effort) with network marketing.

• • •

No matter what your profession is, there is no security in settling for less than you want. And the question remains: if you continue down the path you're on will you reach your goals? Will you be living the life you want in one year, five years, ten years, forty years? Or will you be humming along to the words of some regret-filled ballad? Whatever you decide, I want to caution you to do your research before you dive into what comes next. The time and effort you put in to researching now will pay off in the long-run and may save you thousands of dollars and hundreds of hours in wasted time. And maybe, just maybe, you'll find something worth clapping and high-fiving strangers for.

Case Notes

- There are many ways to earn an additional income. I investigated several before deciding on network marketing.

- Real estate can be a great investment. However, you may have to overcome problematic tenants, capital gains tax, and expensive upfront costs.

- For a very small number of people, investing in the stock market results in incredible wealth. For most, it's part of an overall financial planning strategy that requires skill and a tolerance for risk.

- Franchising is a good option for entry level entrepreneurs who are looking for success systems already in place. However, franchises often come with costly upfront expenses that keep it out of reach for most people.

- Small business ownership can be an exciting venture. You can exercise your creative genius and launch something that is your very own. It often requires that you dedicate most of your time and money, and success is far from guaranteed.

- Working extra hours at your current job is the option exercised by most people. It allows you to do more of what you're already doing. It doesn't require additional skills, just additional time.

CHAPTER 3
THE ACCUSED

The people who know the least about
you always have the most to say.

— Unknown

"I don't even know how to bake," I said.

"You don't have to know how to bake!" Patti stood beside my desk, talking in a half-confidential voice. It was 1997, and she was the only woman in the drug unit. "You just come as my guest and say you want in. Look, you said you want to work undercover, so here's your chance! And it'll be easy. Come on. I need a new Muffin Club member for my case."

I was still working as a uniformed officer at the time but I was very interested in working undercover in the drug enforcement section. I knew that I would have to pay my dues to become an undercover officer but I thought it would be more Charlies Angels and less Martha Stewart.

The Muffin Club—yes, that's what it was really called—was a Ponzi scheme. Most Ponzi and pyramid schemes work the same way: they pay off old investors with the money from new investors. Both schemes are seductive because they promise a high rate of return in a short period with little or no work, a version of the something-for-nothing promised on late night infomercials.

To be a part of the Muffin Club you had to give a "gift" of $5000 cash which was brought to the meeting in a muffin tin. Then you invited friends to join the club and gift their $5000. When new people joined the club, you moved up a spot on the list. When your reached the top, you walked away with your "gift" of $40,000, or eight times the money paid into the club. Once you had your 'muffins' aka $40k, the remaining muffin ladies moved up a space on the list and waited their turn to be crowned Muffin Queen. I can't recall exactly what they called her but I called her the Muffin Queen.

The lead muffin lady, who was hoping to be crowned Queen, explained to us new muffinettes that if you gave the money in a muffin tin as a "gift" no crime was committed. An added bonus was that you did not have to pay tax on that money because it was a gift. This suburban home-maker was so convincing while she offered a smorgasbord of fraud, tax-evasion, and muffins. It was like a James Bond movie starring Julia Child.

"Sounds good to me." I said as I sat cross-legged on a floral sofa that looked a lot like my grandma's. This was not what I expected my first undercover job to be like. I thought we'd be sitting around cocaine and scales in a condemned high-rise, not sipping tea and admiring muffin tins in suburbia. Now don't get me wrong, these were nice ladies; they looked and acted like they would be baking actual muffins and donating them to charity. But they all had that *something-for-nothing* mentality that attracts people to pyramid schemes. I want to share a little bit of legal advice with you: If it sounds too good to be true, it likely is.

When I first started considering network marketing I thought the same thing about it: It seemed too easy to be legitimate. How could ordinary people be making extraordinary money? They didn't have exceptional business skills or an MBA, so it must be a scam. The hype and hoopla splashed over social media was too much to handle. Big checks, fancy cars, and "working" from the beach? Come on, you're either at the beach, or you're working. And who other than Jackie Moon cashes those big checks anyway? Maybe you've felt the same way so you didn't bother to investigate any further. Your skeptical Spidey senses told you to stay away and that's exactly what you did.

I was very skeptical until I put my policing and legal skill set to work. I had to find out the truth behind this network marketing pyramid thing everyone was talking about. So, I went right to the source materials: government websites, including the US Federal Trade Commission (FTC) and the Canadian Competition Bureau, as well as consumer protection agencies. Although there are some variances between countries, the essence of the laws are very similar.

Essentially, legitimate network marketing companies have real products or services that they sell to real people and the distributors are paid on multiple levels, hence the name. At the core of the business model is the premise that commissions are paid for actual sales of real products or services to real people, not for recruiting people into the plan [1]. A pyramid scheme, on the other hand, involves making money from recruiting people, like the muffin club, not from retailing real products or services to customers, like other legitimate businesses.

Per the FTC:

If the money you make is based on the number of people you recruit and your sales to them, it's not. It's a pyramid scheme. Pyramid schemes are illegal. [2]

In other words, if you're just recruiting people to become distributors and you're only selling products to other distributors, not to any retail customers, it is a pyramid scheme. Real customers are a very important part of network marketing. There are several FTC staff advisory papers, legal dicta (a fancy legal term meaning a statement of opinion considered authoritative, not binding) and factums (written legal arguments) that try to define what a customer is as they relate to network marketing. Although there is no legal definition of customer in network marketing, it is inferred from these sources that a customer is a real person, an end-user, that buys the product or service regardless of the compensation plan. In other words, a customer is someone who buys the product or service because they want it, not because they want to participate in a compensation plan. Legally, network marketing companies are required to generate significant revenue from customers outside of the compensation plan. Most companies have a large customer base of eighty-percent or more.

Here's an example to clarify this point. Let's imagine a network marketing company, called Acme Water and they sell amazing bottled tap water. Distributors can buy the water for $100 per unit and can then retail it for $120, earning a $20 profit. Sounds great, right? Not so fast, Serpico. Clearly, there would be little to zero demand for expensive tap water and people who are not a part of the business would not buy the water. As a result, Acme distributors would be forced to focus on finding other distributors and encourage them to buy the over-priced tap water, and then encourage them to find people to do the same. This would be a pyramid scheme because the end-game is to recruit, not to sell viable products.

Many pyramid schemes operate under the guise of gift-giving, or investing to con people, like the Muffin ladies. Some unscrupulous fraudsters have created network marketing companies to mask their pyramid schemes. These companies have a sham product or service with no independent value or they are sold at an inflated cost. The money is made from recruiting others, not from selling products or services demanded by the marketplace.

So yes, some network marketing opportunities are pyramid schemes in disguise. Just like some investment opportunities are Ponzi schemes. Just like some stock market and real estate deals are fraudulent scams. Unethical people will take any legitimate business and twist it to serve their criminal purpose, but that doesn't make the business model fraudulent. Imagine if all investments were considered Ponzi schemes after Bernie Madoff was convicted of orchestrating the biggest fraud in US history. Madoff was a well-respected financier who convinced thousands of investors to hand over their savings, falsely promising a profitable rate of return. Madoff managed to fly under the radar, despite complaints to the SEC, because he was a respected and active investor. Like anything in life, some things are legitimate and others are not. The important thing is to understand and know the difference before you get involved.

What about those network marketing companies that charge membership fees, surely they must be pyramid schemes? Why should you have to pay a membership? That sounds fishy. But think about Costco, or the membership fee that my favorite furniture store, Restoration Hardware, charges. It's quite common to pay a membership fee that entitles you to purchase products at wholesale or discounted prices. Most network marketing companies charge a membership fee that allows people to purchase a product or service at a discounted or wholesale price. This is completely legal and common in many businesses.

The FTC has regulatory authority over many U.S. business activities, including network marketing. The FTC has been instrumental in determining the business standards used by legitimate network marketing companies. Anti-pyramid laws and statutes are very broad in nature so that they can cover all the possible variations of illegitimate schemes that people come up with. What legislator could have ever imagined a "Muffin Club"?

The most often cited definition of a "pyramid" scheme is found in the FTC's decision, *In the Matter of Koscot Interplanetary, Inc.* [3]. The FTC's decision in *Koscot* provided a broad definition of unlawful pyramid schemes; the basic test was that a pyramid rewards recruiting alone "unrelated to the sale of product to ultimate users" through headhunting fees and inventory loading. Inventory loading happens when a distributor (salesperson) is encouraged to stock up on products they don't need to meet sales goals or bonuses.

There is currently no federal statute in America that clearly defines a pyramid scheme. However, decisions made by the FTC and Federal Courts have provided guidance that can be challenging to interpret because they are often case-specific, meaning the decision they make applies to the specific company they are dealing with and don't apply to every network marketing company. The 2016 cases involving Vemma and Herbablife illustrated this. To make things even more complicated, the decisions made by the FTC can be overly broad in scope making it difficult for network marketing companies and distributors to know what is clearly permitted and what is not.

To provide clearer guidance and continuity, US Congresswoman Marsha Blackburn sponsored a bill H.R. 5230 – 114th Congress (2015-2016) to prohibit pyramid schemes. In that bill, the term *"pyramid promotional scheme" means a plan or operation by which a person gives consideration to a participant for the right to receive compensation that is derived primarily from a participant's introduction of another person into the plan or operation rather than from the sale of products to ultimate users.* Essentially this bill is legislating that network marketing companies cannot pay to recruit. At the time of writing this book, the bill had not yet been passed into law.

Canada does have federal legislation dealing with pyramid schemes. Paragraph 55.1(1)(a) of the Competition Act defines *"a scheme of pyramid selling as those situations in which participants give consideration, including cash or any other benefit, to join an MLM* (multilevel marketing, also known as network marketing) *plan, and in turn have the right to receive consideration when others are recruited into the MLM plan. The terms "recruitment bonuses" and "head-hunting fees" are often used to refer to such situations."*

In Canada, the Competition Bureau is an independent law enforcement agency that is responsible for the administration and enforcement of the *Competition Act.* The Competition Bureau can refer criminal matters to the Director of Public Prosecution Service of Canada (my old boss) who then decides if they should prosecute. Of course, I'm sure you can appreciate that when I first became involved in network marketing I conducted prosecutions on behalf of the Federal Crown for the Public Prosecution service of Canada. Although I primarily dealt with laws relating to drug dealers, I also had familiarity with relevant fraud sections. I wasn't dealing with the Wolf of Wall Street, but I did prosecute some drug dealing fraudsters that didn't get movie deals. After reading countless cases, regulations, and papers on pyramid schemes, I was comfortable with my decision to become a network marketer. I understood what illegal pyramids were and how they differed from legitimate network marketing companies. The added upside was I didn't have to attend anymore muffin lady parties.

Let me say it again, legitimate network marketing is not a pyramid scheme. It is a legislated business model based on providing people with real products they need and want at a fair price. Not only do I know this, so do millions of others. There are currently more than 100 million people worldwide involved in direct sales or network marketing, either as a distributor or as a customer. [4] Chances are you've either bought a product or service from a network marketing company, or you know someone who has.

The more I learn about network marketing the more my confidence grows. Over time, network marketing has become one of the most scrutinized and litigated business models in existence. In fact, network marketing has been met with punitive measures unheard of in any other industry. A recent example involved the FTC successfully obtaining a temporary restraining order which temporarily shut down Vemma, a network marketing company. The FTC froze Vemma's assets and placed the company under the control of a court-appointed receiver. This was before Vemma was found guilty of anything. This punitive action was based on charges filed by the FTC that had yet to be proven in a court of law. Yes folks, that's right, guilty until proven innocent. Not only that, punished before proven guilty. A month later, the Court recognized that there was consumer demand for Vemma's products and a rationale for allowing the business to continue so the Court removed the receiver, unfroze the assets, and allowed the company to reopen during the pendency of a trial, but under significant restraints and under the watch of a federal monitor. [5] In September 2016, Vemma and the FTC reached an agreement where Vemma paid a fine and forfeited some real estate and business assets.

Another network marketing company, Herbalife, was also accused of being a pyramid scheme in 2012 by William Ackman, CEO of Pershing Square Capital Management hedge fund firm. Mr. Ackman had a long-standing and very public short position on Herbalife. During this time, he hired lobbyists to alert community groups of the alleged dangers of Herbalife. He set up websites, took out ads, posted notices, and set-up a 1-800 number to warn people about Herbalife. According to the *New York Times*, "Mr. Ackman's staff acknowledges that this crusade is really rooted in one goal: finding a way to undermine public confidence in Herbalife so that his $1 billion bet will produce an equally enormous return"[6]. To date, that has not happened. The FTC ruled that Herbalife is not a pyramid.

However, the FTC did order Herbalife to pay a $200 million dollar fine. Many elements of the settlement are intended to be punitive to Herbalife, meaning that they do necessarily apply to all network marketing companies. Even though the ruling does not apply to network marketing the writing is on the wall: if companies appear to be making deceptive claims about the business opportunity, they need to make some immediate changes to their marketing. Because Herbalife is a giant in the network marketing profession, it is important that we pay close attention to the potential regulatory trends that could arise from the FTC settlement.

At the Direct Selling Association (DSA) Business & Policy Conference in Washington DC in October 2016, FTC Chairwoman Ramirez complimented the DSA's self-regulation and acknowledged that it was a step in the right direction, but that there is still room for improvement. Chairwoman Ramirez stated that the network marketing profession needs to eliminate misleading income and product representations. Of course, network marketing companies and distributors are not the only ones who need to stop the exaggerated claims. Complaints have been filed against many well-known companies like Walmart, McDonalds, and Ford, to name a few. Visit www.consumeraffairs.com and type in your favorite company's name and you will most likely find hundreds of complaints. I'm not trying to make excuses for network marketing companies, just the opposite: if they have done something illegal or unethical they should pay for that. I'm simply pointing out that even well-known traditional businesses receive complaints. However, the government doesn't shut them down, freeze their assets, and appoint a receiver to liquidate the company when a complaint is lodged.

Have you ever heard of the Ford Pinto? The Pinto was a front-engine, rear-drive subcompact car marketed by Ford between the years 1971-1980. When I was around eight years old I remember my uncle being involved in a very serious automobile accident while he was driving a Pinto. I was at my aunt and uncle's house playing with my cousins when my uncle stumbled into the house covered in blood. He looked like he had just come from the prom with Carrie.

"Well, Judy, the car's gone," Uncle Brian gasped in the foyer of their house.

"Where did it go?" Aunt Judy asked, not even acknowledging the blood on his suit.

At the time this did not seem strange to me that the car was gone and my aunt wanted to know where it was. Maybe it didn't seem strange to her that her husband showed up home early from work covered in blood. Aunt Judy was a practical woman who could plainly see that a) her husband was alive and could still walk and talk, and b) he did not have a car with which to drive himself to work the next day.

We later learned that Uncle Brian was very lucky to walk away from the accident. Years later, when I was in law school, I heard about the Ford Pinto again; this time in my ethics class. The Ford Pinto was known to have a defective fuel system that resulted in injuries and fatalities. Ford knew that the car had an unsafe tank placement and didn't change the design because of an internal cost benefit analysis. Essentially, it was cheaper to pay the lawsuits than change the design. The design changes would have cost Ford $137 million dollars. The changes were estimated to save 180 burn deaths and serious injuries per year. However, not changing the flawed design would only cost an estimated $49 million dollars in lawsuit payouts saving Ford approximately $88 million dollars. The dilemma became: save lives or save money. They opted to save money. Ford was indicted on criminal charges of reckless homicide in 1980, the first time a corporation faced criminal charges for a defective product, and the first time a corporation was charged with murder. But Ford was never shut down, their assets were never frozen and they continued, business as usual.

One possible explanation for the microscopic scrutiny that network marketers face is that they are easy targets because they are everyday people, not professional marketers, salespeople, or corporations which traditionally enjoy greater protections. Generally, the people who are the voice of network marketing companies have little to no training and often don't understand compliance policies. I'm not defending pyramid schemes. I despise them. They take advantage of innocent people and have left a trail of destruction that goes beyond money. I am relieved that the FTC monitors companies and is driven to protect consumers. However, legitimate network marketing companies are often unfairly lumped into the same basket as pyramid schemes and that is not only unfair, it's illogical and it's bad commerce. Regulators should be vigilant in protecting consumers from pyramid schemes, and network marketing companies have faced extra scrutiny and penalties unheard of in other industries to ensure the public *is* protected.

To prevent deception, there are laws in place to restrict network marketers from making claims about the income that is, or may be, earned with the compensation plan. Essentially, the law around making income claims is that whoever is making the claim, the company or the distributor, must be able to prove the claims based on what the average distributor earns. That means that network marketers should not post pictures or words that imply that their high-income lifestyle can be achieved by everyone who joins them. Maybe you've seen the photos on Instagram of network marketers sitting in their Rolls Royce's or with their Louis Vuitton bags strategically placed in the picture. Or the "look at my rock star lifestyle" post on

Facebook. Sure, it may be true, but if the picture or story implies that joining them means you will have that too, it's misleading and inappropriate.

Because let's face it, most people don't earn a six-figure income in network marketing. Just like most athletes don't make it to the pros, and most lawyers never become judges. You don't automatically go from point A to point Z with no work, effort, or experience. There is a lot of hard work and skill required to achieve any result and implying otherwise is disingenuous.

Don't get too hung up on this because reputable companies have compliance departments that provide their distributors with guidance that discourages this kind of exaggeration. It's also important to keep in mind that these rules don't only apply to network marketing companies, they apply to all businesses. Whether it's a big box store, global brand, or your local merchant, companies are liable for false or deceptive endorsements or testimonials. For example, in 2016 the FTC filed a lawsuit against Volkswagen for claiming their cars were "clean diesel" vehicles. In 2015 an investigation exposed that VW had been cheating emissions tests on its diesel cars in the US for the past seven years. Thus, VW was ordered to provide up to $10 billion to owners and lessees of VW diesel cars that it claimed had low levels of harmful emissions. In the meantime, VW still operated status quo. They were not shut down, assets were not seized, and media smear campaigns against the entire car industry were not undertaken.

I found countless examples of false advertising but there was one that stood out. The maker of a penis enlargement pill, ExtenZe, agreed to pay $6 million to settle a class action lawsuit in 2010. ExtenZe had claimed that its pills were "scientifically proven to increase the size of a certain part of the male body" on late night TV commercials featuring former NFL coach Jimmy Johnson. In the commercial Jimmy claims the pill worked for him and that consumers should "Go long with ExtenZe".[7] I'm trying to drive home the point that even companies using professional marketing teams and famous athletes sometimes exaggerate and hype up products to the point of ridiculous.

Network marketing is a retail channel used by top global brands who offer all types of goods and services, including jewelry, cookware, nutritional products, cosmetics, housewares, wine, clothing, skincare, energy, insurance, and much more. However, network marketing differs from traditional retail in an important way. Network marketing offers ordinary people an opportunity to build a business with low start-up costs, limited overhead, and a blueprint for success.

Network marketers work on their own, but partner with a company that provides the products or services to the customer. The company handles the research and development, regulatory compliance, packaging, shipping, customer service, and more. Much like a franchise does. That leaves entrepreneurs like me the time to connect with people and forge personal relationships with customers. It allows entrepreneurs to do what they do best, serve their market with products or services in demand.

The way we buy products and services is rapidly changing. Uber is the world's largest taxi company and it does not own any vehicles. Facebook is the world's most popular media owner and it does not create original content. Alibaba is the world's most valuable retailer, and it does not have any inventory. And Airbnb is the world's largest accommodation provider and it does not own any real estate.

Because network marketing is an online business, it continues to grow along with the online shopping trend. According to Pew Research, eight in ten Americans are now shopping online. Amazon is one of the world's largest retailers and is forecasted to be worth more than Walmart, Costco, and Target combined. You don't have to look far to find a mall or shopping center that sits vacant and experts predict that malls will continue to decline over the next decade.

As a result, in this age of social media, network marketing is a go-to strategy that, for many companies and product lines, is more effective than traditional advertising or securing premium shelf space in retail stores. Especially when the stats show that people are 84% more likely to make a purchase when they are referred by a friend. [8] Think about the last purchase you made. Was it based on a friends' recommendation, either in person or on social media? I often use social media to ask for recommendations. Recently I was looking to replace our coffee maker. I posted on Facebook asking for recommendations and received dozens of replies. I loved that people were giving me their recommendations based on personal experience and that I didn't have to trust my decision to marketing spin doctors who've never even used what they were endorsing.

According to Nielsen's 2013 *Trust In Advertising* report, word-of-mouth recommendations from friends and family, often referred to as "earned advertising," is the most influential decision-making factor for people in making a purchase. The report included surveys of global respondents across fifty-eight countries. Word of mouth recommendations are universally more effective than traditional advertising and network marketing is built around word of mouth recommendations. Think about a product or service you are passionate about, I bet you can't keep quiet about it. Maybe it's your new car, a great realtor, or a special vacation spot, you want to tell everyone how much you like it. You're like a proud new parent or a vegan CrossFit blogger, you are loud and proud in your devotion.

But it's not just ordinary people like us who see the value in network marketing. Successful investors like Sir Richard Branson, Warren Buffet, and Carl Icahn support the business model. Respected business owners and best-selling authors Les Brown, Robert Kiyosaki, Jack Canfield, Tony Robbins, and John C. Maxwell all recommend network marketing. Politicians on both sides of the fence support network marketing. Former President Bill Clinton, President Donald Trump, and former Secretary of State Madeline Albright are all supporters of network marketing. But why listen to people who have made billions of dollars in business, written best-selling books, or have been the leader of the free world when you can listen to your cynical neighbor or disgruntled brother-in-law who's telling you network marketing is a pyramid scheme. I prefer to take advice only from people I'd be willing to trade places with, or at the very least are incredibly successful.

Don't take my word for it: reach out to one of the millions of people who are a part of the network marketing profession. Network marketing is part of the fabric of America, touching one in every seven household's in America.[9] When you look at professional sporting franchises, the NHL earns $3.7 billion and the NFL $8.8 billion. Worldwide music sales earn approximately $67 billion, and worldwide movie sales are $34 billion. Network marketing dwarfs all of those combined and is making a huge impact on global commerce by employing thousands of people and contributing billions of dollars to the global economy.

If you are still not convinced that network marketing is a legitimate business model I encourage you to do your own research. Not by reading blogs or simply searching Google online (where anyone can write anything), but by reading real government regulations and transcripts of cases involving network marketing companies, and by interviewing people who are professional network marketers. That is what I have done with this book. Now, let's get into some of the fun stuff!

Case Notes

- Network marketing is a legitimate business model that involves retailing real products or services to real customers.

- Network marketing distributors are paid commissions on multiple levels of sales within their organizations.

- A pyramid scheme, on the other hand, involves making money from recruiting people into the business opportunity

- The FTC has regulatory authority over many US business activities, including network marketing.

- Network marketing sales dwarf professional sports, the music industry, and the movie industry – combined.

- The network marketing industry is endorsed by millions of distributors worldwide and by successful business people like Sir Richard Branson and Warren Buffet.

CHAPTER 4

ADDICTED TO AVERAGE

There is only one thing that makes a dream impossible to achieve: the fear of failure.

— Paulo Coelho, *The Alchemist*

I consider myself a risk-taker. I've jumped out of airplanes and moving cars. I've dealt with drug dealers and bikers. I've performed high-risk takedowns and executed search warrants. I've even been a passenger on the back of a moped in Saigon, without a helmet! I was badass. Kicking in doors and taking names, literally. My friends and family thought hanging around with drug dealers and other criminals on a daily basis was normal. They never questioned my judgment when I shared stories about being locked in an apartment with crack dealers or hiding guns in the cars I drove. We were like any other family at holiday gatherings, "Kevin show my cousin that rib of yours that sticks out from the time those guys jumped you and threw you down three flights of stairs. Oh, and can you please pass the gravy."

Because Kevin and I both spent eight years working undercover, we were never short of good stories to share. When the conversation dragged on about the weather or grandma's cat, we would tell a work story to liven things up. It wasn't until we announced that we were both quitting our jobs because we had replaced our incomes with our network marketing business that they began to worry about us. Once the announcement was made

I could see that the intervention plans were underway: "Set up the chairs and call in the therapist. They've lost their minds!"

"What about Kaleb?" everyone wanted to know, "How will you support yourselves?" "You went to school for so long. Why do you want to throw all of your hard work out the window?" Their unsaid question was really "What will people think?"

Kevin and I have done a lot of risky things in our lives, like the time we ate unusual looking fish hanging in a tree on a deserted Mexican beach with a homeless surfer. Or, the time we vacationed in Pakistan a few days after the assassination of Benazir Bhutto. "Don't stand in one place too long," our driver urged. Then a car bomb exploded a block away. I digress. Needless to say, Kevin and I are not risk-averse. However, we would never risk our son's future. I think our families knew that, but they were concerned nonetheless. Quitting your job for the unknown was way outside of their comfort zone. Education, good jobs, pensions: that was within their comfort zone. Any deviation from this was dumbass, not badass.

The truth is we were taking a huge risk staying where we were. Yes, we had good-paying careers and a comfortable lifestyle. We drove nice vehicles, and lived in a beautiful home. We had wonderful things, but we'd stopped growing. We'd lost the tension between where we were and where we could have been. We had settled for life in the comfort zone: steady pay checks, a mortgage in the suburbs, and two-week annual vacations. We were doing the same things with the same people and getting the same results. We had chosen comfort over possibility. There is nothing wrong with any of that; we just knew that we were meant to do more. We were intended to live full out.

However, living full out meant we had to break out of the fear-based society that makes up what most call the real world. When you live in the real world, taking a leap of faith might be labelled foolish, irresponsible, or even selfish. Hold the phone, you may be saying; "I live in the *real world*. That's what you do in the real world, you go to school, get a job, start a family, and retire to Boca Raton or Elliott Lake. Dreams and goals aren't going to pay my bills or feed my retirement fund. And by the way, I don't have time for all of this. I have enough to do. I'm crazy busy. This network marketing thing you speak of is for people who have time on their hands." Don't worry young Jedi, I'm not telling you to quit your job and become a network marketer because it's not a good idea for everyone. What I'm asking you to do is take a look at your real world, and decide if what you're currently doing is working for you.

Look, there's nothing wrong with the forty-forty-forty plan (work forty hours a week for forty years and retire on a pension of forty per cent of your income) if that's what you want. However, more often than not, the real world is a place where dreams go to die. We all start out with big goals when we're young. Do you remember what you wanted to be when you grew up? I'm going to go out on a limb and say it wasn't a network marketer; me neither. Maybe it was an astronaut, a doctor, or Pat Benatar. Yes, I wanted to be Pat Benatar; I saw myself on stage belting out "Hit me with your best shot!" The fact that my singing sounded like a cat being run over was not relevant to me. Whether or not you still hold those childhood dreams of blasting into space or belting out ballads on MTV, you ended up making choices that have brought you to where you are now. But what if instead of wishing, wanting, and waiting, you found a way to start moving closer to your goals? Would you take action?

My hope is that you're willing to work to achieve what you deserve in life and realize that your destiny is the only real obligation you have. So many people use only a fraction of their ability and rarely strive to reach their *personal legend*. "Personal legend" is how author Paulo Coelho describes your calling in his book *The Alchemist*. If you haven't read that book, please gift yourself a Netflix-free indulgence and dive into this amazing book and awaken the dreams buried inside of you.

Unfortunately, most people are blind to their potential. They want to believe that there's a way to achieve their goals but so far life has taught them that dreaming is for other people. It's much safer to carry on as they have been. It's worked so far. Life's not so bad; I have a roof over my head, food in my cupboards, and the Internet, what's not to love? I'm living day by day. But days turn into weeks, weeks turn into months, and the next thing you know, ten years has slipped by, and you're nowhere close to where you wanted to be.

That's what so many people do; they slip into daily habits that don't serve them. They settle for mediocrity in so many ways every day. Accepting jobs they hate and dealing with people who consistently let them down because they've slipped into a societally induced coma of mediocrity. Dare to dream, and you risk the cost of pain and embarrassment for trying to change. In all my careers, I've noticed that people will cling to a disappointing existence rather than change to get something better because they're afraid of getting something even more pathetic. Or even worse, they're afraid of being judged. A friend once told me that if a person doesn't share your bank account and your bedroom, they're not entitled to a vote in how you live your life. I would take that one step further; you must be happy and excited about the fact that they're sharing your bedroom and bank account to get a vote; a vote that can be vetoed by you without discussion.

A lot of people I dealt with working undercover, in the courts, and as a network marketer are terrified of change, failure, and taking risks. It's far easier to settle than it is to leave our comfort zone, even when our comfort zone is a jail cell. As a drug enforcement officer, one of your jobs is to cultivate informants; people who give you information in exchange for money or leniency. We don't use names when we are dealing with confidential informants; we want to protect their identity for their safety and integrity of ongoing investigations. One of my informants was affectionately known as Smelly Cat. Not because she smelled, but because she looked like Phoebe from the TV show *Friends* (if you haven't seen the show just look up "Smelly Cat" on YouTube), and because she had a penchant for storing things inside a specific body part. I'll let you put the rest of that together.

One day I'm visiting Smelly Cat in jail. She was awaiting trial for a minor drug charge, prostitution, and assault. Smelly Cat called to give me some drug information on a guy that we'd been investigating for a long time. In exchange, she wanted to negotiate a guilty plea for a reduced sentence. Smelly Cat offhandedly told me that she could get her GED (General Education Diploma) while in jail.

"That's great! When do you start?" I asked.

"I'm not going to do it," she said.

"Why not? It's free." I couldn't understand why she wasn't jumping on this opportunity.

"Why should I? It won't help me." And that was the end of the discussion. In her mind, she had achieved what she was capable of, and she wasn't willing to risk the pain or embarrassment of trying harder and then failing. The thought of showing other inmates that she could read at a grade three level was mortifying to her. So what if she could learn, improve, and maybe even change her life? That wasn't enough. The idea of change for the better wasn't in her wheelhouse. Smelly Cat was literally, and figuratively, in a jail cell that didn't permit change. She was a prisoner of her limiting thoughts.

But it's not just people like Smelly Cat that fear change and therefore imprison themselves in mediocrity. I've met doctors, lawyers, athletes, teachers, police officers, business owners, artists, people from every walk of life who made decisions that lead to a life sentence of averageness. Unfortunately, it isn't until the pain of staying where you are becomes so intense that you start looking for a way to move forward. I don't think that we ever truly know what that pain is until it presents itself. For me it was my five-year-old son asking if we were in a hurry again one morning while we were getting ready for our day. It wasn't just that one moment, it was the guilt-filled hours, weeks, months, and years of being away from him that proceeded that comment. It was the realization that nothing was going to change until I did.

Think about relationships that fall apart; it's not usually just one single event. It's several small things over time. Forgetting birthdays or special occasions. Ignoring each other once children come along. Never saying, "I love you" and then actually showing it.

The same with our health, we don't get fat occasionally indulging, it's the daily bad food choices we make. It's not eating one cheeseburger or ice-cream sundae; it's indulging more often than not. We don't become unfit skipping a single workout, it's never working out that leads to degeneration. Tolerating less than you are capable of leads to atrophy. This universal law applies to every part of our lives.

Inaction is a choice that usually leads to the opposite result that we're looking for. That's what happened to Kevin and me. We didn't intend to eat takeout most nights, or sacrifice family time for work, we just let it happen. We said yes to more work and no to time together. We said yes to fast food and no to cooking at home. It was time to start saying yes to what mattered. It was time to make a shift.

When we began our network marketing business, our initial goal was to simply replace Kevin's overtime pay. That worked out to around five-hundred dollars a week. We thought if we could do that we'd have it made. He could take more time off, and we'd have more family time on weekends. That was our big hairy audacious goal: replace around two-thousand dollars a month in overtime pay. At the time, that felt like a huge goal. We started out small and gave ourselves six months to achieve our goal of $500 per week from our network marketing business. We reached that goal a lot faster than we thought possible, but we did not think that we would one day quit our jobs and earn more money as network marketers. That seemed crazy. At first.

But here's what happened, our dreams grew along with our income. Our time freedom increased with our income. And the best part is we didn't do it alone. We partnered with friends who did the same thing. We partnered with strangers who turned into friends. We could make contributions that didn't seem possible before. Many of the people I've met in network marketing have shared similar stories. They had short-term financial goals like buying a car, paying for their kids' education, taking a family vacation, or paying off some credit card debt. Frankly, I've only met a few people who said they got started in network marketing to earn a substantial income. Between you and me, the people who show up just for the money rarely find the success they're looking for. The people who come in with the "get rich quick" mindset fizzle out quickly. You can usually find them standing in line at the 7-Eleven, buying lottery tickets.

Most people get started in network marketing for the products and then decide to try the business. Usually, their goals are small financial ones related to specific things like vacations or debt repayment. But along the way, the magic starts to happen. While they're learning how to run their network marketing business, they're exposed to personal development. For many, it's the first time they've undertaken any personal growth and it's incredible to see what happens.

A few years ago, I was coaching a guy named Jack. Jack is an accomplished engineer with a good career and a beautiful family. When we started working together, I asked him why he wanted to start a network marketing business and his answer has always stuck with me. He said, "I want to change my script. I feel like it was written for me when I was a kid, and I want to write my own script. I finally believe that I can do that." Jack was passionate about his family, music, and his church, and he finally saw a way he could have more time doing what he was enthusiastic about. And it wasn't the money he was making from his network marketing business that made him feel like he was changing his "script" because at the time he wasn't making very much. It was the personal development he was getting through his involvement with network marketing. He was connecting with people in a positive and collaborative environment, who were encouraging him to go for it and he stopped listening to the people who told him he couldn't do it.

So how do people break their addiction to average? There's no simple answer to that question; it's different for everyone. What I do know is that you start by making small changes in your mindset and by letting go of your overwhelming concern about what other people think. Have you ever noticed that you are at your unhappiest when you are dwelling on what other people think? Like Smelly Cat, the greatest prison people live in is the fear of what other people think.

We are social by nature, and we depend on the opinions of others, both their praise and their criticism. Think about how often you check to see if someone liked your social media post. After scrolling through the feed and comparing yourself incessantly with others, you check your post one more time. "Wow, I can't believe that selfie in my bathroom mirror didn't get more likes. It looks like I'd better do the fish face pout next time in my yoga pants." We're constantly looking for feedback on how we're doing, and if the feedback is less than stellar, we're quick to seek the security blanket of average.

When you're kicking the addiction to average, you must decide to be unapologetically you. If that includes bathroom selfies, so be it. However, I believe there's a lot more depth to you than the counter space between you and the mirror. It might be time to let your light shine, and I've learned that everyone can shine when they're in the right light. Sometimes the right light can only be found in a new environment. It may require deleting, unfollowing, and unfriending, both on and offline. Toxic people can be just like cancer, and you must cut them out before they become malignant. It's painful at first, but when you start replacing the toxic with the terrific, you shine even brighter.

This might be a bit cheesy, but think about your personal growth like a houseplant's: we need the right soil, light, and nourishment to grow. But no matter how great all of that is, we'll only grow as big as the pot we're planted in allows. We limit our growth by remaining in a small environment.

Network marketing offers a larger personal growth environment than most people have ever experienced.

When we first decide to kick our addiction to average, we're pretty motivated. We've reached a pain point that screams "I'm sick of mediocrity. I want more!" So, you go for it. You start making sacrifices and tasting success. Now you're inspired. The problem is, as Henry Kissinger once pointed out, that "each success only buys an admission ticket to a more difficult problem." And if you haven't grown to the point where you can take on more challenging problems, your success will flatline or even falter. To keep moving forward, you need to keep growing your skills and protecting your success mindset because the skills that got you to where you are won't get you to where you want to go. This is especially true today in a world that is constantly changing.

Changing careers, starting a fitness routine, cleaning up your diet, eliminating drama, and any other changes you make won't be easy; if it were, everyone would make the changes they need to achieve success. If you start making changes in your life to break free of mediocrity, it's going to freak a lot of people out, especially if one of your choices is network marketing. Everyone will have an opinion, and some will even say it to your face. Pyramid Pam knows these things. The rest will just gossip behind your back. In my best Donnie Brasco voice, I tell you "fuhgeddaboudit." It's easy for people to talk, it's an entirely different matter to act. Which do you want to be known for?

Network marketing allows you to create opportunities for others to shine. That's what makes this business model so brilliant, because you aren't successful until you help other people be successful. Now that's significant, that's what legacies are built on. When we're consumed with staying safe, staying small and average, we are focused within. When we start to grow, we begin focusing on others. We want to achieve something amazing for ourselves and the people around us, but we can't do that without giving something up. And that "something" can be a temporary loss of social acceptance. I say temporary, because the people who leave are replaced with people who are in alignment with the new and improved you.

The author James Allen said: "He who would accomplish little must sacrifice little; he who would accomplish much must sacrifice much." The irony of this is that no matter what choices you make, someone is going to criticize you. And if you're going to be criticized anyway wouldn't you rather be criticized for being bold and pursing your dreams?

Over the years I've learned that sooner or later, some of the people who were trying to pull you down will come to you for advice or decide they want to join you. This has happened at least a dozen times since we walked away from our careers to become network marketers. It's natural for people to want to *wait and see* before they come to you. And if you're consistent in your efforts to achieve your dreams you'll inspire people to join you. Because let's face it, you're awesome, not average and people want some of that. So, get started blazing your path to greatness right now; because if you follow an old path you reach the expected. Light up a new path and you have an adventure.

Case Notes

- The enemy of a great life is a good life. When you allow yourself to settle into your comfort zone you snooze through opportunities. Mediocrity starts with me.

- Most people are blind to their own potential because they've given up on their dreams. This leads to an addiction to average that can only be kicked when you decide to be unapologetically you.

- Daily habits will make or break your success. It's not that one thing you do that changes everything, it's the small things you do every day that add up to failure or success.

- Network marketing is a collaborative business model that rewards you for helping others succeed.

- No matter what choices you make, someone will criticize you – therefore you may as well be bold and go for it!

CHAPTER 5

BREAKING BAD TO BREAKING BUSY

I did it for me. I liked it. I was good at it. And, I was really... I was alive.

— Walter White (*Breaking Bad*)

A long, long time ago, in a mindset far, far away, I wore my busyness like a badge of honor on a girl guide uniform. I used to look down on stay-at-home parents with school-aged kids who complained about being too busy. That was nothing. You want to talk busy? In those days, if you asked me what I was up to, you'd have to brace yourself. "Oh," I'd say, "Kev and I are building our dream house right now! Out of logs. With our bare hands. And we're renovating a rental property we just bought, again, with our bare hands. I'm also working full-time as an undercover police officer in the drug unit, and I'm going to law school full-time in a town four hours away. Did I mention that I'm also pregnant?" Busy? I'll give you busy with a side order of crazy and a single shot of one-upmanship.

Let's just say that I've since recovered from my "what the hell do you do all day?" attitude toward anyone who isn't driving themselves into the ground. I've come to appreciate that we're all busy. We all take on things that we could never finish if we had forty hours a day to do them in. I want to take a moment to apologize to every stay-at-home parent reading this book; having a child brought an entirely new level of busy into my life and I bow to your awesomeness. Becoming a parent helped me appreciate how much busier things are when you have young children to care for. The minute Kaleb woke up, the busy train left the station. Toot toot… breakfast, packing lunches, helping him get dressed (it was hard enough getting myself organized some days) and answering a million "why" questions: "Why do you look so tired Mom?" "Why can't we just play today Mom?" "Why do you have to go to court again today Mom?" Why, why why?

Life is busy for everyone; the struggle is real no matter where you are in your life. Millennials, GenXers, GenYers, Boomers, Foot-in-the-gravers, we're all busy doing our thing. Too often we're so busy we don't see what's right in front of us. I know that's how it was, for me.

A lot has changed since I left my career as a lawyer for a work-from-home network marketing business. One of the best things has been eliminating the 5 am alarms. I know some of you reading this may be very attached to 5 am. There are dozens of books, blogs, and manifestos extolling the virtues of 5 am, but it's still dark out at 5 am. And when I was working full-time my day didn't usually end until after midnight which made 5 am even earlier! Screw 5 am, I'm so over it.

I remember one early morning in particular, like it was yesterday. It was a typical day. Kevin had already left for work, and I was rushing around trying to get everything done before heading out the door with Kaleb. I was shoving files into my brief box on wheels and simultaneously trying to ensure Kaleb's jacket was zipped up and his boots were on the right feet. Like many overwhelmed working moms, I had my Crackberry cradled on my shoulder trying to listen to voicemails while struggling to put my coat on and balance myself in high heels. I was doing everything and nothing at the same time. So, I'm multitasking away, and five-year-old Kaleb looks up at me and asks in his cute little voice: "Mommy, are we in a hurry again today?"

In that moment, everything stopped. Time stood still, and it felt like my heart had been pierced. His innocent question meant that I was teaching my son that life was about rushing around ignoring what was truly significant. Life meant work was important and urgent and that everything else could wait. At that moment, I realized that when I said, "family is the most important thing in my world" it wasn't really true, because my actions demonstrated that work was the most important thing. That saying, "actions speak louder than words" was like a throat punch jolting me into the present. Don't get me wrong; I completely understand that providing financially for our families is an expression of love. This isn't about trying to make anyone feel guilty or wrong for working. You can find studies that show that children who spend more time with their parents at home are smarter and happier. You can find just as many studies that show that kids are more balanced if they have a working parent. You can find stats and surveys to back up any position. My question to you is this: what do you want and why do you want it?

Are you working excessive hours so you can drive a nice car and live in a great neighborhood? Is it because you receive a lot of satisfaction from your job? Or is it because you think that's what you're supposed to do? The reasons are different for everyone. Just take a moment to think about why you do what you do. Why are you living your life the way you're living it right now? What need is it satisfying for you? I know that life isn't all sunshine and rainbows, and we're a long time in the ground, so if the journey above ground sucks, it seems kind of pointless to continue doing what we're currently doing if we don't love it.

I left my career in policing to start a family. I thought that a career as a lawyer would be a more family-friendly job than working undercover was. There would be no more jumping from moving cars and buying cocaine for a living. Now I was going to do a nice family friendly job, I was going to prosecute drug dealers ten hours a day. Yeah, turns out that wasn't very family friendly either. Aside from drug dealers being unhappy with you, the hours are brutal. I finally learned that it's not the job description that's important, it's how you interpret it that matters most. If you love your job, and have a work-life balance, that's great! In my case, I let my job control me. I was so driven to win that everything else in my life took a backseat.

My career managed my time. It controlled the best hours, of the best days, of the best years of my life. I was putting in time away from my family that I would never get back. For me, the return on investment just wasn't balancing out.

I believe that my career as a prosecutor and Kevin's policing career contributed to a safer community. I don't regret that for a moment. But what I was beginning to regret was the fact that other people were spending the entire day with my son, teaching him, helping him grow, and watching him smile. I was missing out on so much. When I slowed down to think about what I was sacrificing it made me feel empty. On the outside, I had it all: great marriage, healthy child, respected career, and good friends. The problem was that all my time was consumed by one part of my life: my career. Like most people, I liked being needed, respected, and challenged, and my job met all those needs. But I had no balance. My choices were beginning to take a toll on my health, my relationships, and my peace of mind.

I tried to juggle so many balls that I always ended up dropping the most important ones: myself and my family. I wasn't doing myself any favors multitasking most days just trying to stay afloat. In fact, it was making me duller than the pot-smokers I would see in court all the time. Researchers at the Institute of Psychiatry at the University of London [1] found that multitasking with electronic media caused a greater decrease in IQ than smoking pot or losing a night's sleep. This doesn't mean you should run out and trade in your iPhone for an iVape, it just means that focusing on one thing at a time is where the magic happens and if you've designed your life so that focusing on one thing seems impossible, it may be time to shake things up a bit.

How do you see your life? Do you find yourself answering "busy" every time someone asks you how you are? The response is almost programmed. We don't even have to think about it. I can tell you that changing careers didn't break my addiction to busy, I had to shift my mindset. It's not what you do for a living that makes you busy; it's how you manage your mindset around what you do. Trust me; it took me a few years of personal development to get over my instinct to reply with "busy" every time someone asked me how I was.

How in the heck did we end up in a society where busy is the most acceptable way to be spending our time? It's time to take back control because we were not put on this earth to be busy. Regardless of your spiritual beliefs, I think that we can all agree that we are here to build relationships, experience life, go places, create things, and help others. Our reasons for "being" are all different, but none of us were put here just to be busy.

I once believed that cramming as many tasks as possible into my day was a way to measure my worth. If you didn't answer with "busy" when asked how you were doing you were a slacker in my universe. What I came to realize was that busy is synonymous with stressed and overwhelmed, and the more we talk about it, the worse it gets. Like that aunt who won't stop talking about her hemorrhoids, or that co-worker who won't shut up about his noisy neighbors—the more they talk, the worse it gets, for them and us. The same applies to busy. It's time to stop complaining and start enjoying. This is almost a commandment according to Pope Francis. He posted a sign on his door that reads "Complaining forbidden. Violators are subject to a syndrome of always feeling like a victim and the consequent reduction of your sense of humor and capacity to solve problems… To get the best out of yourself, concentrate on your potential and not on your limitations. Take steps to improve your life." That advice is right on!

There are many reasons we're overwhelmed in our lives. Taking on too much is a problem for a lot of people. We have this innate desire to please people and as a result we rarely say no. We have become a society of yes-men and -women. "Oh yes, I'll volunteer for that," "Of course I can help you with that," "I'd be happy to host that," and on and on. We resentfully neglect our needs to meet the needs of others. I'm not suggesting that you become a selfish jerk, I'm saying that other people's needs will occupy all your time if you let them. You will have much more to offer the world if you aren't feeling resentful and overwhelmed because you can't say no.

This is something I've had to work on. I thought saying no was rude, and showed that I couldn't handle the extra work. I made it all about me. I wanted to look good in the eyes of others so I agreed to almost every request made of me. But I found that saying yes to things that contribute little to our personal wellbeing or goals leaves very little time for the important things that matter, like pursuing dreams, spending time with family and friends, or nurturing ourselves.

Instead, we spend time listening to that nasty critical voice inside our heads telling us we aren't doing enough, we're not good enough, and we'll never get everything done. We end up placing unnecessary and unreasonable pressure on ourselves through self-criticism and negative self-talk. Sometimes, no matter what we do, or how much we've achieved, there's always something our inner-critic will disapprove of. The same voice of judgment that demands we do more also requires that we do it perfectly. Even if we don't consciously register this, we feel the resulting anxiety and stress in our body. Sometimes we mask this issue by telling others that we're a perfectionist. I loved that label, it made me feel superior somehow. "I'm a perfectionist!" has a nice ring to it. "But no perfection is so absolute, That some impurity doth not pollute." Ah, what would a book about network marketing be without a quote from Shakespeare?

Perfectionism also has an evil twin named Control. This is no comedy of errors; there's only one problem with control: we can't. We need to realize that we can't do everything ourselves; we need others and we can't control them. Learning that I could not control everyone in every situation was a lesson I had to learn many times in each of my careers. As a police officer, I learned that even holding a gun doesn't guarantee that you can control someone. As a prosecutor, the threat of prison does not equate to control. As a wife and mother... well, enough said there.

Not being able to control others has been an exercise in frustration and patience on my part for years. If only everyone did exactly what I said without question, life would be so much easier. Imagine if everyone always did what you told them to? It would be pure bliss. I can see it now: I simply point my finger, utter a command or two, and voila, everything is perfect. Okay, it's time to put away the iVape and let go of this control fantasy. But it's hard to let go because of our lack of trust in the abilities of others. That old saying: "If you want something done right do it yourself" plays over and over in our heads. So, we end up doing, or wanting to do, everything ourselves. It doesn't take long to realize we can't do it all ourselves so we return to that mountain of overwork and self-doubt.

That mountain manifests as workaholism for some people. Workaholism is taking busy to the level of addiction. Working undercover for so long I encountered a lot of addicts, and all addictions have something in common: they destroy lives. Addicts allow their relationships to fall apart and they often have health problems and suffer from deep insecurities. They repeat destructive behaviors despite knowing that they're destructive. Workaholics aren't hard-workers who simply love their jobs, they are people who constantly think about work, and without work may feel anxious or depressed.

Workaholics, like other addicts, are usually trying to escape something even more painful than their addiction. They're usually trying to escape the life they've created outside of work. When I was working undercover, I worked with a guy who volunteered for every overtime shift, every project, every surveillance detail. In short, he always wanted to be at work. He had a wife and three young children and based on his behavior at work, things weren't going well at home. He was doing everything he could to escape the painful reality that his marriage was a mess and his kids didn't really know who he was. Work was the only place he felt truly wanted and appreciated, even though that wasn't true. He eventually imploded and ended up turning to drugs and losing his job. Perhaps you know someone who turned their job into their entire life and the people at home got tired of waiting for them to change. Blaming work for workaholism is like blaming restaurants for food addiction, or Nordstrom for my shoe addiction.

If your commitment to your career is hurting your relationship/work-life balance, it's time to take a serious look at why you're doing what you're doing. I was on a path that led to a life filled with regret because I was missing the important everyday events in my life and I was neglecting myself. I didn't want to be alone and unhealthy, I wanted a vibrant full life. There was a part of me that realized I wouldn't be saying, "Gee I wish I had worked more" when I was on my deathbed. It didn't take network marketing to get me to realize that. I saw it before I became a network marketer. Network marketing simply gave me the vehicle to drive myself away from that inevitable regret.

Being busy is an addiction and it can be just as challenging to quit as other addictions because it's a way to numb yourself. But unlike other addictions, we place a high value on being busy. We are conditioned to believe that being busy equates to being good, worthy, and successful. Like most addicts, people addicted to busy start with a gateway drug. A gateway drug is an introduction. For example, most people don't go straight to heroin, the gateway drug is usually alcohol, cigarettes, marijuana and on from there. The gateway drug to workaholism is skipping lunch breaks, forgoing vacation time, working weekends or extra days. Over time you alienate every other part of your life and you become conditioned to believe that this is okay because it's necessary. Everyone understands when you say "I can't, I have to work." Not many appreciate "I can't, I need to have a day to myself." Unfortunately, your compulsion for busyness will only exacerbate your addiction to average. Because when you are only focused on one thing—i.e. work—the other parts of your life atrophy, leaving you with a boring day-in-day-out existence.

Often we get so caught up in the doing, that we forget why we're doing it, and it takes a painful experience to make us realize we've lost control. If you haven't yet had that wake-up call let me help you out. Instead of being busy and then hoping that it will lead you to what you want, start asking yourself "if I keep doing what I'm doing now, will I reach my goals?" If your answer is yes, great! You're on the right track, keep going. If your answer is no, it's time to consider making a change.

I'm not going to tell you that network marketing will cure your addiction to busyness. What I can say is that it can be part of your rehab. Network marketing is about much more than just the money. It's about reconnecting with your purpose in life. I know, sounds pretty deep. But here's the thing, network marketing helps you to recognize that you don't have to meet expectations set by others. Instead, you can create space and find time to do the things that are important to you. Time is our most precious non-renewable resource and you *should* get to decide how you spend it. It starts with deciding what is most important to you and then figuring out what activities will support that. If spending time with people you love is most important, then figure out a way to make it happen. Like millions of other people, I used network marketing as my vehicle to make it happen.

Along the way I've learned a few strategies to help me, and the people I coach, kick their addiction to busyness. The first one is the most obvious and the most difficult: giving up the need to control everything. We can keep trying to do everything ourselves, or we can delegate the things we don't enjoy and spend the rest of the time doing what's important to us. When my business coach first suggested delegating some tasks, I thought, "What is she smoking? Delegate, sure. To who? How much will this cost me?" It turns out it saved me money, time, and most importantly, my sanity. Ask yourself, "What am I doing that is so menial it could easily be outsourced?" Maybe it's some admin tasks that a virtual assistant could do for $4 an hour. Or some domestic help like someone to clean your house or maintain your lawn for $50 every two weeks. What is your time worth? Really think about that question, and not just from a monetary standpoint. *The 4-Hour Work Week* is a best-selling book by Timothy Ferriss that offers excellent tips and strategies on outsourcing.

If you're ready to break busy, create some boundaries around your time. Start by deciding what's important to you, then figure out activities that will support that. If getting healthier is one of your priorities commit to a fitness routine by scheduling it into your calendar. Even just thirty minutes, four times a week has been shown to dramatically improve our health. The added bonus of getting into shape is you will have more energy and stamina to do more of what you love. If your personal relationships are a priority, then schedule those in your calendar first, not last. Decide that your work will be scheduled around your life, not the other way around. Fortunately, network marketing is very flexible and I've been able to do exactly that.

When we're feeling overwhelmed we often find comfort in doing something mindless like watching TV or surfing the Internet, trolling for the best selfie or organic kale chip recipes. What we forget is that during this time the extra information that comes in becomes noise that further compounds our already overwhelmed state of mind. The best thing we can do when we're feeling overwhelmed is to shut down the electronics and do something that slows the mind down. Consider reading something that expands your consciousness, or listening to music. Think about the things that bring you joy: nature walks, playing with your kids, exploring, sports, hobbies, and then start doing more of those things.

Breaking busy is easier than you think and it starts and ends with deciding to take action. The only way to get control of your time and your life is to plan. I know that's obvious and you've heard it a million times before, but do you do it? When I started planning my day the night before, and my week on Sunday nights, my world changed. I finally started making progress toward my goals because I was in control of my day. I always put one thing on my "must do" list for the day and that gets done first. Of course, the best laid plans often go awry so I leave some buffer time to account for those unplanned things that happen to all of us.

Finally, gratitude is the motherlode of all busyness crushers. When you are in a state of gratitude you're reminded of all the awesomeness that already exists and this helps you believe that there is more where that came from. Every night before we go to bed we ask our son what he's grateful for and Kevin and I share our gratitude with him. It could be something amazing like epic powder on the ski hill, or something we usually take for granted, like clean water. Whatever it is, it helps ground us and remind us of what we already have. There are so many ways to express gratitude I could write another book just on that (lots of people have!) You can send a written note, a text, or a voice message telling someone how grateful you are for them. You can write in a gratitude journal each day. You could take ten minutes to meditate. It doesn't matter how you do it, what matters is that you do it and you can start by being grateful for how incredible you are. And, if you want to, you can drop me a line telling me how great I am too. (Just kidding. Sort of.)

Case Notes

Is your need to be busy exacerbating your addiction to average? Signs to watch for:

- Frequently skipping lunch breaks.

- Forgoing vacation time for more work.

- Working weekends or days off.

- Answering "busy" every time someone asks you how you are.

Strategies to Break Busy:

- Give up your need to control everything by delegating tasks you don't enjoy. If you're on a budget you can hire a student to clean your house or do some gardening. Or, you can trade services. Love to cook? Offer to prepare some meals in exchange for someone to clean your house.

- Create boundaries around your time. Build your schedule around what is most important to you.

- Drown out added noise by turning off the TV or mindlessly surfing the Internet. The best thing we can do when we're feeling overwhelmed is to shut down the electronics and do something soothing or something that brings you joy, like listening to music or playing a sport you enjoy.

- Plan your day out the night before. This one simple thing can be a game-changer in your quest for an exceptional life.

- Practice daily gratitude to be reminded of all the incredible things you already have, reminding you that there is more where that came from. Try writing a few gratitude's in a journal, or sending a hand-written thank you note.

You've got this!

CHAPTER 6

THE HYPE

It is always the novice who exaggerates.

— C.S. Lewis, *The Screwtape Letters*

"This dope is off the charts. Right off the block. Almost pure," Jay enthused. Translation: it was cocaine with very little cutting agent added, making it more potent and valuable. In reality, it was around twenty per cent or less cocaine, and eighty per cent or more cut. Funny that even drug dealers abide by Pareto's 80-20 principle. What I'm getting at here is that drug dealers hype up their product to make the sale. They will tell you anything you want to hear to get you to buy from them.

When you work undercover for a while, you start to notice patterns in people's behavior. The low-level drug dealers frequently exaggerate their abilities and the quality of their product. One of the dealers I came to know quite well was a guy I'll call Jay. I use the name Jay because in every single town Kevin or I ever worked in, there was always a drug dealer named Jay. Go figure. Anyway, Jay loved to brag that he was the best cook, the best fighter, and had the best dope. Yes, they all say that they're the best cooks, fighters, and dealers. Kev and I used to laugh during de-briefs because every single one was the same. I didn't fight any of them or eat their cooking so I can't offer an opinion there. But, I did buy their dope, and they were usually wrong on that count.

Of course, hype is not unique to drug dealers. All sorts of people do exactly the same thing. Have you ever been on a dating website? Me neither. But if you have gone online, you might find people exaggerating their qualities. The tall-dark-and-handsome, turns out to be short-smelly-and-boring. The adventurous super model turns out to be the cat lady you heard about on the news. And it's not just lonely hearts exaggerating their qualities, it's also the saleswoman in the department store who tells you that the outfit is perfect for you, only to go home and see yourself dressed in what resembles a burlap sack. In fact, most human interactions from relationships to spirituality to products and services has likely included some form of exaggeration on the part of the "salesperson". Network marketing is no different. Unfortunately, the hype perpetrated by distributors is even more glaring and easy to criticize because it shows up on your social media, in your neighbor's living room, and around the water cooler at work. With network marketing, it's not just the known salesperson, it's your friends and family members.

If you've been in network marketing for any amount of time you've witnessed the hype. An example I've seen pop up on social media feeds is the statistic that reads "Of the 6% of women in the United States that earn over $100,000 per year, 80% of them are in direct sales." Of course, this is not true. I reached out to the Direct Selling Association to verify this stat the first time I saw it used in a presentation. I was advised that the statistic did not come from them and that there was no way to source that statistic. Even without checking with the DSA let's think about it for a minute. As a professional network marketer, I've met several men and women earning over $100,000 per year. As a police officer, I worked with many officers who, with overtime, earned over $100,000 (I am married to one of them). As a lawyer, I worked with several lawyers who earned over $100,000 per year (I was one of them). Think about your own profession; maybe you know people earning over $100,000 doing that, or you've heard of them. Maybe you're one of them. The point is, people in all professions can earn significant incomes, network marketing is not special in that regard.

The "get in on the ground floor" pitch is another example of exaggerated nonsense that hurts the profession of network marketing. What does this even mean? Jump on board with an untested company in a volatile market? Sure, that sounds enticing. Look, I'm not saying that you shouldn't join a new company because every company was new at one time. What I'm saying is, "ground floor" is not a selling feature. It implies that you can only make money if you get in first and that is nonsense—and oh, that would likely be a pyramid.

What about those "rags to riches" stories promulgated by network marketers? It's like Chris Farley's SNL skit—"I lived in a van down by the river"… until I found network marketing. Even if you are "thirty-five years old, thrice divorced, and live in a van down by the river," it takes the same skill to succeed in network marketing as it does in any business. Yes, there are exceptions to the rule, and some people with limited abilities and challenging circumstances do succeed in network marketing. And some succeed in graduating from medical school, starting the world's largest franchise, or becoming a famous actor, too. It is possible, not probable. The truth is, most people who are struggling in their financial life will bring their lack of skills and abilities with them, making it challenging for them to succeed in anything, including network marketing. The upside is, network marketing gives people a boatload of personal development to help them overcome some of those challenges, something that most other careers do not. This is one of the amazing benefits offered by network marketing, the opportunity for personal improvement, while earning an income.

Of course, people who already possess financial IQ, good personal skills, and are driven to succeed, are more likely to excel faster in network marketing than people who do not have these qualities. The well-known quote, "How you do anything is how you do everything" pretty much sums it up. I'm not trying to discourage the financially challenged from trying network marketing, I'm simply suggesting that your expectations need to be in alignment with your current abilities. Of course you can grow, learn, and develop the skills required to build a successful network marketing company; many people with less talent, fewer skills, and a smaller circle of influence have done it. However, you need to have patience and the fortitude to persevere when things get tough. Patience, passion, and perseverance are all requirements for success in network marketing.

The flip side to hyping up the opportunity, is criticizing the nine-to-five culture. I've heard network marketers say things like "I had a J.O.B. - which stands for just over broke." I have no idea who thought it was a good idea to insult many people sitting in the audience at events, or alienate their social media followers with that kind of messaging. Maybe it was the network marketing equivalent of Jay. Jay, stop it! Demeaning comments like that aren't inspiring or encouraging, they're disparaging and harmful. Who are we trying to attract into our network marketing communities? The guy living in the van down by the river? He doesn't have a J.O.B. so he should be good to go.

I've had my share of careers that are met with public scrutiny and criticism. Almost daily you can find criticism directed at police in the headlines. And those lawyer jokes, I bet you know a few. Although some of the lawyer jokes are funny, almost as funny as blonde jokes complete strangers share with me on airplanes. Yet none of the criticism or jokes come close to those directed toward network marketers. There is probably no other profession that has been as misunderstood as much as network marketing.

I've read countless books on the profession. Some of them are very good, others not so much. The good books tell you the truth about network marketing. Others make up mythical statistics and pad the pages with data that no one can source. Some books tell success stories that imply "anyone" can do it without explaining the difference between possible and probable. Of course, anyone can become a successful network marketer, just like anyone can become a successful doctor, a famous actor, or a professional athlete. It's possible, but not probable for most. However, if you're willing to develop skills, and you have determination, grit, and tenacity it's more likely, or probable, that you will become a successful network marketer.

And the numbers show it's a lot more probable than becoming a pro ball player or famous actor. The NCAA officially estimated probabilities that out of 1,108,441 high school football players, only 255 were drafted. However, even with abysmal odds we don't criticize kids who want to be pro ball players and we don't claim that pro ball is a scam because of these odds. We simply see success for what it is: hard work, talent, and grit. And a bit of luck. From time to time, we can make our own luck, too. You've picked up this book, for instance!

For the profession of network marketing to grow and be accepted and acknowledged for the amazing business model it is, we all need to stop with the hype and start sharing not only what is possible, but also what is probable given the time, talent, and tenacity you bring to the table. We need to stop quoting studies and statistics that don't exist. I love that people are excited about their products and services, and that they want to share their excitement. There is absolutely nothing wrong with loving a product and wanting to tell people about it. However, too often I've seen someone sharing, quoting, and often misquoting statistics to puff up what they're offering. Maybe you've even been corned by one of these people at a cocktail party. You stand there, listening as your eyes glaze over, thinking to yourself "God, why me? It's my only night out and this is what happens!"

Often I don't think they realize that what they've said isn't true, because they simply shared it from someone or somewhere else. And on it goes, the train of misinformation. But here's what happens when you share these inaccuracies: you add to the damaging hype. If you see a quote or a stat that you think you'd like to share, source it first. If it sounds a bit fishy that Warren Buffett says he wishes he were a network marketer, it likely is. If it seems like a bit of a stretch that network marketing produces more millionaires than any other profession, it probably is.

One of the many things I learned as a police officer and as a lawyer is that you always should hear both sides of a story. The same is true with network marketing. Although I've shared some hyped-up network marketing stories, there are just as many on the critics' side of the table. There are hundreds of self-proclaimed network marketing experts who take great pleasure in spewing vitriolic untruths every chance they get. I wrote to the expert who claims that there are disasters and suicides that can be attributed to network marketing. I asked him for specific examples or to cite the source of this information. At the time of writing this, I have been waiting more than two years for a response.

I've also seen posts from everyday people claiming that network marketing is a scam or a pyramid. Again, with zero facts or relevant experience to back up their assertion. They often say things like, "very few people actually make money with network marketing." I agree with them, very few people do. But it's not because network marketing doesn't work; it's because most people are customers, not business builders. On average, if one-hundred people are involved with a network marketing company, approximately eighty-five are customers – meaning they have no desire to make money (and they don't) they simply want to purchase their products at a discount. The remaining fifteen out of one-hundred people try to earn money, and out of those fifteen, most earn enough to pay for their products and a bit more, and some earn a significant income. So when the critics say that only 3% of people are actually making money, they are not evaluating the real numbers and that is dishonest.

The point I'm trying to make is this: there are uninformed people with their own agenda everywhere. If you base your decisions on misinformation and lack of knowledge you are doomed to fail, regardless of which side you choose. So why are some people so hostile toward network marketers, even more than they are toward lawyers? Well, some base their opinion on trying and failing themselves. Others base it on what they've "heard" from others. "Well, my friend tried it and it didn't work. He's still living in a van down by the river." And others are just uninformed because they don't take the time to find out the facts for themselves; they passively rely on social media posts from their friends, or talk around the water cooler at work.

It's time to stop hiding behind words and embrace what network marketing is: it's selling with relationship building. Network marketing emphasizes person-to-person communication and relationship building that doesn't stop with the sale. So, if you are a network marketer, own it. When you're asked what you do simply say, "I'm a network marketer." Or, "I'm a business coach with a network marketing company." Or, "I'm a distributor with network marketing company X." If you're part-time and just getting started you could say, "I'm a _____ (current profession) but what I'm really excited about is my part-time network marketing business." And say it with the same conviction that you would say if you were a neurosurgeon. Be proud. Own it. Please stop hiding behind superfluous explanations about what you do. Here's an example of what I mean:

"What do you do?"

"I create multi-millionaires working from the comfort of their own home." Or, "I sell freedom, prosperity, and growth." What does that even mean? You might as well say, "I corral unicorns and saddle up rainbows." When I was a lawyer and someone asked me what I did, I didn't say, " I'm an advocate for justice" or "I help people find the just and righteous outcome in the war on drugs." I simply said, "I'm a lawyer." Why complicate things? So, if you're new to network marketing and you're being taught to dance around how to answer "what do you do?" throw that approach in the trash where it belongs.

Finally, people who do not want to be network marketers are not haters, they just don't want to be a network marketer. I don't want to be a plumber, that doesn't mean I hate plumbers. When I was in law school I didn't walk over to the med school students and call them haters because they didn't want to be lawyers, I just called them med school students. We do not need to create an us-and-them culture based on our own insecurities. It's time to step up and be proud of what we do. Own it. Whatever it is you do. Whatever it is you're offering to the world, just own it.

Case Notes

- If network marketers want the business model to be revered instead of reviled they need to stop hyping up their products and opportunity.

- Start by eliminating exaggerated quotes and stats on social media: if it sounds too good to be true, it likely is.

- Do not criticize people who are employed by telling them they have a J.O.B. – just over broke. Insulting the very people you are trying to connect with is lunacy and will lead to failure.

- Own what you do. When someone asks what you do, and you're a network marketer, say that you are a network marketer.

- You can increase the odds for your success when you are honest, straightforward, and share information with integrity.

CHAPTER 7

THE DREAM IS FREE - THE HUSTLE IS SOLD SEPARATELY

Talent is cheaper than table salt. What separates the talented individual from the successful one is a lot of hard work.

— Stephen King

"Ready. Aim. Fire!" Sergeant Oliver yelled. He stood so close I could feel his breath on the back of my neck. He was shorter than me, but his voice was so loud it vibrated through my ear protectors. I lost focus for a moment, wishing I had a Tic Tac I could offer him. Seriously, how was I supposed to trust an instructor who thought tuna and garlic was a good choice right before our firearms class?

"Police! Don't move!" I yelled at the paper target down range. And I was as serious as a heart attack, that paper had better not move! I fired all six rounds into what I hoped was the center of mass. It was the very first time I had ever shot a gun. I still have that paper target in a box with other police mementos. I hit the target with every round I fired from my Smith and Wesson .38 Special. Not all my shots hit the center of mass; they weren't perfect but they all hit the target, because I took aim and I pulled the trigger. Each time I fired a round I looked at where the bullet hit and I adjusted, so I could get better. I had zero experience, sweaty hands, and an instructor with halitosis, but I didn't let any of that stop me. I had target and I took the necessarily action to hit it.

We all have enough ability to accomplish anything we want. But we must be clear on what our target is. When you're shooting a gun, your target is obvious. When you're shooting for a goal, obstacles often arise. Most people spend too much of their time getting ready, and when they finally aim, instead of pulling the trigger, they get stuck aiming to be perfect. Then their arms get sore, or they stop seeing the target clearly, or they become paralyzed, believing they have just one chance to get it right. A lot of people, burdened with too much doubt, just put their "gun" down.

They wouldn't put it down if their life depended on it, though, and from this we can learn an important strategy. If your life depended on your firing that gun, you'd fire it and you'd keep firing because perfect doesn't matter when survival is at stake.

If we looked at achieving our goals as a matter of survival, we'd be more likely to pull the trigger and go for it. Aim is less important than letting it fly. And this is where hustle comes into play. Of course, hustle means different things to different people. For some, the word hustle carries negative connotations, but others use it as a business mantra. When you hear the word hustle what do you think of? Do you imagine someone taking advantage of you? Or do you see someone busting their ass until they reach their goal? To me, hustle implies that you're moving toward a goal with the tenacity of a dateless sorority sister on the eve of her homecoming. Like that Pi Beta Phi, the world's greatest entrepreneurs learn how to hustle.

I've hustled as a police officer, a lawyer, a parent, and as a network marketer. Hustling has become a way of life for me because: "Things may come to those who wait, but only the things left by those who hustle." Although this quote is attributed to Abraham Lincoln, there is no evidence to support he actually said it. I don't care, it still applies: if you wait for things to happen you'll get the leftovers from the people who have already made it happen.

There have been many times in my life that I've been afraid to pull the trigger and I got stuck waiting for perfect. This book is a recent example of that. After every speaking engagement, inevitably someone would come up to me afterward and say, "You should write a book." At dinner parties with friends: "You should write a book." Great idea, I thought. How hard can it be? So, I started getting ready. I cleaned up my office, read some books on writing a book, and a thousand other tasks that never resulted in a word on a page. I sat down in front of my computer staring at that blank screen with the blinking cursor. That damn blinking cursor, just flashing at me, daring me to start writing. I can't pull the trigger! What if no one likes it?

It took months to finally start typing words on the page. There were times I wanted to take those pages and use them as target practice. But I didn't. I did something more dangerous. I gave the pages to Kevin to read. He took the pages and read them, lavishing praise after every page. "Sure, you like it. You have to, you're my husband."

"I know, but I don't love everything you do. I don't love your cooking and I don't love your mom jeans."

Point taken.

I hired a book coach to steer me in the right direction. Surely he would be objective, and he'd never tasted my cooking or seen my mom jeans. He gave me some great feedback and was always positive and encouraging. Still, I would take months to send chapters to him, fearful of judgment. This book was important to me and I put this pressure on myself that it had to be perfect. I wanted to provide a pragmatic resource that people could turn to when they were considering the profession of network marketing.

Pulling the trigger on some goals is harder than others, especially when they're important to us and we think that we'll be judged. And finally pulling the trigger and missing the mark sucks. When I first started my network marketing business I sucked at a few key competencies required for a successful business. One of the skills I had to develop was teaching. In my former careers carrying a gun or arguing why someone should go to jail meant I didn't have to teach anyone. I just had to tell them what to do, sometimes with the threat of deadly force or prison. Simple enough, but I needed more when I became a network marketer. Suddenly I had to teach people what to do instead of just telling them to do it. This transition was painful for me, and certainly for some of the people who partnered with me in the early stages of my networking career. Looking back, I'm sure they felt like I was pointing a loaded gun at them at times. I wasn't used to sharing or asking. After a few disappointments and frustrations, I learned how to teach. Now when I connect with new business partners I have a system that teaches them at their pace, not mine. "You think Yoda stops teaching, just because his student does not want to hear? A teacher Yoda is." Yes, I did it. I included a Yoda quote in this book about network marketing. Trust me folks, it gets better.

Although my approach at times was less than ideal, I was still in action, I was still hustling. I came to realize that failure was an important part of the learning process for me. I've made a lot of mistakes in my network marketing business but my failures have been instructive. I've learned to aim, fire, and listen to feedback so I can course-correct along the way. Every person, experience, and event has taught me valuable lessons. One of the most important is that hustle is a key ingredient to success.

Hustle requires persistence, which in turn drives success. "Nothing in this world can take the place of persistence. Talent will not; nothing is more common than unsuccessful men with talent. Genius will not; unrewarded genius is almost a proverb. Education will not; the world is full of educated derelicts. Persistence and determination alone are omnipotent." This quote by America's 30th[th] President, Calvin Coolidge was made even more famous by McDonald's founder Ray Kroc. It epitomizes hustle.

It's often easier to give in than to dig in, especially when people in powerful positions are encouraging you to give in. This happened to Kevin and me several times when we first started building our network marketing business, but we were used to it. When we worked undercover together we had a less-than-ideal supervisor who was afraid of big drug buys, and wanted to keep our drug deals small so he could remain in control. At one point in our undercover project, Kevin and I had finally secured a deal for a couple of ounces of cocaine from a mid-level dealer, let's call him Bob, who could lead us to the bigger fish: the Hells Angels. Bob was a fringe player but he had insulated himself with his minions, making it hard to make a deal with him.

But we were persistent, continuing to connect with the minions and hanging out in the places that Bob liked to frequent. One of the places Bob liked to hang his hat was The Sherwood Forrest, a strip club. I'm guessing that most people reading this book have never stepped inside a strip club, also known as a gentlemen's club. Don't worry you're not missing much, and gentlemen don't really go there.

The Sherwood was dark, smelly, and very icky. I went to that club so many times I became "friends" with most of the dancers and staff. They knew me so well, I didn't have to pay a cover charge and they let me walk into the kitchen area to make my own snacks. Yes, I lived a very dangerous life, eating at strip clubs. Anyway, our persistence paid off. Bob finally agreed to sell to us, hand-to-hand, which is a big deal because that was all the evidence we'd need for a prosecution later on. And it gets better: Bob invited his Hells Angels connection to the meeting. Our hustle was paying off.

The hustle will pay off in your life, too, if you choose a goal that excites you. Maybe that's having zero debt, or retiring early, or simply having enough money that you can spend your days doing what you love, not what you *have* to do.

But there were, and still are, many times when I do not feel like hustling. Sometimes I just want to take a nap, or read a book, or watch an episode of Narcos on Netflix. Everybody has times when they don't feel like working, that's normal. Taking a break is necessary to sustaining the hustle. A study in the journal *Cognition*[1] shows that those who take a break once an hour perform better than those who just keep working without a break.

This break gives you a much needed boost that allows you to see things from a new perspective or find new insights.

Tony Schwartz, author of *The Power of Full Engagement* and *The Way We're Working Isn't Working* warns that "without any downtime to refresh and recharge, we're less efficient, make more mistakes, and get less engaged with what we're doing."[2] I know that's true for me. When I was working as a prosecutor I rarely took breaks. When the judge took a break I would either stay at the counsel table and review my notes, or run to the law library to research an argument. As a network marketer I can take breaks whenever I want, for as long as I want. To date, I've never had a network marketing emergency that required me to work endless hours without time for a break.

There are scientifically proven benefits to taking breaks throughout your day. Something as simple as taking a walk for twenty-minutes can increase blood-flow to the brain and boost creative thought. The fresh air and change of scenery also helps to stimulate our creativity. So does eating the right foods. Enjoying vegetables, fruit, and lean proteins will provide you with a steady source of energy throughout the day. But so often we are pressed for time at lunch so we opt for fast-food that is loaded with sugar, salt, and low-quality proteins that leave you sluggish for the rest of the day. If you're pressed for time try making a delicious smoothie made with a quality protein powder that offers energy-fueling carbohydrates, good fats, and natural ingredients to keep your glucose levels consistent for the rest of the day, saving you from craving that sugary or salty junk offered in the office vending machine.

In addition to physical movement and good nutrition, we also need rest to keep us productive and happy. There are studies that show that a nap of even ten minutes improves cognitive function. Nappers are also known to have improved focus and alertness and a higher tolerance for frustration[3]. So, when you're feeling like you might snap, take a nap. Yes, I'm a poet and I didn't even know it.

Like most other businesses, network marketing requires that you hustle in order to be successful. However, unlike other businesses, network marketing allows you to work around your schedule at your pace, and you're encouraged to incorporate down-time into your schedule. With network marketing you hustle around your life, you don't build your life around the hustle.

Case Notes

- When you set your sight on a goal, take aim and pull the damn trigger. Don't wait. The time will never be just right.

- Be persistent and don't listen to the critics.

- Take breaks each day – they will help you hustle.

CHAPTER 8

"THE BACKEND"-YOUR PARTNER COMPANY

Great things in business are never done by one person. They're done by a team of people.

— Steve Jobs

"Will you be my maid of honor?" Paula asked, as she stared at me with her droopy doper eyes.

"I didn't know that you and Stu were thinking about marriage," I replied. My inside voice was screaming: "Uh oh! How can I be her maid of honor when I'm not really who I say I am?" Sending them to prison for being drug dealers is one thing, screwing up their wedding is completely off-side.

I did what any good fake friend / undercover cop would do: I changed the subject back to cocaine. When in doubt, change the subject. Works well most of the time, unless you're a drug dealer or a spy. Then all bets are off. Hopefully that's not a concern for most of you reading this book.

Drug dealers and spies aside, when it comes to dealing with corporations, things can get tricky because the individuals acting and speaking for the corporation are doing what is best for the company. What does this mean for network marketers? A network marketing business is a symbiotic relationship between corporate ownership and distributors, neither of which can survive without the other. Like all relationships, trust is a critical factor in the success of the corporate-distributor relationship. When network marketing companies demonstrate a commitment to ethics and integrity it trickles down to the field, which in turn instills a sense of trust and confidence to consumers. Of course, all of this leads to a successful business for everyone involved.

As a former police officer and prosecutor, ethics are very important to Kevin and me, and we took a very close look at the integrity of the company we partnered with before launching our business. Using products as a customer is one thing, recommending them as a business is completely different. But I had zero network marketing experience and therefore no idea what I was looking for in a partner company. Fortunately, my first experience with network marketing was with a company that was built on a foundation of integrity and trust. Most network marketing companies also embrace ethics and strive to serve their distributors and their customers. If you're fortunate enough to partner with a company like this you are on your way to success. However, there are some network marketing companies that wouldn't know ethics if it jumped out of the bush and bit them in the ass; stay far away from these companies.

Because companies don't take out ads saying "We're an unethical company run by jerks," my advice on avoiding them is to do a quick Better Business Bureau search. If the company is accredited and receives a good rating, it may be a company worth considering. If you're like I was and don't have a clue what you're looking for, I'll save you some frustration and countless hours of research. I've interviewed several top network marketing leaders, company owners, and regulators, and I've read dozens of legal briefs, books, and articles on network marketing companies. Add in my years of network marketing experience and legal background and I have a pretty good grasp on what to look for, and what to avoid, in a network marketing company.

Because network marketing appeals to many people who have limited or no business experience, there is an increased risk that some will partner with the wrong company. So, what are we looking for when we partner with a network marketing company? Turns out there are quite a few things we should be looking for, and several things we should avoid. What follows is a basic breakdown to help you make your decision.

Product / Service

Network marketing companies offer everything from soup to nuts, literally. Clothing, supplements, skincare, greeting cards, essential oils, technology, utility services, even pepper spray, stun guns, wine, and adult toys. Yes, folks, if you want it, you can likely buy it from a network marketing company. Most people join a network marketing company for the products. That's why Kevin and I got involved: it was strictly for the products at first.

Whichever company you choose to partner with, you must be passionate about the product or service. Why would you ever recommend something you don't really like? We don't recommend movies, restaurants, or stores that we don't like, the same is true for all products and services we consume, that's why network marketing is so great: we get paid for recommending something we truly enjoy and personally use.

Once you've found a product or service you love and feel comfortable recommending, ask yourself "Is this something I could buy and use each month?" Most companies recommend that you purchase a small amount of the product or service consistently. This is referred to as autoship. I wish it was called loyalty rewards because that better describes the requirement. But alas, I do not get to create the terminology. However, companies cannot require you to purchase products as a condition to participate in the income opportunity. In short, autoship as a "pay to play" requirement is illegal. Participation in an autoship program must be optional.

At first, I was a bit freaked out by the thought of autoship. I didn't want them sending me stuff every month, what if my garage started to fill up, proving Kevin right? It turns out I ended up loving autoship because it saved me money (I get a discount when I pre-order) and I never risk running out of my favorite products. Flexibility isn't just for yoga, it's also an important thing to look for in a partner company.

There are a lot of great companies out there, including technology, clothing, and dozens of other non-consumables, and if that's what you're passionate about go for it. However, products that are consumable can be more profitable in the long-run because your customers will need to buy more each month. Choose a product that has a sustainable future. What I mean by that is, will it still be relevant and desirable ten, twenty, and fifty years from now? That is an important question to ask yourself before committing to join a network marketing business. Think about how long you'd like to get paid and use that as your guidepost for evaluating the product or service.

I love technology and admittedly I'm an Apple addict - sorry PC fans. When they release something new, I order it. Apple is great at providing a product that people line up for, some even lineup overnight. (I draw the line at that.) But not all technology is like that. Not all companies are as in tune with public demand as the company created by Steve Jobs. Anyone remember Blackberry, Palm Pilot, or email accounts you had to pay for? What about having your film developed? Or Blockbuster movie rental shops? Technology changes so fast that one minute you're lined up at Blockbuster renting *Back to the Future*, the next minute you're ordering *Star Wars* on your Apple TV or binging on Netflix.

If you choose to partner with a technology company, be sure to think about the long-term sustainability. There are several examples of network marketing companies that created the "next big thing" only to become quickly outdated. Paper maps are now GPS devices or Maps on your phone. Phonebooks, dictionaries, and encyclopedias are on your tablet, phone, or watch. Pay phones used to be everywhere, now even homeless people have smart phones. I, for one, could not have predicted any of this. We are in an era of wondrous new inventions, ideas, and achievements that change moment by moment.

Unbelievable advancements in artificial intelligence and big data will be upon us almost overnight. The doubling of computer processing speed every eighteen months, known as Moore's Law, is just one manifestation of the greater trend that all technological change occurs at an exponential rate. Just think about how much things have changed in the past ten years and then try to imagine how vastly different things will be in 2025, or even 2100.

I recommend trying the product or service before you start shouting accolades from the rooftops, or your living room during a presentation. I'm not saying you should stay stuck in analysis paralysis but you should do your due diligence if you plan on becoming a distributor. The amount of time and information you need will be unique to you. With most products and services, you'll know almost immediately whether it is something you are comfortable recommending. Remember, it's your reputation at stake.

Stability

Network marketing is like all other businesses: some companies succeed and others fail. So what are we looking for in a network marketing company that indicates it's more likely to succeed than fail? There are never any guarantees, but stability is one of the key indicators that a network marketing business has a better chance of thriving and growing. In business, stability is the ability to withstand a temporary problem, like an economic downturn or a key leader leaving for another company. Problems and challenges are inevitable and it's important to partner with a network marketing company that can navigate difficulties effectively.

This often comes from experience. One of the key things to look for in a partner network marketing company is how long they have been in business. Earlier in the book I touched on the "ground floor" hype used by some hypesters (not to be confused with hipsters, hypesters don't require plaid shirts and a beard). Hypesters start talking like they're Elon Musk or a cast member from Shark Tank. This ground-floor statement presents problems on a couple of levels. The first is that if the claim is that you must get in early, or first, to have success, it could be a pyramid scheme, because that's how pyramids work.

The second problem with the "get in on the ground floor" pitch is that is often the riskiest time to join a company. According to the American Small Business Association [1] (SBA), only 30% of new businesses fail during the first two years of starting, 50% during the first five years, and 66% during the first ten years. Only 25% make it to fifteen years or more. I don't know about you, but if I'm going to put time and effort into a business I want to partner with a company that has a proven track record of success.

The experience of the corporate team is also a critical component of a company's stability. The corporate team should be comprised of people who have network marketing experience, both in the field (sales team, distributors, associates), and as members of the corporate executive team. Of course, some companies survive and even thrive without both, but in my experience, and with the research I have conducted, the most successful companies have both. Before starting your network marketing business it's a great idea to check out who's running the company. That's exactly what Kevin did when he flew to Phoenix our first month in business to check out the company ownership and the field leadership during a company-sponsored event. You don't have to invest in plane tickets and hotels to check out the company you are considering; most of your research can be done online and over the phone asking a few questions like:

- Who owns the company?

- What is their experience?

- What did they do before joining / starting this company?

A few minutes on the phone can save you from partnering with a failing team.

86

Company Culture

The ownership of the company dictates the company culture to a large degree. When you are looking at a network marketing company investigate whether they balance the needs of the company with the needs of the distributors and customers. If they do, wonderful - you've found a great company. If they put the needs of the company first, at the expense of the distributors and customers - run away, very fast. Fast and far like Forrest Gump.

Compensation Plan

Let's clear something up right now; there is no one singular compensation plan that is the best. They all have pros and cons. There are people earning significant incomes with all the various compensation plans. I'm not going to offer you a breakdown of every plan offered by every network marketing company out there. Frankly there are so many variations it would be challenging to outline all of them. What I am going to do is outline the basics of the four major plans. Before you start writing me letters telling me that your company operates with compensation plan X and I didn't account for all the nuances and variances your company offers, let me save you some time. There are a lot of variations, and some companies complicate their compensation plan so much that you need a PhD in mathematics just to understand it.

If you are looking at partnering with a network marketing company, please take the time to look at their compensation plan. If it can't be explained in a way that everyone from a high school student to a senior citizen can understand it, then it's too complicated. You should be able to outline your compensation plan in three minutes or less. If you can't, it may mean you don't understand it, and if you don't understand it, how can you expect to make the most of it and earn an income with that plan?

Before computers and the Internet became a part of the average household, network marketing companies had to rely on complicated compensation plans that could be difficult to understand or explain. Now we have computer software that can keep track of hundreds of thousands of customers, distributors, and wholesale customer orders. Compensation plans are easier to understand and easier to master and explain, as they should be.

Maybe you've never heard the term 'compensation plan' before. But compensation plans are not unique to network marketing companies. Law firms have compensation plans with names like Lockstep and EWYK (which stands for "eat what you kill"). I didn't make the names up; they're commonly known and referenced on the Canadian Bar Association's website www.cba.org. Who ever thought lawyers would equate how they get paid with eating what they kill? Don't answer that.

Network marketing companies have kinder, gentler, and cooler names like Matrix, Unilevel, Stairstep Breakaway, and Binary to describe their compensation plans. Briefly, here are some defining characteristics:

With a Unilevel plan, everyone you sponsor comes into the organization directly below you and you get paid a set portion of everything they buy or sell. You are also paid on a certain level of depth (the people added below that initial sponsor). For example, you sponsor Joe, and then Joe sponsors Sally. Joe is your first level and Sally is your second level. Unilevel plans pay unlimited width (meaning there is no limit to how many people you personally sponsor directly below you), so you can earn money on every person you personally sponsor. Depth limitations (how many levels of people you are paid on) varies from company to company.

Binary plans are different from Unilevel plans in that you sponsor two people who form two teams: a left team and a right team, and every person you personally sponsor goes on either your left or your right team. The Binary plan allows you to build and to be paid on unlimited depth. Compensation is paid on group volume (meaning that all the business

88

volume generated by you and your entire team is grouped together in either your left or right team), rather than a percentage of multiple levels of distributors. In other words, payment is volume driven, rather than level driven. Group cooperation is promoted because payout is on group volume.

A Matrix plan, often referred to as a Forced Matrix, has specific depth and width requirements. For example, a 4-by-5 Matrix means that you must sponsor four people to your first level and help them do the same up to five levels of depth (meaning five levels of people below you) Some Matrix plans allow for "spillover" meaning once you fill your width requirement, you can also personally sponsor people to meet the depth requirement.

A Stair Step Breakaway pay model is like a Unilevel pay model in that it focuses on the development of a frontline of distributors with no width limitations. The difference is that once a distributor reaches a certain level of success, he can "break away" from his sponsor, meaning that he keeps more of his income and the sponsor receives less. The benefit of such a plan is that it inspires hard work on the part of each distributor. The problem is that each breakaway event results in an income setback for the enrolling sponsor and it creates a culture of competition that can lead to a scarcity mindset on the part of team members.

All the compensation plans listed above have special bonuses based on performance as outlined by the individual network marking company. Moreover, each plan has pros and cons and network marketers have their favorite, usually based on personal experience. At the end of the day the most important question to ask yourself is "does the compensation plan emphasize getting products and services into the hands of consumers; or does it emphasize making money finding new recruits?" If the answer focuses on recruiting, run away. Fast. Right now. If, on the other hand, it emphasizes products and services, breathe a sigh of relief because it's you, not the compensation plan, that drives success.

Systems

Like franchises and traditional brick and mortar businesses, network marketing companies rely on systems for their success. Most network marketing companies have systems in place that help with online and offline training systems. This is especially important for people with limited or no network marketing experience. When Kevin and I first started, we relied on the online training system our company offered. Because we both had very busy work schedules, we weren't available during the day or early evening to attend training seminars. When you are researching your network marketing company, ask what types of online and offline training they offer and determine whether it fits with your skills and availability.

There should also be systems in place to help you with social media and replicated websites. Replicated websites are company websites that carry your name and allow you to sell retail or sponsor new distributors. Essentially it is your online office. Some companies charge monthly fees for replicated websites, others are free when you are a distributor. Most people have no idea what leads are, much less how to generate them. There should be capabilities within your replicated website, social media, and mobile apps that help you with this. Network marketing is all about making connections and building relationships, and technology is an amazing way to do that. When I first started in network marketing I didn't have a social media presence. I didn't think it was a good idea to let drug dealers have a peak into my private life. However, once I learned about privacy settings, online tools, and apps, I could add to my business by connecting with people online who shared similar interests. There are several amazing books and resources available if you want to learn how to use online systems to build your business. I developed a four-part webinar series that walks a new person through the steps of building a network marketing business. Your company may also have online training systems that you can use.

Beware of scam artists who claim to have "systems" that take all the work out of network marketing. If it sounds too good to be true, it likely is. If it was as easy as blasting on social media or email drip campaigns, the network marketing companies wouldn't need distributors, they would do it all themselves.

Finally, ensure that your company has a system and protocol for handling multilingual and multi-currency business. There should be an easy and fair system in place that allows you to build in multiple countries with different languages and currencies.

Some companies only operate in one country and that's fine, if you are satisfied that a domestic market will sustain your business. Personally, I prefer to partner with a company that does business in multiple countries for a couple of reasons. First, if the economy tanks (which is usually does at some point in time) I can rely on other markets to grow and sustain my business. Think about the financial crisis of 2007-2008 in America. If your business was only operating in the US, your business likely suffered. However, if you had part of your business in Canada, Australia, and some Asian countries, you probably didn't, and you may have even grown during that time. I know that is true for Kevin and me. Our business grew by 700% in 2009 because much of our business at that time was in Canada, even though our partner company is based in America.

Aside from financial stability, another reason to have a global business is for fun. Imagine being able to deduct some of your travel expenses when you visit the countries that your business operates in. I have business partners in Hong Kong, Australia, New Zealand, Malaysia, Taiwan, Indonesia, the UK, Colombia, Mexico, Canada, and the United States, with expansion happening in Europe, and other countries soon. I love travel, and I especially love travel when I get to connect with like-minded entrepreneurs and I can deduct some of my travel expenses from my taxes. That is what's known as a win-win.

Flexibility

I can't walk by the hosiery section in a department store without feeling hot, itchy, and uncomfortable. It gives me flashbacks to those days I spent in court wearing pantyhose, specifically black pantyhose, the choice of smartly dressed prosecuting attorneys in every superior court across the land. I often fantasied about walking into court one day sporting my yoga pants, baggy sweatshirt, and flip flops. Try wearing pantyhose with flip flops, it can't be done. Find me a woman who says she loves wearing pantyhose and you've either found a unicorn or a crazy lady.

So, what do pantyhose or yoga pants have to do with network marketing? I'm glad you asked because it is a big factor in your decision to join, or not to join, a network marketing company. For men, substitute pantyhose for neckties (unless pantyhose are your thing, then hey, who am I to judge?) The point I'm trying to make is that as a network marketer, you can wear what you want to work because work is where you decide. When I say work, I mean you're taking action toward building your network marketing business, you're not snapping selfies of yourself at the beach and calling it your office.

When you're considering a network marketing company, interview some people who are already a part of the business, aside from the person trying to sponsor you, and ask them about their experiences. Are they supported and encouraged to build around their current life situation? Does the company culture support flexibility and work-life balance, or does it encourage rank-advancing, sponsoring, and working unlimited hours? I don't judge either as right or wrong, it's completely dependent on what you are looking for. Some of you are ready to pursue your dreams like a dateless cheerleader on the eve of her prom, others are looking for a part-time gig. Both are fine, if they work for you.

Safeguards

In chapter three we discussed distinguishing a legitimate network marketing business from an illegal pyramid scheme. You can research this further by visiting the Direct Selling Association's website (www.dsa.org) for a list of companies that are part of the Association. The DSA has a rigorous vetting process and each member company must abide by their code of ethics. If a company is not a part of the DSA, ask them why not. A second checkpoint I mentioned earlier in the book is to visit the Better Business Bureau website (www.bbb.org) and put in the name of the company you are considering for a rating. You can also Google it, but please keep in mind that anyone can write anything without facts and with a malicious intent. You are much better to stick to reliable and trusted consumer sites.

Case Notes:

- Before partnering with a network marketing company search them on the Better Business Bureau website (www.bbb.org) and look at their ranking. Also check the Direct Selling Association's website (www.dsa.org) to ensure that the company you are considering is a member.

- Be sure that you love their product or service and are committed to personally using it before you recommend it to others.

- Ask how long the company has been in business and what experience their corporate management team has with network marketing.

- Ensure that the company culture is in alignment with your values.

- If you cannot understand or explain the compensation plan (how you get paid), your income from network marketing will be limited.

- Ensure that there are online training systems offered by the company that you can conveniently access.

CHAPTER 9

SHOW ME THE MONEY

Money and success don't change people; they
merely amplify what is already there.

— Will Smith

I t was just another average day in our little undercover apartment. Susie, one of my favorite drug dealers, opened the 8-ball packet of cocaine (8-ball is an eighth of an ounce, or 3.5 grams) and spread out half a dozen lines onto our coffee table. Being the gracious guest she offered me the first line. (Just in case you're wondering: no, I didn't really snort cocaine. Undercover police officers are taught techniques that are never revealed to the public for obvious reasons). After snorting a couple of lines, Susie said, "I love the money but I hate the risk." Of course, when you're a drug dealer, the risk could include prison, injury, and even death.

"Why do it then?" I asked.

"Money."

Of course, Susie isn't alone in her willingness to risk freedom, relationships, and even her life, for money. Almost every part of our lives is connected in some way to money. Our career choices, relationships, where we live, what we drive, what we eat, where we travel, and so on: all are related in some way to money. Think about your own life. Would you continue to work if you were paid less, or not paid at all? What about your choices at the grocery store or restaurant, does cost play a role in what you choose to buy? How about where you live, what you drive—would you make different choices with more or less money at your disposal? Clearly money is one of the determining factors in almost every choice we make.

Money impacts every part of our lives, especially our relationships. A study by SunTrust [1] found that the leading cause of relationship stress is money. Many people I've worked with didn't need a study to tell them that. Another study found that money issues can predict divorce. According to the study, "Couples who reported disagreeing about finances once a week were over thirty per cent more likely to divorce over time than couples who reported disagreeing about finances a few times per month." [2]

Imagine what your relationship would look like if you did not have any financial stress. Think how juicy and fun a Friday night would be if you weren't arguing about who spent money on what that week. I am not implying that network marketing is going to add sexy spice into your love life or that it's the answer to all your financial woes, because no matter what you do in life there is always one constant: you. What I'm saying is that an added income stream could help take the pressure off, and network marketing provides an opportunity to earn more money without the risks associated with other business ventures like dealing drugs, buying real estate, or investing in the stock market.

In chapter two, I outlined some of the opportunities Kevin and I pursued before finding network marketing. I summarized our foray into working overtime, investing, franchising, and traditional business. If you skipped that chapter, no worries, I'll save you some time. None of those ventures led to financial freedom. Not because they don't work, but because our mindset was not where it needed to be to change our net worth. The problem is that none of what we were trying came with a personal growth plan, like network marketing does.

Personal growth may sound a bit woo woo to some of you. Don't worry, I didn't add coloring book pages to this book or insert chants for you to shout into the bathroom mirror. (Those things are going to be in my next book.) What I have added to this book, however, is this chapter on your money mindset. Initially, we didn't realize that we needed to change the way we thought about money to earn more money. We thought you just went out there and worked for it. We had no idea that our mindset played such a critical role in our financial well-being. To be successful in anything—health, finances, relationships—you need to have a mindset that supports your success.

Because network marketing focuses on personal development and business management, we were able to make a shift. A shift that allowed us to turn up the heat on our financial thermostat. We all have a financial thermostat and most people keep theirs set at "comfortable". Comfortable is relative and different for everyone. For some, comfortable is living in a nice house, earning a six-figure salary, and waiting for vacation time or the weekend to arrive. For others, comfortable is having a roof over their head and being able to afford groceries. For most, it's somewhere in-between. It isn't until the temperature on your financial thermostat drops so dramatically that people feel the need to turn up the heat. That drop can show up in the form of a tragedy like a death, job loss, or a market crash resulting in a drastic dip in cash flow. For others, it shows up in relationships, time away from kids, a lack of time to pursue your real passion resulting in a drastic dip in your enjoyment of everyday life. Whatever it is for you, shifting your money mindset will allow you to turn up the heat without having to freeze your butt off in financial purgatory.

I've read several biographies of wealthy and influential history makers, I've interviewed successful investors and entrepreneurs, and I've spent a lot of time working with and coaching people who earn rock star money as network marketers. Not one person or story has been the same. However, there is one striking similarity that I spotted among these incredible people: their mindset when it comes to money. They all love money. Did I lose you on that last sentence? Love money? How inappropriate, loving your kids, or puppies, or even cupcakes are okay, but loving money, now that's crossing the line! We've come to accept that it's alright to share our story of being down-and-out, but tell someone you're wealthy and people turn up their noses like you just passed gas. Our society has made wanting to have more money a character flaw.

Let's take a moment to sit in judgment of those greedy bastards who love money. Feel better? Good. Have your financial circumstances or the circumstances of people you care about improved? Yeah, didn't work for me either. Armchair quarterbacking the people who are out there in the arena of life never changes anything.

Like Margaret Thatcher once said, *"No one would remember the Good Samaritan if he'd only had good intentions. He had money as well."* I must agree with the Iron Lady on this one, it's hard to help people with only good intentions. We can all help a lot more people with money than we can with judgement, or even good intentions. Try connecting with your favorite charity or non-profit and offer to donate good intentions. Or reach out to your grandmother and offer to pay her medical bills with your "I don't love money" mindset. Unfortunately, good intentions don't feed the hungry or shelter the homeless. If your inside voice is telling you that loving money is greedy, wrong, or immoral, let's rephrase it and see if we can work through this. "I love what money can do for me and the people I choose to help." When you love money, you understand that you must give to receive. Loving money involves gratitude and generosity, not greed and gluttony. When you love money, you understand that there is no virtue in poverty, and that there is nothing wrong with wanting to live a rich and full life.

Many people, without realizing it, repel money from their lives with thoughts of lack, victimhood, and jealousy. When we criticize others for having money it's usually coming from a scarcity mindset. We think that there is a limited amount of wealth and that if you get some, I get less. But here's the thing, others don't lose because you win, this isn't football. There's enough for everyone. We don't have to be jealous of what others have; the fact that you've noticed the success of others is a message for you.

We should be delirious with joy when others achieve wealth and success, because it proves what is possible. If they can do it, so can I, and so can you. "Envy is the ulcer of the soul," Socrates said. So, let's take some Pepto Bismol for the soul and celebrate the wins of others.

This may mean shifting your thought process when it comes to money. Have you ever caught yourself saying or thinking:

- I can't afford that.

- Money isn't important.

- You need money to make money.

- Money is the root of all evil.

- It's more difficult to get rich these days.

- It's selfish to have so much money when there are people who have so little.

I know I used fall back on "Oh I don't need that." Or, "Money isn't important to me." Both were lies I told myself because I didn't get it. I didn't understand that I was sabotaging my success with defeatist self-talk. If you think you're poor, you are. If you think you're rich, you are. "Hold on a minute sistah, I've checked, and my bank balance agrees with me: I'm poor." But that is all relative, isn't it? You can afford the book you're holding in your hand, or you have a person in your life who gifted it to you. That's pretty awesome. You have the time to read it. You have dreams and big goals.

Everything you've done up and until this moment has put you where you are today. The good, the bad, and the mediocre outcomes have resulted from the choices you've made and your choices have been the result of your mindset. If you shifted your mindset from negative self-talk around money to positive self-talk you would become more aware of opportunities happening all around you. Because there are no secret thoughts, everything you think manifests itself in your life.

Have you ever noticed that when you wake up frustrated, or upset, the rest of your day follows suit? Perhaps you're running late for work, then you get stuck in traffic, making it worse. When you get to work, you realize you've missed a meeting. After work you see that you have a parking ticket and then you get home, only to realize you forgot to get groceries and now all you have are martini olives and sour milk. This may or may not have been one or more of my actual days.

How you do things is the direct result of how you think about things. When you think things are going to go wrong, you somehow prove yourself right. On the other hand, when you visualize the day running smoothly, you open your mind to focus on the things that happen to substantiate your belief. You see what you want to believe. Visualization can turn your mind into a cool "attract what I want" magnet. Have you ever heard the story about comedian Jim Carrey? He was broke living in Hollywood, trying to make it big. One day he wrote himself a check for ten-million dollars and kept it in his wallet. Every day he would look at that check. Over the years it became tattered and torn, but he kept it, always reminding himself of what could be. Some actors were making millions, why not him? Then the opportunity of a lifetime came along and he was cast in Dumb and Dumber. That role paid him… you guessed it, ten-million dollars. I'm not suggesting that simply writing yourself a check for millions will literally pay off. What I'm suggesting is that you open your mind to possibilities, ones you may not see if you don't visualize them.

However, you still need to act to achieve what you want. Jim Carrey didn't just write out the check and then sit on a bench all day visualizing. He went to auditions, kept acting, connecting, and doing what it takes to be a success in Hollywood. He had the vision, saw what was possible, and used his drive, talent, and grit to achieve his goal. It's like building a house: you must have the idea and the blueprints before you dig the hole and lay the foundation. You need the foundation before you can build the house, and you must start building before the house becomes a reality. It's no secret that you can't just sit around thinking about it: you must *do* something. But when it comes to money, what to do doesn't come naturally to many people because their mindset is not in alignment with what they want.

I've always had a winning mindset, but I didn't grow up with a wealthy one. Growing up, I didn't see wealth and opportunity, I saw poverty and challenges. I focused on the "haves" and the "have nots," and I fell into the latter group. Maybe you can relate. What did you see and hear about money when you were young? Perhaps you heard your parents argue about money. Maybe you were told things like: "money doesn't grow on trees" or "do you think I'm made of money?" We weren't born with preconceived ideas about money, we developed them over time. Many people associate wanting money with pain because of what they heard and saw as children. These negative thoughts around money became entrenched and when we feel ourselves wanting something we either feel guilty for wanting it or sad because we can't have it. We start to think that we don't deserve wealth, but we can change that when we change our money mindset.

As Bill Gates famously said, "If you're born poor, that's not your mistake. If you die poor, it's your mistake." I completely agree. I also recognize how much mental power it takes to be surrounded by poverty and have a wealthy mindset. It's easy to see abundance when you're already experiencing it. But no one said it was going to be easy, they said it was possible and that's what you need to understand: it's possible. You won't become rich by studying poverty, you become rich by studying wealth and the people who have what you want.

. . .

"Let me give you some advice. Never get on the pipe. It's okay to snort it, just don't smoke it." Jill offered these words of wisdom with a serious tone I'd never heard from her before. When it came to the pros and cons of snorting cocaine versus smoking crack, Jill was usually silent, pretending to be above such discussions. Usually she was on a rant about how Bob spent all their drug money on his personal drug use. Or, she'd tell me about what she would do if she ever found a rat (someone who told the police about her drug-dealing): "I'd rip them apart and feed them to the dog." Jill had an adorable pit bull named Kitty. Kitty wore a spiked collar, was frequently foaming at the mouth, and spent time locked in the bedroom when guests were over so she wouldn't eat them. I had every reason to believe that Jill meant what she said.

For a young woman with a very small five-foot frame, Jill had a loud voice and very scary words. Aside from having a marvelous grasp of the obvious (Don't smoke crack!), she loved to offer advice on just about any topic, from dogs to kids, politics to finances, and of course, drug use and dealing. However, I'd learned long before I ever met Jill that it's a mistake to take advice from people who aren't where you want to be.

Let me give you another example, one that you will likely relate to a lot better than smoking crack, and that is making money. We've all received unsolicited advice on how to make, spend, and invest money. Sometimes this advice comes from someone a paycheck away from living in a van down by the river, and sometimes it comes from a trusted friend whose finances closely match yours. If your goal is to be rich, then listening to people who are not rich doesn't make a lot of sense. Opinions are cheap and plentiful; everybody has one and they're willing to give them to you all day long for free. Essentially, you get what you pay for.

When we listen to the opinions of others who haven't achieved the level of success we are striving for, it stops us from reaching our full potential. Have you ever had an entrepreneurial idea, or wanted to pursue an opportunity but you didn't because your know-it-all brother-in-law or your nosey neighbor said it would never work? "Oh you don't want to do that. My buddy down at the lodge tried that and it didn't work." Even when we know that this sage giver of advice doesn't know the difference between a "quick pick" lottery ticket and a stock pick, we listen because we don't want to be judged, make a mistake, or invest the time and energy to find out for ourselves. At least that was true for me. One time I invested with an acquaintance and lost thousands of dollars. Then I listened to a friend about where to buy rental properties, another major loss. And then there was the time I cashed in part of my retirement savings plan to invest in a "sure thing". Apparently, what they say is true: the only sure thing is death and taxes. Learning, I'm always learning.

Fortunately, I didn't follow the advice from friends who told me that network marketing would never work, that it was a scam and a waste of time. I've learned the hard way a few times that listening to broke people who offer business or financial advice is, well, dumb. Sort of like taking relationship advice from a friend who's been divorced several times, or parenting advice from a colleague whose children no longer speak to him. If we want something more, something better, we need to seek out the people who have it and ask them how they got it.

Before network marketing, I didn't understand anything about real wealth. I'm not saying that you must be a network marketer to appreciate wealth, clearly people from every type of business and profession, in every part of the world, have become wealthy. I'm saying that network marketing gave me the tools, time, and resources to achieve wealth. Working sixty plus hours a week as a lawyer didn't leave me a lot of time to invest in a traditional business. I wanted to keep the security of my job and paycheck and work a business during my off hours. Network marketing fit the bill. The added bonus was all the personal development (mindset training) that came with the business. There are countless other ways to achieve wealth, but network marketing fits into the experience level, skill set, and time constraints of most people. That, and the fact that you can connect one-on-one with successful people who show you what is possible.

I understood the need for security that came in the form of an hourly wage with a good pension and medical benefits. As a police officer, I worked for an hourly wage and as a lawyer I billed by the minute. Time was literally money in the careers that I had chosen, and that gave me a false sense of security when it came to money. I knew that if I worked X hours I would earn X wage, minus taxes (which took almost fifty-percent of what I earned).

Network marketing paid me on my results, not my time. When I finally understood that, my mindset around money began to shift. I started spending time with positive and successful people who provided a model of possibility for me. Don't get me wrong, I learned a lot from the police officers and lawyers I worked with, but understanding wealth was not something we talked about.

Talking about money can be more uncomfortable than talking about sex. (Unless you're talking to your teenage child, then talking about sex can be more uncomfortable.) At the suggestion of Kaleb's grade 6 teacher we bought a book called *What's Going on Down There?* Kevin and I thought it would be a good idea to read it aloud, together, as a family to generate some conversation. If you don't get anything else from this book, know this: twelve-year-old boys are not interested in talking about sex with their mom. Lesson learned. Whoah, getting off track here. Bedrooms and bank accounts, two areas of people's lives that we rarely know the truth about. But here's the cool thing, network marketing—specifically the money I've earned from network marketing—has given me the time to have those awkward conversations with my son and the money to pay for a good therapist should the need arise.

But it isn't all about the money. It's all about you. Success in network marketing isn't measured in the growth of your bank account, it's measured by how much you grow *personally*. Okay, before you freak out and close the book let me be very clear here: personal growth is a big deal and if you're not open to that you will very likely stay exactly where you are.

When I first started my network marketing business I thought it was all about the money. I thought personal growth was for people with a touch of crazy or too much time on their hands. It wasn't for well-educated normal people like me. But I finally realized: it was for me. Growth is for everyone because if you're not growing you're not thriving.

Thriving means you feel healthy, happy, and inspired to be the best you each moment. Maybe that means you want to be able to give more to others. Or maybe it means you want to occasionally enjoy guilt-free time alone. For me it means both and feeling like I don't deserve it doesn't serve me or the rest of the world because I'm not sharing my best.

To improve the world you must first improve yourself. So, if you need money to improve your life, then it's your responsibility to get over yourself and make some money. I've already shared that I think network marketing is one of the simplest ways for the average person to earn an extraordinary income. It's also a great way to add a little extra to your bank account each week.

Jim Rohn once said, "If I wanted to find out how much income you earned, all I had to do was take the average income of your five closest friends and that would be your income." I don't have any studies or stats to back this up but I know it's true in my own life. Check it out in your life. Who are the five people you are closest to? Is your annual income within ten thousand dollars of their incomes? My guess is yes.

A great exercise that I use with some of my clients involves taking out a piece of paper and drawing a line down the center. The left column is entitled "Inspires Me," the right column is entitled "Discourages Me." List the five people you spend the most time with and add them to the column that fits your relationship with them best. For example, if your best friend (or spouse, partner, co-worker, parent, etc.) is always inspiring you to do more or go for it then list them in the "Inspires" column. However, if they do not support your goals or are continually reminding you about the "real world" or tell you things like "You don't have time for that" then they may belong in the "Discourages" column.

Before you get all nuts on me, I'm not asking you to ditch your friends and family. I'm simply encouraging you to become more aware of your circumstances. How can you achieve your goals if you are constantly surrounded by people who are pulling you down?

Imagine surrounding yourself with higher frequency people and experiences. Even reading books like *Think and Grow Rich* by Napoleon Hill or *The Science of Getting Rich* by Wallace Wattles could increase your frequency. It could also mean attending personal development and educational seminars led by Tony Robbins, Marianne Williamson, or any other inspiring speaker. If you're freaked out by wearing a name tag you might have to work through that. Find something that works for you and act on it. Start hanging out with inspiring people who think that making money is a good thing and will help you develop a positive mindset around money and wealth.

Look, you're never going to be able to change if you keep looking for solutions with your present state of mind in your current surroundings. People suffer because they focus on themselves. On what they don't have or what they're missing out on instead of focusing on what they want and going for it.

Although suffering can be beneficial at times. Have you ever noticed that you're able to come up with money when your back is against the wall? When you need money for your child's tuition, a medical expense, or rent, you manage to find it. It's one thing to kick butt when your back is against the wall, it's something quite different when you must treat your dreams with the same urgency and determination. Most people are not able to do that. Which is one of the reasons so many fail at network marketing.

Network marketing is about changing you, not just about changing your income. Why not become the type of person who always has money in the bank? The type of person who can give with no expectation of receiving. The type of person others aspire to emulate. Instead of being the victim, the person with their back always against the wall. The person who is constantly struggling and complaining.

You have the power to change your mindset and become conscious about how you deal with, generate, and receive your money. Wishing is not enough. Visualizing is not enough. You need a plan and you need to take action. Network marketing is the plan I chose.

. . .

"One day I'm going to start a casket bumper sticker business. I'm going to make ones that say 'This Side Up' or 'Return to Sender'. I know I can make a lot of money with those." Rob said matter of factly.

"So you're going to give up dealing?" I asked.

"Yeah. Eventually. I'm never going to be able to retire just dealing drugs and I want to be able to live my perfect average day." He said. Very practical I thought to myself. A dealer with a retirement plan.

"What's your perfect average day?" I asked him. We were waiting for his backend to show up with my drugs so I was trying to kill some time and I had no idea what he meant by "perfect average day".

"I'd spend my day fishing and hanging out at a cabin on the lake. And I'd only spend time with people I like. Have you ever thought about what you would do if you could do anything you want when you want? What would your prefect average day be like?" He asked me.

"I've never thought about it." I said. I didn't know how to answer him but I've spent a lot of time since that conversation thinking about my answer. Sometimes seeds of greatness are planted by the most unusual people at the most unusual time.

Years later I would use Rob's "perfect average day" in conversations with family, friends, and colleagues. Most people I've spoken with have never taken the time to plan what their ideal day would look like because they're too busy repeating their average day on autopilot, like I was. Thanks to an addiction to average, most people spend more time planning the weekend or how to take the perfect pic for Instagram than they do planning what their ideal day looks like.

What would your perfect average day look like? When I say "perfect average day," I'm talking about a typical day that you would be happy to live over and over. To help you think about it answer the following questions:

- Where would you work (or would you work)?

- Where would you live (name the place and why)?

- What would your home look like (apartment, house, farm etc. – be as descriptive as possible – number of bedrooms, bathrooms, unique features like a yoga studio, huge deck with outdoor kitchen, view of mountains, the ocean, countryside)?

- What time would you wake up each day?

- Who would be home when you wake up?

- What would you do first thing in the morning?

- Describe what you would see, hear, smell, and feel when you wake up.

- What would you eat?

- What would you do next?

- The same questions for mid-day and evening – plan out your entire day with as much detail as possible.

- How do you feel?

- What are your favorite daily rituals?

- What kind of vehicle(s) are in the drive or garage?

- Who does the cooking, shopping, and cleaning?

- Do you exercise (when, where, and with who)?

- When you check your bank balance, what number do you see in your savings account, checking account, and credit card balances?

- Which charities or organizations do you donate to and how much?

- If you have children, where do they attend school?

- How often do you travel and where to?

- Add any other details that would make your average day perfect for you.

I recommend getting a journal to write down your answers. Kevin and I do this exercise together during the last week of December. We light a fire, pour a glass of wine or two, and start brainstorming. This is a fun exercise that is limited only by your imagination. Someone out there is living your perfect average day, why not you?

Once you have written out your perfect average day, assign a dollar value and figure out how much money it would take each week to live your perfect average day? Will your current game plan (career, investments, lottery ticket) get you there? If the answer is no, read on.

Something must change if you want your financial situation to change. You need to get really clear on exactly what you want if you are going to achieve it. In *Think and Grow Rich*, Napoleon Hill outlines six steps for turning what you want into a reality. The first step is to determine the exact amount of money you want. Using the above exercise will help you figure out that number. However, you cannot simply say "I want a lot of money", you must have a specific dollar amount. For example, if your ideal day requires $5,000 per week, write down that number.

Once you have your number written down, the second step is to decide how you are going to earn that money. In chapter two I outlined five different options that Kevin and I either tried or investigated before settling on the sixth option, network marketing. I know it's been awhile since you read that chapter so here's a quick refresher:

1. Investing in real estate

2. Investing in the stock market

3. Opening a franchise

4. Starting your own small business

5. Staying where you are (working more hours or asking for a raise)

Of course, you do not have to choose only one option, you can mix and match and add network marketing as a side gig, which is what we did in the beginning.

According to Hill, the third step in achieving your financial goal is to set a deadline by which you will achieve your goal. I mentioned earlier that when Kevin and I started our network marketing business, our goal was to earn $500 per week to replace Kevin's overtime pay, which would allow him to stop working extra hours and make room for more family time. We started building our network marketing business in April 2009 and we set Canadian Thanksgiving (October 12th) as our deadline. That was a huge goal for us and we weren't sure we would achieve it, but we wrote it down anyway. We achieved our goal and received a $2,000 bonus that week for hitting a milestone in our business.

Of course, it takes more than just writing down a number to reach your goal. You must create a plan and put it into action. We didn't just sit around gluing pictures on to a vision board, or writing in a journal, we took some serious action. We built our network marketing business like our lives depended on it, because in a way they did. The life we wanted for our family depended on it.

Hill's fifth step in building riches is to write out a "clear, concise statement of the amount of money you intend to acquire, set a deadline for when you will achieve it, state what you intend to give in return for the money, and describe clearly the plan through which you intend to accumulate it." I kept the statement that I wrote out at the beginning of our network marketing business. Here it is: "I will earn a weekly residual income of $500 on or before October 12, 2009 from my network marketing business. In return for this money I will connect with at least three new customers, follow up with three people, and send gratitude to at least three more. I will work my network marketing business a minimum of ten hours per week with focused connecting time being Sunday - Thursday between 8 p.m. - 10 p.m. I will continue to build my skills and educate myself on the profession of network marketing." I would strongly encourage you to write out your own statement. What do you have to lose?

The sixth and final step is where I lose most people: read your statement out loud twice per day, when you wake up and before you go to bed. As you read it you must see and feel the money in your possession. For some of you this will be more uncomfortable than name tags and high-fiving strangers. I know it was for me. It felt really awkward at first to read something so personal out loud, and secondly to try and believe the money actually existed. So, I printed out a bank statement showing zero debt and a weekly deposit of $500 from our network marketing company (I made up a balance sheet using Word and cut and pasted my bank logo on top). Then I would read my statement out loud as soon as I woke up and then again before going to sleep. The rationale is that it will be the first thing you put into your mind in the morning and the last thing you think about before you go to bed, allowing your subconscious to start working on ways to help you make it happen.

Whatever you choose to believe is true for you. Henry Ford was certainly correct when he said "Whether you believe you can do a thing or not, you are right." It doesn't take any more effort to think that you can do something, so why not go for it?!

It's a fact that if you do not see wealth in your imagination, you will never see it in your bank balance. I know that $500 per week may not seem like much to some of you reading this, but for Kevin and me it was an audacious goal that turned into something much bigger. Setting and achieving this goal helped us believe that we could continue setting bigger goals. We continue to stretch out of our comfort zone every time we set a new financial goal.

I can't promise you that following these steps will result in reaching your goals. What I can promise is that you will never reach them if you don't know what they are; haven't set a date you want to reach them by; and commit to taking action that will lead you to achieving them. Your money mindset will play a huge role in your success or failure using this formula because you will never be ready to receive if you do not believe in your ability to achieve your goals. It doesn't take any more effort to believe in your ability to be rich than it does to believe you are doomed to mediocrity or poverty – both require your thoughts. Why not opt for the belief that you will be rich?

• • •

What would a chapter on money be without a few tips from an accountant and a financial planner? Forget the undercover drug cop stories, these guys really know how to live on the edge. In fact, their motto is "If you're not living on the edge you're taking up too much room which may require paying additional tax." Okay, I made that up, but I didn't want to lose you for the next few pages because I want you to be able to keep the money you make and I'm going to share some tips with you on how to do that. Just remember, it's always a good idea to check with a professional in your area who understands the rules in your jurisdiction. What follows are some general strategies that you can employ no matter where you file your tax return.

Separate Your Business Income from Your Employment Income

When Kevin and I started our network marketing business we thought of it as just more income, so we deposited it into our regular checking account and used the money just like it was extra income. In our minds, we thought of it the same way we thought of Kevin's overtime pay and that's how we treated it. This became an accounting nightmare at tax time and ended up costing us additional bookkeeping fees. If you decide to start a network marketing business (or if you already have one) please do yourself and your accountant a favor – open a separate bank account for your network marketing business and deposit all your income and bonuses into that account. Don't let your banker talk you into opting for a fancy business account – you don't need it. Just a simple checking account with minimal fees will do.

It is also a good idea to have money from your business account automatically withdrawn every month and deposited into a savings account that you do not touch. This savings account will be used to pay the tax you will owe on this income. Talk to your financial planner or accountant to determine how much that should be each month. At the very least, take twenty-five percent of each commission or bonus check and deposit it into this savings account. Many banks will do this automatically as a monthly withdrawal. I wish we had done this when we started our business because after our first year we owed an additional $80,000 in income tax! That was as painful as it sounds, especially since we weren't expecting it.

While you're at it, apply for a credit card that is linked to your business bank account. This will help you track your business expenses and keep them separate from your personal expenses. I would recommend starting with a zero-fee card. Once you start earning more money and using the card more often you can switch to a card that rewards you with points or cashback.

Track Expenses

Tracking your expenses is one of the easiest things you can do to reduce your taxes and keep more of your hard-earned money. I used to shove all my receipts into a shoebox and then deliver it to my accountant every February to prepare my taxes for the April deadline. The upside was I had to purchase a new pair of shoes so I would have a shoebox. The downside was this was not an effective filing system for me or for my accountant.

When I first started my business, I thought everything was a deduction. "Kevin, I need that new handbag for business. It's like a briefcase so it must be a write off." Not quite. I learned that for an expense to be tax deductible it had to be necessary for me to earn an income. Hence, the Prada purse did not qualify.

Some expenses that can qualify include:

- The use of your home. (Is the space you are using used exclusively to earn your business income and do you use it on a regular and ongoing basis?) Expenses related to the use of your home may include heat, water, electricity, insurance, maintenance, Internet, and telephone.

- Your vehicle. Be sure to keep a log book (physical or electronic) and record the number of kilometers/miles at the start of each trip and record if it was business or personal. Expenses related to your vehicle may include fuel, insurance, license and registration fees, maintenance and repairs, interest and leasing costs.

- Office supplies. Things like folders, paper, pens, etc. may be an eligible business expense.

- Meals, travel, entertainment. These expenses must be related to your business. For example, are you taking a new client out for dinner to discuss business, or are you traveling to your company convention? The tax man usually pays very close attention to these expenses so it is always a good idea to write the name of who you were with and what you discussed on the back of the receipt.

- Other expenses may include accounting, bookkeeping, computers, printers, phones, and office furniture.

For a complete list of eligible business expenses and specific guidelines please visit your government website.

I now keep all of these expenses in different colored file folders (according to the type of expense) in a small filing cabinet in my office. If you don't have a dedicated workspace you can use a portable file storage box or bankers box. If you are really tight for storage space, you can use a desktop hanging file folder and store it in your closet. The type of container you use to store your expenses is not important. What's important is that you actually keep your receipts and file them in a way that makes locating them down the road (should you ever get audited) easy. The few seconds that it takes to write on the front of a receipt and file it in a specific folder can save you hours, or even weeks, of struggle at tax time. And, if you're like me you will have a lot of fun shopping for color-coordinated folders and sticky notes. Looking back, maybe my first undercover gig as Martha Stewart was more in character than I thought.

Hire Professionals

When you get started with your network marketing business it may not feel like you have any extra income to hire professionals. Remember my $80,000 tax bill, well, that's nothing compared to my friend's $200,000 tax bill. One night at a network marketing conference we were commiserating over the tax we had to pay and it only took a couple glasses of single malt scotch to realize that if we had hired a professional financial planner and accountant when we first started to make money in our network marketing business we would have saved thousands in tax. In fact, my situation would have been cut by thousands. I would have spent around $2,000 with an accountant and saved more than ten times that amount in taxes owing (not to mention countless hours of stress and searching for misfiled receipts).

It is well worth the money to hire a professional accountant who understands network marketing. Reach out to the person who helped you get started with network marketing for a recommendation. If they don't have anyone they can refer you to, reach out to a leader in your company and ask who they are using. Also, be sure to ask what they charge up front and what is included with their fees.

Case Notes

- Imagine what life without money stress would look like. Write down how your life would be different if you had more than enough money in the bank.

- Is money important to you? Why or why not?

- Who are the five people you spend the most time with? Do they encourage or discourage your dreams and goals? If so, how?

- Expand your money mindset by attending seminars and conferences, reading books that increase your financial literacy, and associating with people who have what you want.

- What would your "perfect average day" look like?

- How much money would you need to earn each week to live your perfect average day?

- Following Napoleon Hill's advice in *Think and Grow Rich*, write out your "clear, concise statement of the amount of money you intend to acquire, name the time limit for its acquisition, state what you intend to give in return for the money, and describe clearly the plan through which you intend to accumulate it." And read it aloud twice each day.

- Hire a professional accountant and follow their advice on how to separate your business income from your personal income and how to track your expenses.

CHAPTER 10

CLOSING ARGUMENTS

*Mediocrity is expensive because you
end up paying for it with regret.*

— Pamela Barnum

Ladies and gentlemen of the jury, thank you for the time you've taken to read the evidence in *A Lawyer's Case for Network Marketing*. Some of you may have started your journey at the beginning of this book with a strong belief that network marketing is a pyramid scheme, while others of you believe network marketing is an incredible business model. My hope is that no matter which side of the argument you believed at the beginning of this book, you've scrutinized the evidence presented and will base your final verdict on facts.

In closing ladies and gentlemen, I ask that you do not compromise what is important for you and that you interpret what you've read based on what it is you want to achieve. Clearly I'm an advocate for network marketing – and I like to tell stories. In keeping with that theme, I present my closing arguments.

• • •

Three flights of stairs lit by one sixty-watt bulb hanging from exposed wires midway up the second flight of stairs. The smell of cigarette smoke, bacon grease, wet dog, and cat urine filled the air.

"OK I have three minutes," I said out loud. I thought I said it in my head but the words came out.

Moments earlier, in the back of the van, Kevin told me I had three minutes to get in, buy the cocaine, and get out. Mike, the other part of my cover team for that night, just nodded and looked straight ahead over the steering wheel. He was usually a man of few words and didn't get worked up about much. He was literally a "silent partner."

Kevin, on the other hand, always had lots to say. A regular advice dispensary. Made sense, considering he'd made hundreds of undercover drug buys and had been beaten unconscious and thrown down two flights of stairs on one of his previous cases. That, and we'd moved from police partners to *partners* in every sense of the word. He was entitled to be worried.

I was about to meet a new and unknown cocaine dealer in a place we'd never gone to before. I had to go in alone. I was afraid. Who am I kidding, I was *terrified*.

"Walk in. Demand to see the coke. Take it and then pay him and get out. You have three minutes before I come in to get you." Kevin opened the back of the van down the block from the house I was going to.

I jumped out and didn't look back. It took the half block for me to start breathing normally. When I opened the door to go into the building it was dark. There were scraps of light on the steps, just enough for me to realize what a slum I was in. The smell. If only this were a scratch-and-sniff book. Then you'd understand that policing involves some of the worst smells you can't even imagine.

The apartment I was going to was inside a Victorian house that in its day must have been spectacular. Now it was a rat's nest on the verge of being condemned. It was a cliché, like a haunted house you see in the movies.

Every step I took made a creaking sound, like I was opening a wooden box with a lock that had rusted shut a hundred years ago. So much for the element of surprise.

I heard a door above me open. I said "Hi" in my friendliest I'm-a-bad-ass-drug-dealer voice.

"Come up," was the response, followed by the door closing again.

When I reached the top of the stairs, it opened again, suddenly. It took a moment for my eyes to adjust to the light as I stepped into the apartment. I didn't notice the guy standing behind me. Another cliché. He wore jeans that exposed his plumber butt, a stained t-shirt, and a black leatherette vest that screamed "wannabe bad guy." He was also about six inches taller than me and a hundred and fifty pounds heavier. So far so good. Then the door shut behind me and I could hear the deadbolt click and the chain slide into place.

Was that sweat I felt trickling down my spine?

I didn't have a lot of time to worry about Wannabe, because two other guys, lets call them Coke One and Coke Two (think Thing One and Thing Two from Dr. Seuss) were seated at a table across the room with cocaine packages between them. Just as I turned my attention their way, one of two Rottweilers raced up to me and jammed his snout into my crotch. Normally a good host would say, "Oh he likes you," or "Don't worry, he's friendly". But Wannabe and Cokes One and Two said nothing, to me or to the dog. The second beast of Satan went and sat beside the cocaine table and stared at me.

"Ahh, Frank?" was all I could say looking toward the Cokes.

"Yeah. You Pam?" Coke One asked.

"Yeah."

"Here you go," he said as he stood and walked toward me.

He held out a sandwich baggy filled with cocaine. I took it barely making eye contact.

"This is the best stuff in town. I guarantee it," he said, holding his hand out.

I took the money out of my pocket and handed it to him. The dog's snout was still pressed against me and he didn't move when I went for the money in my front jean pocket.

"Thanks. If they like it I'll be back," I said.

Once Coke One had the cash in his hand the dog went back to whatever room he came out of. Like he was trained to sniff out the money. More likely he just didn't have any manners.

Wannabe unlocked the door and stepped aside.

All of that in under three minutes. One-hundred-and-eighty seconds of courage. That's all it took.

A few months later our undercover project came to an end and Frank (Coke One) was rounded up and arrested with the other sixty-something people we bought drugs from. Frank did what a lot of people do when they're facing time in prison: they talk to the police and provide information on other dealers higher up the food chain. Of course this is a very dangerous thing to do. As a result Frank was placed in the witness protection program.

Kevin and I went to interview Frank and after he gave us a lot of information, I asked him, "Why did you and your buddies lock the door behind me that night?"

"Because I was afraid you weren't alone," he said matter of factly.

When I look back on that night I thought it was an example of acting despite fear. Now I realize that what it really taught me was that assumptions we make, even when we think we have all of the facts, are often wrong. A drug dealer locked me in a room with two other drug dealers and two Rottweilers. I had never met them before and based on my past experience with drug dealers it was reasonable to think they were going to hurt me, why else would they chain the door closed?

It was just as reasonable for them to be afraid of me – 125-pound woman, alone and unarmed (they could see I didn't have a weapon because

I had nowhere to conceal it wearing a tight t-shirt and jeans). Because they were dealing with a new buyer and they didn't know if I came to rip them off. Someone could follow me up the stairs and rip them off, that's why they locked the door behind me. The fact that I was even more dangerous— an undercover cop—didn't enter their minds. Someone notify the Academy because the best actress goes to …

We've all been in a situation where we thought one thing, only to find out we were mistaken. I thought network marketing was a pyramid scheme because when I told people I was using a network marketing product they said "Oh, it's one of those pyramid things." Granted only a few people said that, but when I added it to Kevin's "fill the garage" statement it equaled pyramid scheme to me, and my nickname had become Pyramid Pam so maybe there was some truth to this pyramid thing. Initially, I didn't understand or care enough to look closer. It wasn't until I started thinking about network marketing as a business that I took the time to investigate the truth. That's usually how things go, you don't open your eyes until you have a vested interest in the outcome.

When I look back on the night I was locked in drug house and on other times I had to do something dangerous, I realize that I wasn't fearless, far from it. I've just learned to step into it. Just one step at a time. Everything I've ever done that required any amount of courage was always a result of taking the first step and then going forward from there.

That's how I went from working as a successful prosecuting attorney to a full-time network marketer. One step at a time. I started using the products. Then I started recommending the products and getting paid when people bought them. Then I started helping other people do the same, and I got paid a percentage of their sales. I didn't just wake up one day and say "I'm going to quit my job as a lawyer to be a network marketer." It was a process.

Although there are countless ways to make money, none offer the possibility that network marketing does, with so little invested and next to zero risk. You can get started with a network marketing business for a few hundred dollars – and that comes with a 100% money-back guarantee and products or services you can use.

People make money every day with real estate, the stock market, franchising, small business ownership, and traditional employment and some earn sizable amounts in these ventures. Yet, they all come with a degree of risk or a significant trade of time for money that in the long-run was not going to work for me. I wanted the ability to earn a significant income in pockets of time without risk, and network marketing fit the bill. Within eighteen months Kevin and I replaced $250,000 in combined salaries working our network marketing business approximately ten hours per week. Not everyone does that, a few earn a lot more much faster, and most earn a lot less. I'm not suggesting a six-figure income is probable for most with network marketing, I'm telling you what is possible when you are committed to growing yourself and hustling to work your business.

Look at where your life is right now. Open your online banking, what does your balance look like? How about your relationships, are they juicy and fulfilling? Take stock of your current career, are you at the top of your game? How you do anything is how you do everything. I'm not suggesting that you have to be a superstar in every area of your life to have success in network marketing, if that was the case it would have never worked out for me and many of the successful network marketers I've met. What I'm saying is that most people need to do a lot of work on themselves before they see results with network marketing.

But that's okay because network marketing comes with a personal development plan that other careers do not. When I started connecting with others in the network marketing profession I received countless recommendations of books to read, podcasts to listen to, event and seminars to attend, and coaches to work with. I did more work on myself than I ever did on my business.

Keeping all of that in mind, I came to the profession of network marketing with a skillset that helped me reach my goals quickly. I don't believe that my education played a huge role because many network marketers who are much more successful than I am came to network marketing with zero post-secondary education. Some didn't finish high school. What my education taught me is how to master the mundane, a necessary skill for network marketers.

I've met hundreds of network marketers earning six and seven figure annual incomes and their backgrounds are as varied as most other careers. Some have PhDs, some didn't finish high school. Some have extensive business experience; others have zero business knowledge. Some are young, others are young at heart. Women, men, gay, straight, single, married, kids, no kids, introverts, extroverts, every faith and religious background from almost every country on the planet. What they all have in common is a burning desire for something more – freedom. The freedom to do what they want, with whom they want, when they want.

It would have been completely reasonable to stay exactly where I was, earning a great salary as a Federal Crown Attorney. It would have been much easier to just stay doing what I was already doing. I'd spent a total of ten years in university and a lot of money obtaining an undergraduate degree and two graduate degrees. I was respected in my community and I was very good at my job. And my profession dovetailed nicely with my husband's twenty-two-year policing career.

Becoming a network marketer was never on my radar. Frankly I didn't know what network marketing was in the beginning and when I started asking about it I was led to believe it was a pyramid scheme. As a result, I initially closed my mind to it. Fortunately, my young son pointed out that my priorities were totally screwed up one morning when he helped me realize that I was putting my career ahead of every other part of my life. I realized that the life I was living was not worth the price I was paying.

How could becoming a network marketer change any of that? How could leaving a respected career in law to become a network marketer, a profession that was (and is) regarded with the same highly questionable legitimacy as fortune tellers and snake oil salesmen be the right decision? I had no idea. But I knew absolutely nothing would change in my life if I didn't do something. I wanted to do something that wasn't going to cost a lot of money, time, or experience. I needed to see what was possible.

I could put up with a little name calling and "Pyramid Pam" wasn't so bad, it could have been worse. I just kept reminding myself that when people were trying to undermine my dreams, and predict my failure, they were telling their story, not mine.

So many people are addicted to a life of mediocrity. Without even realizing that they've settled, they give up and stop striving for more. Kevin and I had both worked hard to have a beautiful home, nice things, great careers, and a happy family life. Even though we were always searching for more, we felt like we had settled. We wanted more but we kept a death grip on the ladder we were trying to climb and that kept us clinging to one rung – our comfort zone. As a result, we weren't able to climb higher. When we finally let go, one hand at a time, we climbed higher than we thought possible. The best part: we could lead the way for others to do the same.

Like most people, we started our network marketing business because we believed in the products we were using. The business came later. What made the business so remarkable was the personal growth plan that is built into network marketing. Nothing I had ever done before emphasized personal development like network marketing does. Fortunately, this helped me break the cycle of busyness I had created for myself. Like so many people I've worked with and coached, I believed that being busy meant I was being productive. It's hard for people to recognize that multi-tasking and busy-work slows down their progress.

But how can we see this? We're so busy trying to control everything and be perfect that we become overwhelmed and filled with self-doubt.

CLOSING ARGUMENTS

This manifests itself as a vicious cycle of doing more of the same and hoping to create a different result. We bury ourselves in our work and busyness to keep us from evaluating what a great life could be. I will never say that network marketing is the cure for busyness, but it can certainly be part of the rehab – it was for me. So if you're ready to break busy, start by deciding – right now – what's most important to you and take some action that will get you closer to that. Whatever "that" is.

No matter where you are in your life right now you're occasionally going to have to step outside of your comfort zone to make changes. Because change is a necessary part of growth. But stepping outside of your comfort zone is scary. Maybe not as scary as being locked in a room with drug dealers and Rottweilers, but scary nonetheless.

Every day we are faced with the choice between excuses or excellence. The choices you've made so far have led you to this exact place in your life. A juicy life filled with excitement and everything you ever wanted. Or, a life of average. For some, a life of yuck. A life like Frank's, where you wish you could enter the witness protection program.

I have good news and bad news. The good news is that change is inevitable. The bad news is that change is inevitable. It's often easier to be stuck in a familiar rut or habit, even a miserable one, than to look outside the habit and have a life that is more desirable. Because people are terrified of change, failure, and taking risks. It's far easier to settle than to leave our comfort zone, even when that zone isn't really all that comfortable, it's only familiar. Like that hideous recliner in the corner of your family room. It doesn't fit, and it doesn't reflect your awesome style, but it's comfortable and familiar. You can't imagine replacing it because it's always been there.

We create endless excuses to justify why we've settled. "I can't add anymore to my life. I'm too busy." "I can't quit my job, that's for dreamers and dreams don't pay the bills." "Oh sure, network marketing will work for him/her, they're _____ (fill in your justification here), and I'm just _____ (fill in your self-limiting belief here)."

127

It's easy to make excuses and give up on your dreams. Heck, we've been conditioned to do that a long time ago. My son pointed that out to me after one of his community classes at school. He came home and told me that he and his class worked on a "Dream List" where they were to fill in what they wanted to be when they grew up and to list all the things they wanted to have. I posted a picture of this on my Facebook wall because I was so captivated by his response. He had written down "Olympic ski racer (gold medal), astronaut, and network marketer" as career choices. Then he proceeded to list all the things he would possess; houses, cars, toys, etc. Then he listed philanthropic projects on par with the Bill and Melinda Gates Foundation. I don't think Kaleb was alone in his big dreams because he came home quite exasperated, telling us that his teacher told the class that they "may have to lower their expectations and shoot for more realistic goals." He said that he told the teacher that they should reach for even more, not shrink their dreams. I wish he paid as much attention when I told him about the virtues of eating more green vegetables and showering every day, but I digress. Kids are always watching and following what they see, not what they hear. Maybe you were told to shrink your dreams. Maybe you tried a few things and they didn't work out so now you're gun shy to go for something more.

The poem "Our Deepest Fear," by Marianne Williamson, eloquently summarizes my position on this.

Our deepest fear is not that we are inadequate.
Our deepest fear is that we are powerful beyond measure.
It is our light, not our darkness
That most frightens us.

We ask ourselves
Who am I to be brilliant, gorgeous, talented, fabulous?
Actually, who are you not to be?
You are a child of God.

Your playing small

Does not serve the world.
There's nothing enlightened about shrinking
So that other people won't feel insecure around you.

We are all meant to shine,
As children do.
We were born to make manifest
The glory of God that is within us.

It's not just in some of us;
It's in everyone.

And as we let our own light shine,
We unconsciously give other people permission to do the same.
As we're liberated from our own fear,
Our presence automatically liberates others.

Maybe you're reading this book because you want more, you're just not sure if you can have it with network marketing. I believe you can, but it's not my belief that will carry you to the finish line, it's yours. I've included an epilogue that shares a few strategies that successful network marketers have used to build their businesses. If the profession of network marketing is something you are interested in pursuing, review the epilogue, keeping in mind that it is not an exhaustive playbook, it is a basic MAP for you to follow in conjunction with the training and resources provided by your partner network marketing company.

If after all of this you've decided that network marketing is not for you, I wish you the best in whatever it is that you are called to do. You deserve a life of excellence and abundance. Go get it! The greatest adventure is what lies ahead.

EPILOGUE:

YOUR M.A.P. (MASSIVE ACTION PLAN) FOR SUCCESS

If you don't know where you are going,
you'll end up someplace else.

— Yogi Berra

nfortunately, Kevin was in jail.

He'd been arrested earlier in the day on a drug charge so he could make "friends" with his cell mate, who was accused of assault causing bodily harm. Kevin had twenty-four hours to get his new friend to talk about the assault. That was an unfortunate turn of events for me because I had made arrangements to buy some cocaine for a snowmobile trip Kevin and I had planned for that weekend. We were supposed to meet with some new drug dealers who just happened to be avid snowmobilers. Now I was going to have to hook up the snowmobiles, load them on to a trailer, and drive to meet one of our dealers who lived outside of town. This presented several problems for me: I had no idea how to hook up the trailer and I didn't know where the drug dealer lived.

But I wasn't going to let these trivialities slow me down from finishing the drug deal on my own. Kev usually took the lead, so I saw this as my opportunity to prove myself as an undercover cop and snowmobile dynamo. How hard could it be? I'd watched Kevin hook up the trailers a few times and although I didn't pay much attention, I knew you had to attach the ball thing to the cup thing and wrap a chain so it didn't drag on the ground. So, that's exactly what I did. After admiring my own genius for a few moments, I jumped into the driver's seat of the Jeep and, towing the sleds on a trailer, headed off to meet our friendly out-of-town drug dealer. Keep in mind this was before GPS, so I was following some directions I'd hastily written down on a scrap of paper.

As I'm driving past the Tim Horton's and contemplating if I'd have the skill to maneuver through the drive-thru, I see two snowmobiles that look exactly like my snowmobiles, sail past me toward oncoming traffic. OMG! Those were my snowmobiles! Fortunately, the road was on an incline and the snowmobiles and trailer coasted into a snowdrift. New problem - they were totally stuck. As I'm mentally cursing Kevin for going to jail at the worst time, I hop out of the Jeep trying to act as casual as any woman in the same circumstances would. I wandered over to the trailer with a puzzled look "I wonder how that could have happened?" I ask out loud – more for the benefit of the onlookers that were gathering than out of genuine curiosity.

"Better call Jerry," a man standing behind me said. "Your hitch wasn't on right and it snapped the coupler. You won't be able to tow it yourself."

"Who's Jerry?" I asked.

"Tow guy. Best in town."

I called Jerry and he was on the scene faster than a speeding bullet. Jerry worked his tow truck magic and within ten minutes of his arrival I was following him back to my undercover apartment to drop off the trailer. I thanked him and took off to meet my dealer before it got too late. I wanted to finish that deal before Kevin got out of jail. After about twenty-minutes of driving down a side road with no end in sight, I pulled over to call my cover team and ask for directions. Mike, one of the cover team officers, was local to the area, and I was sure he could set me straight so I could make it to Joe Dealer's house and pick up my cocaine. I didn't want the day to be a total loss.

"I'm lost. How do I get to County Road 20 from here?"

When Mike answered, he almost couldn't talk he was laughing so hard. "Great to see that Jerry was able to rescue another damsel in distress," he said.

"I'm not a damsel in distress! The coupler thing broke. Thanks for your help by the way. Maybe next time you could do more than just watch."

"You know, the last time I saw Jerry he was being arrested for attempt break and enter."

"What?! How is he still allowed to be a tow truck driver?" I asked.

"It wasn't a real B and E. He was dressed as Batman and he was climbing up a ladder to the bedroom window on the second floor. He was going to "rescue" his wife who he had tied up in bed. The neighbors saw the mask and cape and called it in. They didn't know that Jerry and the Mrs. traded taco Tuesday for tie-me-up Tuesday."

The moral of the story: ask for directions before you get lost and don't try to be a superhero. The same applies to just about everything in life, especially network marketing.

When Kevin and I first started our network marketing business we had no idea what we were doing. Our business didn't come with directions on how to go from ignorance-on-fire to successful network marketer. We listened to podcasts, watched webinars, and attended conferences so we could learn from network marketers who were already successful. We knew from our experience with other endeavors that you need a system for success. Essentially, a map to guide you along your journey. That's what the remainder of this chapter is, a map – or **M**assive **A**ction **P**lan – to help guide you in your network marketing business. These are the steps that we took, and that we've taught to thousands of others, on how to build your network marketing business.

Not everyone can be a successful network marketer. I know you may have heard otherwise, but I'd like to set the record straight. Some people just don't have the skills to be a business owner, but you can learn the skills if you CARE. Don't worry, I'm not going to hug you and start singing Kumbaya. CARE is an acronym for **c**oachable, **a**vailable, **r**eliable, **e**nthusiastic.

Being coachable means that you are open to learning systems and strategies used by successful network marketers. Available means that you set time aside to build your network marketing business. Reliable means exactly that, you do what you say you will. And being enthusiastic doesn't have to mean jumping up and down and running to hug strangers; enthusiastic means you are passionate about what you are doing. Some of what I'm going to tell you may seem obvious – but it wasn't to me. Remember, I was a lawyer and a former police officer. I had never owned my own business and I didn't know the first thing about setting up an office or running a business. So, if you're already a successful business owner, you can skip the "home office 101" section and go right to the M.A.P. section below.

Home Office 101

I thought setting up a home office was all about making it look good. I loved shopping at home-decorating shops and could hardly wait to have an excuse to head over to Home Sense and Restoration Hardware. I'd spent so long working in a drab government office with utilitarian furniture covered in fake walnut and olive green polyester that I could hardly wait to strategically place silk throw cushions on my chairs and a bright wool rug under my modern glass desk. Deciding between teal green and passion pink took up more of my time than I'm willing to admit. Hey, if I'm going to be a business owner, I should have an office that was worthy of my forecasted success! Forget that I'd only made a couple hundred bucks with my network marketing business at that time, I was building an empire and I needed an office worthy of my new title of CEO. Kevin, on the other hand, was content to continue working in the basement on a hand-me-down desk and chair he liberated from his brother's garage. He said he was "all go, no show." Hey, to each their own.

Your home office doesn't have to be featured in the pages of *Architectural Digest* to be effective. It is helpful, however, to carve out a space in your home for your office, even if it's a temporary space. I've heard from network marketing leaders that their home office was a sliver of space on their kitchen table, a small desk in the corner of their child's nursery, or even a card table in their laundry room. Any space can work. However, having a dedicated workspace that has a door you can close is ideal. The lifeblood of network marketing is networking: connecting with people. This is much easier to do if you have a quiet place to work from.

Here's a little pro tip for the keeners out there. Regardless of where you decide to put your home office, it's important that the background looks clean and organized if you are going to use video conferencing (which is how the pros connect). Remember, you are presenting yourself as a professional. It doesn't take a lot of money or effort to clean a small space and stage a nice background (hang a picture or showcase a nice wall shelf of books) so that when people are looking at you they immediately see "professional".

It may seem obvious, but a good computer and Internet connection are also crucial to a successful network marketing business, and if you read the previous chapter on money you know that these are expenses that can be tax deductible. So, if you're just starting out, here's what I recommend as must haves for your home office:

- Reliable laptop computer (your business is portable, so your computer should be portable).

- Access to high-speed reliable Internet. You are running an online business in which you will be accessing your online office, training videos, and video conference calls with customers and business partners.

- Dedicated phone for your business. This can be your personal mobile phone. Ensure that you have an adequate long distance plan that accommodates the countries where you will be building your business. If unlimited global calling is not available, or in your budget, ensure that you know how to use Skype, Zoom, Facetime, or any number of other online systems that will allow you to connect with customers and team members in the various countries you'll be working with.

- Record a professional-sounding voicemail greeting. If you're presenting yourself as a professional businessperson, make sure you sound like one. It's tough to sound professional with a generic robot-generated "Hello. You. Have. Reached. 555-123-4567. Leave a message at the tone." That will leave people asking "Who the heck did I just call?" Take the time to record a professional sounding voice message. Something like, "Hi, you've reached Sam Smith. I'm sorry I missed your call. Please leave a brief message with your name and number. Please include your area code and a preferred time for me to return your call. Thanks and have an awesome day." Stand up while you record it so you have some energy in your voice.

- Use a professional looking email signature. I use Wisestamp because I can link my social media and website to my signature, but there are dozens of free online templates you can use. Or you can create one with your email software. Include your full name and contact info as well as links to your preferred social media – remember, you're a professional networker.

- Use a filing system. I detailed this in the previous chapter, but just in case you skipped it, invest in a small filing cabinet or a portable hanging folder where you can store your receipts and business documents.

Your M.A.P. (Massive Action Plan)

Now that you've set up a successful place to work your empire from, it's time to get to work. When I first started my network marketing business, I felt like I didn't have any time to spare in my already over-scheduled life. You might recall my then-five-year-old's perspicacious comment: "Mommy are we in a hurry again today?" that spurred this whole network marketing thing for me.

Everyone is busy and I've never met anyone over the age of ten who said they had loads of extra time on their hands. We know that we can't make more time, we can only make the best use of the time we have. When Kevin and I started our network marketing business we knew we'd have to schedule it into our calendars to make it happen. We couldn't just wait for time to show up, we had to make working our business a priority. We decided that we would work Sunday through Thursday nights between 8 p.m. and 10 p.m. We put Kaleb to bed every night by 8 p.m., and since we had to get up for work by 5 a.m. we knew we couldn't stay up much past 10 p.m. – hence our 8 – 10 schedule. We were often pulled to adjust this schedule because of work or family but we did our best to commit to at least ten hours a week, two hours per night, five nights per week.

We kept Friday nights open for Pizza Island, a tradition we started when Kaleb was three years old. We put blankets on the floor, creating an island, and ate pizza while we watched a movie. We've continued that tradition but now we have a movie theatre in our home that is our "island." Keeping a family night sacred is so important as you build your business. Kevin and I also reserved Saturday nights for date night, even if that meant getting dressed up at home and ordering takeout to eat by candlelight. Relationship advice is way outside the scope of this book, but I'm going to give it anyway – let's call it a bonus. Your personal relationships are what makes life fun, sexy, interesting, and vibrant. Respect and honor them by making time for them. If you're not in a relationship, spend time with friends and family. You will never regret time spent with people you care about. Okay, now back to our regular programming.

I've heard some network marketing trainers preach the value of working your business every waking moment, and for some that may work. But I didn't want to trade one full-time job in for another full-time overwhelming commitment. My goal was time and financial freedom, not superstardom. Decide what is most important to you and build your schedule around that.

Here's one technique that has worked well for me and hundreds of people I have coached – it is called the mason jar schedule. Imagine you have a mason jar, some large stones, small pebbles, and a pile of sand. The mason jar is your calendar, the large stones are your important "must dos", the pebbles are "should dos" and the sand is everything else. If you want to fit everything in you must start with the large stones, the must dos need to be scheduled first. Then you put the pebbles (should dos) in, they will naturally fill in around the larger more important stones. Finally, add the sand (everything else). The sand will fill in around the stones and pebbles. If you did this in reverse—add the sand first, then the pebbles—you wouldn't have room for the stones. That's what most people do, they let the time-consuming unimportant things (like reading endless emails, watching Netflix, doing chores that could be outsourced, etc.) fill their calendar and then there isn't room for what's important – the things that will give you the biggest ROI (return on investment), like building your network marketing business.

Leave aside for a moment the obligations and complications of the life you currently have. Picture a completely empty calendar with 168-hour time slots. Deduct fifty-six hours for sleep. Yes, I'm asking you to schedule eight hours of sleep each night. If you want to dedicate an hour of that to "date time" go for it. Next, deduct fifty hours for your current job (I've averaged a forty-hour work week with an extra ten hours for either overtime or commuting). That leaves you with sixty-two of the original 168-hours you started with.

From that deduct five hours for fitness or playing sports. If you have a family deduct three-hours from each work day and an additional ten-hours on the weekend for a total of twenty-five hours dedicated to family time. That could be spent helping with homework, attending sports, or just hanging out together. That totals twenty-five hours for the week, leaving you with thirty-seven remaining hours. You probably want to shower, cook, eat, clean, and run errands. Deduct three hours per day for personal maintenance for a total of twenty-one hours, leaving you with eleven hours a week for anything else. I'm not great at math, but somehow that almost works out to the ten hours I dedicated to my network marketing business when I was first starting out.

These are just recommendations, the time allotted is not set in stone. You have complete control and if watching TV, surfing the Internet, or playing Candy Crush is a must do in your world, go for it. It just means cutting into other ways you could be spending your time. Most people can't cut back on the hours they spend at work because they need to pay the bills. Maybe it means cutting back on exercise. Recent polls show that less than one-third of North American's exercise the recommended 2.5 hours (half of what I allocated) per week. Or maybe you cut down on family time. A recent study found that most people are too busy to read to their kids and that working moms and dads clock between one and seven minutes a day reading with their kids. And we're blaming teachers for the lack of literacy in our children? The same study found that dual income couples spend less than twelve minutes a day talking to each other. I was tempted to make a funny comment, but there's nothing funny about that. It's just sad.

It wasn't until I kept a time journal, which is like a food journal, for a week that I realized how much time I was wasting. If you want to see where you spend your time, write down what you're doing, as often as you remember to do so. If you prefer to record it on your phone or laptop, there are countless apps you can use. It doesn't matter how you record it, as long as you record everything you do for a week. Once you have the raw data of how you are spending your time, you can get an honest look at the type of activities you are over investing in, and the ones you are underinvesting in. All this data will clarify what your priorities are, allowing you to make changes if necessary.

At the risk of sounding like Preachy Pam, I want to encourage you to hold yourself accountable to your goals. Big dreams are great, but if you don't create space in your life to make progress toward them, then they're just fantasies. You must be willing to pay a price to achieve your goals, and that might mean giving up screen time, or other unproductive time wasters.

Don't Major in the Minors

It's been said that the road to hell is paved with good intentions, so is the road to failure in network marketing. It's easy to be a good starter because that's when everything is fresh and new. To be a great finisher you must do the work, even when it's hard. But it's not enough to just schedule some time to work at your network marketing business, you must dedicate time to income-producing activities.

Many network marketing leaders allocate their time in their business by following Pareto's 80/20 rule: 80% of their time is spent on income-producing activities and 20% is spent on administration, training, and events. When I started my network marketing business I had two hours—five days per week, for a total of ten hours—to spend on my business.

I spent eight of those ten hours connecting with new people about my products and business and then following up with current customers and team members. I spent 80% of my time on the phone talking to people. Yes, I was spending almost two hours on the phone every night after spending ten hours in the courtroom talking to people. I didn't always feel like talking to more people; sometimes I just wanted to go to bed. But my dream of time freedom was stronger than my desire to sleep. I knew I had to put the work in to get the rewards.

I spent the remaining two hours over the course of the week handling admin (like filing receipts, responding to emails) and working with my growing team (helping them learn and repeat the skills I was discovering). That usually worked out to fifteen to thirty minute increments each day during the week.

In addition to the ten-hours I dedicated to income-producing activities, I fit personal growth in whenever I could. I listened to podcasts and audiobooks on my commute or when I was exercising. I gave up reading fiction before bed and replaced it with personal development books. And one Saturday out of every month, Kevin and I would take turns attending a company event. Many people view this as a hardship – giving up TV, fiction, or the occasional Saturday. We saw it as our ticket to freedom. We knew that we'd have to pay a price for freedom and we were willing to give up a few novels and Saturdays to make that happen.

We believed that working an extra ten hours a week was going to pay off for us, and it did. I often hear from people who say "I already work so much and I don't have time for my family as it is! I can't give up more time for this business. You say it's about freedom but it looks like more work to me." They're right, it is more work and you will have to give up some time during the week and even an occasional weekend to achieve your goals. But imagine what could happen in one year if you dedicated five-hundred hours (ten hours for fifty out of fifty two weeks) of productive work to your business.

Income-Producing Activities

So far so good. You have your home office set up and The Design Guys would be in awe if they saw it. Your calendar has at least ten hours scheduled to work your network marketing business. Now it's time to focus on income-producing activities, or IPAs. IPAs focus on increasing your income by expanding your connections. The lifeblood of your network marketing business is networking and connecting with potential customers and business partners. Don't know who to connect with? No worries. When Kevin and I started our network marketing business we used a "memory jogger" to help us identify our target market (the people we were looking for). If your company doesn't offer a memory jogger just Google it and several will pop up. Choose one that works for you.

Your list of connections can be broken down into three categories: hot, warm, or cold. If you're not a network marketer, the last time you classified someone as hot, warm, or cold may have been after a first date. If you are a network marketer, or have any experience with sales, you've likely heard hot, warm, and cold used to describe leads, or prospects.

HOT MARKET

A hot prospect is someone you have a close relationship with, usually family and friends. Hot prospects are people that you could call in the middle of the night if you needed help, or they may even be someone who cares about you enough to drive you to the airport, or help you move. When you connect with someone on your "hot" list you have three options on how to approach them about your network marketing product and/or opportunity.

Direct Approach

The first way is to be direct. "I called you because I've found some amazing products I think you will want to try." Or you could say something like "I thought of you because the last time we chatted you told me you were looking for _____ (fill in what your product offers). I've started a business that can help you achieve that." Being direct is always a good approach with your hot market because they already know, like, and trust you. At least, you hope they do.

Referral Approach

A second approach with your hot prospects are to ask for a referral from them. "Who do you know that is looking for… (insert one of your product solutions here)?" If you've already spoken to your hot prospect about your business or product in the past and they said "no," you could say something like "I know that you're not interested in _____ (insert your product, service or business opportunity here) but who do you know who is?" If they give you a name, ask them to connect you so that you can help their referral. Kevin and I send thank you cards with a small gift of one of our products to people who give us referrals. You never know, once they try a sample they may decide to become a customer themselves.

Practice Approach

A third approach that works well with hot prospects is the practice method. This is especially useful if you are new to network marketing. You could call them and say something like, "Hi Joe, can I ask you a favor? I'm learning how to present my products and I need to practice. Do you have ten minutes to help me out?" If they care about you they will always say "yes". Then you use that time to present your product or service. I've seen this approach used very successfully and have had team members tell me that what usually happens is the person they are presenting to orders from them.

WARM MARKET

But not everyone you know will fall into the "accept a collect call at 2 a.m." kind of friend, or even family member for that matter. Your warm prospects include acquaintances, colleagues, friends from your past, neighbors, referrals, or anyone else you know, but not well enough to consider them close. One of the best ways to connect with your warm connections is to be a product of your product. If you use your products, people will notice, and they will ask you about them. That's what happened to me. The people I worked with started asking me, "what are you doing?" That led to me sharing my results and them asking how they could get started with the same program.

However, some people in your warm market may not see you often enough to notice a change, (or your product or service is not visual), so it will be up to you to bring it up in conversation. This is as easy as sharing your results in a conversational way. Although it may sound trite, "facts tell, stories sell" is true. When you're chatting with someone in your warm market you can follow this simple formula that I call your anchor story (the story that anchors you to the product or service you are representing).

Anchor Story

- Before using _____ (name of product or service), I was feeling _____ (insert how you were feeling). *This should address the problem your prospect is trying to resolve.*

- I was introduced to _____ (name of company) by _____ (person who introduced you). *This illustrates that it is a referral business.*

- I have used the products for _____ (how long you've been using them). *This demonstrates that your products form part of a lifestyle, not a fad. If you just starting using the products you can say something like, "I just started using the products and my goal is to _____, like my friend Jane who has been using the products for _____."*

- As a result of using _____ (product or service), I have _____ (insert your results). *This presents the solution your prospect is looking for. Again, if you've just starting using the products and you don't have results to share, talk about someone else's results that inspired you to get started.*

- The best part is I am now able to _____ (insert what the results mean to you). *This should focus on the emotional impact of using the product or service.*

Your anchor story must be authentic to you, not a sales pitch. If you find yourself struggling to insert it into a conversation, don't. It must be part of a natural conversation flow. Remember, this is about you helping them find a solution to a problem they've told you about, it's not about you pushing something they don't want or need.

Some of the people I coach are afraid to start a conversation and share their anchor story because they're afraid they will appear pushy or salesy. If this is how you are feeling, please keep this in mind: the right people are looking for what you have and you will only find them if you talk to them. You educate, they decide. So I want to encourage you to do it anyway, because you will only get better and more confident, with practice. Here are some tips to make your anchor story easy for you to share:

1. Be emotionally detached from the outcome. If you focus on "getting" a new customer or distributor you will be constantly disappointed because you cannot control what other people do. However, if you focus on educating people you will have fun and your prospect is more likely to enjoy the experience.

2. Be yourself. This seems obvious but I've seen so many people become a different person when they start connecting, and this makes everyone uncomfortable. Just focus on being the best you, mistakes and all. People will appreciate your authenticity.

3. Bring some passion to the conversation. People are buying your energy, not your product or your business opportunity. Enthusiasm in contagious, people will want what you have.

4. Have a strong posture. I'm not talking about sitting up straight and balancing a self-help book on your head, I'm referring to

self-confidence. It's not up to you to convince them of anything – that's unproductive and a turn off. Instead, communicate the positive outcomes your product or business can offer (no commute, retiring early, feeling better, etc.) in a confident helpful tone.

Another way to start a conversation with your warm market is to use your products in front of them. I remember taking a shaker cup with our company logo into the courtroom and being asked during a court recess what I was drinking; court reporters, judges, defense council and police officers wanted to know what I was drinking. Once, an accused in the prisoner box shouted out "Hey, what are you drinking?" (For the record, he did not become a customer.) Whatever your product is, if you can use it in public – go for it. Or you can wear your company swag. People will ask you questions, opening the door to sharing more information.

One of the arguments people make against network marketing is that they don't want to bother their friends and family. I get it, neither did I, that's why I used the techniques described above. I didn't harass people in person or online by inundating them with "here's my product," "buy my product," "all I talk about is my product." I just shared my results and some people asked about it and some people didn't. You don't have to hassle people to be successful in network marketing. In fact, if you annoy people with hard sales techniques or constant social media posts about your products you won't be successful in network marketing.

COLD MARKET

Even if you are successful with your hot and warm prospects, you will need to continue adding to your connections to grow your business. Please do not confuse cold prospects with cold calls, we do NOT do cold calls. We're not telemarketers or door-to-door salespeople, we're network marketers. Cold prospects are people you do not have a pre-existing relationship with. These are people you meet while you are out and about living life. About half of the people that became a customer or business partner of mine and Kevin's were cold prospects. Here's an example: when we're out for dinner and our server is amazing we say something like, "You're amazing! You obviously love working with people and you'd be great at what we do." Pause. He asks, "What do you do?" "We're with a network marketing company. I know you're busy working. We will send you some info, it might be for you, it might not. What's the best way to connect with you, phone or text?" They reply with either phone or text. Notice I don't ask if they want to be contacted by email because email is easily ignored. I want to be able to connect with them. Then I pull out my phone and hit the contact button and ask them to add their contact info. I've never had anyone tell me they won't give me their contact info. This is because I don't feel weird asking for it because I genuinely think they'd be a great network marketer or could use my products.

I've met cold prospects on airplanes, at ski races, in the lineup at Starbucks, in the personal growth section at the bookstore, at a wedding, in church, on holiday, and countless other places. Essentially, everywhere I go, I'm connecting with new people – because I love people and I love my products and business, so it's natural to talk to people about it. My goal is always to turn a cold prospect into a warm prospect.

There are only three possibilities when you connect with people:

1. You gain a new business partner.

2. You gain a new customer.

3. You make a new connection with a great person who may eventually fit into #1 or #2.

I'm often asked "where can I connect with new people?" The easy answer is everywhere. Although it's true that you can connect with new people everywhere, some people, like Kevin, have taken this to the extreme. When we were first starting our network marketing business, Kevin made it his mission to connect with as many people as possible. One early morning, while I was getting ready for work, I happened to walk by the front window and saw our then-five-year-old son standing in the driveway wearing his PJs and rubber boots, chatting with a strange man wearing a Tilly hat and a fishing vest covered in lures. It was extra strange because we didn't live anywhere near water. Having spent almost twenty-years in the criminal justice system at this point I was somewhat pedophile-paranoid when it came to my young son. Just as I'm rushing toward the door to investigate, Kevin comes barreling past me carrying some product samples saying, "I got another one! Dragged this one out of the bush!" Kevin had been out running with his police dogs on the bush trails behind our house before he left for work. It shouldn't come as a surprise that Bush Man did not order any of our products.

On another "meet and greet," Kevin was alone driving our Jeep home from the grocery store when he saw a woman jogging. She was jogging alone, on a deserted road surrounded by corn fields (we lived in a rural area). He pulled up beside her and as he drove along beside her, he said "I have some great products that will improve your performance on your runs." She started running faster; apparently she didn't need the products. Kevin came home saying, "I don't know why she wasn't interested. Our products are great for runners!" The jogger didn't order any products, but she also didn't file a police report, so there's that.

I'm happy to report that Kevin is still enthusiastic about our products and business but he is no longer chasing down strangers. He's meeting new people and making connections. To keep you from looking like a creepy stalker, here are a few ideas on where to connect with new people:

- Networking events (like BNI or Meetup.com)

- Attending a new class or workshop (always wanted to learn how to play music, paint, write – take a class and meet people with similar goals)

- Gym (go to a different class or workout time if you already go to a gym – this will allow you to meet new people)

- PTA or child's sporting event

- Place of worship

- Leadership or entrepreneurial workshops

- Clubs (social, golf, running, chess, etc.)

- Franchise or small business shows (this is great one – they're already looking for what you have)

- Online seminars or workshops

- Social media (use the search feature to find people with similar interests)

A great way to connect with these cold prospects is to simply say "Hi" and let the conversation naturally progress. Ask them a lot of questions – people love to talk about themselves. It's your job to listen and be genuinely interested. You may have heard that cheesy line "you have two ears and one mouth for a reason." Well, it's true. If you're looking for ideas on what to talk about you can use the acronym F.O.R.M., which stands for friends/family, occupation, recreation, motivation. Starting a conversation is easy if you ask them about their children or friends you may have in common, or about what they do for a living (occupation). Many people love talking about what they like to do in their spare time (recreation). Finally, if you ask the right questions you will discover what motivates them – where they find meaning in their life. For example, you may meet someone who is passionate about art or about missionary work.

Talking about your product and/or business may not happen in that first conversation. That's why it's important to develop a relationship so that the cold connection becomes a warm connection. A great way to do this once you have their contact information is to connect with them on social media. You can do this on the spot when you are getting their contact info. "Hey, are you on Facebook (or Instagram, Snapchat, Pinterest, LinkedIn, etc.)?" Pull out your phone and open the relevant social media platform and add them on the spot. Following you on social media will help them get to know you better. And it helps you to get to know them also. Remember, network marketing is all about building mutually beneficial relationships.

Continue to Build the Relationship

Once I have their contact information I send them a bit of info on my product and business. I use an app that allows me to add them to a CRM (customer relationship management system) so I can continue giving them value while building a relationship through follow up. I never spam people with endless emails and text messages about my products. Quite the contrary, I give them valuable information that's relevant to the goal they are trying to reach. Share information that is helpful for that person to reach their goal. I think it's a good idea to include tips and ideas that have nothing to do with your product or service. Have some articles saved (that don't lead to competing products or other links) that you can share that reinforce the value of your product or service. For example, if you are part of an energy company then share some energy saving tips that they can use even if they don't use your service. If you're part of a skincare company share an article on how exercise or drinking more water improves your skin. Do you see where I'm going with this? Provide value even if they never buy from you.

According to experts, we are bombarded with 35,000 messages a day from family, friends, email, billboards, media, and social media. If you are going to stand out in all of that you must offer value. People determine value based on three questions:

1. Do you care about me? Mutual concern creates a connection.

2. Can you help me? No one wants to be sold to but everyone wants to be helped.

3. Can I trust you? Experts assert that we decide whether we trust someone within the first seven-seconds of meeting them. Therefore, how you present yourself will greatly impact your connection.

To make your message stand out in the crowd avoid hype. I talked a lot about this in chapter six but that was several pages ago. Here's a quick refresher:

- Tell the truth, the whole truth, and nothing but the truth.

- The rules of business do not change merely because the distribution channel does.

- Use official materials provided by your company. This ensures that you are sharing compliant materials.

- Don't exaggerate - be honest and transparent.

- Don't guarantee results. Guarantee satisfaction.

- Share all important information.

- Be careful not to set unrealistic expectations around your product or business opportunity.

Remember, the facts are enough. If you believe in your products and business opportunity you won't need to hype them up.

I'm often asked, "Who are you looking for in your network marketing business?" The answer is "not everyone." You are not going to want every person in your hot, warm, or cold market to be a partner in your network marketing business because the thought of working with them makes you want to poke a hot stick in your eye. Of course, everyone deserves the opportunity to use your products but that doesn't mean that everyone deserves to work with you. As a mentor of mine once said "Bless and release." I found that I had to do a lot less "blessing and releasing" (and mumbling inappropriate things under my breath) when I learned how to connect with the people best suited to me. Instead of trying to partner with anyone with a pulse and a credit card, figure out what qualities you are looking for in a business partner. Who do you love to work with? What qualities do they have? Personally, I work best with people who C.A.R.E. (coachable, available, reliable, and enthusiastic).

Follow Up

Once I've connected with someone I would like to work with (as a customer or business partner), I schedule a follow up appointment during the initial contact. For example, after you've connected with a hot or warm contact and advised them that you are going to send them some information, ask them when a good time to follow up would be. "When do you think you'll have time to check out the info I send you?" "Great, let's connect at X p.m. so I can answer any questions you may have." I like to send them a quick reminder text an hour before we are supposed to talk that way they are reminded, and I'm already demonstrating great customer service by doing what I said I would do.

Sometimes they don't respond and they don't answer their phone. If this happens I leave a message, "Hi, I thought we had a call scheduled. Something must have come up for you. No worries, I know how busy life gets. Please give me a call or text with a time that works better for you. If I don't hear back I will try you again later this week." If they don't call back, it doesn't mean they are avoiding you, it could mean any number of things. I had one woman who told me she was interested and when I called her back she didn't answer. I left a similar message to the one above and I tried back later that week. Still no reply. I left a text, no reply. So, I left another message "Hi Sarah, I know you said you were interested in trying our products. I've left a couple of messages and haven't heard back from you. I hope everything is okay, because you don't strike me as someone to ignore people. If you've changed your mind, no worries, just let me know." She called me back a couple of days later and told me she had been camping in the mountains and did not have cell service. Other times people never call you back. Remember Donnie Brasco: "fuhgeddaboudit." When in doubt, be Donnie.

Objection! Overruled.

When I was working as a prosecutor I dealt with objections every day. They were part of my job description. When you become a network marketer you will also face objections. The more you connect with people, the more objections that will come your way. Objections are normal and should be expected if you are building a network marketing business. I've dealt with thousands of objections as a network marketer, and although they are as varied as the people making them, they can be boiled down into six broad categories:

1. Money

2. Time

3. Don't like sales

4. Research

5. Approval

6. Pyramid scheme

These objections are legitimate and real in the mind of your prospect. Instead of arguing with them or trying to convince them otherwise, start by agreeing with them: "I know how you feel. I felt the same way. But what I found was…"

Let's use the money objection "I can't afford it" as our example. You could respond with "I know how you feel. I felt the same way. But what I found was I actually saved money by replacing _____ (fill in what your product or service is replacing) with this program / or these products / service."

You could also respond by asking the question, "If I could show you a way to get your products for free would you be interested?" People always answer yes to this question which allows you to outline your compensation plan and quick start bonuses – showing them how they can get paid.

You can avoid the money objection completely if you do a great job presenting the value of your products early in your presentation, and you ask them what their budget is to achieve their goal. For example, "We offer a variety of getting started packages. What is your budget to achieve _____ (the solution they are looking for)?"

For many others, time is much more valuable than money. One of the objections I had to starting a network marketing business was "no time." I thought that network marketing would take a lot of time because every other business model I had considered was very time consuming. I didn't realize that I could build the business around my life. The "no time" objection can be answered with "How much time do you think it will take?" They often think it's going to take a lot more time than it really does. You could also ask them what they would do with more time, painting the vision of what real freedom could look like. A part-time commitment changed my life and I'm excited to show other people how they can change their life.

Another common objection is "I don't like sales." I usually reply with "Did you feel sold to during our conversation?" The answer I always get is "no." I used to have an issue around sales until I understood what it is. Sales is simply supplying a solution for a problem. If you believe in your product wouldn't you want to tell people about it? Most people seem to be okay buying from a traditional store, and online, but make it all about "sales" when it comes to network marketing. The distribution model should not impact how we feel about sales. You want something, you pay for it – that's commerce.

If you've been in network marketing for any amount of time, you may have heard "I have to research it first." This objection often comes from people who don't research anything. For example, if you approach them with a health and wellness product, they have to research it – they want triple blind studies and peer reviewed articles that they can review while they chow down on a Big Mac and fries. I deal with this objection by asking "what specifically do you want to research?" then I supply them with information to help them in their research. For some people, it doesn't matter how much documentation or information you give to them – they will continue to stall. Let them go, you're not in the convincing business. Keep the door open and let them know you will continue to follow up to see if you can help them in the future.

There are some people who need approval before making a purchasing decision. "I need to check with my _____ (spouse, partner, friend, mom, dad, healthcare provider, tarot card reader, hairdresser, neighbor, dog-walker, guy who hangs out on a lawn chair in his garage… .)" You can respond with, "Great idea! When can we all meet / get on a call, so I can answer all of your questions?" However, you can avoid this objection alto-gether if you ask during your presentation "Do you need to check with anyone before trying _____ (whatever your product or service is)?" Most people will answer "no."

My favorite objection, and the one that inspired this entire book: "is this a pyramid scheme?" Of course my answer is "no" but I recommend asking "what do you mean by that?" Let them answer. Then respond with "no, that's not what this is. This is a legitimate business model." I've found that people don't ask this question to be disagreeable, they truly don't understand what network marketing is, so let's work on educating them.

Once you think that all the objections have been asked and answered, it's up to you to ask the most important question of all: "Do you have any other questions before I help you get started today?" This question accomplishes a lot. First, it ensures that you answer all their objections and provide them with the information they need to decide. It also presumes that they are going to get started with you – today. If they answer "yes, I have more questions" find out what they are and answer them. If they answer "no" reply with "Great! We take Visa, Master Card, and American Express, which would you like to pay with?" and take their order. Continue to provide amazing customer service and help them reach their goals.

More than 85%, people are only interested in being a customer, they do not want to be a distributor for a network marketing company. But the 15% who are interested in partnering with you as a distributor deserve some extra attention and it's your job to show them how to build their business.

People who are successful in network marketing understand:

- Goal setting.

- Basic success skills: connecting, sharing their anchor story, presenting, and dealing with objections.

- Scheduling.

- The importance of belief in the products, company, network marketing, and in their abilities.

- The numbers – how much business volume is required to reach their goals.

Goal Setting

When I start working with a new business builder, one of the first things I want to discuss are their goals. If I understand why they are interested in building a network marketing business I am in a better position to help them succeed. I interview them and ask questions like:

- What are your specific financial goals (how much money would you like to make with your network marketing business and when would you like to make it by)?

- Why is this important to you?

- Who will benefit if you reach your goal?

- Imagine what life is like once you've reached your goal – describe that to me.

- On a scale of 1 (very low) to 10 (very high), how committed are you to reaching your goal?

- How many hours are you committed to working each week on your network marketing business?

- What are the biggest obstacles you are facing (unsupportive spouse, busy schedule, lack of skills, limited network, etc.)?

Once I know the answers to these questions, I'm able to serve them better as they build their business. This interview also tells me what their expectations are and if they are in alignment with their skills and their schedule. For example, if someone tells me they want to earn a six-figure income from their network marketing business in the next six months, yet they are only committed to an hour a week and they lack the basic skills required, I know that their expectations are out of alignment with their current abilities.

Success Skills

Once I have clarity on what they hope to achieve, I review the basic skills that they need to be a successful network marketer. I have them watch a four-part webinar series where I train people on connecting, sharing their anchor story, presenting, and dealing with objections. After they watch each segment, they connect with me to review what they've learned and go over any questions they may have. I also encourage them to attend a company training event so they can further develop their network marketing skills.

Scheduling

One of the keys to success with network marketing is making time for income producing activities like connecting and presenting. We discussed scheduling earlier in this chapter and I can't stress how important it is to manage your time. If you struggle with time management, remind yourself why you started a network marketing business.

Belief

To build a successful network marketing business you need to have rock-solid belief in your products or service, your company, network marketing, and most importantly – yourself. On a scale of 1 (low) to 10 (high) what is your belief in:

- The products/service you represent?

- The company you've partnered with?

- Network marketing as a business opportunity?

- Your ability to be successful with network marketing?

If you're not a 10 out of 10 in each area you will struggle to succeed in network marketing. If you don't believe in the products/ services and/ or company, you may need to make a change because if you don't believe, how can you inspire confidence in others? It's also important to believe in network marketing. If you lack belief in network marketing – re-read this book. Just kidding. You can download the audio version and I'll read it to you.

The area where most people lack belief is in themselves and their ability to be successful in network marketing. Everyone faces obstacles and moments of self-doubt that must be overcome to succeed – network marketing is no different. If you lack confidence you're not alone, we all do at one point. I wish I had the power to simply wave a magic wand that would eliminate the noise telling you that you're not good enough, or that you don't deserve it. But there is no magic wand – if there was I'd start my own magic wand network marketing company. I can see the marketing material now: my face superimposed on an "I Dream of Jeannie" poster.

Part of the network marketing business model is personal growth. So, if you don't have faith in yourself yet, don't worry: it will come. That's the beauty of network marketing, you're working on yourself as you work on your network marketing business.

The Numbers

Every business owner knows how important it is to track, test, and measure customer conversion rates. It helps you figure out your baseline performance and ensure that you are improving over time. When Kevin and I began our network marketing business we kept track of how many people we spoke with about our products and business opportunity. In business, it's important to understand how well you are doing, or where you need to improve. And you can't improve if you don't measure. We used old-fashioned pen and paper to keep track. Here's what our tracking sheet looked like.

Name	Phone	Email	Contact Date	Status	Comments
Joe Smith	555-123-4567	joe@hotmail.com	15 Mar 2017	Follow-up pay day	School friend
Jill King	555-123-8954	jill@gmail..com	15 Mar 2017	YES!	Nurse
Sam Wells	555-123-4095	sam@anymail.com	15 Mar 2017	Follow-up more info	Shoe dept Nordstrom
Jackie Car	555-123-8367	Jackie@mail.com	16 Mar 2017	Follow-up biz info	Server at restaurant
Kelly Kay	555-123-3456	Kellyk@hotmail.com	16 Mar 2017	Follow-up ask wife	Wt loss – 25+
Sally Ems	555-789-1987	salems@gmail.co	16 Mar 2017	YES!	Co-worker skincare

Each sheet has space for ten contacts because we wanted to know if we had ten conversations, how many would say yes and get started on our program. We keep a separate sheet for each person that we place behind the contact sheet depicted above. For everyone we connect with, we record their name, date we contacted, and a note for each time we speak with them. We record things like "wants to lose weight before vacation in June," "check with wife – call back next week." When we need to follow up we schedule it in our calendar. In this example, we would add "call Kelly Kay 555-123-3456, re: weight loss for holiday, checking with wife." Every time we follow up, we record a point or two about what was discussed, or we make note if they didn't answer and we left a message.

Kevin and I committed to talking to at least three new people about our products and opportunity every day. After tracking our numbers for a month, we learned that with our hot market we had a conversion rate (number of yeses) of four in ten. So, for every ten conversations with our hot market, four people would say yes and start using our products. For our warm market, we had a conversion rate of three in ten. When we moved to our cold market our conversion rate was two in ten. That means we needed to have at least ten conversations to get two people started with our products. This number factors in that it takes between 6 and 8 "touches" before someone is ready to buy. According to the Online Marketing Institute, one reason it takes a multitude of touches (or exposures) to generate a decision-ready lead is because they are inundated every day with so many messages, they may need to hear (or see) the same message multiple times in order to make a decision.

It may seem strange that as we gained more experience and better network marketing skills that our conversion rate went from four in ten to two in ten. It's because we had a large circle of influence when we started and the people in our hot market didn't care what we knew or didn't know about our products – they trusted us and wanted to do what we were doing. We burned through our hot market (no pun intended) within our first six months and now connect with warm and cold. Or course, we continue to build relationships that take cold to warm and warm to hot but we are not starting with a huge hot market this far into our business build.

We also keep track of how many of our product users (customers) become business partners. That number is roughly 1.5 in 10 (15 out of 100). For every ten people that start using our products, one or two will become a distributor and help other people get started with the products. Those are the people that we spend time training and coaching. These are average numbers across the network marketing profession. Talk to your upline or leaders and you will likely find similar numbers. I share this with you because so many people become disappointed and quit when they hear a few nos or their customers don't jump on the business bandwagon. I'll say it again, not everyone wants to try your products, and even fewer want to build a network marketing business. This does not matter. You can build a successful and lucrative network marketing business on the yeses you receive. As my mentor and network marketing leader Jimmy Smith said "The yeses built my business and the nos built my character."

I've included a visual M.A.P. at the end of this chapter. If you are new to network marketing, this resource will guide you through the process of connecting right through to sponsoring a new customer or business partner (distributor).

Celebrate Success

"All work and no play makes Jack a dull boy." It also makes network marketing sucky. Oftentimes we get so wrapped up in working toward a goal that we forget to celebrate along the way. One of the questions I ask customers when they get started with our products is "how are you going to celebrate when you reach your goal?" People are a lot more focused and committed if they are working toward something that has a reward attached. Of course, reaching the goal is a huge reward, but a nice new pair of shoes, or a quiet afternoon with a good book (like Simon Sinek's *Start With Why*) and a latte are pretty nice, too.

Making a family reward is also a great way to keep you striving toward your goal because your family will be more likely to encourage you along the way. When Kevin and I started our business, we told Kaleb that if Mommy and Daddy reached their goal we would take him to Great Wolf Lodge to celebrate. He was really excited about this and every day would ask us, "Did you reach your goal? When are we going to Great Wolf Lodge?" This daily reminder of why we were working so hard was coupled with a great reward. This kept us in action, even when we didn't feel like it. I would encourage you to choose a personal reward (spa day, housecleaner, round of golf at a new club – whatever floats your boat), and a family reward (movie night, amusement park, vacation – something everyone would like) that you will gift yourself when you reach your goal.

Be sure to celebrate smaller milestones along the way to keep you going. If you set a big goal and have a big reward at the end, the time in-between can feel never-ending and you may be tempted to give-up. What you decide to give yourself is only limited by your imagination and it doesn't have to cost much, if anything.

Even more important than celebrating your personal accomplishments is celebrating the wins of your customers and business partners along the way. Imagine how excited your customer would be to receive a handwritten note of thanks or encouragement from you in the mail. Or seeing a celebratory post on social media. Letting them know that you are grateful for their business is critically important to your long-term success. It's good karma too, and we could all use more of that.

Celebrating your team and business partners is amazing! Nothing feels better than watching someone achieve their goals. Think about how you feel when someone you care about accomplishes something – it's fantastic! But don't just be a bystander cheering from the sidelines, actively reward your team when they win.

Again, the ideas are only limited by your imagination, and they don't have to be expensive! When Kevin and I started to see our business partners achieve their goals we added their name to a trophy we had made. It's grown over the years and now we call it the Stanley Cup for our team. People love to post pictures on their social media of this huge trophy, highlighting their name.

We also send handwritten gratitude cards and gifts to team members congratulating them not only for performance, but for perseverance. Network marketing can be challenging and we want people to know that we appreciate them for trying and sticking with it. We get to know our team and send them gifts to celebrate life milestones like weddings, birthdays, and their network marketing anniversary. During the holidays we send special gifts to all of our top leaders and those we've personally sponsored. It's important to show your gratitude to the people who work so hard to help you achieve your goals.

The first-time Kevin and I received a handwritten note and gift in the mail from our team leader (upline) we couldn't believe it. In twenty years working in the criminal justice system I don't ever remember receiving a handwritten thank you card, let alone a gift. Showing appreciation goes a looooong way! And it feels really great to give and receive.

Pro Tips

Never take advice from a quitter. If you start a network marketing business you will hear from people who say things like "Oh, I tried that. It doesn't work." They're like those women who like to share unsolicited pregnancy and labor horror stories with pregnant women. They take their personal story and turn it into a universal law. When you meet that person who is anxious to give you some uninvited advice ask them a few questions for clarity. Ask:

- What was your product experience? Did you follow the directions / system? Why or why not?

- Did you receive mentoring / coaching around your product use?

- How long did you try it for?

- How much time did you invest in learning how to do the business?

- What events did you attend?

- What books, webinars, programs, did you invest in?

I don't necessarily recommend this next question, but it can be floating around in your head: "How many other things have you tried and been unsuccessful?" After coaching hundreds of people and training thousands in network marketing, I've found that the universal truth "how you do anything is how you do everything" applies. For some reason people think that this law of success doesn't apply to network marketing. If you're taking advice from someone who has had limited success in most areas of their life, it may be time to reevaluate who you're listening to. If you want to succeed in any area of your life, model those who have had success. If you want a healthy body you will model someone with a healthy body, not someone who has their own table in the food court. If you want a juicy sexy relationship you will model people who have an incredible partnership, not the Hollywood train wreck who's on husband or wife of the week. The exact same applies to finances, spirituality, parenting, business, and of course network marketing. Follow success, not failure.

Case Notes

- Set up a quiet workspace equipped with a reliable computer, high-speed Internet, and a dedicated phone.

- Follow Pareto's principle and spend 80% of your time on IPAs (income-producing activities) and 20% on admin and skill building.

- Your most important IPA is continuously building your list and connecting with hot, warm, and cold prospects.

- Develop and practice an inspiring anchor story.

- Learn to overrule objections.

- Know the numbers and keep track of your conversion rate so that you can improve.

- Practice gratitude. Every. Single. Day.

- Model success and steer clear of the quitters.

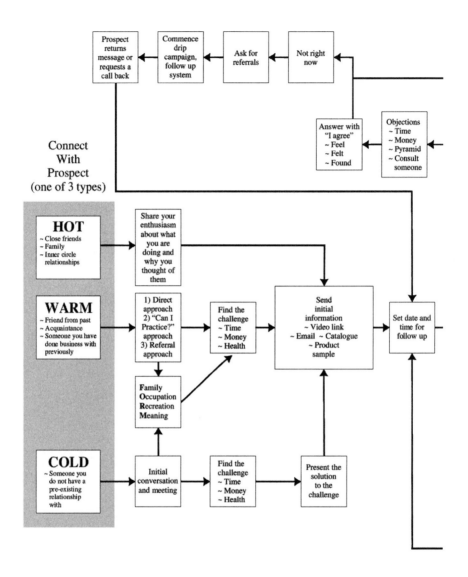

Connect
With
Prospect
(one of 3 types)

HOT
~ Close friends
~ Family
~ Inner circle
relationships

WARM
~ Friend from past
~ Acquaintance
~ Someone you have
done business with
previously

COLD
~ Someone you
do not have a
pre-existing
relationship
with

Prospect returns message or requests a call back

Commence drip campaign, follow up system

Ask for referrals

Not right now

Answer with "I agree"
~ Feel
~ Felt
~ Found

Objections
~ Time
~ Money
~ Pyramid
~ Consult someone

Share your enthusiasm about what you are doing and why you thought of them

1) Direct approach
2) "Can I Practice?" approach
3) Referral approach

Find the challenge
~ Time
~ Money
~ Health

Family
Occupation
Recreation
Meaning

Send initial information
~ Video link
~ Email ~ Catalogue
~ Product sample

Set date and time for follow up

Initial conversation and meeting

Find the challenge
~ Time
~ Money
~ Health

Present the solution to the challenge

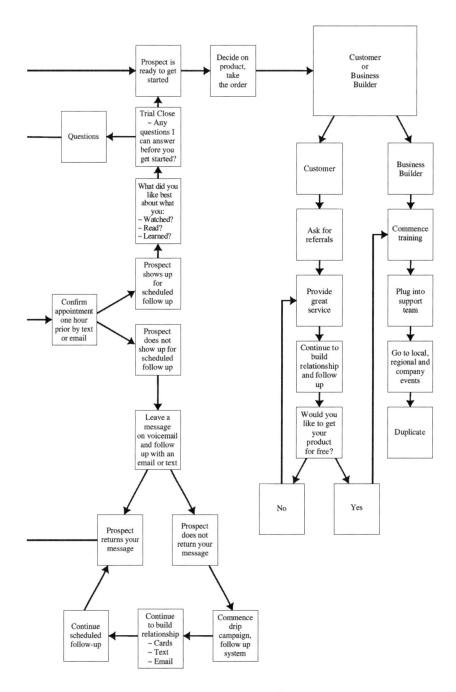

CASE CLOSED

W hat if the next time someone asks, "What do you do?" you replied with confidence, "I'm a professional network marketer." Imagine what your life could look like if you put the MAP into action. Imagine.

No matter where you are in your network marketing journey you can make a difference. Not only in your life, but in the lives of countless people who follow your lead. Whether you decide to do anything is completely up to you. My hope is that you stop allowing yourself to make excuses for why you can't have success. Because you can – and you deserve it!

Whether you are just starting out, or you are a seasoned network marketing leader, people are looking for what you have to offer. Let's commit to impacting as many lives as we possibly can by offering the gift of network marketing. Together, we can change the world. And that's pretty inspiring.

• • •

My goal with this book was to inspire, educate, and validate the profession of network marketing. If you received value from this book, please pass it on to someone you want to encourage.

Cheers,

Pamela Barnum

ACKNOWLEDGMENTS

A Lawyer's Case for Network Marketing grew out of several presentations I have made as a professional network marketer. Following each presentation, very generous souls would tell me that I should write a book. To all of you, I humbly say "Thank you." Because without your encouragement I would have never stretched outside of my comfort zone to write this book.

Countless people believed in me and helped me on my network marketing journey. First, my incredible husband and business partner, Kevin. No one has ever believed in me as much as you do. You're the never-ending source of joy, love, and entertainment in my life. Words could never communicate my sincere appreciation for the clearing you created which allowed me the time and energy to write. To our son Kaleb – thank you for inspiring me every single day. Without you, none of this would be possible.

To my network marketing partners, thank you for your tireless work and continued trust and support. You continue to set the bar for what is possible, inspiring others with your drive and determination.

Thank you to all the network marketing coaches, mentors, and leaders who not only show the way but go the way. Your integrity moves me to always strive for improvement. To my first business coach Sonia Stringer, whose friendship and guidance has helped grow and succeed as a network marketer.

The earliest draft of my manuscript was critiqued by New York Times best-selling author, Stephen Mansfield, and I am forever grateful for his guidance. I also owe special thanks to my brilliant editor, Michael Redhill – who laughed at some of my jokes.

Finally, to all the people who read this book and pass it on to someone you believe it will inspire, thank you. I know that if enough of us learn how to be professional network marketers and work hard to help others along the way, we will change the world.

NOTES

Chapter 2 – The Investigation

[1] http://www.franchise-law.com/Franchise-Law-Overview/A-Brief-History-of-Franchising.shtml

[2] 45% percent of Canadians surveyed put saving for a holiday as their most important savings goal.

[3] Forbes Dorie Clark "Job Security is Dead, and Here's Why That's Awesome" Sept 18, 2014.

[4] USA Today 2007

[5] http://www.businessinsider.com/americans-want-to-work-for-themselves-intuit-2013-3

[6] Business Insider

Chapter 3 – The Accused

[1] "Pyramid Schemes: International Monetary Fund's Seminar on Current Legal Issues Affecting Central Banks" Washington DC May 13, 1998. Debra A. Valentine, Former General Counsel.

[2] http://www.consumer.ftc.gov/articles/0065-multilevel-marketing

[3] 86 F.T.C. 1106, 1180 (1975).

[4] Global Direct Selling -2014 Retail Sales dsa.org

[5] Jeffrey A. Babener "Vemma Preliminary Injunction Order"

[6] https://www.nytimes.com/2014/03/10/business/staking-1-billion-that-herbalife-will-fail-then-ackman-lobbying-to-bring-it-down.html

[7] https://www.youtube.com/watch?v=WTDnEUIRYw0

[8] http://www.nielsen.com/us/en/insights/news/2013/under-the-influence-consumer-trust-in-advertising.html

[9] DSA.org

Chapter 5 – Breaking Bad to Breaking Busy

[1] http://articles.chicagotribune.com/2010-08-10/opinion/ct-oped-0811-multitask-20100810_1_iqs-study-information-overload

Chapter 7 – The Dream is Free – The Hustle is Sold Separately

[1] Atsunori Ariga, Alejandro Lleras, *Cognition* Vol. 118, Issue 3, March 2011, pgs 439-443

[2] http://fortune.com/2012/11/08/the-case-for-taking-a-real-lunch-break/

[3] Daniel Levitin "Hit the Reset Button in Your Brain" The New York Times, August 9, 2014

Chapter 8 "The Backend" – Your Partner Company

[1] http://www.investopedia.com/slide-show/top-6-reasons-new-businesses-fail/

Chapter 9 – Show Me the Money

[1] http://www.cnbc.com/2015/02/04/money-is-the-leading-cause-of-stress-in-relationships.html

[2] https://www.psychologytoday.com/blog/communication-success/201304/how-money-issues-predict-divorce-how-prevent-them

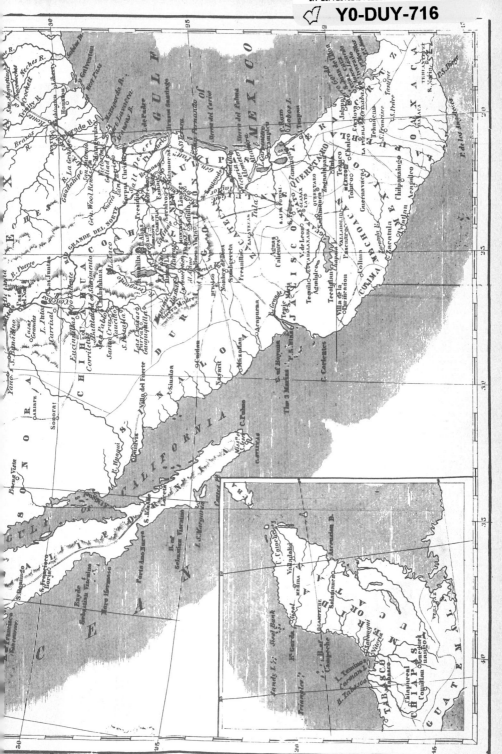

MEMOIR

OF

A TOUR TO NORTHERN MEXICO,

CONNECTED WITH COL. DONIPHAN'S EXPEDITION,

IN 1846 AND 1847.

Litho by Walsworth Pub. Co., Inc., Marceline, Mo.

30th Congress,
1st Session.

[SENATE.]

Miscellaneous.
No. 26.

MEMOIR

of

A TOUR TO NORTHERN MEXICO,

CONNECTED WITH COL. DONIPHAN'S EXPEDITION,

IN 1846 AND 1847.

BY A. WISLIZENUS, M. D.

[WITH A SCIENTIFIC APPENDIX AND THREE MAPS.]

January 13, 1848.—Ordered that 5,000 copies be printed for the use of the Senate, and 200 additional for Dr. Wislizenus.

The Rio Grande Press, Inc.

GLORIETA, NEW MEXICO · 87535

First edition from which this edition was
reproduced was supplied by
L. E. Gay, Books,
P. O. Box 548,
Lordsburg, N. M. 88045

A RIO GRANDE CLASSIC
First Published in 1848

Library of Congress
Card Catalog
74-85495

1969

The Rio Grande Press, Inc.
GLORIETA, NEW MEXICO · 87535

Publisher's Preface

This is the 45th title in our continuing series of books that we call
The Beautiful Rio Grande Classics—basic source books of American
history. Our 43rd title was by the same author, entitled *Journey to the
Rocky Mountains 1839*. These two titles together constitute not a "set"
of books, but a pair that are certainly complementary (like our Reichard
titles and our Bourke titles). It should go without saying that no library
or collection, anywhere, should have one Wislizenus title and not the
other.

While *Journey to the Rocky Mountains 1839* was pristine Americana, this title is a little bit of something else. About half the text deals
precisely with places and distances along the old Santa Fe Trail in
what is now Kansas and New Mexico, and the rest describes places,
distances and events in old Mexico during the Mexican War. Still, the
title is Americana by any definition, and in the opinion of most schol-
ars, it is an important and reliable report from a no-nonsense
scientific writer.

The first edition of this title was published originally in 1848 as
Senate Miscellaneous Document #26, 30th Congress, 1st Session. Apparently, only a total of 5,200 copies were printed as a paperbound
pamphlet ephemera #1. By midsummer 1969, 121 years later, one can
only surmise at the few copies that may be left. Those that do remain
are as brittle and fragile as fresh potato chips. We encountered some
difficulty reprinting this title, for pages 65 through 80 (inclusive) were
badly "foxed" in our first edition. This is a technical term, meaning
that the oils used in printing inks of 1848 have spread and impressed

discoloration from one page to the next throughout the book—but especially so in the 16 pages mentioned. Our printers tell us that originally this one 16-page signature was printed on even poorer paper stock than the rest of the book; it is this 16 pages in our edition that may not be as well printed as the rest. We tried several technical experiments to filter out the foxing, but the result we came up with is the best we could do without resetting the type. Had we done that, we might have had better pages but we would not have had a facsimile first edition.

The first edition from which this copy was reproduced was supplied by our friend L. E. Gay, dealer in rare books, at Lordsburg, N. M. One day last March, 1969, we answered the telephone.

"McCoy?" a voice asked.

"Si," we replied, making unlimited use of our limited Spanish.

"Larry Gay here. You interested in a couple of good books to reprint?"

"Always," we answered. There was, of course, more to the conversation than this, but this is the gist of the talk.

"Have you ever thought of reprinting the two Wislizenus titles?"

"One," we were happy to report, "is presently in production. We'll be releasing *Journey to the Rocky Mountains 1839* in July."

"Well," Gay replied. "I have a copy of *Memior of a Tour to Northern Mexico,* and I thought if you wanted it, you could have it."

"Not for free, I'll bet. How much?"

He told me; I said we'd take it and then fainted. It was not cheap, believe me. We subsequently discovered, in our contacts with the rare book 'grapevine', that it was the first copy to change hands on the open market in several years. In about 5 years, we'll sell this first edition back to Mr. Gay for twice what we paid for it.

As The Rio Grande Press is now indexing all of its reprints, we turned once again to our friend William B. Farrington of the State Library at Santa Fe, N. M. Indexing is a tiresome, tedious and time-consuming task; it is part of the drudgery of publishing. But some people have a knack for it, and even like it, and such a one is Mr. Farrington. So as his off-duty time permitted, he indexed this book in his own deft and meticulous way.

We had some discussion about whether or not the botanical words in the appendix should be indexed to their latin names, and ultimately decided against it. It was our thought, finally, that any botanist using the book for research would probably want to read Dr. George Engelman's report in full anyway, and the latin names would be of no interest to a non-botanist. But the appendix is properly indexed otherwise, and hence, our congratulations and thanks to the tireless, indefatigable Mr. Farrington for another tough job expertly done.

In passing, it is worth mentioning that our other Wislizenus title, *Journey to the Rocky Mountains 1839* was also indexed by Mr. Farrington.

Last, but emphatically not least, we invite the reader's attention to the informative and delightfully-written introduction that follows these pages. It was prepared by the scholarly Armand W. Reeder of Denver; Mr. Reeder also wrote an introduction for our other Wislizenus title, and that, together with this introduction, gives a most lucid and comprehensive 'overview' of the two Wislizenus titles and to the good Dr. Wislizenus himself. Although these two volumes are not related, and are sold separately, they should be side by side on the shelf of every library with an Americana or Southwest collection. Thus, any researcher, student, scholar or historian interested in the Wislizenus titles or the author himself could read Mr. Reeder's two introductions and the sum of the two parts would be greater than the parts themselves.

Our warm thanks to Mr. Reeder for his scholarly, interesting and highly informative notes on Dr. Wislizenus, his works and his times.

We have one final note. The first edition of this title carries one map, a geological sketch and an elevation profile chart in a pocket at the back of the book. Because of the universal tendency these days for loose materials to disappear from library books, we have had the three pieces "tipped" into the book permanently. We don't suppose this medicine will cure the disease, but *most* people are loathe to mutilate a book to obtain something from it.

Now, back to the workbench, and on with our program of reprinting books—our Beautiful Reio Grande Classics—basic source books of American history.

Robert B. McCoy

John T. Strachan

Glorieta, N. M. 87535
August 1969

A Tour of Northern Mexico with Colonel Doniphan

by

Armand W. Reeder

Frederick Adolphus Wislizenus had to flee his native Germany because of political liberalism. He went to Zurich, Switzerland, where he studied medicine and earned his M.D. degree. He practiced medicine for awhile in Zurich; he later practiced in Paris and New York, then moved to the village of Mascoutah, Illinois. A competent geologist and a naturalist of substantial standing, he made the Oregon passage as far as Fort Hall in 1839, and wrote a book about the venture; *A Trip to the Rocky Mountains in 1839* is a standard source book, and was recently reprinted by The Rio Grande Press. Upon Wislizenus' return he entered into partnership with Dr. George Engelmann for the practice of medicine in St. Louis and stayed with the practice until 1846, when he could no longer resist the temptation of further exploration.

On May 4, 1846, Wislizenus left St. Louis and on arriving in Independence, Mo., on May 9th, he joined the caravan of Santa Fe trader Albert Speyer. The caravan consisted of 35 men, 22 wagons each drawn by 10 mules, and some smaller vehicles. Wislizenus intended going over the Santa Fe Trail to Santa Fe, thence to Mexico and finally to Upper California. He expected to return in the Fall of the following year. His object was scientific, for he wanted to examine the geography, natural history and resource statistics of the country. He outfitted himself for the trip by private means. This time, unlike his

Rocky Mountain adventure, he had the help of a servant and in his wagon he carried an adequate scientific laboratory.

On his trip over the Santa Fe Trail, as on his journey to the Rocky Mountains, Wislizenus' perceptiveness went along with him. Towards the east he perceived the blessings of civilization—fine farms with cornfields, orchards, dwelling houses and all the sweet comforts of home. Towards the west, he saw the lonesome, far-reaching prairie, without houses or culture, the abode of the restless Indian, the highway of the adventurous white man. He examined every rock, every flower, every plant he saw in an endeavor to identify it. He examined the terrain, he judged the soil, he made barometric measurements and he made notes.

What Wislizenus and Speyer did not know until they reached Santa Fe was that war had broken out between the United States and Mexico. Nevertheless, when they had completed their business in Santa Fe, Wislizenus and Speyer obtained the necessary passports and went tranquilly on into Chihuahua, quite as though nothing out of the ordinary was going on. The Mexican War had reached a critical pitch by this time and on arrival at Chihuahua, Wislizenus was taken prisoner and removed along with some other American prisoners, to the Sierra Madre Occidental, 90 miles to the west. Here he was permitted, on parole, to wander as far as two leagues from Cosihuiriachi. During this enforced stay he was indefatigable in gathering scientific information on various topics. On the slopes of Bufa Mountain, for example, he found remarkable plant species, some of which are still little known in our herbaria. Evidently his colleague, Dr. Engelmann, a noted naturalist, had tutored him in the correct collection procedures with the result that he brought home some remarkable specimens.

After six months, American victories brought liberty to the prisoners at Cosihuiriachi. They left for Chihuahua and Wislizenus, seeing the impractibility of continuing his journey as far as he had intended, joined Col. Alexander W. Doniphan's regiment as a surgeon and returned with it by way of Monterrey to the United States. On the homeward journey he made such scientific investigations as his medical duties permitted.

Wislizenus' tour was mainly scientific in its purpose. As far as the Mexican War was concerned, he considered his historical allusions only as a contribution to future history of the campaign. The resulting memoir contains a considerable amount of original and valuable data on New Mexico as well as the regions further south. He made large collections and brought home many specimens from his tour.

The value of his report is further enhanced by the Botanical Appendix prepared by his colleague Dr. Engelmann, who went on to become a very famous naturalist. Engelmann's important private herbarium became the nucleus of the world-renowned Missouri Botanical Gardens in St. Louis, and the Engelmann spruce is named after the good doctor. Engelmann characterized his fellow physician and townsman Wislizenus as an "unbotanical collector" who often picked up some remarkable plants missed by the botanist.

Among those interested in the trip of Wislizenus was Senator Thomas Hart Benton of Missouri. At his instance the United States Senate ordered printed 5,000 copies of Wislizenus' journal, together with accompanying maps and tables and Dr. Engelmann's report on the flora of the trip, with 200 extra copies for Dr. Wislizenus' personal use. While lager scientific investigations superseded this one in detail, they have only emphasized the reliability and keen observations of Dr. Wislizenus.

This is a basic source book of American History, and an indispensable one for this particular period. The Rio Grande Press is to be commended for reprinting it.

Armand W. Reeder

Denver, Colo.
August 1969

30th Congress,
1st Session.

[SENATE.]

MISCELLANEOUS.
No. 26.

MEMOIR

OF

A TOUR TO NORTHERN MEXICO,

CONNECTED WITH COL. DONIPHAN'S EXPEDITION,

IN 1846 AND 1847.

BY A. WISLIZENUS, M. D.

[WITH A SCIENTIFIC APPENDIX AND THREE MAPS.]

JANUARY 13, 1848.—Ordered that 5,000 copies be printed for the use of the Senate, and 200 additional for Dr. Wislizenus.

WASHINGTON.
TIPPIN & STREEPER, PRINTERS.
1848.

In the Senate of the United States,
January 13, 1848.

The Committee on Printing, to whom were referred the resolutions submitted by Mr. Benton, viz:

" *Resolved,* That there be printed, for the use of the Senate, —— copies of the tour, or memoir, of Dr. Wislizenus through the northern parts of Mexico, as physician to Col. Doniphan's column, being a history of the expedition of Col. Doniphan, with scientific observations upon the face of the country:

" Also that there be engraved, or lithographed, for the use of the Senate, —— copies of the superficies map which accompanies the same; also the same number of the barometrical map of the profile of elevations above the level of the sea from St. Louis, in Missouri, on the line of march of said expedition, to Santa Fe in New Mexico, and thence by Chihuahua, the Bolson de Mapimi, Parras, Saltillo, and Monterey, to Reynosa, on the Rio Grande; also the same number of the geological map, and the same number of the table of meteorological observations, which accompany the same:

" *Also, be it resolved,* That —— copies of the said memoir, with the accompanying maps, be printed for the use of Dr. Wislizenus:"

report, that there be printed for the use of the Senate 5,000 copies of the tour, and that there be lithographed a like number of the maps accompanying the same; also 200 copies for the use of Dr. Wislizenus.

Attest:

ASBURY DICKINS, *Secretary.*

PREFACE.

Instead of the many apologies generally offered to the public by an author who has the hardihood to present them what, in spite of all prefaces, it will either accept or refuse, I take the liberty to explain at once to the reader with what intention I undertook my excursion, and under what circumstances I pursued it; and he will accordingly be enabled to perceive if the records of such a journey may suit his own taste or not.

In the spring of 1846, I left St. Louis, Missouri, with the intention of making a tour through Northern Mexico and Upper California, and of returning in the fall of the next year. The principal object of my expedition was scientific. I desired to examine the geography, natural history, and statistics of that country, by taking directions on the road with the compass, and by determining the principal points by astronomical observations. I made a rich collection of quite new and undescribed plants. I examined the character of the rocks, to gain insight into the geological formations of the whole country. I visited as many mines as possible, and analyzed some of the ores. I made barometrical observations, to ascertain the elevations above the sea. I kept meteorological tables, to draw general results from them for the climate, its salubrity and fitness for agriculture, and took memoranda in relation to the people—their number, industry, manners, previous history, &c. The intention, in short, for which I started, was to gain information of a country that was but little known. All that I can, therefore, offer the public in the following pages is, what I have sought myself—a collection of matters of fact, related not in the exciting description of an historical novel, but in the plain narrative form of a journal, through which the incidents and adventures of the trip are but occasionally interwoven.

How far I have succeeded in it, the reader must judge for himself at the end of the work; though I am myself free to confess, that, for various reasons, the result of my expedition has by far not satisfied the expectations I entertained of it at the beginning.

After having outfitted myself for the trip by private means, and being already on the road, the war between the United States and Mexico broke out, very untimely for my purposes, and deranged my plans considerably. By the arbitrary government of the State of Chihuahua, as the reader will perceive in the course of my narrative, I was detained for six months in a very passive situation; and after the arrival of the American troops in Chihuahua, seeing the impracticability of continuing my journey as far as intended, I accepted a situation in the medical department of the army, and returned with it, by way of Monterey, to the States. My connexion with the army enabled me to become acquainted with the principal events of that campaign; but not having been an eye-witness to all of them, I consider my historical allusions only as a contribution to a future history of the campaign; a task that will soon be accomplished by a more competent friend of mine in St. Louis, a late officer in Colonel Doniphan's regiment.

As unsatisfactory, however, as the fruits of my researches have generally been to myself, I must content myself for the present with the reflection of having been one of the first scientific pioneers through a great part of that country; and as the log-cabin of the pioneer of the west disappears in coming years before the more imposing residences of advancing civilization, so will my little work have fulfilled its purpose, when, in later years, scientific men, under more favorable circumstances, shall explore thoroughly that country, and open its treasures as well as its deserts to the knowledge of the whole civilized world.

In one particular I have to ask the indulgence of the public. I am a German by birth, and an American by choice; and though well aware that by study and daily practice one may acquire the use of many languages, there are few who can express their thoughts as freely and distinctly in one language as in another. The usual language of our youth generally leaves the deepest impression on our mind, and unconsciously influences the more extensive knowledge of later years. If the reader should, therefore—as I have no doubt he will—discover some Germanism in my English style, I hope he will not judge me with the severe criticism of an English grammarian, but with the philanthropic liberality of a citizen of the world.

Finally, it affords me great pleasure to acknowledge the co-operation of many scientific men in the furtherance of this publication. Among them, I am mostly indebted to my friend and former partner in medical practice, Dr. G. Engelmann, of St. Louis, for the arrangement of my botanical collection; to Professor Goebel, for the most exact calculation of my astronomical and barometrical observations; to W. Palm, esq., for the skillful drawing of the maps; to Dr. I. Gregg, for an exchange of his astronomical observations from Chihuahua to Matamoras, against my barometrical ones; to Lieutenant C. Kribben, of the artillery, for his aid in sketching the road from Chihuahua to Monterey; to Dr. H. King, of St. Louis, and to Dr. S. G. Morton, of Philadelphia, for their assistance in the geological department.

Last, though not least, I am indebted to the distinguished and learned Senator from Missouri, Thomas H. Benton, for the favor of laying my little work before the Senate of the United States, and of having given it publicity under the auspices of that eminent body.

This generous protection does not relieve me, of course, of the responsibility for the individual opinions and conclusions formed and expressed by me in the work. As they emanate only from my own observation and judgment, I am alone to be blamed for them when incorrect; but however erroneous they may be considered by some, the impartial reader will concede, at least, that they are based upon facts, and apparently intended to promote the best interests of my adopted country.

A. WISLIZENUS.

WASHINGTON CITY, *January*, 1848.

MEMOIR.

INDEPENDENCE, Mo., *May* 9, 1846.

Having left St. Louis on the 4th of May, I arrived to-day here in this well known frontier town of Missouri, the usual starting place of the companies going to Santa Fe, Oregon, or California, though some of the latter select Westport or Kansas. Seven years ago, when I returned from an excursion to Oregon, I had seen Independence as a small village. I now find it very much improved, and the great throng of emigrants to the " far west," and of Santa Fe traders, at present there collected, gives it quite a lively appearance. This varied crowd of strangers was composed of the most different materials—all united in one object; that is, to launch themselves upon the waste ocean of the prairie, and to steer through it in some western direction. My own object was, to join the first large company destined for Santa Fe, and my enterprising countryman, Mr. A. Speyer, whose name is very well known in the Santa Fe trade for his energy, perseverance and fearlessness, afforded me all the facilities of doing so. Mr. Speyer's preparations not being quite finished, and longing myself for the prairie, I left Independence on the 14th of May for Big Blue camp, the first camp in the prairie, about 20 miles west of Independence. My barometrical observations during my stay in Independence gave as its elevation above the sea 1,040 feet.

Big Blue Camp, May 15.—A charming spot is this first camp in the prairie. It lies just on the western boundary line of the State of Missouri, the military road from Fort Towson to Fort Leavenworth passing by it. This road forms the dividing line between the last settlements and the Indian country. Situated thus at the very junction of civilization and wilderness, we could overlook them both with a single glance. Towards the east we perceived the blessings of civilization—fine farms, with corn-fields, orchards, dwelling-houses, and all the sweet comforts of home: towards the west, the lonesome, far stretching prairie, without house or cultivation—the abode of the restless Indian, the highway of the adventurous white man. The scenery was enlivened by thousands of stock grazing around us, and by the daily arrival of new wagons and prairie travellers, who take their final start from here to the prairie. Amongst this bustle and activity of the whole caravan, I had to remain about a week. I made some astronomical and barometrical observations of our camp. The first gave me 38° 59′ 27″ north latitude; the latter, an elevation of 1,020 feet.

May 22.—Our whole caravan started, consisting of 22 large wagons, (each drawn by 10 mules,) several smaller vehicles, and 35 men. I had provided myself with a small wagon on springs, to carry my baggage and instruments, and as a comfortable retreat in bad weather. The confusion and bustle of such a first start, the inexperience of some of the drivers, and the fractiousness of the mules, render it advisable to make the first day's march merely a trial. If everything works well, one may go ahead afterwards. For that reason, we marched to-day but five miles on the Santa Fe road, and encamped in the prairie, with good grass and near water.

May 23.—We started in the morning for "*Lone Elm-tree*," or "*Round Grove*," (10 miles.) The prairie over which we travelled looked more beautiful than I had ever seen it. The grass had all the freshness of spring, and the whole plain was so covered with flowers, principally with the blue-sky *Tradescania Virginica*, and the light-red *Phlox aristata*, that it resembled a vast carpet of green, interwoven with the most brilliant colors. The road was excellent. This long trail through the prairie, the Santa Fe road, made only by thousands of large wagons that have travelled over it, is really a better road than is met with in a great part of Missouri and Illinois. The higher elevation of the prairie, with a most gradual ascent and descent, and the facility of leading the road over the most favorable part of the ground, explains it sufficiently. At "Lone Elm-tree" we halted at noon: rather a poor camping place, with bad water, scanty grass, and a single elm-tree; some brushes growing along the water. How long the venerable elm-tree, that must have seen many ages, will yet be respected by the traveller, I am unable to say; but I fear that its days are numbered, and that the little valley will look then more desolate than ever. We started again in the afternoon, and camped, after five miles, near a water-pool in the prairie. At every camping place the wagons were formed into a " corral;" that is, so as to embrace an oval space with but one opening. The animals were turned loose to graze, at the time of starting driven into the corral, and caught there in the Mexican fashion, with the lazo.

May 24.—This morning we passed the road to Oregon, that leaves, about eight miles from Round Grove, the Santa Fe road, and turns to the right towards the Kansas. A way post had been put there, marked: "Road to Oregon," (to Japan, China, the East Indies, etc., might have been added.) At noon we reached *Black Jack Point*, (12 miles.) In our camp, and still more to our right, we saw plenty of those dwarfish oak-trees, the so-called black jack, whose dark green leaves contrast strikingly with the livelier green of the prairie. The black jack grows rather on wet ground and poor soil, and the locality seemed to answer. In the afternoon we marched eight miles to *Hickory Point*, and four miles beyond to *Wackarussi Point*, a well wooded camp, with a fine spring, in the timber. Before reaching our night camp, going over high ground, we enjoyed a beautiful view over a valley towards the north, containing many hills resembling Indian mounds, and with the distant bluffs of the Kansas in the background. I understood that it is a favorite hunting ground of the Kansas Indians.

May 25.—Noon halt, after five miles, near water; night camp, ten miles further on *Rock creek*. On the latter we found good grass, tolerable water, but no wood. For the first time since our start, I saw to-day limestone in the prairie, cropping out on the creek of our noon halt, as well as on Rock creek. At both places it was a yellow compact limestone, with encrinites and other fossils of the carboniferous limestone formation.

May 26.—We reached at noon 110-*miles creek*, (10 miles,) with fine timber, but no running water. The name of the creek refers to its distance from the old Fort Osage. Eight miles further, on *Bridge creek*, we found a beautiful night camp. A severe thunder storm came on in the night, during which some of our mules took it into their heads to run back to cultivated life; but our Mexican mule boys (the best set of men for that purpose) brought the prisoners to camp in the morning.

May 27.—Made eight miles in the morning, to *Switzler's creek,* a fine running water. In the afternoon we passed three small creeks, and encamped on the fourth, *Fish creek,* (10 miles.)

May 28.—Passed in the morning two small creeks, and halted at noon on the third, *Pleasant Valley creek,* (15 miles.) The camp deserves its name: there is good grass, and plenty of water and timber, the three great requisites of a prairie camp. On the opposite bluffs exist two kinds of limestone: one is compact, white, like the carboniferous limestone near St. Louis, with some indistinct fossils; the other an argillaceous, soft, earthy limestone without fossils, resembling in appearance rocks of the cretaceous formation, but probably the same first limestone in a state of decomposition. On account of rain we marched in the afternoon but three miles, and encamped in the prairie, as we had taken wood and water along.

May 29.—Went five miles to *Bluff creek,* also a beautiful camp, with clear water, plenty of timber, and bluffs of limestone; but the finest camp, so so far, we met with in the evening. After having passed Big John creek, we reached the well known *Council Grove,* (six miles,) and encamped on the right bank of the small stream running by it. The valley in which Council Grove lies, affords peculiar advantages. It is better wooded than any other on this road. A strip from half a mile to one mile in width of timber skirts the water-course; the trees are full grown and of good size, and consist mostly of oak, hickory, walnut, elm, ash, etc. The vegetation is quite luxuriant, and the soil very fertile. For agriculture, as well as raising stock, the place would be excellent. The bluffs on both sides of Council Grove consist of a grayish argillaceous limestone, without fossils. Several graves of Indians, as well as of white men, are here erected in the usual prairie manner, with rocks heaped upon the ground.

Council Grove forms, as it were, a dividing point in the character of the country east and west of it. The country east of it is formed of prairie, with slight ascents and descents—constant undulations, as I might call them; sometimes shorter and more rapid; sometimes larger and fuller, resembling the waves of the ocean, which no doubt once covered those plains, and partly moulded their present form. Of those slight undulations, the barometrical measurements will give evident proof. Big Blue camp was 1,020 feet elevated above the sea; Council Grove is 1,190; and the highest intermediate point is 1,420 feet, on the divide between the waters of the Osage and the Neosho or Grand river. This eastern portion is well watered, and along the water courses sufficiently timbered to sustain settlements. The soil is generally very fertile, and, to judge from the higher elevation, more exempt from fevers, the plague of the bottom-land. Let us take a prospective view now of the country west of Council Grove. A short distance west, the country rises suddenly to the elevation of 1,500 feet, and ascends gradually towards the Arkansas to 2,000 and more feet above the sea. The intermediate country yet exhibits sometimes the short, wavelike form of the eastern portion, but oftener it resembles already the plateaux or high plains between the Arkansas and Cimarron, those representatives of the calm, immense high seas, where the horizon extends further, the soil becomes dryer and more sandy, the vegetation scantier, timber and water more rare. The country between Council Grove and the Arkansas forms the transition to the sandy plains on the other side of the Arkansas; the soil is generally less fertile than in the eastern portion, but all along its watercourses (as Cottonwood creek, Little Arkansas, Walnut creek, Ash creek,

Pawnee Fork, and along the Arkansas,) settlements might succeed, though they would have to depend more upon stock-raising than agriculture.

May 30.—We went in the forenoon 15 miles from Council Grove, to *Diamond Spring*, gradually ascending. We killed on the road some large snipes, probably the long-billed curlew, (*Numenius longirostris*—Wilson,) and saw the first antelopes. In the evening we travelled seven miles further, and encamped in the prairie, without water: soil generally good, and grass fine.

May 31.—Passing the " Lower springs," we travelled 14 miles to *Willowgreen*, over a high plain, where no prominent object relieved the eye from the distant horizon of the prairie. In the afternoon we encountered a severe thunder storm, and it rained all night.

June 1.—In rather a drenched condition, we started this morning for *Cottonwood creek*, (six miles,) a fine camp, with cotton trees, *(Populus Canadensis,)* the first on this road, and willows along the creek, which forms, by a semicircular bend, a natural corrál. The *Malva papaver*, with its violet flower, was here very common. In the evening we travelled six miles further, and encamped near a water-pool. On the road to our night camp I found some bog-ore in the prairie, and a great deal of yellow, brown, and bluish sandstone, combined with the hydrated oxyde of iron; which sandstone, as I have often to mention it, I will for brevity's sake call ferruginous sandstone. For the first time, we that night put guards out, as we were then approaching the country of hostile Indians.

June 2.—Travelled the whole day again over a high plain, the favorite resort of the antelope; halted at noon near *Little Turkey creek*, (12 miles,) and camped beyond Big Turkey creek, in the prairie, without water, (10 miles.)

June 3.—Reached at noon the *Little Arkansas*, (12 miles.) On the march we perceived for the first time, to our left, at a distance of about 10 miles, the low sandy bluffs of the Arkansas river, partly wooded with cotton trees. The Little Arkansas, its tributary, was now a small, very fordable creek; but when swelled by rains it becomes a wild torrent, overflowing its steep banks, and the whole valley. The soil is sandy; grass rather indifferent. For the first time on our road I found to-day the representative of a dry sandy region—a prickly pear, or *cactus*—that constant companion of mine in my travels through Mexico. It was the *Opuntia vulgaris*, with its bright yellow flower. Charming as are all the brilliant flowers of the cactus family, more charming yet, to use no harsher expression, are their thorns, hooks, and prickles. A man collecting them ought either to provide himself with nerves of iron, to become insensible against pain; or, better still, with iron gloves, to handle them unpunished. On the bluffs near the Little Arkansas I found a spotted, yellow, calcareous sandstone, without fossils, and loose pieces of ferruginous sandstone. In the evening we travelled six miles, and encamped in the prairie, without water. On the road me met with a train of 22 wagons from Bent's Fort; they reported to us that the Camanches and Pawnees were very hostile, and had killed one of their men on Pawnee Fork.

June 4.—The morning was very chilly; we passed several " *Little Cow creeks*," near one of which the Mexican trader Chavez was robbed and killed in 1843, and halted at noon at *Big Cow creek*, (14 miles:) soil was sandy, grass small and dry. In the evening we started again, and arrived late in the night at *Camp Osage*, (16 miles,) the first camp near the Arkansas. To-day we saw signs of the buffalo, and the first prairie dog village.

June 5.—Along the Arkansas, about two miles north of the river, we marched eight miles, up to *Walnut creek*, another of its tributaries, to make our usual noon halt. On the road we met with the first buffaloes, in small bands, but they were too wild for us to approach them.

Half way on our morning march, about three miles north of the Arkansas, there is a slight chain of hills in the prairie, mostly overgrown with grass. Attracted by a prairie grave on this elevation, made of a heap of rocks, I was astonished to find these rocks not to be lime or sandstone, but to resemble a volcanic formation; and upon further examination, I discovered the same rock *in situ*, cropping out at the southern end of the hill: the rock is a porous, red, black, and yellow mass, as if earthy substances containing iron had been baked together by strong fire. It shows great similarity to the burnt rocks in the cretaceous formation on the upper Missouri, specimens of which the late Mr. Nicollet brought back from his expedition; but the latter are blacker and lighter. The character of the rock, as well as of the surrounding country, excludes the idea that it was thrown up from the depths by volcanic action; but it is more likely that it was produced by pseudo-volcanic fires, or subterraneous fires near the surface, (" Erdbraende," as the German geologists call it,) such as are generally called forth by spontaneous or accidental ignition of underlying coalfields.* When, in the evening of the same day, I found the same formation again on Pawnee Rock, it was in so intimate connexion with the ferruginous sandstone that it left no doubt in my mind that this scoriaceous rock is the product of action of such fires upon the ferruginous sandstone.

In the afternoon we started again for *Ash creek*, (19 miles.) Our road went through a sandy plain, with short and fine grass, the so-called buffalo grass, *(Sessleria dactyloides;)* the Arkansas river running a few miles south of the road. The whole plain through which we passed was really covered with bands of buffaloes; their number must have been at least 30,000. The hunting fever soon became epidemic; all rifles and pistols were put into action, but the huge animals were more frightened than injured. The level of the plain did not allow us to take them by surrounding, and only the hunters, who chased them on fast horses, had the good fortune to kill any. About six miles east of Ash creek there is a prominent rock seen to the right of the road, connected with a small chain of hills, and known under the

---

* *John Bradbury*, (Travels in the Interior of America in 1809, '10, and '11 : Liverpool, 1817,) p. 153, says : " I observed a vein of fine coal, about 18 inches thick, in the perpendicular bluff, below the fort—(the Missouri Fur Company's fort, on the upper Missouri, above the Mandan village.) On showing some specimens of it to some of the hunters in the fort, they assured me it was a very common substance higher up the river, and that there were places on which it was on fire. As pumice is often found floating down the Missouri, I have made frequent inquiries of the hunters if any volcano existed on the river or its branches, but could not procure from them any information that would warrant any such conclusion. It is probable, therefore, that this pumicestone proceeds from these burning coalbeds."

Major *Stephen H. Long*, (Account of an Expedition from Pittsburg to the Rocky Mountains, in 1819 and '20 : Philadelphia, 1823, vol. ii, p. 80,) when passing through the Raton mountains, remarks : " This sand rock, disclosed at the bottom of a ravine, is of a slaty structure, and embraces narrow beds of bituminous clay slate, which contains pieces of charcoal, or the carbonized remains of vegetables, in every possible respect resembling the charcoal produced by the process of combustion in the open air. In the ravines and over the surface of the soil we observed masses of light, porous, reddish brown substance, greatly resembling that so often seen floating down the Missouri—by some considered a product of pseudo-volcanic fires, said to exist on the upper branches of that river."

name of Pawnee Rock. It is a yellow sandstone, overlaid and surrounded by ferruginous sandstone and the scoriaceous rock. The gradual transition of the ferruginous sandstone into the scoriaceous rock is here very distinct, and leaves no doubt as to the origin of the latter. Having no other light but the moonshine, I was not able to examine the surrounding hills closer. Late in the night we reached Ash creek; there was plenty of wood, but not a drop of water in the creek: it did not, however, prevent us from enjoying first some roasted hump-ribs, and then sleeping soundly in our blankets.

June 6.—Went in the morning but six miles, to *Pawnee Fork*. Near that place I discovered again yellow and red sandstone, uplifted, as it were, from southwest to northeast, by the scoriaceous rock. The ferruginous sandstone itself is here more compact, and deep red. Pawnee Fork is an excellent camp. The short buffalo grass is rather dry, as everywhere else now, but there is plenty of timber, and fine running water, containing fish. In the evening we left again, and travelled through the same plain till late in the night. Having passed several dry creeks, we camped at last about 16 miles from Pawnee Fork, in the prairie, without wood and water, and with but tolerable grass. On the road we saw the grave of the unfortunate man who but a week ago had been killed by the Indians, as his companions, from Bent's Fort, had already told us.

June 7.—We reached in the morning *Little Coon creek,* (six miles,) and rested near a water-pool. In the evening we travelled on; and finding no water in *Big Coon creek*, we camped again in the prairie, without water, (15 miles.) Although we travel yet through the same plain, with the Arkansas to our left, less and less buffaloes are seen every day.

June 8.—After a few miles march we found in the morning some standing water in a creek, probably a branch of *Big Coon creek*. The bluffs of the creek consist of common sandstone below, and a white, fine-grained marl, without fossils, above it. This marl also resembles some specimens brought by Mr. Nicollet from the upper Missouri, and belonging to the cretaceous formation. Having refreshed our animals, we travelled in the forenoon 10 miles further, gradually ascending till we reached the Arkansas, and halted at noon. The *Arkansas*, like all prairie rivers, is rather monotonous and tiresome: broad, but shallow and sandy, with low bluffs or none at all, bordered sometimes with cotton trees, but generally quite bare, it hurries its waves rapidly through the open prairie, as if it were itself very anxious for a change. However, after having travelled for some 100 miles through the prairie, one is contented even with a less beautiful river, and considers it an improvement in the scenery. On the place of our noon halt I found low bluffs on the river, formed by a grayish limestone, with some very small and rather indistinct fossils, and granulated, like a fine conglomerate. In the afternoon we went about 12 miles up the river. The valley of the Arkansas is here several miles wide, the soil sandy, and the bluffs mere hills, covered with grass. Our night camp was on the " *Caches;*" so called from a party having, in 1822, hid their goods here. Near this place, it is understood, passes the hundredth degree of longitude west of Greenwich, but I had no chance to make an observation.

June 9.—Moved about 20 miles up the Arkansas; sometimes travelling in the valley, sometimes on the bluffs, and over a high plain into which they run out. The bluffs to-day were formed by a coarse conglomerate

of sand and quartz, united by cement of lime. On the afternoon we arrived at the usual fording place of the Arkansas, and, to our great satisfaction, we perceived on the other bank of the river a corrál of wagons,
belonging to some smaller companies that had started before us. Riding
over on horseback, we shook hands with our friends and joined them in a
hearty buffalo dinner. The crossing with the wagons was deferred till
next day. The river is here several hundred yards wide, very sandy but
not deep, and generally easily forded. The road, which continues to run
up the river on its northern bank, leads to Bent's Fort, and is considered
more practicable for an army, while the more difficult but shorter route
by crossing here the Arkansas, and striking southwest for the Cimarron,
is preferred by the Santa Fe traders.

June 10.—The whole morning was spent in crossing the wagons. To
each of the large wagons from 8 to 10 couple of mules were put, and in
about six hours all stood safe on the other shore. We rested yet till
evening, and provided ourselves with wood and water, because it was
doubtful whether we should find any within 50 miles in the sandy region,
equally destitute of wood and water, that lay now before us. My barometrical observations, made on the river bank of the Arkansas at the crossing place, showed an elevation above the sea of 2,700 feet, the highest
point yet got on the road. From here our ascent will be more rapid, and
without interruption, till we reach, near Santa Fe, an elevation of 7,000
feet.

Towards evening we started again. Our road led through deep sand.
Grass was very scanty, but there was quite an abundance of sand-
plants; and the ground was so covered with the most variegated flowers,
especially the gay *Gaillardia pulchella*, that it looked more like an
immense flower garden than a sandy desert. At first ascending a little,
we travelled afterwards over a high plain, with good road, and pitched our
night camp on "*Battle Ground*," (15 miles from Arkansas,) with poor,
dry grass, but a small water-pool. The name of this camp refers to the
small band of Texans under Colonel Snively, who, in 1843, here fell in
with the vanguard of General Armijo's army. With their rifles and
bowie knives they made a dreadful havoc among them ; and the few
Mexicans who escaped frightened Armijo so with their reports, that he,
with his whole army, ran back to Santa Fe.

June 11.—Travelled about 18 miles before we halted, without seeing
wood or water. Buffalo have entirely disappeared ; not even buffalo
chips, the usual substitute for fire-wood, were to be seen. The high
plain between the Arkansas and Cimarron, whose elevation above the sea
is about 3,000 feet, is the most desolate part on the whole Santa Fe road,
and the first adventurers in Santa Fe trade stood many severe trials here.
Within the distance of 66 miles, from the Arkansas to the lower springs
of Cimarron, there is not one water-course or water-pool to be depended
upon in the dry season. The soil is generally dry and hard; the vegetation
poor; scarcely anything grows there but short and parched buffalo grass
and some cacti. Though the horizon is very distant, there is no shrub
or tree to fix your eye upon, and no other game attracts your attention
except once in awhile a wild antelope, which is apt to allure you to a useless chase. But, for one quality this desert is distinguished. When your
patience has been worn out by the long ride, and by the monotonous
sameness of the scenery; when your lips are parched from thirst, and a
friend at your side, in cruel consolation, reminds you of the luxuries of

cultivated life—to all of which you would nevertheless prefer a refreshing draught of cold water—there emerges in the plain before your astonished eyes a beautiful lake. Its surface looks like crystal; the wind moves but slightly the wide sheet of water; but the faster you hurry forward, the nearer you approach it, the sooner you will be disenchanted; the lake disappears again before your presence; and when you arrive at the very spot, you perceive nothing but the same hard, dry, parched soil, over which you have travelled all day. This is the celebrated *"mirage," (false ponds; fata morgana.)* Though it also appears in other parts of the prairie, it is nowhere so common, so deceptive, and so well developed, as here. In examining the causes which produce it at this high plain, I have arrived at the following conclusions:

The phenomenon of mirage requires—

1. A wide high plain, with extensive horizon, and but slight undulations of the ground.

2. A dry, hard ground, either quite barren, or but coated with parched and isolated vegetation, like the short buffalo grass.

3. Dry and warm weather, with a clear sky. On such days, and less in the morning and evening, but rather when the sun has the most power, mirage is the most frequent and the plainest.

4. A slight hollow in the undulating plain, however insignificant it may be, producing a background. Where this low background is interrupted by the horizon, on that place the mirage grows more dim and disappears entirely.

5. The distance of several miles from the stand of the observer. The nearer one approaches, the more indistinct becomes the mirage, and it changes at last into a glimmering of the air, such as can be seen on hot summer days upon dry, solid, macadamized roads, from which the rays of the sun are powerfully reflected.

6. The mirage is therefore the effect of a strong reflection of the rays of the sun from the ground, seen out of a certain distance, on certain localities.

7. That objects, being near the mirage, as trees, animals, men, &c., are seen double, can also be explained by the following law of reflection:

When two strata of air, one of common middle temperature and density, and the other hotter, meet together, an observer, standing also in a common temperature and looking at an object near where the two strata meet, will see that object double, directly in the stratum of common air, in which he stands himself, and indirectly by reflected light in the hotter stratum. The direct image will stand upright; the reflected one inverted.

But let us return to our caravan. While we were travelling to-day over the lonesome plain, men and animals quite tired and exhausted, on the rising of a hill before us quite suddenly appeared a number of savage-looking riders on horseback, which at first sight we took for Indians; but their covered heads convinced us soon of our mistake, because Indians never wear hats of any kind: it was a band of Ciboleros, or Mexican buffalo hunters, dressed in leather or blankets, armed with bows and arrows and a lance—sometimes, too, with a gun—and leading along a large train of jaded pack animals. Those Ciboleros are generally poor Mexicans from the frontier settlements of New Mexico, and by their yearly expeditions into the buffalo regions they provide themselves with dried buffalo meat for their own support and for sale. Their principal weapon is the lance, which in riding they plunge so adroitly into the buffalo's flanks, that they seldom miss their aim. They are never hostile towards white men, and seem to be afraid of the Indians. In their manners, dress, weapons, and faces, they resemble the Indians so much, that they may be easily mistaken for them. The company which we met with consisted of about 100 men and some women, and they felt rather disappointed when we told them how far they had to travel to find the buffalo. We left our noon camp again towards evening, determined not to stop any more before we should reach water. Late in the night we arrived at *Sand creek*, (17 miles,) and were fortunate enough to find here some muddy water and tolerable grass.

June 12.—Early in the morning we were honored in our camp with the visit of five Indians, (Shayenes,) who reported that 500 lodges of their people were camped near the Cimarron, to trade with the Camanches, and they would be happy to see us this evening. The messengers themselves had "dreamed" that we would regale them with a good breakfast; their dream was granted, and they left us contented. We started very late this morning, and reached about noon the *lower springs of Cimarron*, (eight miles,) a small green valley, spread out like an oasis in the desert. The water is fresh and running, and rushes grow on the banks. We had not been a long time in our camp, when a whole crowd of Shayenes—warriors, squaws, and papooses—made their appearance. The warriors sat down to a smoke and talk, were fed, and received some presents; the squaws, some of whom were quite handsome, sold ropes, moccasins, &c., to our men, and we parted all in friendship. In the evening we marched eight miles more, and encamped near the Cimarron, on which we shall ascend for several days. The *Cimarron* is here a mere dry bed of sand; but after digging some feet deep, the hole will soon be filled with water.

June 13.—Went 18 miles in the morning over a dry plain before we halted on the Cimarron, from whose dry bed we drew again some water. In the evening we reached the *middle springs of Cimarron*, (8 miles,) with tolerable water. For the first time I saw some rocks again, a sandy limestone, above a pure sandstone.

June 14.—Next morning we marched but three miles and rested near a water-hole made in the Cimarron. The soil has now become entirely sandy; different species of artemisia, those shrubs with bitter taste and terebinthine flavor, cover the whole plain; horn-frogs, lizards, and rattlesnakes find a comfortable abode in the warm sand; thousands of grasshoppers occupy all shrubs and plants, mosquitoes and buffalo gnats the air;—what a great place for settlements this would be! We travelled in the evening about 10 miles, and camped without water, but with tolerable grass, considering that we were on the Cimarron.

June 15.—Went up the Cimarron for about six miles, and halted at noon. For the first time we saw here running water in the creek, but of bad, brackish taste. The plains through which we travel are often coated with alcaline salts, in a state of efflorescense. The soil is less sandy, and the grass decidedly better; flowers, which I had not seen since we left the Arkansas, reappeared. In the afternoon we passed *Willow creek*, and encamped on the *crossing of Cimarron*, (eight miles.) On the road to-day we saw the skulls and bones of about 100 mules, which Mr. Speyer had lost here several years ago, when he travelled over these plains late in the fall, and a snowstorm overtook him in the night. The poor animals (so he told me) crowded all around a little fire which he had kindled, but the cold was so intense that most of them died the same night; and others, in a state of starvation, commenced eating the ears of the dead ones.

The Cimarron at our night camp is a fine running creek, with good grass, but without wood. The elevation of our night camp is 3,830 feet. To-morrow we shall leave the Cimarron entirely, for better regions. In looking back from here towards the Arkansas, it is hardly necessary to remark, that this whole country, from the crossing of the Arkansas to the crossing of the Cimarron, will never be settled, from the scantness of grass, the scarcity of water, and the entire want of wood. But westward from here we shall come to regions more favored by nature, and more accessible to human industry.

June 16.—Started in the morning, passing by the *upper springs of Cimarron*, (12 miles,) to *Cold spring*, (17 miles.) The road becomes more gravelly. To our right we perceived distant, table-formed hills, with timber—a refreshing sight to a traveller who comes from the Cimarron.

About five miles from the crossing, light bluffs rise in the prairie, con-sisting of a yellow and reddish sandstone below, and a spotted sandstone, combined with lime and argyle, above. Five miles further, to the right of our road, rises a small mountain, formed by masses of rocks heaped up in irreg-ular shapes to the height of nearly 100 feet. Ascending over those blocks to the top, I found them all to consist either of pure quartz or a very compact silicious sandstone of different colors, from white to deep red, (colored by oxyde of iron.) For a moment, I was at a loss to explain the presence and origin of this mountain. There was common sandstone all around it in the prairie, even at the foot of the mountain, but I could dis-cover no connexion at all between this sandstone and the isolated mountain, and nowhere else could I perceive igneous rocks. This mountain could not therefore be *in situ;* it was an immense mass of boulders, transported here from more distant places by water, ice, or whatever theory one may accept for the explanation of those heavy masses of rocks, found very dis-tant from the place of their origin, and known under the name of *boulders.* My opinion was confirmed by some polished surfaces that I found on the southwest side of the blocks, even of those lying on the top of the moun-tain. Some miles further I met with many isolated blocks of the same character; also with erratic rocks of serpentine and amygdaloidal basalt.

Cold Spring, where we halted, afforded us the best water we have tasted since we left the Arkansas; it breaks out of the sandstone that prevails here, and has a refreshing coolness. In the evening we marched six miles on our road, and encamped in the prairie. Towards evening we enjoyed the most beautiful scenery, which but a landscape of so mixed a character, where prairie and mountains meet, can produce. In the distant moun-tains before us, and to our left, a thunder-storm was gathering; and the set-ting sun illuminated the fast sailing clouds with so many tinted colors, changing their hues every minute, that it would be impossible even for the pencil of a Salvador Rosa to do justice to the grandeur of the scenery.

June 17.—We started this morning in a thick fog, with drizzling rain, but at last the sun overcame the clouds. The road is good, gradually as-cending, and leads through the plain, while mountains, timbered with cedar, are on our right, a distance of 10 miles, and the rabbit-ear mounds about 40 miles before us. At noon we halted at *Cedar creek*, (eight miles.) Some cedars and cotton trees grow here; sandstone prevails; the water is good; grass tolerable. In the afternoon we marched to *McNees' creek*, (12 miles,) but found not a drop of water in it.

June 18.—At our noon halt to day we met with water again on *Cottonwood branch*, (12 miles.) Here, as well as on McNees' creek, a yellow sandstone prevails. The road is approaching nearer and nearer to the mountains. In the afternoon we passed to the right of the rabbit-ear mounds, whose resemblance to rabbit-ears, with some stretch of imagination, one may discover very easily, and arrived on *Rabbit ear creek*, (12 miles,) a camp with good grass and water, and cotton-trees and willows along the creek. On the right bank of the creek rise steep bluffs, formed by that porous, black looking basaltic rock, known as amygdaloidal basalt, and so common throughout the whole of Mexico. This is the first place where I have seen it *in situ*. It forms perpendicular walls, and is found strewed over the whole river bank. Below is a compact quartzose sandstone, as if common sandstone had been changed by volcanic action. The basalt, as well as the sandstone, lay horizontal.

June 19.—For want of water we marched 20 miles without rest, to *Rock creek*. About eight miles from Rabbit ear creek a mountain rises in the prairie, nearly one mile south of the road—the so-called *Round mound*. I ascended it, and by barometrical measurement found the difference between the foot and the top of the mountain to be 610 feet, or its absolute elevation above the sea 6,655 feet. So rapid has been our ascent since we left the Cimarron. On the top of the mountain grow cedars. The rocks composing it appear to be basaltic, in a state of decomposition; they look brown, and are sometimes very compact—sometimes more granular and friable. The view from the Round mound over the surrounding country is beautiful. The Taos mountains, in the west, are quite conspicuous; and towards the northwest I discovered high mountains—some of them with snowy summits—probably the Spanish peaks. On Rock creek I saw the amygdaloidal basalt again *in situ*, with its underlying sandstone.

June 20.—In the morning we made but five miles, to *Whetstone creek*, and halted, with good grass and water. The sandstone here contains some lime, and may be used for coarse whetstones. The amygdaloidal basalt, which I found near our noon camp, is intermixed with silicious particles, glittering like mica. In the afternoon we made 14 miles, to *"Point of Rocks,"* the projecting spur of a chain of mountains, to our right, that here approached the road. In going to our night camp we passed extensive strata of yellow quartzose sandstone, dipping gently towards the northeast. Point of Rocks itself is a mass of large blocks of sienite, towering to the height of several hundred feet. A clear mountain spring comes out of the rock. Here we camped.

June 21.—Travelled in the morning eight miles over excellent road, and halted at noon in a ravine, or cañon, 6,486 feet above the sea. During the whole day we enjoyed a beautiful view of the mountains before and around us, the most distant of them being covered with snow. In our afternoon march I met, in the plain, with a hill of a very compact black basalt, underlaid by sandstone. In the evening we reached the *Rio Colorado*, (12 miles,) the principal headwaters of the Canadian river, and found an excellent camp. The Rio Colorado is a clear mountain stream, with fine grass and good soil; cedars grow on the neighboring hills, and further down on the creek. A settlement would succeed very well here.

June 22.—We left the Colorado this morning for the *Ocaté creek,* (six miles.) The Ocaté contained but little water at that time, but its bed of sandstone and its steep banks seemed to be made for a big river, which form it assumes sometimes. On Ocaté creek there are some pines, the first we have seen close on the road. The elevation of the Ocaté above the sea is about 6,000 feet. We started in the afternoon for *Wagon mound.* Our road, as usual, runs through a wide plain, with the constant view of the northwest mountains before us. Half way a hail-storm overtook us, and forced us to camp in the prairie, (12 miles.)

June 23.—Made this morning 12 miles, to *Santa Clara.* We are travelling still over a high plain, though more encompassed by mountains than before. The western mountains before us are all covered thickly with pine timber. Some isolated mountains rise in the plains through which we travel. The road passes at the foot of the highest of them, the so-called *Wagon mound,* which I ascended as far as the rocks would allow. On the Wagon mound I found for the first time a dry specimen of the *Opuntia arborescens,* (Eng.,) so common throughout Mexico, and whose porous stems are used in the south as torches. The rock composing the Wagon mound is a compact black and spotted basalt, that rises on the top to steep, perpendicular, indented columns of about 100 feet. During my excursion the caravan had come to a halt, and camped on a spring near the Wagon mound, called the *Santa Clara.* On riding to camp I was taken by surprise at hearing suddenly the warlike sound of a trumpet, and seeing a captain, with 30 Mexican soldiers and a flock of sheep, encamped near the caravan. The soldiers looked as poor and miserable as they could be. Some wore pieces of uniform; some were dressed in mere rags; some seated on mules, and some walked barefooted. All of them were armed with short lances, like the Ciboleros, but few had rusty guns. After all, they made no formidable appearance; and had no use for it, neither, because they appeared with the most friendly intentions. . It was the usual escort sent out by the Governor of Santa Fe to receive the caravans, to protect them from the Indians; to sell his sheep to them if they wanted to buy some, but especially to prevent smuggling. The Mexicans reported that everything was quiet in Santa Fe, and that General Armijo was at the head of government in New Mexico. We travelled in the afternoon about eight miles, and camped in the plain without water, the Mexicans some distance from us.

June 24.—Went in the morning but five miles, to *Wolf creek.* The descent on the river bank is very steep and rocky. The creek, as well as the whole neighborhood, exhibited again the amygdaloidal basalt, with quartzose sandstone below, both horizontal. Pine, cedars, and sundry shrubs, grow along the creek; the grass and water are good.

Travelling this morning quietly over the plain, we heard in the distance of several miles a singular, awful noise, like a combination of falling rocks, breaking of bones, screams of anguish and cries of children, but the deep impression which the mysterious concert had made upon my ears was but surpassed by the surprising effect, when with my own eyes I descried the wonderful machine whose action produced that unearthly music—a Mexican carréta. Imagine to yourself a cart, made without any nails or iron of any kind, with two solid wheels formed out of the trunk of a big tree, and in the circumference rounded, or rather squared, and with a frame of ox-skin or sticks fastened together by rawhide, and this machine then put in motion by three yoke of oxen, and carrying a load, which on a better vehicle one animal could transport much faster and easier, and you will have an idea of this primitive and only known vehicle used in Northern Mexico. The present carrétas were loaded with maize, for which Mr. Speyer had sent to the nearest settlements; and our animals, somewhat exhausted by the journey, enjoyed for several days a sumptuous dinner, which the poor Mexican soldiers, whose only food was beans, seemed to envy them. A plain and good road led us in the afternoon through mountains to our right and left, covered with pine.

About eight miles from Wolf creek we reached the *Rio Mora*, a fine mountain stream, and a charming valley was spreading out before us. Soil, grass, and water, are excellent; the surrounding mountains furnish an abundance of pine, and protect the valley at the same time from severe cold in the winter. Stock increases here very fast; nevertheless, there are vere few settlements at present in this part of the valley, because they are constantly exposed to the depredations of Indians. We stopped a short time at the first settlement, belonging to Messrs. Smith and Wells. The house (quite a new sight to us since we had left Missouri) was built in the Mexican fashion of sun-dried bricks or *adobes*, and with a flat roof. Delicacies of milk, butter, and pie were offered to us, and of course not refused. We marched about six miles beyond Rio Mora, and encamped in the plain.

June 25.—Made in the morning 12 miles as far as *Gallinas creek*. Half way, we had a beautiful view over the whole chain of mountains through which we have now to travel. The descent on the left bank of the creek is very steep. The bluffs here consist of a dark-bluish, shistose limestone, with fossils belonging to the cretaceous formation. About a mile from the creek lies the small town of las Vegas, or Gallinas, a village of 100 and odd houses, and poor and dirty-looking inhabitants, who cultivate some fields around town by means of irrigation, and raise some stock. The valley of Vegas is not so fertile as that of Mora, and more exposed to the rigor of the winter. In the afternoon we passed through town and turned immediately into the mountains. Instead of over a high plain, we shall now travel mostly in narrow valleys, and through mountainous passes, surrounded by high precipitous rocks, so called *cañons*. Through such a cañon we travelled on that same afternoon. The steep rocks overtowering our road sometimes, consisted of common and silicious sandstone, red, white and grayish. Two species of pine grow on the mountains, both of them undescribed yet. The one (*Pinus brachyptera*, Eng.) is the most common pine of New Mexico, and the most useful for timber; the other, (*Pinus edulis*, Eng.) or so-called *piñon*, contains in the cones seed of small nuts, that are roasted and eaten. We encamped at the end of the cañon, in a small valley, about five miles from las Vegas; our camp was on all sides surrounded by rocks. The grass brought out by the late rains is very fresh and tender, but had a singular bluish green color, probably the effect of light reflected from pine timber. Our night camp, as I understood afterwards, is the place where General Armija, in his late memorable campaign, had at first collected his troops, with the intention to attack the Americans in the cañon.

June 26.—Travelled in the morning through a mountainous and timbered country to *Tecolote Abajo*, a small village of about 30 houses, and halted some miles beyond it on a small creek, (seven miles.) A coarse, conglomerate sandstone prevailed here, and pine and cedar grew all around.

2

In the afternoon we ascended first a steep, very rocky hill; passed after-wards by Ojo de Bernal or San Miguel spring, surrounded by a dozen houses, and camped some miles east of San Miguel, (10 miles.) The rocks near our night camp are a coarse conglomerate of decomposed granite, sand-stone, and lime.

June 27.—Passed this morning through *San Miguel,* or the Rio Pecos. The place seems somewhat larger and wealthier than las Vegas. A church, built of adobes, is the prominent building in town. San Miguel is the most southern point on the Santa Fe road, and from here our mountain road takes a northwestern direction. About three miles beyond San Miguel we halted at noon, and started again in the afternoon for the mountains. Ac-cording to my custom, I rode ahead to examine the country. The day was excessively hot; and with the design to reach the watering place of our to-night camp, I rode faster on and passed it unperceived, because it lay aside of the road. Determined, however, to find water ahead, I rode 20 miles, till I reached the *Rio Pecos,* opposite the old Pecos village. The bed of the creek above was entirely dry, but where the road crosses it two springs come out of the sand, whose clear and cold water my horse enjoyed not less than myself. A little below I selected my solitary night camp. My horse, which I had picketed when he got tired of grazing, laid down close at my side, and the night passed without any disturbance.

June 28.—I awoke rather chilly this morning, as I had no blanket with me, but a good fire soon made me comfortable. To spend my time till the caravan should arrive, I walked along the bed of the creek and examined the rocks; it was granite in a decomposed state. While knocking with my hammer some specimens from the heavy granite blocks, I suddenly per-ceived an Indian on horseback, galloping over the hill straight towards me. Having kept my horse always saddled and near me, I was mounted in a minute, but the Indian was already at my side, followed by about 20 others. Without saluting or showing any marks of friendship, he at once told me by signs, in a rather commanding way, to dismount. I refused it as posi-tively, giving him to understand that I had to ride far yet, and left before all his followers could come up. The old chief (such he was apparently) looked at me for some minutes, as if irresolute what to do; but having no doubt perceived my rifle gun and pistols ready for emergency, he grum-bled something like an oath, and let me pass. I rode on, not very fast, till I was out of their sight, and then turned back into my old road, and waited in the timber for the arrival of the caravan; which reached the place about noon, and halted at the Pecos spring. The Indians, as I understood after-wards, were a party of Camanches.

About one mile north of the Pecos springs lies the *old Pecos village.* When the caravan started in the afternoon, I rode aside to examine this interest-ing place. The village is entirely deserted. The most remarkable house in it is an old, spacious building, of adobes, two stories high, with strong doors and columns of cedar, ornamented by carved work. This old build-ing is the temple of Montezuma, in whose subterranean vaults an eternal fire was kept up by the tribe of Pecos Indians, in consequence of an old tradition prevalent amongst them, that Montezuma himself had kindled this sacred fire, and that he would return finally, if the fire was kept burn-ing by his followers. For centuries they have been careful to preserve their sanctuary; but their tribe has dwindled down at last to a trifling number, and either from necessity or shaken faith, they left some six years ago the home of their fathers, and joined another tribe.

From Pecos springs we went that afternoon six miles, over a very mountainous road, to *Cottonwood branch*, a small valley amidst high mountains, where oaks, maple (*Negundo fraxinifolia*,) common and bitter cottonwood, (*Populus Canadensis* and *angustifolia*) grow, surrounded by pine trees. This is the highest point on the Santa Fe road; according to my barometrical measurements, it is 7,250 feet above the level of the sea.

June 29.—Travelled in the forenoon eight miles over rough road, through a narrow valley, or rather a cañon with a ravine running through it. We halted at noon on a clear mountain stream. From Cotton branch to this camp, all the rocks around us consisted of sandstone in the most varied forms—of common, silicious, and calcareous sandstone, white, red, grayish, striped, and spotted—sometimes looser and coarse grained; sometimes finer and very compact. The strata were generally horizontal, except near our noon camp, where they seemed to have been uplifted from southwest to northeast, in an angle of nearly 100 degrees. From our noon camp the caravan started through another cañon about six miles long, while I preferred, for better examination of the country, to ride over a mountain path, that cut off several miles. This mountain path was extremely steep, and strewed all over with blocks of granite and some gneiss. This is the first place on the Santa Fe road where I found the granite undoubtedly *in situ*. On Rio Pecos, and some other localities, the granite was always in a decomposed and conglomerate state, and was most likely transported there in the course of centuries by the yearly risings of the river. But here I stood upon firm granite ground, thrown up from the bowels of the earth in one of the grand revolutions which, in time immemorial, have changed the nature of our globe. This granitic formation extends without interruption from here to Santa Fe. At the highest point of the road is a small plain with good grass, and a fine view over the mountains. Many wooden crosses are here erected upon heaps of granite rocks—a sign that many travellers have met here with an untimely grave by the hand of robbers. Descending again, I reached the common wagon road on the other end of the cañon, and waited for the wagons, which soon afterwards arrived, and we encamped near some springs. Our night camp is the same spot where, some months after this narrative, Governor Armijo was encamped with his whole army, prepared for a battle with General Kearny. On a small eminence at the outlet of the cañon he had put his batteries, intending probably to molest the Americans through the whole length of the cañon, and to give here the decisive battle. The ground was easy enough to be defended. The whole mountain road, in fact, from las Vegas to Santa Fe, is by nature so fortified, that the Americans may congratulate themselves not to have encountered a more energetic enemy, who, without fighting any great battle, by mere skirmishing and harassing might have destroyed the whole army.

June 30.—In the morning we travelled six miles over a sandy and gravelly road, surrounded, as usual, by thick pine timber, and halted at a small creek. From here Santa Fe is but four miles distant. Riding ahead, I passed several hills, and overlooked then at once the beautiful wide valley, environed by nearer or more distant mountains, in which *Santa Fe*, the celebrated capital of New Mexico, lies. My expectations of seeing a fine city had already been cooled down by previous accounts of travellers, and by the sight of the Mexican country towns through which we had passed. However, when I perceived before me that irregular cluster of low, flat roofed, mud built, dirty houses, called Santa Fe, and resembling in the distance more a prairie-dog village than a capital, I had to lower them yet for some degrees. After a short ride, I came to the " plaza," or public square of the town, and met there with some of my friends, who had gone in advance of me.

The first important news which I heard in Santa Fe was an account of the battle of Palo Alto, that had reached Santa Fe from the interior of Mexico one day previous to my arrival. When we left the frontier of Missouri, the latest newspapers reported the first skirmish, near Matamoros, that preceded this war, and the requisition of General Gaines for more troops; but there was no war declared yet, and the general impression prevailed, that if war at all should grow out of these difficulties, it would be finished in a short time. I myself, unacquainted with the obstinacy of Mexican character, and confident that our government would take energetic measures to finish the war at a single blow, shared their opinion. Under this conviction, I started for New Mexico, and the present joyful news rather confirmed me in it. The people in Santa Fe appeared indifferent to the defeat at Palo Alto; no excitement prevailed; only Governor Armijo felt alarmed, because he had been informed that troops would be sent over the plains to occupy New Mexico. All the information we could really give him on that account was, that such a plan had been thought of; that no troops were ready when we left; and that if they started at all, they could hardly reach New Mexico in less than two months hence. In the meanwhile, Governor Armijo treated the traders as usual. After some bargaining, they agreed to pay $625 duty on each wagon; those who wanted to go into the interior received the usual passports from him, and everything went on as in perfect peace. While the traders were occupied with the arrangement of their mercantile business, I availed myself of this delay to take a look at the strange life in Santa Fe, to make some scientific observations, and to collect as much information about the country as circumstances would allow, the summary of which I insert here as an abridged statistical account of New Mexico. My short stay, as well as the general want of statistical documents in this State, and the very unpropitious time to ask insight into the few that existed, render it impossible for me to give any more definite account for the present.

Statistics of New Mexico.

To define the *boundaries of New Mexico* is no easy task, for the reason that they never seem to have been clearly defined; and the recent controversy in relation to the boundaries of Texas, makes them more indefinite still. To come to a clear result, we must begin with the facts, known as such. Towards the north and northeast, New Mexico meets with the boundary of the United States, as agreed upon the 22d February, 1819, between the United States and Spain, to wit: that part of the line which runs from Red river in the 100° longitude west of Greenwich, up to the Arkansas; then along the Arkansas to its sources; from thence in a straight line north to the 42° north latitude, and following the 42° west to the Pacific. The southeastern boundary of New Mexico is directly connected with the still still undecided question of the boundaries of Texas. The limits of the Mexican province Texas, previous to its revolution, are generally considered the Nueces river in the southwest, the Red river on the north, the Sabine on the east, and the gulf of Mexico on the southeast.* The State of Texas, after its declaration of independence from Mexico in 1836, resolved, as a matter of expediency, to extend the southwestern boundary of Texas from the mouth of the Rio Grande along the river to its source, and up to the 42° north latitude.† The settlement of this question would therefore change the boundary of New Mexico towards the north, east, and southeast, at the same time. Towards the south, the State of Chihuahua forms the principal boundary of New Mexico. This State claims as its northern boundary towards New Mexico 32° 30' latitude north; this line to be protracted towards the east to the Rio Pecos or Puerco, and towards the west to the headwaters of the Gila, and descending this river to its junction with the San Francisco‡ This northwestern angle of the State of Chihuahua is by Mexicans supposed to be in 32° 57' 43" north latitude. The northern boundary of the State of Sonora that comes from hence in contact with New Mexico has never been exactly defined, but

---

* Under the Spanish government, Texas, with Coahuila, New Santander, and New Leon, belonged to the general commandancia of the provincias internas orientales. This division was made in 1807. In 1824, when 19 independent States and some territories formed themselves into the present republic of Mexico, New Leon and New Santander became two of those States, the latter having changed its name into Tamaulipas, and Coahuila and Texas united formed a third State. The boundaries of those States continued to be the same as under the Spanish government. All the authorities which I had an opportunity to compare, in regard to the then southern boundary of Texas, seem to agree in a line along the Nueces; but the respective boundary between Coahuila and Texas appears to have been somewhat indefinite from the earliest settlements. Humboldt, in his Essay Politique sur le royaume de la Nouvelle Espagne, v. i, p. 282, says : " J'ai tracé les limites de Coahuila et Texas près de l'embouchure du Rio Puerco et vers les sources du Rio de San Saba, telles que je les ai trouvées indiquées dans les cartes spéciales conservées dans les archives de la viceroyauté, et dressées par des ingénieurs au service du roi d'Espagne. Mais comment déterminer des limites territoriales dans des savannes immenses où les métairies sont eloignées les unes des autres de 15 à 20 lieues, et où l'on ne trouve presque aucune trace de défrichement ou de culture." •

A late German work on Mexico by Muehlenpfordt, published in 1844, contains the following comment upon the same object : " The boundaries of the present State of Coahuila towards Texas in the north and northeast are rather indefinite, but we presume that towards the north the boundary of the State of Coahuila extends from the mouth of the Rio Puerco to the small lake of San Saba, near the 32° north latitude." And in another place the same author says of the State of Tamaulipas : " This State, formerly called the colony of New Santander, and belonging to the intendance of San Luis Potosi, but since the revolution of Mexico an independent State, is bound on the north by the State of Coahuila and the present republic of Texas, and on the east by the gulf of Mexico, from the Laguna de Tampico to the Nueces river, or from the 22° to the 28° north latitude !"

† This revolutionary title of Texas to the Rio Grande seems to me far superior to the doubtful right acquired by the forced promise of Santa Anna, while a prisoner in Texas, to acknowledge such a boundary. The right of revolution has already become sanctioned in this part of the globe; the existence of the United States is based upon it, and the whole continent will be regenerated by it. But the revolutionary right includes, in my humble opinion, *eo ipso*, the right of conquest, whenever the oppressed party, in its strife for republican existence, shall consider it necessary or expedient to secure its victory by such means.

‡ In the " Ensayo estadistico sobre el Estado de Chihuahua," published in Chihuahua, 1842, I find (p. 10) the following passage :

" El Rio de Pecos forma la linea divisoria del Estado con el de Coahuila y Tejas, desde los 32° 30' latitud norte, hasta se desemboque en el Rio Grande del Norte."

" The Pecos river forms the dividing line between the State of Chihuahua and that of Coahuila and Texas, from 32° 30' north latitude, down to its mouth, into the Rio Grande."

In the same work, p. 11, is said :

" Los vertientes del Rio de Gila nacen en la Sierra de Mogoyon, y forman el lindero mas boreal del Estado hasta su reunion con el Rio de San Francisco ; recorre hasta este punto 27 leguas."

" The headwaters of the Rio Gila come from the Mogoyon mountains, and form the most northern line of the State (of Chihuahua) until their junction with the San Francisco, a distance of 27 miles."

generally the Rio Gila is considered to form it. Towards the west of New Mexico an immense country is spread out between the Rio Colorado and the Gila, inhabited only by wild Indian tribes. This whole wide country is sometimes allotted in the Mexican maps to Sonora, sometimes to Upper California, but generally to New Mexico, while the large waste desert northwest of the Colorado is generally attributed to California.

If we accept now in all directions the widest boundaries for New Mexico, it would extend from 32° 30' to 42° north latitude, and from 100° to about 114° longitude west of Greenwich. But as the country of the wild Indians has never been under any jurisdiction or control of the Mexicans, and settlements have never extended over the whole territory, the name of New Mexico has generally been applied only to the settled country between the 32° and 38° latitude north, and from about 104° to 108° longitude west of Greenwich. In this limited extent, whose lines are drawn by custom, gradual development, and natural connexion, it will be most convenient at present to consider New Mexico.

New Mexico is a very mountainous country, with a large valley in the middle, running from north to south, and formed by the *Rio del Norte.* The valley is generally about 20 miles wide, and bordered on the east and west by mountain chains, continuations of the Rocky mountains, which have received here different names, as Sierra blanca, de los Organos, oscura, on the eastern side, and Sierra de los Grullas, de Acha, de los Mimbres, towards the west. The height of these mountains south of Santa Fe may, upon an average, be between six and eight thousand feet, while near Santa Fe, and in the more northern regions, some snow covered peaks are seen that may rise from 10,000 to 12,000 feet above the sea. The mountains are principally composed of igneous rocks, as granite, sienite, diorit, basalt, &c. On the higher mountains excellent pine timber grows; on the lower, cedars, and sometimes oak; in the valley of the Rio Grande, mezquite.

The main artery of New Mexico is the Rio del Norte, the longest and largest river in Mexico. Its headwaters were explored in 1807 by Captain Pike, between the 37° and 38° north latitude; but its highest sources are supposed to be about two degrees farther north in the Rocky mountains, near the headwaters of the Arkansas and the Rio Grande, (of the Colorado of the west.) Following a generally southern direction, it runs through New Mexico, where its principal affluent is the Rio Chamas from the west, and winds its way then in a southeastern direction through the States of Chihuahua, Coahuila and Tamaulipas, to the gulf of Mexico, in 25° 56' north latitude. Its tributaries in the latter States are the Pecos, from the north; the Conchos, Salado, Alamo, and San Juan, from the south. The whole course of the river, in a straight line, would be near 1,200 miles; but by the meandering of its lower half, it runs at least about 2,000 miles from the region of eternal snow to the almost tropical climate of the gulf. The elevation of the river above the sea near Albuquerque, in New Mexico, is about 4,800 feet; in el Paso del Norte about 3,800; and at Reynosa, between three and four hundred miles from its mouth, about 170 feet. The fall of its water appeared to be, between Albuquerque and el Paso, from two to three feet in a mile, and below Reynosa one foot in two miles. The fall of the river is seldom used as motive power, except for some flour mills, which are oftener worked by mules than by water. The principal advantage which is at present derived from the river is for agriculture, by their well managed system of irrigation. As to its navigation in New Mexico, I doubt very much if even canoes could be used, except perhaps during May or June, when the river is in its highest state, from the melting of the snow in the mountains. The river is entirely too shallow, and interrupted by too many sand bars, to promise anything for navigation. On the southern portion of the river the recent exploration by Captain Sterling, of the United States steamer Major Brown, has proved that steamboats may ascend from the gulf as far as Laredo, a distance of 700 miles. Although said steamboat did not draw over two feet of water, yet the explorers of that region express their opinion, that "by spending some $100,000 in a proper improvement of the river above Mier, boats drawing four feet could readily ply between the mouth of the Rio Grande and Laredo." Whenever a closer connexion between this headpoint of navigation and New Mexico shall be considered, nothing would answer but a railroad, crossing from the valley of the Rio Grande to the high table-land in the State of Chihuahua.

The *soil* in the valley of the Rio del Norte, in New Mexico, is generally sandy and looks poor, but by irrigation it produces abundant crops. Though agriculture is carried on in a very primitive way, with the hoe alone, or with a rough plough, made often entirely of wood, without any particle of iron, they raise large quantities of Indian corn and wheat, beans, onions, red peppers, and some fruits. The most fertile part of the valley begins below Santa Fe, along the river, and is called "rio abajo," or (the country) down the river. It is not uncommon there to raise two crops within one year. The general dryness of the climate, and the aridity of the soil in New Mexico, will always confine agriculture to the valleys of the water courses, which are as rare as over all Mexico—such, at least, as contain running water throughout the year. But this important defect may be remedied by Artesian wells. On several occasions I remarked on the high table-land from Santa Fe south, that in a certain depth layers of clay are found, that may form reservoirs of the sunken water-courses from the eastern and western mountain chain, which, by the improved method of boring, or Artesian wells, might be easily made to yield their water to the surface. If experiments to that effect should prove successful, the progress of agriculture in New Mexico would be more rapid, and even many dreaded "Jornadas" might be changed from waterless deserts into cultivated plains. But at present, irrigation from a water-course is the only available means of carrying on agriculture. The irrigation is effected by damming the streams and throwing the water into larger and smaller ditches (*acéquias*) surrounding and intersecting the whole cultivated land. The inhabitants of towns and villages, therefore, locate their lands together, and allot to each one a part of the water at certain periods. These common fields are generally without fences, which are less needed, as the grazing stock is guarded by herdsmen. The finest fields are generally seen on the *haciendas*, or large estates, belonging to the rich property-holders in New Mexico. These haciendas are apparently a remnant of the old feudal system, where large tracts of land, with the appurtenances of Indian inhabitants as serfs, were granted by the Spanish crown to their vassals. The great number of human beings attached to these haciendas are, in fact, nothing more than serfs; they receive from their masters only food, lodging, and clothing, or perhaps a mere nominal pay, and are therefore kept in constant debt and dependence to their landlords; so that if old custom and natural indolence did not prevail upon them to stay with their hereditary masters, the enforcement of the Mexican laws against debtors would be sufficient to continue their servitude from generation to generation. This actual slavery exists throughout Mexico, in spite of its liberal constitution; and as long as this contradiction is not abolished, the declamations of the Mexican press against the slavery in the United States must appear as hypocritical cant.

Besides agriculture, the inhabitants of New Mexico pay a great deal of attention to the *raising of stock*, as horses, mules, cattle, sheep, and goats. Their stock is all rather of a small size, because they care very little for the improvement of the breed; but it increases very fast, and as no feeding in stables is needed in the winter, it gives them very little trouble. There are large tracts of land in New Mexico too distant from water to be cultivated, or in too mountainous parts, which afford, nevertheless, excellent pasturage for millions of stock during the whole year; but unfortunately here, as well as in the State of Chihuahua, the raising of stock has been crippled by the invasions of the hostile Indians, who considered themselves secret partners in the business, and annually take their share away.

A third, much neglected branch of industry in New Mexico are the *mines*. Great many now deserted mining places in New Mexico prove that mining was pursued with greater zeal in the old Spanish times than at present, which may be accounted for in various ways, as the present want of capital, want of knowledge in mining, but especially the unsettled state of the country and the avarice of its arbitrary rulers. The mountainous parts of New Mexico are very rich in gold, copper, iron, and some silver. Gold seems to be found to a large extent in all the mountains near Santa Fe, south of it in a distance of about 100 miles, as far as Gran Quivira, and north for about 120 miles up to the river Sangre de Cristo. Throughout this whole region gold dust has been abundantly found by the poorer classes of Mexicans, who occupy themselves with the washing of this metal out of the mountain streams. At present the old and the new *Placer*, near Santa Fe, have attracted most attention, and not only gold washes, but some gold mines too, are worked there. They are, so far as my knowledge extends, the only gold mines worked now in New Mexico. But as I have made from Santa Fe an excursion there for the special purpose of examining those mines, I must refer the reader, in relation to them, to that chapter of my narrative. As to the annual amount of gold produced in New Mexico, I am unable to give even an estimate. But as nearly all the gold of New Mexico is bought up by the traders, and smuggled out of the country to the United States, I believe that a closer calculation of the gold produced in New Mexico could be made in the different mints of the United States than in Mexico itself. Several rich silver mines were, in Spanish times, worked at Avo, at Cerrillos, and in the Nambe mountains, but none at present. Copper is found in abundance throughout the country, but principally at las Tijeras, Jemas, Abiquiu, Guadelupita de Mora, etc. I heard of but one copper mine worked at present south of the Placers. Iron, though also abundantly found, is entirely overlooked. Coal has been discovered in different localities, as in the Raton mountains, near the village of Jemez, southwest of Santa Fe, in a place south of the Placers, etc. Gypsum, common and selenite, are found in large quantities in Mexico; most extensive layers of it, I understood, exist in the mountains near Algodones, on the Rio del Norte, and in the neighborhood of the celebrated "Salinas." It is used as common lime for whitewashing, and the crystalline or selenite instead of window-glass. About four days travelling (probably 100 miles) south-southeast of Santa Fe, on the high table-land between the Rio del Norte and Pecos, are some extensive salt lakes, or "salinas," from which all the salt (muriate of soda) used in New Mexico is procured. Large caravans go there every year from Santa Fe in the dry season, and return with as much as they can transport. They exchange, generally, one bushel of salt for one of Indian corn, or sell it for one and even two dollars a bushel.

Not far from these salinas the ruins of an old city are found, of the fabulous "la Gran Quivira." The common report in relation to this place is, that a very large and wealthy city was once here situated, with very rich mines, the produce of which was once or twice a year sent to Spain. At one season, when they were making extraordinary preparations for transporting the precious metals, the Indians attacked them; whereupon the miners buried their treasures, worth 50 millions, and left the city together; but they were all killed except two, who went to Mexico, giving the particulars of the affair and soliciting aid to return. But the distance being so great and the Indians so numerous, nobody would advance, and the thing was dropped. One of the two went to New Orleans, then under the dominion of Spain, raised 500 men and started by way of the Sabine, but was never heard of afterwards. So far the report. Within the last few years several Americans and Frenchmen have visited the place; and, although they have not found the treasure, they certify at least to the existence of an aqueduct, about 10 miles in length, to the still standing walls of several churches, the sculptures of the Spanish coat of arms, and to many spacious pits, supposed to be silver mines. It was no doubt a Spanish mining town, and it is not unlikely that it was destroyed in 1680, in the general, successful insurrection of the Indians in New Mexico against the Spaniards. Dr. Samuel G. Morton, in a late pamphlet, suggests the probability that it was originally an old Indian city, into which the Spaniards, as in several other instances, had intruded themselves, and subsequently abandoned it. Further investigation, it is to be hoped, will clear up this point.

The climate of New Mexico is of course very different in the higher, mountainous parts, from the lower valley of the Rio del Norte; but generally taken, it is temperate, constant, and healthy. The summer heat in the valley of the river will sometimes rise to nearly 100° Fahrenheit, but the nights are always cool and pleasant. The winters are much longer and more severe than in Chihuahua, the higher mountains are always covered with snow, and ice and snow are common in Santa Fe; but the Rio del Norte is never frozen with ice thick enough to admit the passage of horses and carriages, as was formerly believed. The sky is generally clear, and the atmosphere dry. Between July and October, rains fall; but the rainy seasons are here not so constant and regular as in the southern States. Disease seems to be very little known, except some inflammations and typhoidal fevers in the winter season.

The history of New Mexico lies very much in the dark. The Spaniards, it seems, received the first information about it in 1581 from a party of adventurers under Captain Francisco de Levya Bonillo, who, upon finding the aboriginal inhabitants and the mineral wealth of the country to be similar to those of Mexico, called it New Mexico In 1594, the then viceroy of Mexico, Count de Monterey, sent the gallant Juan de Oñate, of Zacatecas, to New Mexico, to take formal possession of the country in the name of Spain, and to establish colonies, missions, and presidios, (forts.) They found a great many Indian tribes and settlements, which they succeeded in christianizing in the usual Spanish way, with sword in hand, and made them their slaves. The villages of the christianized Indians were called *pueblos*, in opposition to the wild and roving tribes that refused such favors. Many towns, of which only ruins exist now, were established at that time; many mines were worked, and the occupation of the country seemed to be secured, when quite unexpectedly, in 1680, a general insurrection of all the Indian tribes broke out against the Spanish yoke. The Indians massacred every white male, and the then Governor of New Mexico, Don Antonio de Otermin, after a hard fight, had to retreat with his men from Santa Fe, and marched as far south as Paso del Norte, where they met with some friendly Indians, and laid the foundation of the present town of that name. It lasted ten years, until Spain recovered the whole province of New Mexico again. Several other insurrections took place after that, but none so disastrous as the first. However, the deep rancour of the Indian race against the white has continued to the present time, and in all the frequent and bloody revolutions of later years in New Mexico the pueblos generally acted a conspicuous and cruel part. There is constantly some distance between them and the rest of the Mexicans. They live always isolated in their villages, cultivate the soil, and raise some stock, and are generally poor, frugal, and sober. Their different tribes, of which about twenty yet exist, are reduced to about ten thousand souls. They speak different Indian dialects; sometimes, too, broken Spanish. All of them know the old tradition of Montezuma, mentioned already in the account of the old Pecos village; but none have carried the veneration of their expected Saviour so far as this faithful tribe. For the regulation of their communities they select a chief or cacique, and a council, and in war a capitan. Their religious rites are a mixture of Catholicism and Indian paganism; the Spanish priests themselves favored this combination, from policy. Their villages are built with great regularity; sometimes they have but one large house, with several stories, and a great many small rooms, in which the whole village is quartered. Instead of doors in front, they use trap-doors on the roofs of their houses, to which they climb up on a ladder, which is withdrawn in the night for greater security. Their dress consists of moccasins, short breeches, and a woolen jacket, or blanket; they generally wear their hair long. Bows and arrows and a lance, and sometimes a gun, constitute their weapons.

The whole *population* of New Mexico was in 1793, according to a census, 30,953; in 1833 it was calculated to amount to 52,360, and that number to consist of $\frac{1}{20}$ Gapuchines, (native Spaniards,) $\frac{4}{20}$ Creoles, $\frac{5}{20}$ Mestizes of all grades, and $\frac{10}{20}$ of pueblo Indians. In 1842, the population was estimated at 57,026, and at present at about 70,000 souls.

The *manners* and *customs* of the New Mexicans proper are very similar to those over all Mexico, described so often by travellers to that country. While the higher classes conform themselves more to American and European fashions, the men of the lower classes are faithful to their serapes or colored blankets, and to their wide trousers with glittering buttons, and split from hip to ankle to give the white cotton drawers also a chance to be seen; and the ladies of all classes are more than justified in not giving up their coquetish rebozo, a small shawl drawn over the head. Both sexes enjoy the cigarrito or paper cigar, hold their siesta after dinner, and amuse themselves in the evening with monte, (a hazard game,) or fandangos. Their dances are, by-the-by, very graceful, and generally a combination of quadrille and waltz. The principal ingredient in the Mexican race is Indian blood, which is visible in their features, complexion, and disposition. The men are, generally taken, ill-featured, while the women are often quite handsome. Another striking singularity is the wide difference in the character of the two sexes. While the men have often been censured for their indolence, mendacity, treachery, and cruelty, the women are active, affectionate, open-hearted, and even faithful when their affections are reciprocated. Though generally not initiated in the art of reading and writing, the females possess, nevertheless, a strong common sense, and a natural sympathy for every suffering being, be it friend or foe; which compensates them to some degree for the wants of a refined education. The treatment of the Texan prisoners is but one of the many instances where the cruelties of the Mexican men were mitigated by the disinterested kindness of their women.

The *rulers of New Mexico,* under the Mexican government, used to be a governor and a legislative power, (junta departmental;) but as the latter was more a nominal than a real power, the governor was generally unrestrained, and subject only to the law of revolution, which the New Mexicans used to administer very freely, by upsetting the gubernatorial chair as often as the whole republic did that of the President. Governor Armijo, the last ruler of New Mexico, before it was invaded by the Americans, has already received his full share of comment from the public press. He is one of those smart, self-confident men, who, like their prototype Santa Anna, are aware that the wheel of fortune is always turning, and that the Mexicans are a most credulous and easily deceived people; and though at present he is a fugitive from his country, and subdued, I have no doubt he will before long appear once more on the stage, and by some means come into power again. The judiciary power in New Mexico has always been as dependent as the governor was independent. Besides that, the clergy, as well as the military class, had their own courts of justice. In relation to the general government of Mexico, New Mexico has always maintained greater independence than most of the other States—partly from its distance from Mexico, and partly from the spirit of opposition in the inhabitants, who derived very little benefit from their connexion with the republic, and would therefore not be taxed without an equivalent. Several times the general government tried to introduce in New Mexico the so-called estanquillas, or the sale of tobacco in all its forms, as a monopoly of the general government; but it never succeeded. In the same way the introduction of copper coin was resisted. This loose connexion with the mother country will aid a great deal its annexation to the United States, provided that the latter will bestow upon it what the Mexican government never could—stability of government, safety of property and personal rights, and especially protection from the hostile Indians.

Finally, we will take a view of the capital of New Mexico. *Santa Fe* is one of the oldest Spanish settlements in New Mexico; its origin dates probably as far back as the end of the sixteenth century. It lies in 35° 41′ 6″

north latitude, and 106° 2' 30" longitude west of Greenwich.* Its elevation above the sea, according to my own observations, is 7,047 feet.

Santa Fe lies in a direct line about 20 miles east of the Rio del Norte, in a wide plain, surrounded on all sides by mountains. The eastern mountains are the nearest; those towards the northeast, the Taos mountains, the highest: some of their snow-capped peaks are supposed to be from four to five thousand feet higher than Santa Fe. A small creek, that comes from the eastern mountains, provides the town with water, and runs about 25 miles southwest from it into the Rio del Norte. There is no timber on the plains, but the mountains are covered with pine and cedar. The soil around Santa Fe is poor and sandy; without irrigation, scarcely anything can be raised. There is no good pasturage on the plains; stock is generally sent to the mountains, and only asses, mules, and goats—the stock of the poorer classes—are kept near the settlements.

The climate of Santa Fe is rather pleasant; not excessively warm in the summer, and moderately cold in the winter, though snow is a common occurrence. Nearly all the year the sky is clear, and the atmosphere dry. All the houses in Santa Fe are built of adobes, but one story high, with flat roofs; each house in a square form, with a court or open area in the centre. The streets are irregular, narrow, and dusty. The best looking place is the "plaza;" a spacious square, one side of which the so-called palacio, the residence of the Governor, occupies. The palace is a better building than the rest; it has a sort of portico, and exhibits two great curiosities, to wit: windows of glass, and festoons of Indian ears. Glass is a great luxury in Santa Fe; common houses have shutters instead of windows, or quite small windows of selenite, (crystallized gypsum.) The festoons of Indian ears were made up of several strings of dried ears of Indians, killed by the hired parties that are occasionally sent out against hostile Indians, and who are paid a certain sum for each head. In Chihuahua, they make a great exhibition with the whole scalps of Indians which they happen to kill by proxy; the refined New Mexicans show but the ears. Among the distinguished buildings in Santa Fe, I have to mention yet two churches with steeples, but of very common construction.

The inhabitants of Santa Fe are a mixed race of Spanish and Indian blood, though the latter prevails. The number of inhabitants was in former times reported as high as 4,000; at present it contains at most 3,000; and with the surrounding settlements belonging to the jurisdiction of Santa Fe, about 6,000. The manners and customs of the inhabitants of Santa Fe are those of whole Northern Mexico; they are indolent, frugal, sociable, very fond of gambling and fandangos, and the lower classes, at least, exceedingly filthy. As in most Mexican towns, I was at a loss to find out by what branch of industry the mass of the people support themselves; and I came at last to the conclusion, that if from natural indolence they work as little as possible, their extreme frugality, too, enables them to subsist upon almost nothing.

---

* This is the result of the most numerous astronomical observations made by Lieut. Emory, of the engineer corps, during his stay in Santa Fe, and which he has kindly allowed me to refer to. The result of my own observations for latitude, made during my short sojourn in Santa Fe, differs from his but in seconds. Dr. J. Gregg had already determined it as in 35° 41'. There can, therefore, be no doubt as to the real latitude of Santa Fe. Nevertheless, all the Mexican maps have generally laid it nearly one degree further north. This northern tendency of Mexican maps I observed on many other points where I made observations for latitude.

Since the commencement of the Santa Fe trade, the Mexicans there have been accustomed to see strangers among them; and the trading compa-. nies from the United States are anxiously looked for by the government and people of Santa Fe, because they fill the empty pockets of the one, and pro- vide the other with the necessaries and comforts of life. Santa Fe receives nearly all its goods from the United States, and some foreigners, mostly Americans and Frenchmen, generally reside there for commercial purposes. Among the then foreign residents of Santa Fe, it affords me pleasure to recollect Mr. Houghton, Mr. Alvarez, and others, who gave me in relation to the country all the information in their power to give.

As to the Santa Fe trade carried on between the United States and New Mexico, I cannot add anything to what has been published already by Dr. J. Gregg, in the "Commerce of the Prairies," to which interesting work I refer the reader, in relation to it. I will mention, only, that on an average the annual amount of merchandise carried there is estimated at half a mil- lion of dollars.

———

After a week, Mr. Speyer had finished his business in Santa Fe, and re- solved to go on to Chihuahua. No further news had during that time been received either from below or from the plains. In this state of uncer- tainty, I thought it best, instead of waiting idle in Santa Fe for the pos- sible arrival of an army over the plains, to spend my time more usefully by extending my excursion as far as Chihuahua, where, according to all ac- counts, everything was as quiet as in Santa Fe. Besides, I had a passport from Governor Armijo, drawn up in the usual form, and securing my retreat in case of necessity.

Mr. Speyer's caravan was encamped five miles west of Santa Fe, in Agua Fria, and was ready to start on the 9th.

July 8.—I left Santa Fe for the camp in Agua Fria.

July 9.—The caravan started on the usual road, by Algodones, for the Rio del Norte. But being anxious myself to examine the celebrated gold mines of New Mexico, the old and new Placer, in a range of mountains southwest from Santa Fe, I intended to make first from here this out of the way excursion, and to join the caravan afterwards on the Rio del Norte, near Albuquerque. I started, therefore, in this direction, riding alone and taking nothing along but my arms and a pair of saddle-bags.

The distance from here to old Placer is about 25 miles; from Santa Fe, 27. In a southern direction I rode through the valley that separates the mountains east of Santa Fe from the chain of the Placers. This valley is about 25 miles broad, very sandy and sterile, covered with artemisia, and nearer the foot of the Placer mountains with dwarfish cedars. Travelling along a low chain of hills that form an outward wall to the mountains of old Placer, I passed by two springs, on the first of which I found sienite; on the other a fresh-water limestone. Ascending afterwards to the hills, I met everywhere with a red and brown sandstone, looser or more compact, and with large masses of petrified wood. From here the ascent to the mountains is rather rapid till a plain is gained, from which a fine retrospect- ive view is enjoyed towards Santa Fe, and over the whole valley. Pine and cedar cover the mountains all around. Slightly ascending from the plain for some miles, a narrow ravine between high walls of mountains sud- denly opposes further advance, and about 20 houses are seen hanging on both sides of the narrow valley. This solitary place is el Real de Dolores, or, as it is commonly called, old Placer. Several foreigners live here. The first one I saw was Mr. Watrous, a New Englander, but for many years a resident of this country. He received me very hospitably, and invited me to his dwelling. Some fresh skins of grizzly bears were spread out on scaffolds, the sure American rifle stood in the corner, and everything else bore the character of the backwoodsman; but by his intelligent conversation he showed himself a man of very good sense, and as an acute observer. Though Mr. Watrous had not himself been engaged in mining, he paid attention to his whole neighborhood, and showed me many specimens of gold ores, which in his rambles through the mountains he had collected. I took a walk with him to the nearest gold washes. The first instance of this operation I witnessed on the small creek that runs through old Placer. From the bed of the creek, which was in most places dry, they took up some of the ground—gravel, sand and earth—put it in a spacious, rather flat wooden bowl, (batéa,) added water, removing first, by stirring with the hand, the coarse pieces of gravel, and then, by well balanced shaking, all the earthy and sandy particles, till at last nothing is left at the bottom but the finest sand, from which all the visible portions of gold are picked out. The poorer class of Mexicans are generally occupied with those gold washes in the creek; and they divide for that purpose the creek with the water amongst themselves, in lots, which often call forth as many claims and contests as the finest building lots in our cities. As the gold is apparently carried here by the waters of the creek from higher auriferous regions, the gain from these washings is different according to the season. The most gold is generally found in and after the rainy season, and it diminishes with the failing of water. Occasionally they discover a larger piece of gold in the sand; but generally the gold is so divided, that a whole day's work will amount on an average to not more than a quarter or half a dollar. Every evening they sell their small gains to the storekeepers, and take provisions or goods in exchange, or receive cash for it at the rate of sixteen dollars per ounce. This is the most common but least profitable way of gold washing. It may be practised on all the water-courses in those mountains, provided that there is sufficient water to wash with. In going from this to some other gold washes in the neighborhood, I took notice of the prevalent rocks in old Placer; they are white and yellow quartzose sandstone, quartz, hornblende and quartz, sienite and greenstone, (diorit.) The second place where I saw the process of gold washing was on a high piece of ground not far from a creek. They had opened here a great many pits to the depth of from 50 to 60 feet, and raised the ground, a sandy earth mixed with iron ochre, to the surface, where it was washed for gold in the same way, in batéas. These gold washings are said to be profitable, but they would in my opinion be more so where a regular mining was done by sinking a shaft, and by separating the gold by quicksilver, or in some other way than mere washing.

On the next day I went to see a gold mine, near the upper part of the town, belonging to Mr. Tournier, a French resident of the place. The mine lies between one and two miles west of the town, on the slope of some mountains. It was discovered several years ago by Mr. Roubadoux, who commenced working it, but for some reason gave it up. Mr. Tournier had worked it for one year, and found it very profitable. The gold vein runs from SSE. to NNW., with a very slight dip. It is generally from two to four feet wide. Mr. Tournier has sunk a shaft already in the entire depth of 40 varas, and with the drift of about 30 varas, and the ore promises to hold out very fairly. The vein is found in sienite and greenstone, the gang consists of argillaceous iron ore, (yellow and brown iron ochre,) with which the native gold is very intimately mixed. A yellow or brown earth, a decomposition of the same rocks and found among them, is con- sidered peculiarly rich in gold. The ores are carried in bags to the sur- face, and on mules to the amalgamation mill in town. After the ores have been ground, by hand, (pounding them with rocks,) they are put in the mill, a small circular basin formed with rocks, with one or two mill- stones, which are constantly turned around in it by mule power. These millstones are placed on their face, revolving round a centre pole, which is turned by the animal. To the coarsely powdered ore, water, and then quicksilver, are added, and the amalgamation goes on in the usual way. Mr. Tournier told me that he worked in this way every day about two and a half cargas (750 pounds) of the ore, and that he draws, on an aver- age, three-quarters of an ounce (about $12 worth) of gold out of it. Although the whole work at present is done on a very small scale, and would allow yet many improvements, Mr. Tournier makes nevertheless a smart business of it, and will soon turn his gold mine into real gold. Near Mr. Tournier's gold mine is a copper mine, (sulphuret of copper,) said to contain gold ore, and worked for some time, but now given up. Several other specimens of copper ore from the vicinity were shown me; a very rich iron ore I saw myself in the neighborhood; but neither of them is worked.

The old Placer is a very promising place for mines. The gold ores there were discovered by mere accident in 1828, and gold washings established; but besides that, the ground is barely touched, and will yet open rich treasures to the mining enchanter, who knows how to unlock them.

In the afternoon of the same day I left old Placer to pay a visit to the other mining place, southwest from it, called new Placer, and about nine miles distant. I rode there with Mr. Nolan, a French resident of new Placer. Our way lay through fine pine timber, over steep mountains, and through narrow ravines; the road is so rough, that no wagons can pass it. After having reached the highest point, an extensive plain is seen towards the south; and towards the west a small valley opens, in which new Placer, or Real del Tuesto, a town of about 100 buildings, is situated. Several foreigners reside here, generally storekeepers. In the house of one of them, with Mr. Trigg, I found a kind and hospitable re- ception.

The gold in new Placer is also got in two ways, by washing and by mining. The principal place for gold washing is about one mile south- west from the town, at the foot of a naked granitic mountain, the so-called "Bonanza." A cluster of houses, or rather huts, form here a small vil- lage, whose inhabitants live exclusively by gold washing, but look as poor and wretched as if they never handled any gold of their own. The whole place is excavated with pits, from whose depths they dig the same yellow auriferous ground as in old Placer, and they wash it also in the same way. Not a drop of water is found here; all the water for washing must be brought in barrels from new Placer. The wash gold obtained from new Placer is generally considered inferior to that of old Placer, as being more impure. To ascertain the correctness of this opinion, I examined some wash-gold from new Placer, and found it to contain:

Native gold	-	-	-	-	-	-	92.5
Silver	-	-	-	-	-	-	3.5
Iron and silex	-	-	-	:	-	-	4.0

100.0

I am sorry that I have no wash-gold from old Placer at hand for a comparative analysis, but the above mentioned result shows that if any difference exists between the two ores, it cannot be considerable.

Two gold mines are worked at this time in new Placer; one by Mexicans, the other by an American. They are said to be very similar to each other. I visited but the nearest, belonging to Mr. Campbell, an American resident of new Placer. Mr. Campbell commenced mining only a short time since. His amalgamation mill was not yet in operation; but he had already collected heaps of gold ores, and invited me to see the mine that he had opened. It lies about one and a half mile southwest from the town,ʹ near the top of a high mountain, to which a rough and steep road leads, accessible only to pack-mules. The gold mine is found, as in old Placer, in sienite and greenstone; it runs horizontally from east to west: the gang is iron ochre and crystallized quartz. The vein was from eight to ten feet wide, and explored only to the length of about 20 feet, and to the depth of about 10 feet. The ore seems to be very rich in gold, and the prospects it offers to Mr. Campbell are certainly very flattering.

The new Placer adds to the attraction of the gold ores, which seem to be found in this whole range of mountains, that of a better situation as a town than old Placer, and of more passable roads. But many other mining places will no doubt spring up in this neighborhood as soon as the state of the country allows it. Up to this time many causes have existed to prevent rather than to encourage mining enterprise. Though the law in New Mexico was generally very liberal in granting lots for mining, the instability of Mexican laws, and their arbitrary administration, have neutralized and annihilated it. When a New Mexican wants to work a gold or other mine, not yet occupied by another, he has to apply to the nearest alcalde; (justice of peace of the district,) who, according to the means and intended work of the individual, allows him a smaller or larger tract of land, measured only in front, and reaching in depth as far as the owner pleases to go. The price of the land is trifling; but if the owner does not work a certain portion of the mine every year, it falls back to the government. Foreigners were, in consequence of the eternal revolutions and new law-codes in Mexico, sometimes excluded, sometimes allowed to participate in this privilege. By taking a Mexican as partner, they obviated the law; but the most dangerous enemy was generally the avaricious Mexican government itself. Often when a foreigner had opened a profitable mine, those trustees of justice interfered for some reason or other, and ejected the owner of his property. Several instances of such proceedings are known. If we add to these causes the isolated situation of New Mexico, the thin population, the want of good mechanics and real miners, the hostilities and depredations of Indians, it will not astonish us at all, that notwithstanding the great mineral resources of the country, so few mines are worked at present.

The annual production of gold in the two Placers seems to vary considerable. In some years it was estimated from 30 to $40,000, in others from 60 to $80,000, and in latter years even as high as $250,000 per annum.

July 11.—Loaded with specimens of gold ore, I started this morning to join the caravan again, which expected to reach Albuquerque within four days. The road from here to Albuquerque leads at first through a cañon in a SSE. direction, because a chain of granitic mountains to the west does not allow a more direct course. Tall pines, cedars, and sometimes a small oak tree, grow in the narrow valley, and all over the surrounding mountains. After having travelled six miles, I passed by a small Indian village or pueblo; they cultivate some fields by way of irrigation, but look exceedingly poor. The entrance to their houses was, as usual, a hole on the top, to which they climb on a ladder. Riding on through a solitary valley, I met with a Mexican soldier, who recognised me at once as a "Tejano," and, professing great friendship, bothered me so long with his Spanish that I put my horse in a trot and left him, with his mule, behind. About 10 miles farther I reached a Mexican town, San Antonio; my horse was tired, and I would have wished, myself, to stop; but everything looked so mean and filthy that I passed through the town, and rode three miles farther. Here I met with a little stream, and followed it some distance into the mountains; and grass and water being excellent, I resolved to camp here for the night. I picketed my horse to the best grass, and prepared for myself a supper. In the night my horse, watchful as a dog, disturbed me several times by getting frightened and running towards me, but it was caused by nothing but wolves, deers, and other innocent animals.

July 12.—Following the course of the creek, I went in a southern direction about six miles through the valley, hemmed in on both sides by rugged granitic mountains. Turning then towards the west, I left the mountains for a plain, at the western end of which, in a distance of 10 miles, Albuquerque and the Rio del Norte lay before me. The plain affords good pasturage, and a great deal of stock was grazing here. The first view of the Rio del Norte was not imposing: it is a flat, shallow river, with bare and sandy banks, and with no mountains towards the west to form a background. *Albuquerque* is a town as large as Santa Fe, stretched for several miles along the left bank of the Rio del Norte, and if not a handsomer, is at least not a worse looking place than the capital. It is the usual residence of Governor Armijo; whenever he was out of power, he retired hither to work himself into power again.

Having ascertained in Albuquerque that the caravan had not passed yet, I retired to a rancho (small farm) near the town, to await its arrival. For several days I looked in vain for the caravan; but as it had rained in the latter days, I attributed their delay to the impaired roads. My poor but hospitable ranchero in the meanwhile did all in his power to make me comfortable. He picketed my horse to the fattest grass, and provided myself with milk, beans, and "tortillas," *ad libitum*. Those rancheros or small farmers seemed to me generally to be more honest than the rest of the population. They do not work to excess, because it is anti-Mexican; but at the same time they are so frugal, that they raise all they want. The country around Albuquerque appears to be well cultivated. Though the soil is sandy, and apparently not fertile, by irrigation they produce abundant crops, often twice a year. They cultivate mostly maize, wheat, beans, and red pepper, (*chile colorado*.) The fields are without fences. A canal, by which water from the river is led into the plain, provides by its ramifi-

3

cations the whole cultivated ground with the means of irrigation. How quick this sandy, apparently sterile soil in the valley of the Rio del Norte is by affluence of water changed into the most fertile, is astonishing; and the granitic character of the surrounding mountains, whose decomposed parts are carried into the valley and form a portion of its soil, may have some influence upon it, as it is well known how much decomposed granite, and principally decomposed feldspar, favors vegetation; but, for its complete decomposition it requires more water than the climate affords by rain.

On *July* 15, at last I discovered from the top of the house, my usual observatory, the approach of the caravan. They had been detained, as I supposed, by the falling of rains, which made part of the road along the river nearly impassable. Riding up, I found them in the worst kind of miry bottom, and it took them one day and a half to reach from here a higher and better road running east of Albuquerque. As I had left my barometer and other instruments in the wagon, it was not in my power to make an observation for elevation above the sea since my excursion to the gold mines. The place at which I made the first observation again was about three miles north of Albuquerque, in a level plain about one mile east of the Rio del Norte, and it resulted in 4,813 feet elevation above the sea. Santa Fe I had found to be elevated 7,047 feet. The usual road from there, by Agua Fria and Algodones, to Albuquerque, does not amount to more than 63 miles. In about two thirds of this distance the road descends towards the river, and in the last third it leads along the river, through its valley. The descent, therefore, from Santa Fe to the Rio del Norte (a distance of about 40 miles on this road) must be very rapid, as it amounts to about 2,200 feet.

July 17.—Weather and road improved to-day. We passed Albuquerque this morning and halted two miles beyond, at *Sandival's hacienda*. We had taken the upper eastern road, which was very sandy, but drier. From here, advised so by Mexicans, we intended also to take a higher road, leading over the hills; but when we arrived in the evening at the height of the hills, after a good deal of trouble, the road some distance ahead was found impracticable. We had to camp here in a sandy plain, covered with artemisia and similar shrubbery, but without grass.

July 18.—Commenced this morning with a retreat to Sandival's hacienda, and travelled then on the usual road along the river three miles further before we camped. Some of the wagons got again mired, and prevented us from going any further. Our camp was close to the river, and on its left bank. Some caravans prefer to cross the river at Albuquerque, and recross it again near Socorro, but we thought it best to continue always along the left bank. The Rio del Norte is here about 100 yards wide, and, as usual, sandy, shallow, everywhere fordable and nowhere navigable, not even for canoes. In the river we saw an abundance of geese, ducks, and pelicans; the latter bird is very common all along the water. Fishes and shells appear to be very scarce. On the banks of the river, heretofore quite bare of trees, occasionally a few cotton trees are seen. West of the river rise light hills, while east of it, in the distance of 10 miles, a rugged chain of granitic mountains confines the valley. Vegetation, except on the water course, is poor, the soil generally sandy and dry. Everywhere in the sandy regions of New Mexico most various kinds of lizards are seen, but their swiftness makes it very difficult to catch them.

July 19.—Following the usual road along the river, we travelled about three miles in the forenoon, and but two in the afternoon. · The caravan of Mr. Speyer had increased to about 40 wagons; and the larger the caravans, the more delay is commonly produced. The country on the left side looked very barren and sandy, while opposite, on the right bank of the river, we saw several fine ranchos and haciendas—Padillas amongst them. Our night camp was at the foot of some sand hills, nearly opposite to a pueblo on the other side, called *Isleta*. The small village, with its church, green fields, and cluster of cotton and orchard trees, looks quite picturesque in the desert around us. The Indians from the pueblo brought some apples to our camp, small and sour; but having tasted none for a long time, we relished them.

July 20.—After having crossed with some difficulty a chain of sand hills, we reached a fine grove of cotton trees, called *bosque*, or *alamos de Pinos*, and halted there, (five miles.) It is about one mile from the river, and quite a fine camp. The shade of the trees was the more welcome as the thermometer in the few last days stood very high, generally about 95° Fah., in the afternoon. In the evening we went but two miles, to the *hacienda of Mariano Chavez's* widow. This hacienda is the largest we have yet seen. It embraces a large tract of land, with cornfields and an extensive pasture, shaded by cotton trees, and fenced in by a wall made from adobes, and by a ditch with running water. The comfortable dwelling-house of the owner, with the opposite huts of the Indian serfs, bore a striking resemblance to a southern plantation in the United States. The late Mariano Chavez was (to mention it by the way) the brother of the ill-fated Antonio José Chavez, murdered in the prairie on the Santa Fe road.

July 21.—About one mile from Chavez, on the road, lies *Ontero's hacienda*, or *Peralta*. He is another of the rich nobility of New Mexico. His land is also very extensive, well cultivated and fenced in with adobes. He raises a great deal of maize and wheat, and owns a large stock. We passed in the morning through *Valencia*, and having travelled about six miles, soil and road getting better, we halted at noon about one mile from the river, near a pond. In the afternoon we passed a long-stretched town, *Tomé*, with extensive and remarkably fine maize and wheat fields, well irrigated, but not fenced in except by a ditch. Camped at the southern end of the town, about three miles from our noon camp.

July 22.—Made five miles in the morning, and halted at noon on a sandy hill, with 95° Fah. in the shade. Our night camp was in *Casas Coloradas*, (six miles,) a town near the river, and with high sand hills.

July 23.—Travelled about four miles, and halted half a mile from the river, with tolerable grass. West of us, on the right bank of the river, rises a chain of high mountains, while in the east the same steep chain that we never lost sight of continues parallel with the river in a southern direction. The mountains on both sides are too far for me to examine them; but to judge from their form, they are granitic and basaltic. On the river bank no rock is to be seen. Made in the afternoon about three miles, and camped on a hill near the river.

July 24.—Noon camp (three miles,) with good grass, about one mile from the river. We met here with a party of Americans from Pitic, in Sonora, where they had been engaged in mining; they were returning at present to the States, and reported that everything was quiet when they left. We passed in the afternoon *Joyita*, a small town, and camped two miles beyond (four miles,) on the river. Near Joyita, mountainous bluffs reached for the first time the Rio del Norte; they consist of black amygdaloidal basalt.

July 25.—Camped at noon in *Joya*, (five miles,) another small town, near the river. In the afternoon we had to cross a steep hill. On such occasions the teams had to be doubled, and one wagon after the other to be pulled up, causing a delay of many hours. In the afternoon we went about three miles, and camped again on the river.

July 26.—Passed in the morning through the town *Sabino*, and camped beyond it on the river, (10 miles.) Our night camp was five miles further, (near *Parida*.) The vegetable creation in the valley of the Rio del Norte, characterized principally by a great many sand plants, exhibits since a couple of days two specimens of shrub, which for their extension over the greatest part of Mexico, and their daily appearance hence, deserve a particular notice. The one is the so-called *mezquite*, a shrub belonging to the family of the mimmoseæ, and a species of algarobia. It resembles in appearance our locust tree; is very thorny; bears yellow flowers and long pods, with a pleasant sour taste. The wood is compact and heavy, and here, where they grow but as shrubs, used only for fuel. The mezquite requires a sandy, dry soil, and is no doubt the most common tree in the high plains of Mexico. Pleased as I was with the first sight of the shrub, which I knew only by description, I soon got tired of it, when daily and hourly I saw it around me, and the more particularly when passing afterwards from Chihuahua to Monterey and Matamoros, through endless chap- arrál, of which it forms the constant companion. It grows here seldom higher than from five to ten feet, but in the southern parts I have seen them as large trees, from 40 to 50 feet in height.

The other new companion to which I alluded is the *yucca*, resembling in appearance the palm tree, and therefore commonly called palmilla. There are many species of this family, but they all have very fibrous, straight, pointed leaves, forming a crown on the top, and leaving the stem bare, and a cluster of white, bell-shaped, numerous flowers, hanging down generally, from their weight, in a bunch of from one to two feet in length. The first very diminutive species of this plant, from two to three feet high, (*yucca angustifolia*,) I had seen on the Arkansas and near Santa Fe; but here a much larger species begins, which becomes every day now more common and taller. We see it here already at a height of from six to eight feet, while south of Chihuahua, especially between Parras and Saltillo, a still larger species is found, growing as trees, of several feet diameter and from 40 to 50 feet elevation. The root of the palmilla is in this country often used for washing instead of soap, and called *amole;* it is a fibrous, spongy mass, containing mucilaginous, and probably even alkaline parts. The wood of the palmilla is too porous and spongy to become very useful; nevertheless, in the south the poorer classes build their huts entirely of this tree.

July 27.—Having made but two miles in the morning, we met with good grass on the river and halted, as our animals had fared very badly last night. In the afternoon we had to ascend a steep, sandy hill; some of the wagons were upset, and after long delay we camped again near the river, (three miles.)

July 28.—Opposite to our road this morning, on the right bank of the Rio del Norte, was the town *Socorro*. As Mr. Speyer had some business with the priest of that place, I rode along. Señor el cura was a Mr.

Chavez, and apparently a man of pure Castilian blood, and of education. He presented me with some specimens of very rich copper ore from the celebrated copper mines near the headwaters of the Gila, and about 100 miles southwest from Socorro. As I understood that some copper ore and some old mines, worked in former times, were found on the mountains west of the town, I engaged a guide and made an excursion to the place. These mountains are about four miles from Socorro, and they consist principally of porphyritic rocks. The supposed copper ore proved to be but a green trachytic rock. The abandoned mines appeared to have been gold mines, but probably exhausted. The ore is found with iron and quartz. I found in those hills, too, a new species of yucca, with large, oblong and edible fruits. The pulpy mass of the fruit tastes like paupau; the grains are larger and thicker than those of the common yucca. For the first time, also, I saw here opuntias, with ripe, red fruits, which are as sweet and refreshing as the great many small prickles with which they are coated are troublesome. Crossing the river again, I met with the caravan about five miles from our last camp. In the afternoon we travelled two miles more over a very sandy road, and camped one mile north of Lopez.

July 29.—Made on better road this morning six miles; passed *Lopez*, a small town, and halted near a rancho. The mountains on both sides of the river, which generally heretofore were from 10 to 20 miles distant from each other, seem to approach now. The soil, though always sandy, exhibits the same peculiarity as above noticed—that, when irrigated, it produces abundant crops. Vineyards ought to succeed very well on the hills. Travelling in the evening six miles, we camped about one mile from the river. To-day we have passed the last settlements above the much dreaded Jornada del Muerto.

July 30.—Went this morning over sandy road six miles, and camped in a fine grove of cotton trees near the river. Examining in the morning the nearest bluffs on our side, I found them to consist of a dark brown, nodular sandstone, without any connexion with other rocks. In the evening we travelled six miles further; passed the "*ruins of Valverde,*" (in prosaic translation, the mud walls of a deserted Mexican village,) and camped at the foot of some sand hills, in a beautiful grove of cotton trees. By the accession of several traders and travellers our caravan was increased to 50 wagons, and made quite a respectable appearance. When the whole caravan was encamped here under the many broad cotton trees, and the camp fires illuminated the different groups of wagons, horses, and men, belonging to most different nations, it made quite a romantic picture, worthy of being sketched.

July 31.—In crossing the hills this morning, the deep sand, in which mezquite and other sand shrubs are flourishing, made the assent rather difficult. Some black-looking hills between our road and the river consisted of amygdaloidal basalt. Descending again to the valley of the river, we halted, (three miles.) Along the river spreads a broad seam of cotton timber, in which many wild turkeys are found. In the afternoon we passed more hills, and camped about one mile from the Rio del Norte, (seven miles.) During the march I found several sulphur springs on the river; the formation of the hills was the same black basalt. Late in the night an alarm took place in our camp. The Indians tried one of their favorite games—that is, stealing animals; but our mule boys being alert, the whole camp was soon in motion, and prevented their mischievous designs. But one mule was lost.

August 1.—Travelled this morning about five miles, and camped between one and two miles off the river. This camping place is known as *Fray Cristobal;* but as there is neither house nor settlement here, and one may fix his camp close on or some distance from the river, the limits of Fray Cristobal are not so distinctly defined as those of a city, and generally the last camping place on or near the Rio del Norte before entering the *Jornada del Muerto** is understood by it. This awful Jornada, a distance of about 90 miles, with very little or without any water at all, has to be resorted to because the Rio del Norte below Fray Cristobal takes not only a very circuitous bend, but rough mountains, too, alongside of it, make it most difficult to follow the water-course. In the rainy season there is generally plenty of water in the Jornada, as everywhere else, but in the dry season often not a drop is found. The ridge-like elevation of the Jornada del Muerto above the surrounding country, as may be seen in the barometrical profile, seems to allow less accumulation of water on the surface than on other localities. Although the rainy season had not commenced, some showers had already preceded it, and we expected, therefore, to find *some* water at least, but were prepared for the worst. Having watered our animals once more on the river, and filled all our water casks, we started in the evening, and having travelled about 12 miles over a good firm road, we encamped without water. The general direction through the Jornada is nearly due south. To the right, or west of our road, in a distance of about five miles, runs a chain of mountains extending to the river; towards the east the Sierra Blanca, a long, high and steep mountain range, distant about 30 miles, is always in sight of us. The wide country between those two mountains, through which we have to travel, is a high plain, in the elevation of from four to five thousand feet above the sea, with dry, hard soil, tolerable grass, and an abundance of mezquite and palmillas. The latter grow here already to the height of from 10 to 12 feet, and give to the scenery some peculiar impression, reminding one of African landscapes. No other tree grows in the Jornada. The palmilla and mezquite furnish the only fuel.

August 2.—Started early this morning, and halted, after 10 miles, near a place called *Laguna del Muerto,* because sometimes a water-pool is left here by the rains, but at present it was perfectly dry. About five miles west from here, at the foot of the mountains to our right, is a good spring, with running water, the so-called *Ojo del Muerto.* Whenever a traveller through the Jornada will not risk to rush through it in the shortest time, he drives his animals from here to the Ojo, and back to the road, because it is the only water to be depended upon. We left, therefore, all the wagons, with half of the men, in the camp, and the other half drove the whole stock of animals, from 400 to 500, to the Ojo. I joined the latter party. We rode at first over a sandy plain, where we saw many antelopes, and killed one, and then through a narrow gorge, or "cañon," till we reached the desired spring, under a cluster of cotton trees. The water was pure, but too warm. The bluffs were formed by a conglomerated granitic rock; the real mountain chain was more distant. On our return to

---

* Jornada del Muerto means, literally, the day's journey of the dead man, and refers to an old tradition that the first traveller who attempted to cross it in one day perished in it. The word Jornada (journey performed in one day) is especially applied in Mexico to wide tracts of country without water, which must for this reason be traversed in one day.

camp we understood that an accident had happéned. In one of the wagons a small cask of powder had, from some cause or other, taken fire, and had scattered the contents of the wagon over the plain. It was fortunate that nobody was near enough to be injured seriously, and that the scattered goods were mostly articles of hardware; the loss was therefore not so important. Towards evening we started again, and went about 10 miles before we camped, without water.

August 3.—Started early, and reached within six miles *Alamos*, a place where sometimes a water-pool is found, but which was now perfectly dry, and went four miles further before we nooned, without water. Our camp was on a hill, near a prairie grave, distinguished by a cross. The grass was tolerable, but our animals were too thirsty to eat. After some hours rest, we started again and went 16 miles, as far as *Barilla*, another camping place, where we had the good fortune to find, for the first time, some stagnant water, sufficient to water our animals. The eastern mountains send here some spurs into the plain. The soil is good and firm, and, with more water, would no doubt become very productive.

August 4.—Travelled in the morning but five miles, and halted, because we found another water-pool with stagnant water, and good grass. In the afternoon we went about 18 miles, and encamped without water.

August 5.—This morning, at last, after having travelled eight miles, we reached the river once more. The camping place, where we struck it, is called *Robledo.* The country here looks very mountainous. The eastern mountain chain has a very broken, pointed, basaltic appearance, whence they are called Organon mountains. Opposite our camp, too, on the right bank of the river, steep mountains rise. From here to *Doñana*, the first small town again, it is about 12 miles. Before reaching Doñana, I met on the road with the largest cactus of the kind that I have ever seen. It was an oval Echino cactus, with enormous fishhook-like prickles, measuring in height four feet, and in the largest circumference six feet eight inches. It had yellow flowers, and at the same time seed, both of which I took along with some of the ribs; but I really felt sorry that its size and weight prevented me from carrying the whole of this exquisite specimen with me. Dr. Engelmann, perceiving that it was a new, undescribed species, has done me the honor to call it after my name.

August 6.—Made in the forenoon five miles, in the afternoon three miles. Night camp near river.

August 7.—This morning Mr. Wiek, a merchant from Chihuahua, and myself, started ahead of the caravan, to reach el Paso some days before it. We took our small wagons along; went that morning 15 miles, and halted about noon, near the river.*

In the afternoon we started again; and travelling through the night, we made 28 miles more, and halted near the *" upper crossing of the Rio del*

---

*This camping place, according to all descriptions given to me afterwards in relation to it, is the famous battle-ground, *Brazito*, where some months later Colonel Doniphan's regiment celebrated Christmas day by its first engagement with the enemy. 1,200 Mexicans attacked here, quite unexpectedly, 450 Americans; but notwithstanding the black flag, unfurled before the battle, the Mexicans were in less than 20 minutes so completely defeated, that they ran " in less than no time" 130 miles, as far as Carrizal. Our brave volunteers had stood their ground like men. They received the first charges of the enemy without firing a gun ; but when the word was given, the deadly-aim of their rifles decided the battle at once. This first successful skirmish taught them their own strength and the weakness of the enemy, and imbued them with the daring, invincible spirit that marked their long, conquering march through Mexico.

Norte.'' The road was very good, in the latter part descending; on both sides of the river rose mountains, which converge above el Paso, and confine the river for several miles to a narrow pass, hemmed in by precipitous rocks.

August 8.—*El Paso del Norte* lies about six miles from the upper crossing, and two roads lead to it. One road crosses here the river, and leads over hills, covered with deep sand, to the plain, on which the town lies. The other continues on the left side of the river, ascends over a rocky, broken country to a considerable elevation, and descends from here to the valley of el Paso, crossing the river below, at the town. We selected the first road, and crossed the river, therefore, at once. The water was very low, and we passed it without any difficulty. My barometrical observations, made here on the flat river bank, gave an elevation above the sea of 3,797 feet; about 1,000 feet lower, therefore, than I had found the river nearly 300 miles north from here, near Albuquerque. Supposing that the circuitous course of the river in that distance amounts to 400 miles, the fall of its water would, on an average, be $2\frac{1}{2}$ feet per mile. After some rest on the right bank of the river, we started for the sandy hills. but the sand was by far deeper, and our animals more exhausted, than we had anticipated; and seeing the impossibility of getting through on this road without fresh animals, we retraced our way to the river, crossed again, and took the other road, which was rough, broken and rocky, but without sand. To our right was the river, running through a cañon; to our left rose high, steep walls of mountains; the road always ascending from hill to hill, till we gained at last the highest point and perceived the charming valley of el Paso del Norte spread out before us. The Rio del Norte, having escaped the mountain pass, runs here into an open, fertile plain, at the beginning of which el Paso is situated. The town is principally built on the right bank of the river; but few houses are on the left. Stretched out along the river to the length of many miles, all the houses surrounded by gardens, orchards, and vineyards, and rich settlements, with cornfields, as far as the eye can trace the stream, lining its green bank—such a scenery will always be attractive; but to a traveller, who has passed over the lonesome plains and through the dreary Jornada del Muerto, it appears like an oasis in the desert. Descending from the hills in the valley, we crossed the river on the lower ford opposite the town, and were soon in the middle of it, on the " plaza."

I rested in el Paso for about a week, to recruit my animals, and take some view of the town and surrounding country. Unfortunately, the rainy season came on and prevented me from making many excursions and observations. What information, however, I was enabled to collect, I will render to the public.

The settlement of el Paso was commenced about 1680, when Governor Otermin, of New Mexico, and his party, were driven from Santa Fe to the south by a revolt of the Indians. Some Indian pueblos, which received them well, already existed in the fertile valley, but this seems to have been the first Spanish settlement.

El Paso belonged under the Spanish government to the province of New Mexico; at present, to the State of Chihuahua. The latter State claims as its northern limits towards New Mexico, as already stated, 32° 30' latitude north, a line which by Mexicans is supposed to fall near Robledo, our first camp on the river in coming out of the Jornada. El Paso itself, according to my own observations, lies in 31° 45' 50'' north latitude. In most maps it is as many minutes north of the 32d degree as it really is south of it; a fact which may deserve consideration, if the suggestions of some statesmen, to make the 32d degree of latitude our southern line towards Mexico in that quarter, should be adopted. The position of el Paso is in many points an important one. It is distant about 340 miles from Santa Fe, about 240 from Chihuahua, and is the largest town between these two capitals. At the same time, the road by el Paso is the only practicable wagon road leading from Santa Fe to Chihuahua. Another circuitous road might in case of necessity be taken from the right bank of the river, on the northern end of the Jornado del Muerto, to the copper mines near the sources of the Gila, and from there, by Carmen, to Chihuahua; but it is by far more mountainous, circuitous, and difficult, than the direct road by el Paso; that has become the high road, and in fact the only thoroughfare between these two States.

As to natural advantages for a military station, I have not seen a better point on the whole road from Santa Fe to Chihuahua. Appropriate fortifications erected on the mountain pass above el Paso would command the fords of the river, and the roads leading to the north; and a garrison well provided with provisions and ammunition, could hold out there against a ten-fold stronger force. If the Mexicans, instead of attacking the Americans at Brazito, like mad-men, and running like cowards, had prepared themselves here in these hills for defence, they would no doubt have been also defeated by the Americans, but probably not in so disgraceful a manner.

But besides all those advantages, the valley of el Paso is the most fertile country that we have seen along the river. Besides maize and wheat, they raise a large quantity of fruits, as apples, pears, figs, quinces, peaches, &c., but especially an excellent grape, from which they prepare the celebrated " el Paso wine," and a liquor called by the Americans " Pass whiskey." The grape, which they cultivate extensively, is of Spanish origin; blue, very sweet and juicy, and produces a strong, sweet, southern wine of straw-color. For want of barrels they preserve it generally in large earthen jars, or in leather bags of ox-skin. The wine contains a great deal of body; when improved by age, it tastes like Malaga wine. Besides the blue grape, they raise sometimes also a white one, tasting like Muscadine grapes, but I have not seen any wine made of it. Their manner of cultivating the grape is very simple; they cover them with earth in the winter, keep the vineyards clear from weeds, hoe and prune them at the right season, but do not stake them. The soil and climate seem to be so favorable, that less labor is wanted than in most other countries. A great deal, if not most of the fertility in the valley must be ascribed to the ingenious system of irrigation, which they have introduced by a dam constructed in the river above Paso, and turning a considerable quantity of water into a canal. This canal, spreading into numerous branches and reuniting again, provides all the cultivated land with a sufficiency of water. Wine and fruits are the principal articles of exportation from here; they are carried to the north and south, and enrich the people of el Paso, some of whom are very wealthy.

The *population* of the town proper, which is but a small place, and of the long line of settlements that extend for 20 miles down the river, is estimated at from 10 to 12,000.

The *elevation* of the town above the sea is at the Plaza 3,814 feet. Some *mines*, I understand, have formerly been worked here in the mountains; several copper and silver ores were shown me as being found there yet, but none are worked at present. To examine the geological character of the surrounding country, I made, one day, an excursion to the mountains, southwest of the town. I was astonished to find them to consist almost entirely of limestone, the first I saw in the valley of the Rio del Norte. Below the limestone at the foot of the mountains were horizontal layers of compact quartzose sandstone, such as I had seen for several hundred miles in the prairie towards Santa Fe, underlying the basaltic and granitic rocks. The limestone rose upon it to the height of the mountain chain, but on its sides granitic and porphyritic rocks seemed to a small extent to have burst through the limetsone and overflown it. After a long search I was lucky enough to find near the top of the mountain some fossils in the limestone, belonging to the Silurian system. Where the limestone and the igneous rocks meet, a few old abandoned mines exist. With the aid of my lazo, which I had fixed outside to a rock, I descended into one of the pits about 30 feet deep, and found a large vein of calcspar, and some pieces resembling gold ore, but no further trace of it in the depth.

Of the many plants growing on the mountains near Paso, I will mention but two as the most common and useful. The one is the so-called lechuguilla, a species of agave, whose long, stiff, indented leaves, somewhat similar to those of the common agave, are used for making of their fibres a very good quality of ropes; the other, a species of dasylirion, is the bushy so-called sotol, whose pulpy roots are roasted and eaten, and from which also an alcoholic liquor is prepared.

During my stay in el Paso, General Ugarte marched through it with 400 men and some cannon, to oppose the Americans if they should invade New Mexico. This was the only hostile demonstration I saw or heard of. No further news had arrived from the south. The people of Paso seemed very indifferent as to who should be the conqueror. The authorities of the place had neither asked my passport nor inspected the contents of my wagon; and all foreigners then in Paso were treated in the most civil way. Under such circumstances I did not hesitate to continue my journey to Chihuahua, as had been at first my intention. Mr. Speyer's caravan had in the meanwhile passed through el Paso; but knowing that, on account of the large number of wagons, their progress was very slow, Mr. Wiek and myself resolved to join from here to Chihuahua a smaller but faster travelling company that left el Paso a few days afterwards. It consisted of about 20 Mexicans and five foreigners. Most of the Mexicans were engaged by Mr. Jacquez, a gentleman of Chihuahua, who travelled with his family.

On *August* 15, we left Paso and the Rio del Norte at the same time. I had no idea then of the molestation that awaited me, and that in the course of next year, instead of travelling along the Pacific, I should see the same river again on its mouth into the gulf.

From el Paso there are two roads leading to Carrizal, an intermediate town between it and Chihuahua. The one follows the river yet for about 40 miles, and unites with the other road near lake Patos; the second leaves the river at Paso, and leads over the so-called sand hills, to Carrizal. The first is more circuitous, but the only practicable road for loaded wagons; the second is shorter, but on the sand hills quite impassable for common teams. On both of them water is rather scarce, but more so on the first, where from the last camp on the river to lake Patos, a distance of 60 miles, no water can be expected in the dry season. Mr. Speyer had taken the first road; our company preferred the second, because we had but four small wagons along, and we would gain from 20 to 30 miles travelling by it. From want of water we had nothing to fear, as the rainy season had commenced, and daily showers provided us with a greater abundance of it than we liked.

On the first day we started rather late from Pasó, but yet made 24 miles without rest. To our right was a mountain chain running, probably of limestone: to our left, the receding valley of the Rio del Norte, which takes here a southeastern direction, and from which a high chain of mountains will soon separate us entirely. Our road passed over a wide sandy plain, covered with mezquite, and similar shrubbery. It was strewn with two kinds of limestone; the one of the same character as I had seen in Paso, and the other of a chalk-like appearance, probably a fresh-water limestone. Pieces of the first were frequently enveloped by a white crust of the latter. We camped near the road in the plain, with tolerable grass and plenty of rain-water.

August 16.—Travelled this morning but eight miles, and halted, with good grass and rain-water. Ahead of us were the much-dreaded sand hills, *(los médanos,)* an immense field of steep sand ridges, without shrub or vegetation of any kind, looking like a piece of Arabian desert transplanted into this plain, or like the bottom of the sea uplifted from the deep. Several springs, I am told, are found near the sand hills; and it is not at all unlikely that this whole ground was once covered by a lake. One spring in particular, forming a water-hole at the foot of the sand hills, and called *ojo de malayuque,* is known as a usual camping place on our road, but we stopped before reaching it. Though we shall pass but the lowest depression of the hills, near their western limit, it will nevertheless be a hard day's work, and we prepared our animals for it by a long rest.

About noon, while we were encamped, a thunder-storm came on, as usual in the rainy season. It rained awhile, and towards the end of the shower, the thunder disappearing in the distance, I perceived a most remarkable phenomenon in the mountains to our right, about 10 miles distant. Three pointed flames, apparently from one to two feet high, and of whitish lustre, were seen at once on a high barren place in the mountains; they lasted for about 10 minutes, and disappeared then as suddenly. The Mexicans told me that this phenomenon is not uncommon in these mountains, and that such a place had once been examined, and a crevice found, around which the grass was burnt. The popular opinion amongst the Mexicans seems to be, that such flames indicate silver mines. There can be hardly any doubt that the phenomenon is connected with electricity; but whether an inflammable gas, that emanates from a crevice, is ignited by lightning, or an unusual quantity of free electricity is developed by local causes, or superficial metallic layers should have some influence in producing it, are questions that can only be solved by a repeated and careful examination of the localities and circumstances. In the afternoon we commenced our march for the sand hills. For six miles we had to travel over a sandy and hilly country, before we reached the sand hills proper, which are here six miles wide. On the first part of the road I saw rocks of a reddish brown porphyry, encrusted sometimes with chalk-like limestone, but no more pieces of limestone. · The form of the mountains, too, on our right, more resembles igneous rocks than limestone. Having arrived at the foot of the sand hills, we commenced travelling very slow. There was nothing around us but the deepest and purest sand, and the animals could only get along in the slowest walk, and by resting at short intervals. At last my animals were exhausted; they would move no more, and we had not yet reached half of our way. In this dilemma I put my own riding horse to the wagon. Mr. Jacquez lent me some additional mules, and forward we moved again. In the meanwhile dark night had come on, illuminated only by lightning, that showed us for awhile the most appalling night-scene—our wagons moving along as slow and solemn as a funeral procession; ghastly riders on horseback, wrapped in blankets or cloaks; some tired travellers stretched out on the sand, others walking ahead, and tracing the road with the fire of their cigarritos; and the deepest silence interrupted only by the yelling exclamations of the drivers, and the rolling of distant thunder. The scene was impressive enough to be remembered by me; but I made a vow the same night, that whenever I should undertake this trip again, I would rather go three days around, than travel once more over the sand hills with a wagon. About midnight, at last we reached the southern end of the sand hills, and encamped without water.

August 17.—On better road, we travelled this morning about 12 miles, and halted at a pool of rain-water. The soil becomes now firmer, contains more clay than sand, and makes as good a wagon road from here to Chihuahua as if it were macadamized. The plain through which we travel is east and west, lined by mountains, and is 15 to 20 miles wide. The mountains are timbered with a few scanty cedars, and some pine trees; the geological formation is granitic and porphyritic. The grass becomes every day better, and looks as fresh as in spring. The so-called gramma grass, which grows here very fine, is especially liked by our animals. A small caterpillar covered it in great numbers. On the mezquite shrubs, too, some insects become very common, a great many *spectra* especially, and a large *centipede* of flattened form and dark brown color.

In the afternoon we travelled 15 miles more and camped again in the prairie, with plenty of rain-water. About five miles before we went to camp, I made an excursion to a cave to the left of our road. The cave was in a small isolated mountain, composed of amygdaloidal basalt and porphyritic rocks. It was towards sunset when I approached it, and the mountain, with the grotto, looked quite mysterious. Two ravens, sitting before it on high palmillas, seemed to guard the entrance, and an owl flew screaming over my head as soon as I dared to enter it. Inside I found a small lake of pure fresh water, with sediments of limestone, but it was already too dark for further examination.

August 18.—Made in the morning 15 miles, and camped again in the prairie, on a water-pool. In the forenoon we passed *Ojo Lucero* (Venus spring,) and *Laguna de Patos*, (lake of geese.) The first is a fine spring, only a hundred yards to the left of our road. The water comes out of a small, sandy basin in the prairie, but with considerable force; it is clear and soft of taste; the temperature of the spring was 77.5° Fah., while the atmosphere in the shade was 81° Fah. A little creek, formed by it, crossed the road, and spread to the right of it into a small lake. Some miles ahead, to the left of our road, but more distant from it, a larger lake is seen in the plain, the Laguna de Patos; it is the outlet of the Rio Carmen. Between the Ojo Lucero and lake Patos, but to the right of our road, rises a square mound, some 20 feet high, and on its level top a warm spring boils up in the very centre. The presence of many similar springs in this valley proves that there is no absolute want of water here, and Artesian wells would most likely strike a large subterranean water basin.

Near the lake Patos the two roads from el Paso meet again. Opposite to our noon camp to-day, in the western mountain chain, rose an isolated mountain of very singular form; at the base conical, on the top flat, and sufficiently large for a fort. This conspicuous mountain is seen for a long distance. In the afternoon we travelled 12 miles more, and reached *Carrizal*, the only town on the road from Paso to Chihuahua. We camped in the place. Carrizal is a small country town: it was formerly a presidio or fort, and has therefore a wall yet around it, and some soldiers in it; but for all that, it is not safer from the Indians than without them.

August 19.—We stayed this morning in Carrizal, because one of the wagons had to be repaired, and started about noon. Made 15 miles, and camped again near the road. In the distance of about 10 miles we passed the *Ojo Caliente*, (warm spring.) It is a clear, pure water, in a large basin of porphyritic rocks, with sandy bottom, out of which many warm springs come to the surface. The thermometer, placed in the springs, showed 82° Fah.; the atmosphere, 84.5°. As an outlet from the basin, a creek runs into the Carmen below. Near the springs is a whole ridge of porphyritic rocks, containing some limestone, and no doubt connected with the springs. The basin, with its lukewarm water, affords a most comfortable bath, but we had no time to try it. About one mile south of the Ojo, we crossed the *Rio Carmen*, quite a river at that time, but in the dry season generally without a drop of water. The Carmen comes southwest from the mountains, and taking from here a northern turn, runs into lake Patos, as above mentioned. This peculiarity of Mexican water-courses in drying up entirely, and swelling to rivers again, must be ascribed partly to the regularity of the dry and rainy seasons, partly to the deep sandy beds of the creeks, and to the general dryness of the country in soil and atmosphere.

August 20.—Travelled to-day in rainy weather, without stopping, about 30 miles—a most fatiguing march. We camped, as usual, in the prairie, with plenty of rain-water, excellent grass, and sufficient wood from shrubs. Near our night camp, I understood, some miles west on the mountains, is a fine spring, called *Chaveta* spring. The grass in the rainy season grows wonderfully fast, much more so than in other countries in the spring, because the season is warm. The rainy season is here the real spring for vegetation. In the spring months the grass, though it may grow some, will always be dry and fallow; but as soon as the rainy season commences, a good observer can almost see its daily growth.* The rainy season brings forth at the same time most of the flowers of the prairie, and resembles in that respect, also, the spring of other climates.

August 21.—Took an early start and marched 20 miles before we halted in the prairie. Passed this morning the *Oj de Callejo*, (at present a creek,) which comes from the near mountains to our left and crosses the

---

*That the common phrase, to "see the grass grow," is not an absurdity in itself, the following fact, mentioned in Alex. von Humboldt's Kosmos, may show:

"The celebrated Spanish botanist, Cavanilles, was first taken with the idea of seeing the grass grow by directing the horizontal micrometer-thread, in a powerfully magnifying telescope, sometimes upon the shoot of a bambusa, sometimes upon the flower stalk of the agave americana, which develops itself very rapidly.

road, but in the dry season a mere spring, that must be followed up to the mountains. About four miles south of it, and about one mile east of the road, I was informed, exists another spring in the mountains, the Callejito spring.

The prairie was to day covered with more flowers and of more brilliant colors than I had seen for a long time. The grass was fresh as ever; the mountains, too, heretofore naked, cover themselves with a green coat of grass. This whole valley, or rather plain, from Paso to Chihuahua, seems fertile enough to raise many millions of stock, and in former times they raised large numbers; but at present the wild Indians are the lords of the country, and the Mexicans are becoming impoverished more and more.

Our noon camp is the highest point, according to my barometrical observations, on the road between Paso and Chihuahua; its elevation above the sea is 5,317 feet. Every afternoon, generally, we encountered a thunder storm, with rain; but to-day, while we were on the march again, it was severer than ever; the rain poured down in torrents, and quite a creek to the depth of several feet ran over the road, whose firm soil, however, allowed us to travel on till we arrived on a hill near the head of the Laguna de Encinillas, and camped, (eight miles.) There was neither wood in our camp, nor any use for it, as it rained all night.

August 22.—The rain ceased in the morning, but the road was worse than yesterday. The plain over which we travelled was about 15 miles wide, and a large lake was on our right. This "*Laguna de Encinillas*," as it is called, is one of those remarkable lakes so common in Northern Mexico, with considerable afflux of water, but without any outlet. With the freshets of the affluent waters they rise of course, and fall again in the dry season. Although the water of the creeks and rivers that run into them is fresh, the water in the lakes has generally a salty, brackish taste, and the surrounding country is covered with *tequesquite*, or alcaline salt in a state of effervescence, which is used for fabrication of soap. The peculiarity of these lakes allows of similar explanations as those I have given in relation to the rivers. The extensive sheet of water formed by lakes on level ground and the great dryness of the atmosphere cause an unusual evaporation, and the dryness and porosity of the soil a rapid imbibition. The lake of Encinillas extends in its greatest length from north to south, and is, according to the season, from 10 to 20 miles long; at present I estimated it about 15; the breadth, on an average, is three miles. West of the lake of Encinillas, our road was winding through a level plain, elevated about 5,000 feet. In the afternoon it commenced raining again; and after a most tiresome march, during which I had to put additional mules to my wagon, I arrived late in the evening at "*el Peñol*," a large hacienda, (28 miles from last night's camp.) The creek of the same name passing by the hacienda is the principal affluent of the lake of Encinillas; by the rains it was swelled to a torrent, and its roaring waves, rushing over all obstacles, sounded in the stillness of the night like a cataract.

August 23.—The distance from el Peñol to Chihuahua is about 40 miles. The Mexicans of our company prepared to go there in one day; Mr. Wiek and myself preferred to make it in two days, and we stayed therefore, with our wagons and servants, behind. We travelled in the forenoon about 12 miles, weather and road getting better. Near the western mountain chain we perceived several settlements, haciendas, and villages—*Encinillas*, for instance, on the southern end of the lake, and *Sauz* further south. In the afternoon we made 10 miles more. In the latter part of our march we reached a creek called *Arroyo Seco*, (dry creek,) but it was now so far from being dry that we could hardly cross it. This creek flows towards the east, and falls some miles below into the Sacramento. From Arroyo Seco we travelled about three miles, till we reached the valley of the *Sacramento*, the famous battle field six months afterwards. Of this valley, since that time, so many accounts have been given, with drawings and illustrations, that I consider it useless to expatiate on the locality; but a few remarks may not be out of place, to recall it to the reader's memory.

The mountains above the Sacramento approach each other from the east and west, and narrow the intermediate plain to the width of about six miles; and on the Sacramento itself, where new spurs of mountains project, to about three miles. The road from the Arroyo Seco to the Sacramento leads at first over a high plain; but as soon as the Sacramento comes in sight, it descends abruptly to its valley and to the left bank of the creek. Near where the road begins to descend, a ravine, with an opposite long hill, runs to the left or east of it, and a level plain spreads out to the right or west of it. On the hill towards the east was a continuous line of batteries and entrenchments, and the principal force of the Mexican army was there collected. On the opposite plain from the west, the American troops, who had above the Arroyo Seco already turned to the right of the road to gain a more favorable position, advanced in open field against their entrenched and by far more numerous enemies. How the American artillery with the first opening of their fire struck terror into the Mexican ranks; how the brave Missourians, then on horseback and on foot, acted by one impulse, rushed through the ravine up to the cannon's mouth, and, overthrowing and killing everything before them, took one battery after the other, till the whole line of entrenchments was in their possession and the enemy put to complete flight; how they crossed from here to the Sacramento and stormed on its right bank the last fortified position, on a steep hill, till not a Mexican was left to oppose them, and all their cannon, ammunition and trains abandoned to the victors—these are facts well known in the history of that campaign, and will immortalize the brave volunteers of Missouri. Little did I dream, when I reached on that evening the lonesome valley, that six months afterwards the cannon would roar here, and that the blood of the Mexicans would stain the clear water of the creek. My only trouble then was the same creek, which had swollen to such an extent that wherever I rode in, my horse had to swim. It was therefore impossible to cross it with the wagons to-night, and we camped on the left bank near a small enclosure of rocks, containing some springs and cotton trees. The springs, which I examined with the thermometer, had a temperature of 67° Fah., while the atmosphere was at 59° Fah. The elevation of this place above the sea is 4,940 feet, which makes it 300 feet higher than Chihuahua. For the first time we had a clear night again, and without rain.

August 24.—During the night the river had so considerably fallen that I could this morning ride over without swimming; and having found a good ford, we crossed with the wagons. There is a farm-house on the other side, el rancho de Sacramento; it lies at the foot of the steep hill, where the last defence was made by the Mexicans. I examined the rocks composing the hill; they were porphyritic and trachytic of many different colors—red, blue, white, and gray. From here it is about 20 miles to Chihuahua. The road leads over a level plain, widening again below the Sacramento mountains. In the plain grows mezquite and other shrubbery; the mountains east and west of the valley are steep, rough, and apparently formed by igneous rocks. About half way from Sacramento to *Chihuahua* we got the first sight of the city. I was taken at once with the beautiful site of the place. The mountains from both sides meet there in the middle, as if they intended to shut up the valley; and amidst this circle of mountains lies Chihuahua, with its churches and steeples, with its wide and clean streets, with its flat roofed, commodious houses, with its aqueduct and evergreen alameda—there it lies, as bright, shining and innocent, as if it were a city of "brotherly love"—but my enchantment should not last very long. In the afternoon we entered the city. A crowd of ragged loafers and vagabonds received us at the entrance as "Tejanos," (Texans,) the usual abusive appellation to Americans. The officers of the custom-house examined the contents of my wagon very carefully, and were rather at a loss how to account for the various instruments, packs of plants, and heaps of rocks that I carried with me; however, they let me pass. I stopped at the American hotel in Chihuahua, kept by Messrs. Rittels & Stevenson, and became soon acquainted with most of the foreign residents there. From them I learned, for the first time, that there was no prospect of peace; that General Wool was ordered to Chihuahua, and that in consequence of it great excitement existed in town. There was a Mexican war party in Chihuahua, and a more moderate party. The then governor of the State belonged to the latter party; but on the next day after my arrival he abdicated, or was rather forced to abdicate, to make place for the leader of the other party. Such bloodless revolutions, brought on by intrigue and money, had been so common in Chihuahua, that the State was sometimes ruled every month by a different governor. Under present circumstances the change of government was more important to the State, as well as to the foreign residents of Chihuahua. The new governor, chosen by the war party, was Angel Trias, a man conspicuous for his wealth, for his hatred against the Americans, and for his ambition of power. His inauguration took place with military and ecclesiastical pomp, patriotic sentiments increased rapidly, and occasionally a "death to the Americans!" was heard. The war fever soon grew very high; volunteers were drilled every day, and paraded through the streets; a foundry for cannon was established, ammunition provided for, and threats against the lives and property of foreigners became very common. Paying no more attention to those warlike preparations than I could help, I pursued, in the meanwhile, the scientific object of my excursion to Chihuahua by collecting plants, examining the geological character of the surrounding country, and making in the yard of my dwelling barometrical and astronomical observations. The prospect of the continuation of my journey to California was at present rather gloomy. However, General Wool's army could be expected in Chihuahua within a month; and if the excitement during that time should become too high, I intended to retire to some more quiet place. As I had presented the passport which I received in New Mexico from Governor Armijo to the authorities of Chihuahua, and they had acknowledged and countersigned it, I entertained no doubt that I was at liberty to leave the place again whenever I chose.

On *August* 29, five days after my arrival in Chihuahua, an occurrence, trifling in itself, brought me in contact with the Mexican authorities.

Several days back I had told my servant to clean my guns and pistols, which still remained loaded, and I had advised him to do it on the first sunny day. When I asked the landlord, an old resident of Chihuahua, for a suitable place to discharge them, he showed me to a corner of his court-yard; and upon my inquiry if there was not anything illegal or improper in shooting them off here, he made light of my scruples and assured me that neither the one nor the other was the case, and that travellers were almost daily in the habit of doing so. My servant accordingly discharged the guns this morning, and he selected this day for no other reason than because it was the first clear and sunny morning. Unfortunately, on the same day an express arrived from New Mexico with the intelligence that the American troops under General Kearny had taken possession of Santa Fe. The citizens of Chihuahua, not expecting any thing less from Governor Armijo than that he would make all the Americans prisoners, as he had formerly that handful of famished Texans, were quite exasperated at the news, and could explain this result but by treachery. Their patriotism was as its height, and looked for some vent. Some either malicious or stupid Mexicans, seeing in my barometer probably a courage meter, and in my sextant a paixhan, had several days ago spread a report over town that my scientific observations aimed at a military plan of the open and unfortified city, and that I was sent ahead of the American army as a spy. The discharging of my guns afforded a new opportunity for their lying propensities. Though the guns had been fired off in a remote corner, without any knowledge of the recent news, without any spectators except some Mexicans who passed through the yard, and without the least demonstration of any kind to warrant such an opinion, the same Mexicans reported that a salute had been fired in honor of the victory in Santa Fe; whereupon fifty brave Mexicans applied to the governor for permission to break into my appartments and take away my arms by force. The privation of my arms would have exactly suited their plan of a general mob against the Americans, which they had fixed already for to-night. But the governor, whatever blunders he may have committed, being a man at least of nobler feelings than the Mexican rabble, refused their request and preferred the legal way. A warrant was then issued by a judge for the man who had fired off the guns. As my servant had done it in accordance with my orders, I took the responsibility of course upon myself, and appeared before the court. Having examined several witnesses, pro and con, the judge perceived that there was not the least foundation for such a denunciation, and acquitted me. Notwithstanding this, the long talked of mob against the Americans came off that same night. I have been somewhat minute in relating these trifling matters—more, perhaps, than will interest the public—for the reason that a young *Englishman*, from *Missouri*, who arrived some weeks after me in Chihuahua, and was protected there by his *English* passport, wrote an exaggerated, and in many particulars untrue account of it to St. Louis, Missouri, where it was published, and found its way into several newspapers.

But let us return to our mob. A Mexican mob is not that short, offhand, killing affair that it is in the "far west" of the United States; it is rather an uproarous meeting, a somewhat irregular procession, arranged with a certain decency, and executed more from love of plunder than thirst of blood. In the evening, after dark, a large crowd assembled on the "plaza;"

4

haranguing speeches were made, the alarm-bell was rung, and with tremendous enthusiasm the mass moved towards the Americal hotel, selected
as the first point of their attack. The large front-door was forthwith
bolted, and we awaited their attack within the yard. Our whole garrison,
myself included, consisted of but four men, all well armed, and resolved
to defend themselves to the last. The mob commenced by throwing rocks
against the door; but when they found it too strong, they satisfied themselves
with abusive language and with patriotic songs. At last the governor interfered, and the crowd, though for hours yet collected around the hotel,
abstained from further violence. I must so far do justice to the governor
as to say that he disapproved in public of the mob, and blamed the Mexicans for these outrages; but, at the same time, I cannot conceive why he
did not entirely prevent the mob, as it had become a topic of conversation
during the day, and he must have known about it.

Although the first mob had failed, the excitement continued, and new
threats and insults were of daily occurrence. Six American residents of
Chihuahua, mostly merchants, who were principally exposed, applied
therefore to the government of Chihuahua, which either could not or
would not afford sufficient protection for passports to retire to Sonora.
After some negotiations they received passports for Cosihuiriachi, an out-
of-the-way place about 90 miles west of Chihuahua, under the condition
that they had to stay there under the control of the prefect, and that they
were not allowed to leave the place without special permission from the
governor of Chihuahua.

On *September* 6, the Americans left Chihuahua for Cosihuiriachi, es-
corted there by a military detachment. I thought it time now for myself
to leave the place, which had become too hot for scientific researches, and to
look out for some safer point; but when I asked for my passport, I was for
the first time informed that I could not at present leave either the State
or the city of Chihuahua; in other words, I was a prisoner of state,
without knowing it. Mr. Speyer had in the meanwhile arrived with his
caravan, and was also exposed to numerous vexations. His men were all
disarmed before they entered the city. At first, he should not leave Chihuahua at all; at last, they allowed him to go to the southern frontier of the
State, but without any Americans in his service, &c. Mr. Speyer was too
well acquainted with Mexican manners and character, and had too much
at stake, not to hold out against all those molestations; and by management he gained one concession after another, till he was at last out of
their power and on his way towards the south of Mexico. But, I for my
part had no inducement to go further south. Some of my friends, respectable merchants of Chihuahua, called once more, in my behalf, on the governor, and offered even their personal security for me, but to no avail. In
this dilemma I considered myself privileged to take " French leave," and
had already made my preparations, when, on the eve of starting, an English resident of Chihuahua, Mr. J. Potts, offered me his intercession with
the governor. Mr. Potts is proprietor of the mint. I had made his acquaintance in Chihuahua, and found him quite a scientific and obliging
gentleman; besides that, he was, of all the foreigners there, the most influential with the governor. From the short acquaintance I had with him,
I could not ask such a favor; but when voluntarily offered to me, I did not
hesitate to accept it. By his kind intercession I received that same day a
passport for Cosihuiriachi, under the same conditions as the other Ameri-

cans, with the additional clause to abstain from all correspondence injurious to the interest of the State of Chihuahua; a proof that my commission as a "spy" still occupied their minds. I received my passport on the evening of

September 11.—The same night I left Chihuahua, the sprightful city, which I had loved at first sight, but had now become disgusted with on account of the unjust treatment from the Mexican authorities and the licentiousness of the cowardly mobocracy. Within two days I was at the place of my exile, in *Cosihuiriachi.*

Gentle reader, whenever in the course of your life you should feel tempted to pronounce a foreign, jaw-breaking word, or to visit a strange-looking, incomprehensible, awful place, I would recommend to your kind attention Cosihuiriachi, because it includes everything that human imagination may conceive of—a combination of difficulties in words, appearances, and naked reality. Most willingly I would have saved to your eye the trouble of travelling so many times over the whole length of the unpronounceable word, which in old Indian language means, no doubt, a great deal more than we know of; but, as ill-fortune wished me to be confined there for six long months, I must ask you the favor to bear as patiently with the name, as I did (yielding to necessity) with the place itself.

The town of Cosihuiriachi, to come to the point, is about 90 miles west from Chihuahua, in 28° 12′ latitude north. The road to it from Chihuahua is always ascending, very rough and mountainous, and leads to the very heart of the Sierra Madre. The only considerable town on the road is San Isabel, about 35 miles west of Chihuahua. Only a part of the road can be travelled with wagons; pack-mules furnish, therefore, the means of transportation. Steep mountains of igneous rocks rise in all directions. The mountains are generally intersected by small valleys and high plains, fit for agriculture, and more yet for raising of stock; but on account of the Indians, who roam over the country, but few settlements exist. The mountains are principally formed by porphyritic rocks, and covered with oak, cedar, and pine. Travelling west of Chihuahua, one will soon perceive in the western mountain range a prominent point that is seen for a great distance, and may serve as a guide. This high mountain is called the "Bufa," and at its very foot lies the town of Cosihuiriachi. Coming close to it, the road descends for a couple of miles to a narrow ravine, between high, steep, sometimes perpendicular mountains, on both sides; and through the ravine, along a creek, stretches but one street of several hundred mud-built houses, representing the town of our banishment. The seclusion and closeness of the place, together with the poverty and filthiness of the greater part of its inhabitants, make it a very fit place to control prisoners of state and prevent them from being too comfortable. Two Americans, Mr. Phristoe and Mr. Carlysle, happened to live at that time in Cosihuiriachi, engaged in mercantile business; they received their exiled countrymen very hospitably, and extended the same favor to me on my arrival. In their dwelling-house, more commodious than the rest, we all took our lodgings, while Bill, our colored cook, attended to our board.

The names of the Americans who had been sent from Chihuahua to Cosihuiriachi before me, are the following: Messrs. East, Messervi, Weatherhead, Stevenson, Douglass, and Litzleiter. Our common impression then was, that our banishment could not last longer than one, or at the utmost two months, on account of the most positive news we had of

General Wool's march towards Chihuahua. But, instead of that, ill-fortune wanted us to stay there six long months, which I consider the most tedious of my whole life.

The day after my arrival I presented myself, with my passport received in Chihuahua, to the prefect of Cosihuiriachi, a respectable old man, who treated us throughout very kind, and executed the strict orders which from time to time arrived from Chihuahua for our better control, with all the humanity that his official station allowed. Though we were not permitted to leave Cosihuiriachi for another residence, we considered ourselves at liberty to make excursions in the neighborhood. Most of us were experienced hunters; and as the surrounding mountains contained a great many deer, we roamed almost daily over our hunting ground, to kill time as well as to provide our table with venison. On such excursions I paid constant attention to the botany of the country, and made in the first month a rich collection of mountain plants, most of them undescribed as yet. But with the approach of winter the flowers disappeared; the geology of the country was most uniform. To extend our excursions further was forbidden by a new order from the Governor of Chihuahua, which limited them to two leagues at the utmost; nearly all my books and instruments I had left behind; society was confined to ourselves; communications from Chihuahua were but seldom received, and, according to all accounts, there was no more prospect of General Wool's march towards Chihuahua. So we spent the winter in a state of constant expectation and weariness, interrupted sometimes only by a small patriotic excitement from a part of the Mexicans, most of whom hated us as foreigners, but did not dare to attack us. But instead of expatiating upon these trifles, which can afford no interest to the reader, I will rather insert here the few statistical accounts which I was able to collect in relation to Cosihuiriachi.

The town of Cosihuiriachi, or, with its full name, Santa Rosa de Cosihuiriachi, (also written Cosiguiriachi and Cusihuiriachic,) was established in the beginning of the latter century, in consequence of the accidental discovery of silver mines. The mines must have been very productive, because the population of the town in Spanish times was estimated at 10,700 souls; while at present, with the surrounding settlements, it hardly exceeds 3,000. The mountain chain on which it is situated is called Sierra de Metates; and forms a part of the Sierra Madre, which occupies the whole western portion of the State of Chihuahua. The mines are all in the mountain chain, west of town. Renowned among them were the mines of San Antonio, Santa Rosa, la Bufa, etc.; the first of them had been worked to a depth of near 300 varas. The mines are all found in porphyritic rocks, the prevailing formation in this part of the country. Silver occurs as sulphuret, in combination with sulphuret of iron and of lead. At present very little mining is done, more from want of capital than from exhaustion of the mines. Some of the mines have been abandoned on account of the water in them. The few wealthy families that live here, and attend to mining on a small scale, are unwilling to risk anything by expensive machinery, and foreign capitalists and miners have in the last 20 years been more attracted by the rich mines of Jesus Maria, further west. The ores of the few mines that are worked yet, contain, on an average, from three to four ounces of silver in the carga, (300 pounds.) The silver is extracted by fire. With the decline of the mines, the town also decayed, and the greatest part of the population looks at present wretchedly poor. Besides that, they are afflicted with two diseasês, very common among them, and not apt to promote propagation, syphilis and lepra. In Cosihuiriachi itself they cultivate only a few gardens, but in the neighborhood are some villages and settlements, with cornfields and orchards; and if it were not for the scourge of the country, the hostile Indians, all the plains might be cultivated, and the people might get richer by the raising of stock than by the mines. But the Mexicans are at present so under fear from those savage highway robbers, that they dare not even pursue them. During our stay in Cosihuiriachi, a party of Apaches stole away a drove of mules and killed six persons in a neighboring village, but nobody thought of pursuing them till they saw us determined to do so. A few badly armed Mexicans joined us then, and we followed all day the trail of the Indians, who were ahead of us for six hours, till we convinced ourselves that they had already retreated into the deepest recesses of the mountains, where it would have been more than temerity to have followed them in the night. One company of American rangers, roaming about like the Indians themselves, would soon sweep these enemies of all cultivated life out of the country; but the Mexicans, with the resignation of fatalism, rather suffer than take up arms and fight to the last.

The elevation of Cosihuiriachi above the sea is, according to my own observations, 6,275 feet, and the height of the "Bufa," the highest mountain in the chain, 7,918 feet above the sea, or 1,643 feet above Cosihuiriachi. The climate is, notwithstanding the high elevation, more temperate than cold; during the winter we had sometimes ice, but no snow.

In the beginning of the year 1847 our prospects began to brighten. The battle of Brazito had been fought, and the relief which we had in vain looked for from below seemed to approach now from the north. But, for two long months yet, we were kept in a dreadful state of suspense, the more excruciating the nearer the time came when a decisive battle between the two armies could be expected. Of the American troops we had no reliable information, but on the part of the Mexicans we witnessed all the strenuous exertions which they made for a vigorous resistance. They had procured a goodly number of cannon and small arms, with ammunition; new taxes had been gathered by a forced loan; about 4,000 men were pressed into the service; in the public press and from the pulpit, the people were excited against the " perfidious Yankees;" heroic deeds, and death for the fatherland, became every-day phrases. But to what, after all, could such theatrical display avail against the cool, determined bravery of the Missouri volunteers, which sought no vent in words, but in actions? Near the time of the expected battle, our suspense was of course on the highest point; but only vague rumors penetrated into our distant, isolated mountains, till, two days after the battle, some fugitives of the Mexican army returned as the first indication of a lost battle; and soon after, an express, sent out by our friends in Chihuahua, informed us positively of the glorious victory at Sacramento. There was no further authority in the place that would have tried to retain us under such circumstances. A part of the Mexican population, whose conscience was not quite clear from self-reproach, fearing revenge, fled even to the mountains, while we in the meanwhile prepared in all haste our baggage and animals, for our return to Chihuahua. Next morning, on

March 3, 1847, we left the place of our exile. Having taken leave of our old prefect and several better minded Mexicans of the town, and embraced, à la Mexican, some of the fair señoritas who had never given us cause for offence, we moved off in a body as happy as freemen, under such circumstances, can be, and two days afterwards we entered Chihuahua again. The city looked rather differently from what it did formerly, but not for the worse. One half of the Mexican population had left the city, from fear that the Americans would, after their victory, act as meanly and overbearing as they had done themselves before it; but in that they were disappointed—no excesses were committed, and the Mexicans were treated as mercifully as ever a vanquished enemy was by a generous victor.

But, really, what a ragged set of men those brave Missouri boys were! There was not one among them in complete uniform, and not two in the whole regiment dressed alike: each one had consulted either his own fancy or necessity, in arranging the remnants of former comfort, to produce a half decent appearance. Some of the resident Americans in Chihuahua, I understood, when after the battle the first American companies entered the town and halted on the Plaza, were so thunderstruck by the savage exterior of their own countrymen, that they ran back to their houses to ascertain first to what tribe or nation they belonged. But, notwithstanding their raggedness, there was some peculiar expression in their eye, meaning that they had seen Brazito and Sacramento, and that Mexicans could not frighten them even by ten-fold numbers. Among the troops I met with some old friends from Missouri, and during our stay in Chihuahua I became acquainted with many officers and men whose knowledge and bravery would do honor to any army, and whose gentlemanly deportment I shall always recollect with pleasure. But, for the present, we will leave Colonel Doniphan with his regiment in their comfortable quarters in Chihuahua, and take a review of the State and city of Chihuahua, before our final return to the United States.

Statistics of the State of Chihuahua.

The territory of the State of Chihuahua contains an *area* of 17,151½ square leagues, or 119,169 English square miles, and reaches from 26° 53′ 36″ to 32° 57′ 43″ north latitude. Its boundaries are, towards the north, New Mexico; towards the east, Coahuila and Texas; towards the south, Durango; to the southwest, Sinaloa; and to the northwest, Sonora. The great mountain chain of Mexico, the connecting link between the Rocky mountains of the north and the Andes of the south of this continent, is known here as *Sierra Madre*, and occupies chiefly the western part of the State, where it ascends to a considerable height, and then abruptly descending into deep ravines, (barrancas,) is lost in the rich plains of Sonora and Sinaloa. The highest point of the Sierra Madre (at Cumbres de Jesus Maria,) is, according to Mexican observations, elevated above the sea 3,004 varas, or 8,441 English feet. The mountain ranges, running generally from the north to the south, are intersected towards the east by fine valleys and plains. The eastern portion of the State is less mountainous, containing wide plains, and lying for the greater part on the broad and high plateau, the flattened crest of the Cordilleras that extends from New Mexico as far south as the city of Mexico. The average elevation of this plateau in the State of Chihuahua is between 4,000 and 5,000 feet.

The *water-courses* of the State are those that run, first, into the Gulf of Mexico; second, into the Pacific; third, into lakes within the State. To the first class blongs the Rio del Norte, running from northwest to southeast through the State, and its two tributaries, the Rio Conchos and Pecos. The water-courses that run into the Pacific all have their origin in the Sierra Madre, and are the following: the San Miguel, Refugio, Moris, Papigochic, and Gila. Of the latter, the Gila, the State of Chihuahua claims only the sources flowing from the Sierra de Mogoyon, until they unite with the Rio de San Francisco, a distance of 27 leagues. The third class of rivers discharge themselves into those peculiar lakes without outlet, which I have mentioned already in passing lake Encinillas, above Chihuahua. The following rivers empty into such lakes: the Rio de Casas Grandes into lake Guzman; the San Buenaventura into lake Santa Maria;'and the Carmen into lake Patos. It appears as if those lakes are principally produced by the physical properties of the'ground, to wit: a wide, very level plain and great porosity of the soil. Some of the lakes are supposed to have been formerly connected.

Common and mineral springs are very frequent in the State; the latter are mostly sulphurous, but are seldom used for medical purposes.

The *climate* generally is temperate. The influence of the more southern latitude of the State is counterbalanced by its high elevation above the sea. In the mountainous parts of the Sierra Madre, there is of course a greater variety in the seasons: hot summers; rainy seasons, and severe winters, often follow each other. But on the plains of the plateau, between 4,000 and 5,000 feet above the sea, there prevails a delightful, constant climate, with moderate temperature in summer and winter, with a clear sky and dry atmosphere, interrupted only by the rainy season, which generally lasts through July and August. The thermometer in the city of Chihuahua, I am told, seldom rises higher in the summer than about 95 degrees Fah., and of the moderate cold in the winter I can speak from experience. Some breezes prevail throughout the year. The barometer exhibits in the city of Chihuahua most regular daily oscillations, but very slight variations throughout the year. In the many observations which I have made there in the rainy season, in the winter and spring. there is a difference only, between the highest and lowest stand of the mercurial column (reduced to 32° Fah.) of 0.580 inch.

The great dryness of the atmosphere produces, of course, a very free development of *electricity*. By rubbing the hair of cats and dogs in the dark, I could elicit here a greater mass of electricity than I had ever seen produced in this way. Some persons, entitled to confidence, informed me that by changing their woollen under-dress in the night, they had at first been repeatedly frightened by seeing themselves suddenly enveloped in a mass of electrical fire. The remarkable flames that appeared after a thunder-storm in the mountains south of el Paso, already mentioned by me, were no doubt connected with electricity. I recollect also, from an account published in relation to the battle of Buena Vista, that during a sultry evening electrical flames were seen on the points of bayonets among the sentinels stationed in the mountains. Experiments made on the high table-land of Mexico with a fine electrometer, would no doubt give interesting results.* As to

---

* In Major Z. Pike's expedition to the sources of the Arkansas, etc., I find the following interesting comment upon the same subject: "The atmosphere had therefore become so electrified, that, when we halted at night, in taking off our blankets the electric fluid would almost cover them with sparks; and in Chihuahua we prepared a bottle with gold leaf, as a receiver, and collected sufficient of the electric fluid from a bear skin to give a considerable shock to a number of persons. This phenomenon was more conspicuous in the vicinity of Chihuahua than any other part we passed over."

the relative dryness of the atmosphere, my observations for the dew point will give some information.

The *productions* of the cultivated soil in the State of Chihuahua are maize, wheat, beans, peas, red pepper, apples, peaches, onions; and in the less elevated regions, figs, granates, melons, grapes, &c. Cotton, too, has been tried with success in the southern part of the State. Generally taken, the country seems to be more fit for raising stock than for agriculture, as a great portion of it is either too mountainous, or too scantily supplied with water, to become very productive. But notwithstanding, the State has sufficient arable land in the valleys and plains along the water courses to produce all the crops that are wanted for a much denser population than the present. In the mountains of the Sierra Madre there is an abundance of pines, which grow the finest and tallest, at an elevation of from eight to nine thousand feet above the sea; while in an elevation of five and six thousand feet more, oak and cedar are found, and in the plains mezquite and shrubbery furnish the necessary fuel. In the city of Chihuahua oak is used, carried there on pack mules from the mountains.

The *annual produce of agriculture* in the State is estimated at the value of $880,062. The following is a list of the items:

Maize	-	-	-	246,399 fanegas.
Barley	-	-	-	830 do.
Wheat	-	-	-	62,660 do.
Beans	-	-	-	30,713 do.
Peas	-	-	-	730 do.
Red pepper	-	-	-	5,694 do.
Cotton	-	-	-	12,957 arrobas.
Wine	-	-	-	23,652 frascos.
Whiskey	-	-	-	28,900 do.

More important than agriculture is the raising of *stock* in the State. Horses and mules, cattle and sheep, thrive and increase very rapidly, and the wealth of the proprietors of large "haciendas" consists mostly in their innumerable stock, which is never kept in the stables, but during the whole year is allowed to roam about. In former years, it is said, the stock was so numerous that large proprietors never knew the extent of their own herds; and whenever it was necessary for them to realize some money, they would send droves to the south, even as far as the city of Mexico; and they often cleared as much as $100,000 in one such trip. But since the last 20 years, the wild Indians have become so hostile, and committed so many depredations, that the stock is diminishing every year. An official but rather incomplete account valued the stock of the State, in 1833, at $3,848,228.

Another most important branch of industry in the State of Chihuahua is *mining*. Its many and rich silver mines have been celebrated for several centuries. They are principally found in the western part of the State, throughout the length of the Sierra Madre, and in a mean breadth of 30 leagues. The silver ores occur generally as sulphurets, with iron or lead, sometimes as native silver and muriate of silver, and are found either entirely in porphyritic rocks, or in stratified rocks, (limestone,) passing in greater depth into igneous rocks. They are worked either by amalgamation, or by fire in common furnaces. For the latter process they need generally an addition of greta, (litharge, or oxyde of lead,) which forms, therefore, a valuable article of trade. Besides the silver mines, rich mines also of copper, and some of gold, lead, iron, and tin, are found. The most distinguished mines of the State, of older and more recent date, are the following:

The mines of *Santa Eulalia*, near Chihuahua, have during the last century produced immense masses of silver, as the following fact may prove. The cathedral in Chihuahua, a most splendid building, was within the last century erected from a fund created from the proceeds of the Santa Eulalia mines, by a grant of one real (12½ cents) on every marc of silver (worth $8 25) obtained from the mines. This fund was created in 1717, and in 1789 the cathedral was finished, at an expense of $800,000. The amount of silver taken in these 72 years from the mines would, therefore, be $52,800,000. The abundance of lead found in Santa Eulalia makes the smelting of the silver ore very convenient. The mines are at present not yet exhausted; but from intrusion of water, want of capital, and the attraction of new mines, they are but little worked.

The mines of *Parral* (Hidalgo) are the oldest of the State, and have also been extremely productive in silver; but for want of regular mining, most of them, though not exhausted, are made inaccessible and worthless.

The mines of *Santa Barbara*, discovered in 1547, were renowned for both silver and gold ores, but are now entirely abandoned.

The mines of *Batopilas* were celebrated for the large masses of native silver, and the unusual richness of the ore.

South of Batopilas lies the rich mine of *Morelos*, discovered in 1826, where one mass of native silver was found weighing 230 marcs.

The mine of *Sierra Rica*, west of the old Presidio de San Carlos, was begun to be worked by a company in 1829. The prospects at first were most flattering: the superficial layers of the silver ore produced from one to a hundred marcs in the carga, sometimes 150, and in one instance even 327 marcs; but at the depth of 80 varas the mine seemed to give out, and the invasions of hostile Indians became at the same time so troublesome, that the mine was abandoned.

Such extreme richness of the ore is of course not a common occurrence; and the result, found by comparison of Mexican and European mines, that the mines in Mexico are generally poorer as to the relative amount of silver, but far superior as to abundance and extent of the ore, seems also to correspond with the mines in the State of Chihuahua; because a silver mine furnishing from three to four ounces of silver in the carga, is generally considered good enough to be worked with advantage; and many with less per cent. are rendered profitable.

In recent times, the mines of *Guazapares* and of *Jesus Maria* have attracted most of the capital of the State. The latter, southwest from Chihuahua, on the height of the Sierra Madre, were discovered in 1821; and so many valuable silver mines, and some gold mines, too, have since that time been opened, that it promises to be for a long time one of the richest mining districts in the State.

Of the copper mines in the State of Chihuahua, the most celebrated is the " *Santa Rita de Cobre*," in the western angle of the Sierra de Mogoyon, near the headwaters of the Gila. The mine, known for a long time to the Apaches, passed through the hands of several proprietors, till in 1828 it was effectually worked by Mr. Coursier, a French resident of Chihuahua, who is reported and generally believed to have cleared in seven years about half a million of dollars from it. The ore looks extremely rich; it is a remarkably pure oxyde of copper, accompanied sometimes with the native metal, and said to contain some gold. Mr. Coursier soon monopolized the whole copper trade in Chihuahua; and as the State at that time coined a great deal of this metal, he made a very profitable business of it: but at last the mine, which seems to be inexhaustible, had to be abandoned on account of hostile Indians, who killed some of the workmen, and attacked the trains. These copper mines are claimed by the State of Chihuahua, as belonging to its territory; but as not even the latitude of the city of Chihuahua had been well determined by the Mexicans, more exact astronomical observations may perhaps prove that they fall within the territory of New Mexico. This question may become of importance, because this whole range of mountains is intersected with veins of copper and placers of gold. Cinnabar also, says rumor, was discovered there in 1824, but nothing positive is known in relation to it.

Coal has been found at present only on two places in the State, near the mines of Carmen and near the mines of Sierra Rica; but it will probably occur in other localities.

After this short review of the mines in the State of Chihuahua, the question of course will arise, What is *the annual production of these mines?* The only data to which I can refer, are the following: In the 24 years from 1738 to 1761, the amount of silver produced in the State of Chihuahua was 3,428,278 marcs, or $28,283,293; and in the 17 years from 1777 to 1793, 1,394,161 marcs, or $12,501,828. The following is the estimated amount for later years:

In 1824	-	-	-	-	69,816 marcs, or	575,982 dollars.
1826	-	-	-	-	138,015	1,138,623
1827	-	-	-	-	129,402	1,067,566
1828	-	-	-	-	142,785	1,177,976
1830	-	-	-	-	128,747	1,062,163
1831	-	-	-	-	138,916	1,146,057
1832	-	-	-	-	117,484	969,243
1833	-	-	-	-	116,802	963,616
1834	-	-	-	-	109,419	902,707

More recent dates I was unable to get, though I understood from competent persons that the amount of silver had in the last 12 years considerably increased. The computator of the above tables estimates that the annual average amount of the production of silver and gold in the State of Chihuahua is 125,000 marcs, or $1,031,251; but he supposes that but 100,000 marcs of that sum pass through the mint, and that 25,000 marcs are every year smuggled out of the country.

There is a well-managed mint (casa de moneda) in Chihuahua, coining gold, silver, and copper. Mr. J. Potts and brother are the present proprietors, in consequence of a contract made with the government of Chihuahua. As all the silver ore in the State contains more or less gold, they separate it before coining, in large platina vessels, with sulphuric acid. For coining a marc of silver without separating the gold, they receive two reals, (25 cents;) for coining and separating the gold, five reals; but the marc of silver from which the gold is to be separated must contain at least 16 grains of gold.

Of the *commerce* of the State very little can be said at present. A

State so isolated in the interior of a large country, with a very thin population, without any navigable river, receiving most of its merchandise
either by the long Santa Fe trail from the United States or far from the interior of Mexico, or but occasionally by direct importation from the seaports
on the Pacific, has certainly no claim to commercial advantages. But if,
in the course of years, a shorter communication should be opened with
the seashore by a good direct road to the Rio Grande; if the indolent
Mexicans should be spurred on to greater industrial energy by their go-
ahead neighbors; if the Indians, the very scourge of the country, should
be driven out or extirpated by some companies of Texas rangers; if op-
pressive laws and monopolies should be supplanted by free competition of
industry, the State would soon be productive and rich enough to exchange
ever year many millions of goods with the seashore, as well as with the
interior.

The *population* of the State, exclusive of the wild Indians, was

In 1827	120,157
1832	138,133
1833	139,081
1842	147,600

At present it is estimated at from 150 to 160,000 inhabitants, which
number would give about 1.3 for each English square mile. The greater
part of the people are of Indian descent, though some have preserved
their pure Castilian blood. The settlements generally commenced and
progressed with the discovery of mines. The oldest town in the State is
Santa Barbara, (near Parral,) whose mines were discovered in 1556. About
1600, the town contained 7,000 inhabitants, who were mostly occupied
in the gold mines, which produced then from 12 to 14 ounces of gold in the
carga. Afterwards Parral was settled, Santa Eulalia, Cieneguilla, Cosihuiriachi, etc. The numerous *Indians* that in former years occupied the
country have greatly diminished. Some of them have become Christians,
and lead in their separate villages (pueblos) a poor and miserable life;
others are untamed yet, and roam restless about, living by hunting and
depredations upon the Mexicans. Those hostile Indians are principally
the *Apaches*, a very general denomination, comprising the following related
tribes : Tontos, Chirocahues, Faraones, Llaneros, Navajoes, Gileños, Mim-
breños, Mezcaleros, and Lipanes. The four latter tribes live only within
the State of Chihuahua, and carry on a continual warfare against its inhabitants. All the warriors of these four tribes are not estimated at more
than 1,400; nevertheless, this small number has ruined the industry
and impeded the progress of the State so completely, that if more energetic measures are not taken, the Mexicans will yet become the vassals of
these savage hordes.

In the northwestern part of the State of Chihuahua some *old ruins* are
found, built, no doubt, by a cultivated Indian tribe that has passed away.
They are known as *Casas Grandes*, and lie near the village and creek of
the same name, between Janos and Galeana. Ruins of large houses exist
here, built of adobes and wood, squared, three stories high, with a gallery
of wood, and staircase from the outside, with very small rooms and narrow doors in the upper stories, but without entrance in the lower. A canal
led the water of a spring to the place. A sort of watch-tower stands two

leagues southwest of it, on an elevation commanding a wide view. Along the creeks Casas Grandes and Janos a long line of Indian mounds extends, in some of which earthen vessels, painted white, blue, and violet, have been found; also weapons, and instruments of stone, but none of iron. The same artificial construction of houses is yet found amongst the Moqui Indians, northwest of the State of Chihuahua. But an old tradition reports, that the Aztecs, in their migration from the north to the south of Mexico, made three principal stations—the first on the lake de Teguyo, (great Salt lake?) the second on the Gila, and the third at Casas Grandes. The ruins of Casas Grandes are only distant about four days' travel from Cosihuiriachi, and I felt very anxious to examine them; but as the government of Chihuahua, following the precedent of Dr. Francia, in Paraguay, considered a scientific exploration of the country as endangering the welfare of the republic, I had to forego the pleasure, and to confine myself to the reports given to me in relation to it. *

Finally, let us look into the capital, the largest and finest city of the State. *Chihuahua* was settled about 1691. The number of its inhabitants is said to have been much greater about the middle of the last century than now; at present it is estimated at from 12 to 15,000. Chihuahua has a most beautiful situation in a valley, open towards the north, and surrounded on the other sides by the projecting mountains of the Sierra Madre. The city is regularly built; has wide and clean streets—in some of them quite handsome and convenient houses; plenty of water from the Chihuahua creek, and from an aqueduct; fine gardens around the town, and a delightful public walk, (Alameda,) shaded with cotton trees. The finest place of the city, as usual in Mexico, is the Plaza, or public square. It is very spacious; has a public fountain in the middle, and foot walks on the side, with benches and pillars of a white porphyry, which is found in the neighborhood. Three sides of the square are occupied with public buildings and stores; on the fourth stands the cathedral, a very imposing building, which I have mentioned already in connexion with the mines of Santa Eulalia. Although the style of the building is not throughout Gothic, it shows nevertheless great finish and elegance of construction; the two equal and parallel steeples in front of it are elevated 52½ varas above the Plaza. Another expensive work of architecture, erected in Spanish times, is the aqueduct, built of rocks, with arches; it extends 6,533 varas, and provides the southern part of the city with water, while on the north side the Chihuahua creek runs, which unites below with the "Nombre de Dios," and falls into the Conchos. Another remarkable building in town is the church of San Felipe, commenced by the Jesuits, and left unfinished after their expulsion. In this building the patriotic Hidalgo and his associates were confined before their execution; also the Texan officers of the ill-fated Santa Fe expedition, on their march to the south; and in more recent times it was converted into a foundry, at which were cast the cannon taken by Colonel Doniphan's regiment at the battle of Sacramento, and since transported to the distant capital of Missouri. In the interior of the building the Americans had their hospital established, during their occupation of Chihuahua. Near the old church, on a public square, stands a simple monument, in honor of Hidalgo, Allende, and Jimenez, the revolutionary heroes that were shot here by the Spaniards.

---

*In Clavigero's Historia antigua de Mejico, quite a similar account of these ruins is given.

The elevation of Chihuahua above the sea is, according to my numerous observations, 4,640 feet. Its geographical latitude I determined to be in 28° 38′ N.; its longitude, according to lunar observations made by Dr. Gregg, is in 106° 30′ west of Greenwich. The climate is delightful. Of diseases I have seen there dysenteries in summer, typhoidal fevers and rheumatic affections in the winter. Intermittent fevers and scurvy, which prevailed then among the American troops, are not common to the Mexicans.

Part of the population are very wealthy, but the majority are quite poor. The lower classes are ragged and filthy, and as to thievishness they might excel in London or Paris. The manners of the people are generally polite, (except in patriotic paroxysm;) the señoritas are celebrated for their beauty and natural grace; and fandangos and montebanks, cockfights and bull-fights, flourish as well here as over all Mexico.

———

Let us return now to the American troops in Chihuahua. When Colonel Doniphan's regiment left Santa Fe for this place, it was done in consequence of a previous order from headquarters to march south and report himself to General Wool, who was at that time marching towards Chihuahua. General Wool's destination was afterwards changed, but no news of that event nor contrary orders reached the troops at Santa Fe, and the "lost" regiment marched towards the south to meet with General Wool, in Chihuahua or somewhere else. In el Paso they ascertained, for the first time, that the General had not yet come to Chihuahua, and that the government of that State had made formidable preparations for defence. At the same time, news reached them of the revolution in New Mexico, exaggerated, for purpose, by the Mexicans. In this dilemma—surrounded in the rear and front by enemies—thrown in the middle of a hostile country—cut off from all communication and support of their own country, they took the only resolution that could avail in such emergency; they marched on, to conquer or die.

Having conquered Chihuahua, and not finding General Wool there, an express was sent from here to his camp near Saltillo to ask further orders. John Collins, esq., of Boonville, Missouri, a trader, who had volunteered in the battle of Sacramento, undertook the dangerous excursion with only 12 men. The regiment was stationed in the meanwhile in Chihuahua, and indulged in the luxuries of the town. Towards the end of March the first news of the battle of Buena Vista was received. Although Santa Anna claimed, in his official report that reached Chihuahua, a victory on his part, the Americans were too well versed in translation of Mexican reports not to consider themselves privileged to fire a salute on the Plaza in honor of *our* victory.

Most men of the regiment got at last tired of the inactive life in Chihuahua, and in a council of war an expedition to the southern part of the State was agreed upon. Some negotiations with the old Mexican authorities of Chihuahua, who had fled in this direction, failed to produce any result; they kept up, on the contrary, a shadow of Mexican government in the south of the State, at Parral. A march of the American troops there would have broken up that government at once, and being nearer to the seat of war, the regiment might, according to circumstances, have either thrown itself upon the State of Durango or marched towards Saltillo.

On *April* 5, 1847, 600 men, with 14 cannon, left Chihuahua for that purpose, while about 300 men, with some pieces of artillery, were left behind for the safekeeping of the city. As there was at that time a want of surgeons in the regiment, an appointment to that effect was offered to me, which I accepted. I left Chihuahua with the troops, moving towards the south.

Passing through Mapula and Bachimba, we reached within three days *San Pablo*, 50 miles southeast of Chihuahua. Here we were met by an express, sent from Americans below, and reporting that a large Mexican force was approaching from the south to reconquer Chihuahua, that the Mexican government had fled at the first news of our march, and that General Taylor had left Saltillo, etc. Upon these reports Colonel Doniphan resolved to return to Chihuahua, and defend that place at all hazards. With some reluctance the troops returned; the chivalric sons of Missouri relied so much upon their own bravery and good fortune, that they disliked every retrograde movement, although policy might command it. Two days afterwards we entered Chihuahua again, to the astonishment of friend and foe. Many Mexican families that had stayed in town left it now, from fear of a new battle. But, for two weeks we waited in vain for the large army from the south, till we became convinced at last that it was but a hoax—invented, perhaps, in Chihuahua, by some persons whose interest it was to keep the troops there as long as possible. As the prospects of a battle diminished, the regiment, whose term of service came near expiring, and which during the campaign had received glory enough, but neither pay nor clothes, became every day more anxious to return to the United States, and a day was at last fixed for the final departure of the whole regiment, if the express sent to General Wool should not return up to that time. Our route in that case would have been by Presidio del Norte and the Red river, to Fort Towson. But in due time Mr. Collins made his appearance. In about 30 days he had travelled, with a mere handful of men, about 1,000 miles through a hostile country, with no other passports but their rifles. In going out, his party consisted of but 12 men; on his return it was increased to about 40. The gallant Squire was received in Chihuahua with enthusiastic joy. He brought us definite orders from General Wool to march at once, and on the most direct road to Saltillo. Within two days our troops were on the march. Colonel Doniphan, before he left, called the Mexican authorities of the place and made them promise to treat the American residents of Chihuahua in a decent manner, and threatened them, in case of disorder, with a return of the American troops and a severe chastisement. The Mexicans promised everything. Many American and other foreign residents, however, had so little confidence in Mexican faith, that they preferred to accompany the army.

On *April* 25, 1847, our vanguard, with the artillery, left Chihuahua. They made on that day but 14 miles, and encamped at Coursier's hacienda, near *Mapula* This place is to the right of the usual road, and about five miles out of the way, but has to be resorted to for want of water, if one does not intend to go in one trip as far as Bachimba, the nearest watering place on the road, and 32 miles from Chihuahua. I was still detained this day in Chihuahua, and started in the morning of

April 26, to meet the troops in *Bachimba*. When, in the distance of about four miles, in crossing a chain of hills that encompass Chihuahua on the south, I looked for the last time over the interesting city in which I had seen within the last eight months a whole drama performed, and had been forced myself to act a rather passive part in it, I could not help admiring once more its romantic situation, and my first, favorable impression returned. But there was no time now for reflections: bidding farewell to the fair valley and to the distant Sacramento mountain, that rose like a massive tombstone over the battle-field, I crossed the hills and was soon in another valley, through which the road runs in a southeastern direction. This valley was about 10 miles wide, with a mountain chain towards the east and west, and but a few settlements on the right, (Mapula and Coursier's hacienda.) The grass was very dry, and the bed of several creeks which I passed contained not one drop of water. About 20 miles from Chihuahua the mountains, projecting from east to west, hemmed in the valley and changed it abruptly into a narrow pass (cañon) of five to six miles in length, and from half a mile to one mile in breadth. The pass is in some places so narrowed by steep rocks on both sides, that with some fortifications it could be made impregnable; but I am informed that the cañon would be evaded by taking a mountain road west of it that leads also to Chihuahua. Nearly in the middle of the pass lies a rancho, with a spring, but too scanty water. Lower down we passed a deserted rancho destroyed by Indians. Several Mexicans, killed by them, were buried here so superficially, with rocks heaped upon them, that their limbs were sticking out. At the other end of the cañon another much wider valley opened, through which we have now to travel. Bachimba lies about five miles off the cañon, in the plain; it is a hacienda with about one dozen houses, and a fine running stream. We encamped here to-night.

April 27.—Marched to-day 20 miles, to *Santa Cruz*, through the same wide valley, running from northwest to southeast. The mountains to the left of our road, towards the east, are about 25 miles distant; the Conchos river runs along that chain. The mountains to the right, or the west, are from five to 10 miles off. The whole wide plain is covered with mezquite and other shrubs, forming the so-called chaparrals. Walking and riding are both difficult through those thickets of thorny brush, and a man lost in a chaparral is by far worse off than one lost in the prairie. In the chaparral I met with different species of cacti in blossom; a small odd tree, (*Koeberlinia*,) seemed to be entirely composed of long green thorns; some *yuccas* raised their crowns, with a cluster of snow white flowers, above the shrubbery; also the purple-flowered *Fouquiera splendens*. I had seen the latter shrub already in the Jornada del Muerto, above el Paso, but not in blossom. As it is one of the most common and obnoxious plants in the continued chaparrals which will now surround us daily in our march to Monterey, I will give a short description of it. It grows in long branchless stalks, but a dozen of them standing sometimes together, covered all over with thorns, with few and quite small leaves, and at the upper end of the stalk a cluster of purple flowers. They grow generally from 10 to 20 feet high; sometimes I have seen them to the height of 30 feet. Their peculiar appearance, their height and red flowers, make them very conspicuous objects in the chaparrals. The Mexicans use them sometimes for hedges.

The soil was rather sandy, and grass scanty and poor, but the road firm and level. About 10 miles from Bachimba the road forks: the one to the left leads southeast to San Pablo; the other to the right, SSE., to Santa Cruz.

Both roads meet again before Saucillo. The San Pablo road is several miles nearer; but as we understood that a miry plain near San Pablo, covered with tequesquite, had by rains become impassable, we took the Santa Cruz road, arrived there in good time, and camped about one mile south of the town. Santa Cruz is a tolerably good looking town, and is said to contain, with the surrounding settlements, about 5,000 inhabitants. The *San Pe-dro creek* runs by the town; it is a clear mountain stream, that comes from the western mountains about 100 miles west of Santa Cruz, and takes a semi-circular turn from southeast to northwest, through the plain, till it falls, some distance below San Pablo, into the Conchos. Cotton trees grow along its borders. *San Pablo,* the town which we had reached in our first excursion from Chihuahua, lies about eight miles below Santa Cruz, on the San Pedro, and seems to be a flourishing place, with about 4,000 inhabitants. There is rich cultivated land along the stream, upon which they raise a good deal of maize and some cotton. Near our camp stand a flour mill and a cotton-gin. The latter seemed to be abandoned, but a basin in which the cotton used to be washed, with a water fall of about 10 feet, afforded us a refreshing shower-bath. We stayed here also the next day.

On *April 29*, we left for Saucillo, (23 miles.) We travel our day's march always without a noon halt, which is certainly the most convenient for an army. Our way led through the same valley, covered with chapar-rál; the road was good, but not quite so level as heretofore. Near Saucillo the mountains approach each other, and form south of it a wide gap lead-ing into another valley. Saucillo itself is a town on the *Conchos.* This river, whose water-courses extend over one-third of the State of Chihuahua, comes from the northwestern height of the Sierra Madre, takes first a south-ern, then an eastern and northeastern, and at last a northern direction, and falls, near Presidio del Norte, (therefore also called Presidio de las Juntas,) into the Rio Grande. Its whole course is about 400 miles, and its charac-ter as changeable as that of the Mexican rivers; at present it was rather a small stream.

In the mountains southwest from Saucillo some silver mines are worked, the ore of which is smelted here; it is combined with lead, and affords but from one to one and a half ounce of silver in the carga, but the simul-taneous production of "greta" (oxyde of lead) makes it nevertheless quite profitable. For the first time since we left Chihuahua, here I saw lime-stone, instead of the prevailing porphyritic rocks.

April 30.—Went 30 miles to-day, to *Santa Rosalia.* The gap, leading from the former valley to a new one, is about five miles wide; the road over it is hilly. Nearly half way we passed through *la Cruz,* a small town, and further below through *las Garzas,* a smaller place yet, where we crossed the Conchos, and followed its course up to the point at which the Florido river flows into it. There we camped, opposite to the town of Santa Rosalia, which lies on a hill in the angle between the two joining rivers. Southwest from the town, and from our camp, rises a chain of mountains in the distance of about five miles; the rocks are apparently strat-ified, and no doubt limestone; the Conchos runs along that chain. Near the river in this direction some sulphur springs are found, which are resorted to by the Mexicans for cutaneous and other diseases. I was not at leisure to visit them, but Dr. Gregg, who made an excursion there, informed me that the temperature of the different springs had been from 105 to 108° Fah., while the atmosphere was 85° Fah. Sediments of pure precipitated sulphur are found at the bottom of the springs. The mountains at the eastern side of the valley are more distant, about 10 miles. The intermediate plain is for the greater part covered with chaparrál. The *Rio Florido,* which comes from the State of Durango, and takes generally a northern course, runs here in a northwest direction through the valley into the Conchos, coming from the southwest. Santa Rosalia is a town of about 5,000 inhabitants; it lies on a hill about 100 feet higher than the river, and towards the south spreading out in a small plateau. Here, on the southern end of the town, the Mexicans had 'erected a fort against General Wool, when his division was expected to march towards Chihuahua. The fortifications consist of a very spacious square, built of sun-dried bricks or adobes, with redoubts, loop-holes, and trenches. Such fortifications of adobes have the advantage, that cannon balls will pass through them without making a breach. The fort is directly on the road leading to the town, and occupies very favorable ground; but a hostile army might turn the fort entirely, by going through a wide plain east of it, though they would have to march through chaparrál.

. On *May* 1, we rested on the same camping ground, to give to the last companies that left Chihuahua after us a chance to come up with the army.

May 2.—The whole regiment being together, we left this morning our camp at Santa Rosalia for *la Ramada,* (24 miles.) Lieutenant-Colonel Mitchell went to-day ahead with a small party, to reconnoitre the country between here and Saltillo; the road was more sandy, but nevertheless firm and easy to travel. Our direction was ESE.; the Rio Florido always to our left, and chaparral all around us. In the evening we had a thunder storm, with rain. La Ramada is a small place on the Florido.

May 3.—Made a strong march to-day of 33 miles, to *Guajuquilla.* The road was constantly winding itself through endless chaparrál; the Rio Florido on the left, and mountains and hills east and west, in the distance, from 10 to 20 miles. About half way we passed a rancho with some water; farther on, the road forks: the right hand road leads directly to the town; the other by a large hacienda. Before Guajuquilla we crossed the Florido, and passing through town, encamped south of it. Guajuquilla looks more like a town than any other place we have seen so far, on the road from Chihuahua; its population is from 6 to 7,000. The surrounding country is well cultivated, and seems well adapted for raising cotton. The produce of the cotton crop was in the last year 140,000 arrobas. Some copper and silver mines, I understood, are worked in the neighborhood, but I could not see any of the ores.

May 4.—Marched this morning but three miles south of Guajuquilla, to the *Hacienda de Dolores,* a large estate with well irrigated and cultivated fields. From here we will have to travel 20 leagues without meeting water. The prospect of this "Jornada" made us rest here till evening. Two Mexican loafers, suspected as spies, were made prisoners to-day; they confessed to have been sent out by General Ugarte; that he was roving about in that neighborhood, and intended to attack us in the Jornada. The news received very little credit on our part. One of the spies was taken along, but he made his escape during the night.

About 4 o'clock in the evening we started for the Jornada, and travelling through 'chaparrál and very uniform plain, we made that evening yet 20 miles, and encamped about midnight in a small valley without water.

5

May 5.—We started early in the morning, and went over a hilly country, till we ascended a table-land that divides the water courses of the Conchos and Rio Grande. A barometrical observation, made on the height of the table-land, gave an elevation above the sea of 4,700 feet. The plain was strewn with pieces of limestone, of common quartz, and of calcedony. Instead of mezquite, there was more grass around us; and instead of mountains, only hills, rolling towards east and west. From this table-land we descended again into a chaparrál valley, running from northwest to southeast, and surrounded by high mountains of limestone. The chaparrál had been set on fire, and thick masses of smoke rolled over us; but it did not in the least interrupt our march, although it made the heat in the valley more suffocating. I could not ascertain if this fire had originated from accident, or if Ugarte's bands had raised it to molest us; or if, perhaps, a disciple of Professor Espy's doctrines, travelling ahead of us, had the kind intention to produce a rain-shower for us in the Jornada;—at any rate, the experiment failed, and ended but in smoke. Some distance ahead, we met with arriéros, (muleteers,) carrying a large stock of brown sugar from Saltillo to Chihuahua. They sold the " piloncillo," a small loaf, weighing about one pound, as cheap as one medio, (sixpence.) About eight miles from our to-night camp, we passed a spring, with a water-pool, in a ravine to the left of our road; but the water was so muddy and brackish, that the animals refused to drink, or rather to eat it. This spot is known as *San Antonio camp.* Three miles further, a few deserted houses, and a spring on the right hand of the road, (*San Blas,*) are found; but the water is equally bad, and of sulphureted taste. The first good water, and in sufficient quantity, is met about five miles beyond San Blas, in *San Bernardo,* a deserted rancho, with willows and cotton trees, built against a steep mountain wall, from whence a fine creek takes its origin. A small plain half a mile below the rancho contains also some springs and water-pools, and good grass. We pitched our camp in this plain. We have travelled to-day, according to my estimate, about 40 miles. The long distance, as well as the want of water, the excessive heat, and especially the tremendous dust in the narrow road between the chaparráls, made to-day's march one of the most fatiguing.

May 6.—We started late to-day, and made but 10 miles, to the *Cerro Gordo,* or *el Andabazo* creek. Having crossed the mountain, at whose foot San Bernardo lies, we went for a mile through a cañon, with mountains of limestone on both sides, and from there into another valley, watered by the el Andabazo. This considerable creek seems to run from southwest to northeast; but whether it is connected with the Nasas river, or, what is more likely, runs into lake Paloma, a small lake northeast from the large Laguna de Tlagualila. I was unable to ascertain.. The Mexicans are generally so indifferent as to the geography of their neighborhood, that a traveller is often at a loss how to reconcile the many different statements. On the left bank of the river was a deserted rancho: we crossed the water and encamped on the other side, amidst chaparrál.

May 7.—Made 25 miles to-day, to the hacienda de *San José de Pelayo.* The country over which we travelled is a wide plain, with distant hills towards east and west. Chaparrál shrubs, and on the higher places a great deal of lechuguilla and sotol, cover the ground. A good-sized *Echino cactus,* of which 1 took a specimen along, was very common; and the *Opuntia arborescens,* with its straight stem and great many horizontal branches, grew as a tree of from 20 to 30 feet in height; and its numerous red flowers and unripe yellow fruit gave it the gay appearance of a large Christmas tree.

Pelayo is a small village, or hacienda, with several good springs around it; some of common, others of higher temperature. The creek formed by them is, according to the Mexican statements, afterwards lost in the sand. Pelayo belongs to the State of Durango; but I am not sure whether the el Andabazo, or some other point, forms here the boundary line between the State of Chihuahua and Durango. In Pelayo, a small but steep hill was fortified on the top, by walls of stone. This fortification was probably intended against General Wool's army. Two days before us, Lieutenant Colonel Mitchell had arrived here with the vanguard, and seeing the inhabitants of the place organized as a military company, he made 30 of them prisoners, and took their arms from them; but upon their representation that they would by this act become a prey to the surrounding Indians, he restored them their arms, under the condition that they be used only for defence against Indians.

May 8.—A rough mountainous road brought us to day into another valley, in which *Cadena* lies, a large hacienda belonging to the Governor of Durango, (18 miles.) About three miles east of our camp, in Cadena, rises a steep chain of mountains; another to the west, the Sierra de Mimbres, from which a creek comes, which runs through Cadena, in an eastern direction. About half way on our road, to-day, we passed a deserted hacienda, *Oruilla*, where copper ores used to be smelted. I saw there some pieces of very rich green carbonate of copper.

May 9.—Our road, this morning, led at first to the eastern mountain chain; and a narrow but very good pass brought us then into another wide valley, about 20 miles broad, and about 35 long from north to south, encircled on all sides by high mountains. This whole part of Mexico over which we travel at present, seems, as it were, but one large network of encased valleys, connecting with each other by good mountain passes and defiles. The mountains at the pass of Cadena (*puerta de Cadena*) consisted of a very compact limestone, dipping from west to east, at an angle of about 30 degrees. A Frenchman, an old resident of the country, informed me that he found coal in this mountain range; but while I passed through I could discover neither fossils nor coal. From the pass, the road turns through the level valley, due east, to *Mapimi*, 21 miles from Cadena. This town lies in an eastern corner of the valley, surrounded by high mountains, in which silver mines are worked. Two springs, called Espiritu Santo and Agua de Leon, form here a creek, which runs through the town in an eastern direction, and is lost afterwards, according to Mexican account, in the sand. One or two miles east of the town is a large smelting establishment for silver ores, found in the mountains near Mapimi. The silver is combined with lead. The poorest ore, I was told, contains three ounces, the richest one marc of silver, in the carga; besides which, they make at the same time much greta, and sell it at $12 per carga.

The town of Mapimi was rather deserted. In the evening our artillery fired a salute, in honor of the anniversary of the battle of Palo Alto.

May 10.—Leaving Mapimi this morning, our road went at first three miles to the eastern mountain chain, wound itself then about two miles through a cañon, and led us into a new very open and level valley, which belongs to the famous " *Bolson de Mapimi,*" which commences here. To the right of our road, or east, at the distance of from three to five miles, a steep and high mountain chain of limestone rises; and another chain to our left, distant from 10 to 15 miles. Both chains gradually diverge, but especially the eastern, which seems to run towards the northeast, and to return thence towards the southwest, at an angle, leaving a large *cul de sac*, or pouch, in the middle, from which form the country has probably received its name, as Bolson means pouch, or pocket. The barometrical profile will elucidate, better than a description, this pouch-like slope of the country, which extends most likely as far towards the north as the Rio Grande. Passing over a ridge, on our road, I enjoyed the most distant view over the Bolson de Mapimi, at the southern base of which we are at present travelling. All around us was an immense chaparrál plain, and in the distance of from 15 to 20 miles ahead of us the *Rio Nasus*, which runs towards the north, into the abovementioned pouch, and forms there the large *Laguna de Tlagualila*, (on maps generally called lake Cayman.) Neither the lake nor the northern end of the Bolson was to be seen from the place of my observation; but the outlines of the surrounding mountains, disappearing in the most distant horizon, seemed to extend towards the north to about 80 miles in length, and towards east and west to an average breadth of 30 miles. The limits of the Bolson have never been clearly defined, either in geographical or political regard. The northern part of it belongs to the State of Chihuahua; the southern, to that of Durango; but no certain boundary line seems to exist. As to the physical properties of the Bolson, the general impression is, that it represents a low, flat, swampy country, and a mere desert, which is but partly true. The two terminating points of our march through the Bolson are Mapimi, where we entered it, and el Pozo, or rather a point between Pozo and Parras, where we left it. At Mapimi, the elevation above the sea was 4,487 feet; in the valley of the Nasas, at San Sebastian, 3,785; at San Lorengo, 3,815; at San Juan, 3,775; and towards the eastern edge of the Bolson, I found el Pozo 3,990, and Parras 4,987 feet above the sea. We perceive, therefore, that the valley of the Nasas river, which may be called the vein and centre of the Bolson, has a mean elevation of 3,800 feet; and though from 500 to 1,000 feet lower than the surrounding country, it occupies nevertheless a considerable absolute elevation above the sea. The soil in the Bolson is less sandy and better than in the higher country; in the valley of the Nasas, especially, is a black rich soil, and most luxuriant vegetation, as we shall see hereafter.

From the ridge, from whence I overlooked the valley, the road descends slightly about five miles to a hacienda, where formerly silver ores used to be smelted. They have a large and deep well here, from which the water is drawn by a mule, and in peaceable times sold to the thirsty traveller: we of course refreshed ourselves, gratis. Some miles further, two more ranchos lie on the road, where, also, wells have been sunk. Although the soil looks everywhere dry, and the nearest water-course is the distant Nasas, good water is got everywhere in this valley by digging to a certain depth. Near these ranchos the road forks, and a more northern or southern route can be taken from here. The northern route leads by Alamito, San Lorenzo, and San Juan, (all settlements on the Nasas,) to el Pozo; while the southern goes to San Sebastian, (on the Nasas,) and by Matamoros and Laguna de Parras, to el Pozo. The latter route is considered the shortest; we selected it, therefore, and marched on the right hand road as far as *San Sebastian,* where we encamped. The nearer we approached San Sebastian and the river, the richer became the soil, though scarcely anything was to be seen but weeds and mezquite. The latter had changed here from shrubs into trees, reaching to the height of from 50 to 60 feet, and with trunks of a man's size. San Sebastian is a hacienda on the left bank of the Nasas river, and about 35 miles from Mapimi. The *Nasas* is here quite a deep and respectable stream, while further down it becomes flat, and disappears sometimes even entirely in the sand. It comes about 150 leagues from the western part of the State of Durango, from the so-called Sianori mountains, and runs in a northwestern and northern direction in the Bolson de Mapimi; ending as a lake. The Nasas is the Nile of the Bolson de Mapimi; the wide and level country along the river is yearly inundated by its risings, and owes to that circumstance its great fertility. Besides wheat and corn, they raise a good deal of cotton in the valley of the river, and wine has been tried, too, with success. The climate, I understood, is so mild, that the root of the cotton-shrub is seldom destroyed in the winter, and continues to thrive for many years. In San Sebastian we were informed that, for the want of water, it would be impracticable to continue the southern route, which would have passed from here to el Gatuño, Matamoros (la Bega de Maraujo,) Santa Mayara, Alamo de Parras, St. Domingo, and Peña, to el Pozo. The Laguna de Parras, which we would have also passed on that route, is formed by the Guanabal river, but was then entirely dry. It was therefore resolved to turn back into the northern route, by going from here, along the Nasas, to San Lorenzo. We shall lose in this way about 12 miles.

The inhabitants of San Sebastian had been hostile towards Mr. Collins's party, when they passed it on their express trip; they were punished for it, by our taking a lot of maize for our animals without pay.

May 11.—We crossed the Nasas below San Sebastian, on a good ford, and marched on its right bank, though generally a great distance from the river, 24 miles, to *San Lorenzo.* Our road went mostly through fine mezquite timber. Several settlements are along the river, as Rancho del Muerto, Hacienda de Concepcion, and Alamito. The latter lies about half way between San Sebastian and San Lorenzo, on the river, and six miles north of our road; it is the point where we ought to have camped last night, on the northern route. The proprietor of Alamito is an intelligent Spaniard, (Gapuchin,) Señor de Gaba, who rode along with us for some distance and gave me a good deal of information in relation to the country.

On the right hand, or south of us, a chain of limestone mountains was running parallel with the road. At the foot of a hill belonging to that chain, Señor de Gaba pointed out a place to me where some years ago a remarkable discovery had been made. In the year 1838, a Mexican, Don Juan Flores, perceived there the hidden entrance to a cave. He entered; but seeing inside a council of Indian warriors sitting together in the deepest silence, he retreated and told it to his companions, who, well prepared, entered the cave together, and discovered about 1,000 (?) well preserved Indian corpses, squatted together on the ground, with their hands folded below the knees. They were dressed in fine blankets, made of the fibres of lechuguilla, with sandals, made of a species of liana, on their feet, and ornamented with colored scarfs, with beads of seeds of fruits, polished bones, &c. This is the very insufficient account of the mysterious burying-place. The Mexicans suppose that it belonged to the Lipans, an old Indian tribe, which from time immemorial has roved and is yet roving over the Bolson de Mapimi. I had already heard in Chihuahua of this discovery, and was fortunate enough there to secure a skull that a gentleman had taken from the cave. At present, I was told, the place is pilfered of everything; nevertheless, had I been at leisure, I would have made an excursion to it.

San Lorenzo is a town of about 1,000 population, and lies on the right bank of the Nasas; but the waters of the river had here so far disappeared that only some pools were left, and in the dry sandy bed of the river some wells had been dug. In these wells, from 10 to 20 feet deep, I saw below the sand a layer of clay; Artesian wells might therefore succeed here. Such disappearance and reappearance of a river in the sand is a very common occurrence in Mexico, and seems to depend mostly upon the greater or less absorption by the soil. The course of the river is not interrupted thereby; it runs but deeper through the sand—perhaps, too, through crevices, instead of on the surface; and with the rising of the river the water returns as gradually as it has receded. Most of the property in San Lorenzo belongs to a Señor Sanchez, a rich Mexican, who received us well and seemed to be favorable to the Americans. While we were encamped at San Lorenzo, a rumor reached us that the Mexicans at San Sebastian had cut off some of the American traders in the rear of the army. A party at once started back; the more willingly, as an interesting and respectable American lady, sharing all the hardships and dangers of such an expedition, with her husband, were concerned in it; but fortunately, all proved to be a false alarm. Some other rumors were spread, about a Mexican army marching against us from Durango. We gave, then, very little credit to the last rumor, but ascertained afterwards from the public papers that they really had sent a force against us; but being informed that we turned, instead, to Durango, in the direction of Saltillo, they presumed, of course, that their unknown and distant presence had frightened us out of the State of Durango, and published a gasconading report about their bloodless victory. Some suspicious Mexicans, prowling about our camp to-day, were made prisoners.

May 12.—Starting this morning for San Juan, our vanguard discovered three armed Mexicans running from us. After a short steeple-chase through the chapparál, the Mexicans were made prisoners, and, as no plausible account could be elicited from them, taken along to our night camp in San Juan Bautista, a rancho on the Nasas, 15 miles from San Lorenzo. The road to-day was sandy, and mountain chains towards west, south, and east. The Nasas contained here plenty of running water again.

As we shall leave the river at this place, I will communicate what I could ascertain from Mexicans in relation to its course further down. The river takes from here a generally southern direction. About five or six leagues below San Juan there is another and the last settlement on its bank, called San Nicolas; from there it runs yet about eight or ten leagues, till it spreads out at last into the Laguna de Tlagualila, a lake of fresh water, but without outlet. In the dry season, this lake often contains no water, while in others it forms a sheet of water of thirty and more leagues in its greatest dimensions, from south to north. Some branches of the lake bear particular names, as Laguna de San Nicolas, de las Aguas, de los Muertos, etc., but the general name is lake Tlagualila. The denomination lake Cayman is quite unknown to Mexicans. From San Lorenzo the lake is about 15 leagues distant; and starting from there, the circuit of the lake, and return, may be made in four days' travelling (of Mexican riding.) About 16 leagues northwest from lake Tlagualila two other smaller lakes lie in the Bolson, called Laguna de Palomas and Jacque; their water is salty, and the salt found on the shore is used in the amalgamation process of silver mines.

May 13.—We travelled to day 25 miles, from San Juan to *el Pozo.* The road was more gravelly than sandy, at first quite level, afterwards slightly ascending. A few miles to our right a steep mountain chain was running parallel with our road; to the left rose more distant mountains. The mountains are formed of a compact gray limestone, without fossils, intersected with large veins of calcspar. About half. way we passed by a deserted rancho, "Refugio," with a well. Near el Pozo the valley becomes narrower; its width there is about five miles.

I had been riding ahead this morning, and reached Pozo early, though not in time to take part in a skirmish between our vanguard and a party of Indians. When I arrived, some Mexicans were engaged in lazoing several dead bodies of Indians and dragging them into a heap together. The skirmish had taken place under the following circumstances: Two days before, a party of Lipan Indians, upon one of their predatory excursions, had stolen from a hacienda near Parras several hundred mules and horses, and killed several men. The proprietor of the hacienda, Don Manuel de Ibarra, applied to Captain Ried, of our regiment, (who was then ahead of us with Lieut. Colonel Mitchell's party,) for aid against these Indians. The captain, one of our most gallant officers, took but eight men along, and, accompanied by the Don himself, went back to el Pozo, where the Indians, on their march to the mountains, had to pass, being the only watering place in that neighborhood. There they hid themselves in a corral, to wait for the arrival of the Indians. Quite unexpected, about 20 men of our vanguard came very early this morning to el Pozo, and increased their party to 30 men. Soon afterwards the Indians appeared—from 40 to 50 warriors. When our men rushed on horseback out of the corral to attack them, the Indians (probably supposing them to be Mexicans) received them with sneering and very contemptuous provocations, and their confidence in their bows and arrows was increased when the Americans, firing their rifles from horseback, killed none at the first charge. But as soon as our men alighted, and took good aim with their rifles, the Indians fell on all sides. Nevertheless, they fought most desperately, and did not retire till half of them were either dead or wounded. But at last they had to run for their lives, and to leave all their dead and all their booty behind. Besides the stolen stock, thirteen prisoners, Mexican women and children, whom they had carried along, were retaken and released from the brutality of their savage masters. Fifteen Indians were lying dead on the field. On our side, Captain Ried was wounded by some arrows, but not dangerously. Most of the dead Indians had fine blankets; some even carried gold; all were armed with bows and arrows, and a few with elegant shields of leather; and the "medicine man," who was foremost in the action, and fought most bravely, wore a head-dress of feathers and horns. Our men, of course, took of these curiosities whatever they liked; and the Mexicans stripped them of the rest, and dragged their bodies together. The fallen Indians were all of medium size, but well proportioned and very muscular; their skulls and faces bore all the characteristics of the Indian race, but their skin looked whiter than I have ever seen it in Indians. The dead bodies were lying there all day; neither Americans nor Mexicans seemed to care about them, and their burial was no doubt left to the wolves. I saw, therefore, no impropriety in taking another curiosity along for scientific purposes—to wit, the skull of the medicine man, which I have, since my return, presented to that distinguished craniologist, Professor Samuel G. Morton, of Philadelphia. In relation to the tribe of Lipans, I could only ascertain from the Mexicans that they live in the mountains of the Bolson, extend their stealing and robbing excursions very far south, and have the reputation of being a most brutal and cruel set of Indians, though brave in battle.

El Pozo (the well) is a hacienda, belonging to Don Manuel de Ibarra, and consists of but one large building, in which many families live. The place is distinguished for its ingenious water-works. It consists of a deep and very spacious well, from which the water is drawn by mule power in the following way. Over a large wheel in the upper part of the well a strong and broad band of leather is stretched, moving around with the wheel; to the band, in regular distances, many buckets of leather are attached, which, by the equal circular motion of the wheel and the band, are descending on one side to the well, and fill themselves with water, while they are drawn up on the other side, and; emptying their water into a basin, return again to the well. To receive the drawn water, two large basins of stone, about 40 feet wide and 100 feet long, have been made, and on the outside of the basins runs a long line of troughs, all of stone, for the watering of the animals. Part of our vanguard have been ordered ahead this morning to see the basins filled; and when the regiment arrived, all our animals were watered in less than an hour. The same Indians which our men fought here, the Lipans, used to frequent this well very freely, and carried their impudence even so far that they notified the Mexicans at what time they wanted to have the basins full, and the Mexicans did not dare to disobey. Although the idea of this water-wheel is by no means a new one, it is certainly very simply and well executed, and the more gratifying to the traveller, as this is the only watering place between San Juan and Parras, a distance of about 50 miles. On the threatened invasion of General Wool, the Mexicans, amongst other preparations of defence, had proposed to fill up this well on the approach of the American army, to expose them to starvation for want of water. This would certainly have proved a most wanton destruction, as the Mexicans must have found out by this time that a Jornada of 50 miles is not capable of stopping an American army.

May 14.—We left this morning for *Parras*, in the State of Coahuila. On most maps the Laguna de Parras is laid down as the western boundary between Durango and Coahuila; some Mexicans told me that in the Bolson de Mapimi the Rio Nasas is considered as the boundary line. Our road run parallel with a near mountain chain to the right, and was mostly ascending. In the latter part of our march we saw from a hill Parras, at the foot of the same chain, which makes here a bend towards southeast. The first sight of the town reminded me of el Paso, on account of the great many gardens and vineyards that surround it. Entering the town, I was struck with the luxuriant growth of pomegranates, figs, and fruits of all sorts, and with the enormous height and circumference of the common opuntias and agaves, which I had seen already in the State of Chihuahua, but much smaller. The opuntias had trunks of one foot diameter, and the agave americana grew to the height of from 10 to 15 feet, making excellent hedges. The town itself was much handsomer than I had expected. It has some fine streets, with old substantial buildings, a large "plaza," and a general appearance of wealth and comfort. We encamped in the Alameda, a beautiful public walk, shaded with cotton trees and provided with seats of repose. Early in the morning a concert of thousands of birds, many mocking birds among them, that live here quite undisturbed, awoke us from our slumber. These Alamedas, fashionable in all the Mexican cities, do honor to the general taste of the Mexicans for flowers, gardens, and natural embellishments. To prevent any injury to the trees, our horses were kept outside the Alameda. Parras was probably built towards the end of the seventeenth century, and received its name from its vine, parra meaning vine-branch. The cultivation of the vine is at present a principal object of industry in Parras. The vineyards are mostly on the hilly slopes of the limestone mountains west of town. They produce a white and a red wine, both of very pleasant taste, resembling somewhat the vine of el Paso, but more heating and stronger, though I doubt very much if the wine would stand a long transport by land. I tried, at least, with a friend of mine, to take a sample of it to the States, but from some cause it had nearly all evaporated when we reached Saltillo. The population of Parras is estimated at from 8 to 10,000, and with the surrounding settlements at nearly double that number.

When General Wool arrived here last year, the citizens of Parras were very well treated, and formed a very favorable opinion of the Americans; but those friendly relations came near being interrupted at present by a fatal accident. One of our wagon drivers, a very quiet man, had been assaulted by a Mexican loafer, and received several wounds, from the effect of which he afterwards died. As the prefect of Parras was not able to find out the guilty person, the friends of the wounded man took revenge on some Mexicans, and more disturbance would have grown out of it if we had stayed longer. We rested in Parras two days, and left it on the morning of

May 17, on our road to Saltillo. From Parras we marched about five miles in an eastern direction, through a plain, to *San Lorenzo*, or, as it is commonly called, *Hacienda de abajo*, a large, splendid hacienda, belonging to the above mentioned Don Manuel de Ibarra. The road from el Pozo leads directly to this place; by going to Parras, several leagues are lost. The hacienda has all the appearance of a large and rich village, and Don Manuel, who resides here, lives, no doubt, quite comfortable. From here the road was winding over a hilly and rocky country, till we arrived in *Cienega Grande*, a hacienda of Don Rey de Guerrero, (25 miles from Parras.) The mountains consisted yet of the same compact limestone; but sometimes, on the road, pieces of fresh-water limestone are seen, and roots and other objects in the creek were incrustated by lime.

May 18.—Through a wide valley, with mountains to the north and south, we went to day (18 miles) to *Rancho nuevo*, and encamped about one mile southeast of it, in a valley. On our road we saw a great deal of lechuguilla, and very large *palmettos*, a species of yucca with branches in the crown. Some miles from our camp, in a corner, amidst mountains, lies *Castañuela*, an old but small town, from which a shorter but very rough road leads over the mountains, to Parras. A fine creek runs by it, descending from the southwest mountains and turning towards the northeast.

May 19.—Marched 25 miles, to *Vequeria*, a small place on a creek of the same name. The very tortuous road led over a hilly and broken country. From one of the hills we perceived, towards the ENE., the distant mountains of Saltillo. About five miles from Vequeria we passed a creek with very clear water, the San Antonio, which unites below, near Patos, with the Vequeria creek. In several places to day, but principally in small valleys, we met with groves of yuccas, or palmettos, of unusual height, exhibiting sometimes a dozen branches in the crown, and growing from 30 to 40 feet high.

Northeast from Vequeria is an opening in the surrounding mountains, through which the mountain chain of Saltillo appears again. The route through this pass is the shortest and most direct for Saltillo, but with wagons one has to take a southeastern course to avoid the mountains. About one mile from Vequeria, in the pass leading to Saltillo, lies Patos, a small town.

May 20.—Made 22 miles to-day, from Vequeria to *San Juan*. Having ascended for some time, we came to an elevated and wide plain, surrounded on all sides by high mountains. Towards the east we distinguished already the mountains of Encantada and Buena Vista. We passed several ranchos and haciendas on the road, among them the Hacienda de los Muchachos, where all the houses of the "péons" were built entirely of the yucca tree. From the thickest trunks they had made the doors; from the smaller and the branches, the walls; and the roof was covered with the leaves. While I stopped in one of the huts to taste some tortillas, my horse came near unroofing another by eating it up. Such a simple and primitive structure of houses would authorize us to presume a very mild climate, but I am told that the winters are generally very rough in this high plain.

We encamped at San Juan, a place renowned by the battle fought here in the revolutionary war against Spain. At present, nobody lives here. On a hill of limestone stands a deserted rancho, and below is a green spot, with fine spring-water, and some miry places around it. Here we camped. General Wool's camp is about 15 miles from here, in Buena Vista.

May 21.—As we expected to meet General Wool to-day, there was a general brushing up this morning in the camp; but as it was impossible to create something out of nothing, we looked as ragged as ever. In the marching line, too, an improvement was tried. Usually, during the march, the men selected their places more according to fancy than military rule, and it was not uncommon to have our line stretched out to five miles, or three-fourths of the regiment marching in the vanguard. But, to day, to my utter astonishment, the heroes of Sacramento fell into regular line, and marched so for nearly half an hour, till the spirit of independence broke loose, and the commanding voice of Colonel Doniphan had to restore order again. However, after about 10 miles march over the plain, we arrived in "*Encantada,*" where some Arkansas troops were encamped. According to orders from headquarters, we encamped here also. The battle field and General Wool's camp at Buena Vista were five or six miles from here, and visits were soon exchanged between the two camps. With some friends from the Illinois regiments, I rode in the afternoon over the battle-field and to General Wool's camp.

Encantada is the southern opening of a pass that is here about five miles wide, and narrows itself towards the battle-field to about two miles.

On the east side of the pass a steep and rough chain of limestone rises, that may be about 1,000 feet higher than the pass, while towards the west a chain of hills, connected with more distant mountains, forms a barrier. A wagon road leads through the narrow valley, and between this road and the western chain of hills runs at first a small creek that comes from Encantada, and nearer the battle field a deep, dry ravine, formed probably by torrents of rain. Towards the battle-field the high mountains on the east form at their foot a small table land, ending in many gullies towards the road, or west. On this small table-land, from half a mile to a mile wide, the battle was fought; but in the narrow gullies and precipitous ravines the bloodiest mêlées took place. This locality was certainly the most suitable for a small army against a far superior force, and the selection of the battle-field bestows as much credit upon General Wool, as does the battle itself, which has been sufficiently commented upon by eye-witnesses, upon General Taylor and the whole army. The Mexicans call the place, very appropriately, *Angostura*. Buena Vista is a rancho about one mile north-east of Angostura, on the road to Saltillo. General Wool had fixed his camp there since the battle.

May 22.—The General, with his staff, rode to-day to our camp to review our regiment. A salute was fired, and he expressed himself highly satisfied with the martial appearance of the great marching and fighting regiment of Missouri, though he seemed not to admire our uniform. We received orders to march from here to Saltillo, Monterey, and Matamoros.

Before leaving Encantada I will remark, that the elevation of this camping place is 6,104 feet, which is the highest point on our road from Chihuahua. From here we shall descend very abruptly to Monterey, which is but 1,626 feet above the sea, and may be considered as the eastern limit of the high plains and mountains of this part of Mexico.

On *May* 23, in the morning, we left Encantada, passed by the battle-field and General Wool's camp, and marched through Saltillo and six miles beyond it before we encamped. In Wool's camp the old American cannon belonging to our regiment were left, while the conquered Mexican pieces were taken along as trophies, to Missouri.

Saltillo, or *Leona Victoria*, the capital of Coahuila, lies at the commencement of a wide plain, covering the sloping side of a hill which hides the view of the city in approaching it from the southwest. The city is very compact, shows half a dozen steeples, has clean streets, a beautiful church, &c.; but at the same time it has something narrow and gloomy, and the wide plain around it does not improve its rather awkward position. The population of the city was in 1831 about 20,000, but it seems to have diminished since that, and at present a considerable portion of the inhabitants had absented themselves. I stopped for some hours in the hotel of the " Great Western," kept by the celebrated *vivandière*, honored with that *nom de guerre*, and whose fearless behaviour during the battle of Buena Vista was highly praised; she dressed many wounded soldiers on that day, and even carried them out of the thickest fight.

Through a long, sloping, ill-paved street we proceeded on our way to camp, which was near some ranchos, on a dam. In going there, I perceived for the first time a plantation of *maguey, (agave americana,)* the same plant which we had seen, from Chihuahua down, often enough used for garden fences, or growing wild on dry and sunny places; but here it was raised and planted for the especial purpose of preparing *pulque*, a

whitish, slightly alcoholic beverage, which I had already tasted in Saltillo and found it quite palatable. Some of the plants were just in the
state of production. The white liquid was collected in the heart of the
plant, where, by cutting the stem out in the right season, a cavity is formed,
into which every day about one gallon of a sweet, saccharine juice exsu-
dates, from which, by short fermentation, the pulque is prepared. By a
more protracted process they obtain from it also a spirituous liquor, that is
very freely used in Mexico, and called *Mezcal, (Mexical.)* From the
fibres of the thick blades of the agave americana the old Mexicans prepared a very fine paper, on which they printed their hieroglyphic figures.
At present they work these fibres into ropes, bags, and thread, though for
the latter purpose a smaller and related species of agave (lechuguilla?) is
more used, whose finer and stronger fibres are called *pita.* The juice of the
agave contains before the season of flowering an acrid principle, which is
applied to wounds for cauterization. As the maguey is a perennial plant,
and useful in a variety of ways, a plantation of it in the southern part of
Mexico is generally considered a good investment.

May 24.—We left our camp this morning for *Rinconada,* (25 miles.)
Having marched about 18 miles through a wide plain, we reached some
deserted ranchos which had been destroyed by a part of the American
troops. From here the road winds itself through a mountain pass, with
precipitous mountains of limestone on both sides; the pass is, on an average,
two miles wide, and a creek with clear water runs through it. The way
leads mostly over a very hilly and broken country, and the scenery is wild
and romantic. About three miles from Rinconada there is a place in the
pass where it is scarcely more than 500 yards wide. General Ampudia had
commenced here some fortifications by throwing up redoubts and other
works; and from the narrowness of the pass, and the steepness of the road
ahead of it, the position is undoubtedly most formidable; but, after the
battle of Monterey, the place was abandoned by the Mexicans.

Rinconada belongs to the State of Nuevo Leon, which we have entered
now, and is a deserted rancho, in a corner of the mountain pass, on the same
creek. Although every thing there is at present in a state of desolation, it
seems to have been a well cultivated place, judging from the long line of
cotton trees along the water, and the many pomegranates and fig trees in
the garden. Rinconada is 3,381 feet above the sea; we have therefore
descended from Encantada, within 48 miles, 2,723 feet.

May 25.—Always descending, we still marched for some time through
the pass, which widened successively into a large valley, surrounded towards the north and south by high barriers of mountains. Passing by
Santa Catarina, a village to the right of our road, and by a large mill,
Moleno de Jesus Maria, we encamped within about four miles of Monterey, (24 from Rinconada,) with the bishop's palace in sight. In the afternoon we had a thunder storm, with rain, the first good shower since we
left Chihuahua.

May 26.—Started this morning for *Monterey,* the celebrated capital of
Nuevo Leon. The road passes at the foot of the bishop's palace. This
building of stone looks more like a chapel than a palace; around it some
walls and retrenchments were erected. The hill which it occupies is a
projecting spur of the nearest mountains, about 100 feet higher than the
road, but very steep and rocky. General Worth's charge upon this fort
does not stand the lowest among the many gallant deeds which this Murat

of the American army has performed in the present war. From the height of the bishop's palace a beautiful view is enjoyed over Monterey, lying about one mile east of it, over the black fort a little to the north, and over the whole wide plain which spreads out northeast of Monterey. The city looks to great advantage from here; the many gardens in the suburbs give it a lively appearance, and the more compact centre forms a fine contrast with this green enclosure. Riding through along suburbs, we arrived at last on the Plaza, where the Mexican troops had been pressed together before they capitulated. Many houses in the streets, principally on the corners, yet showed the marks of cannon and grape shot. A great many of the Mexicans must have left the city: it seemed, at present, to contain more Americans than Mexicans. Most of the stores, at least, belonged to Americans. The population of Monterey, in peace, is estimated at from 15 to 20,000. Many of the houses are built of limestone, instead of adobes; in the suburbs they are generally covered with stone. The climate of Monterey is very mild. With an elevation of but 1,626 feet above the sea, it is protected on three sides by the mountain chain of the Sierra Madre, whose eastern ramification ends here rather abruptly; and towards the east, where the country is hilly but not mountainous, it lies open to the breezes of the gulf. Oranges and other southern fruits grow here in the open air. In one of the gardens I saw, too, a very tall and high palm tree. The country around Monterey is generally very fertile.

Our regiment marched that day four miles beyond Monterey, to General Taylor's camp, on the *Walnut Springs*. In riding there, I passed by the "black fort," a strong fort in the plain, northeast from the city, commanding the main road and a great part of the city. The fort had been repaired by the Americans, and most of the conquered cannon found a place in it.

When I came to camp, a crowd of officers and men was collected about a simply dressed and plain looking individual, covered with a straw hat, that could not belong to any other person than to the "old Ranchero" himself, as the Mexicans used to call him—to the hero of Palo Alto, Monterey, and Buena Vista. When introduced to him, I found him as plain and easy in his conversation as in his appearance; and he was so kind as to give us some interesting details in relation to the battle of Monterey. General Taylor seems to be very partial to his camping ground, on the Walnut Springs; and the fresh spring water and fine timber are sufficient reasons for it.

On *May* 27, about noon, we left General Taylor's camp for *Marin*, (20 miles.) We marched through a wide plain, the mountains changing into hills. Chaparral of course covers the ground, but the soil seems to be richer and more fertile than heretofore. We passed several ranchos and villages on the road, as San Domingo, San Francisco, Agua Fria, which were inhabited, and others that had been destroyed by the American troops. Marin is a small town, on an eminence near the *Rio Meteros*, which seems to be the northern headwater of the San Juan.

On *May* 28, we marched 35 miles, to Carrizitos. The country was hilly, and all around us thick chaparral; but the chaparrals in the lower country, from Monterey to the sea-shore, are rather different from those on the high plains and mountainous parts of Mexico. Although sundry species of mezquite prevail in both of them, other shrubs disappear here entirely, or diminish at least, while new shrubbery and small trees take their place. So, for instance, disappears here the Fouquiera splendens; yuccas become very scarce; cacti in general diminish in number, but in place of them new shrubs and several trees appear, as the so-called "*black ebony*" tree; a Mimosea, with very solid wood; the *Leucophyllum texanum*, a shrub, with violet flowers of delicious odor, &c. As a change, too, in the mineral kingdom, I have to mention that we saw in the plain, east of Monterey, the American partridge, or quail, (ortyx Virginiana) again, which is never found in the higher regions of northern Mexico; but instead of it, a related bird, the ortyx squamata, (Vigors.)

About six miles from Marin is the spot where General Canales, with his guerilla bands, had captured, some months past, a rich train of the American army, and killed most of the unarmed wagon drivers. The bones of these ill fated men, which were either not buried at all or dragged out by the wolves, were scattered about in all directions. Another more horrid spectacle offered itself to our eyes near *Agua Negra*, a deserted village, where a man (and, to judge from pieces of clothing, an American) had been burnt to ashes, some bones only being left. In seeing such horrors, known only in old Indian warfare, can any one blame the American troops for having sought revenge, and burning all the villages and ranchos on their route which gave refuge to such bands of worse than highway robbers? The right of retaliation, as well as expediency, command, in my opinion, such measures against such unusual warfare; and when carried out with some circumspection, it will break up these guerilla bands much sooner than too lenient a course.

About half way on our road we passed a deserted rancho, with water; but we marched on to Carrizitos, a place with several burnt ranchos, but with a fine creek, excellent grass, and plenty of wood.

May 29.—In the forenoon we went but seven miles, through chaparrál plain, to *Cerralbo*, a tolerably good looking town, with many houses of stone, and some silver mines in the neighborhood. We made a noon halt to-day. Some troops of North Carolina and a company of Texan rangers were stationed here. The latter had captured this morning a well-known chief of a guerilla band, who was said to have committed many cruelties against Americans. He was sentenced to be shot, but refused to make any confessions. He boasted of having killed many men, and that he did not expect any better fate for himself. The execution took place on the Plaza. When led there, and placed against the wall of a house, he requested not to be blindfolded, or shot in the back, according to Mexican custom, which was granted. After a short conversation with a priest, he prepared and lit a cigarrito with a steady hand, and had not quite finished smoking it, when some well-aimed balls pierced his heart and head. He died instantly. His name was Nicholas Garcia; and whether guilty or innocent, he died like a brave man. Some rumor was afterwards started that he was the brother of General Canales, but in Cerralbo I understood that he was well known there; that his mother lived there yet, and that he had no other connexion with Canales than having belonged to his bands.

From Cerralbo we marched that afternoon 15 miles, to *Puntiagudo*, a burnt village on a creek, which is one of the headwaters of the Alamo. Cerralbo is 1,000, Puntiagudo but 700 feet above the sea. Since our descent from Monterey, we have constant east and southeast winds coming from the gulf, and heavy dews wet our blankets every night. Since we have left the higher regions, we perceive often in the sandy parts of the road a very large black spider, reminding me of the bird-catching spider of South America; the Mexicans consider it poisonous.

May 30.—We marched to-day through endless chaparrál 30 miles, to *Mier,* celebrated by the Texan invasion in 1840. It is a town with from 2,000 to 3,000 inhabitants, and has many stone buildings, while others are mere huts covered with straw. It lies on the right bank of the *Alamo* or *Alcontre,* a small river that runs, five miles below, into the Rio Grande. On the Plaza, the corner house was shown to us where the Texans, in their memorable expedition, fought against the ten-fold number of Mexicans. We encamped outside the town, near the river.

May 31.—Took a very early start this morning for *Camargo,* (25 miles.) Our road left here the river, but I followed its bank yet for some miles, be- cause I had learned that some singular, large oyster-shells were found there. I had to cross many deep ravines to continue along the river, and met there with bluffs consisting of a gray limestone without fossils; but for a long while I perceived only a great number of recent shells, living yet in the river or on the shore, till I discovered at last, in a clay bank of the river, a whole bed of the supposed oyster-shells, which were in fact very large spe- cimens of the genus *Ostrea,* belonging undoubtedly to the cretaceous for- mation. The place where I found them is close to the river, about two miles from Mier, and about three from its mouth in the Rio Grande. Ac- cording to similar accounts of large oyster-shells on the upper Rio Grande, this cretaceous formation seems to extend higher up on the Rio Grande as far as Laredo, and it is most likely connected, too, with the same formation lately discovered in Texas. Loaded with specimens, I turned into the road again, and, passing several creeks, ranchos, and villages, arrived at the left bank of the Rio San Juan, opposite Camargo. The San Juan, whose headwaters we passed at Monterey, is here a broad and respectable stream that falls into the Rio Grande about nine miles below Camargo, near San Francisco. In high water, steamboats drawing five feet go from the mouth of the Rio Grande up to Camargo, and a large depot has therefore been es- tablished here by the War Department; but at present the water was too low for such craft, and we were told that we would have to march, prob- ably, as far as Reynosa before we could find steamboats. A ferry boat, managed by a rope drawn across the river, brought us to the opposite shore, where Camargo lies. This is a town of 1,000 or at most 2,000 in- habitants at present, with some stone houses and a great many huts. The American depots and stores are generally kept in large tents or in large shanties, with wooden roofs and walls of canvass. The situation of the town, in a sandy plain, offers nothing the least attractive; but if we also add to the deep sand that covers all the streets a constant disagreeable wind, and the brackish, sulphureted water of the Rio San Juan, it must be considered a very unpleasant place.

On *June* 1, we left for *San Francisco,* (nine miles from Camargo.) I had been detained in town by some business till all the troops had left, and rode therefore alone, behind them. The road was very sandy, and the head wind filled the air so with dust and sand, that it was most painful to the eyes; on both sides of the narrow road was thick chaparrál. Riding ahead, therefore, with half-shut eyes, and reflecting upon the good chance that the guerillas would have to put an end to my scientific rambles forever, I was met by a return party of our regiment, reporting that one of our men, Mr. Swain, who stayed behind the troops, had just been killed by some

Mexicans near the road. The death of the unfortunate man had no doubt saved my own life. We soon came to the fatal spot. The body had already been removed by his friends, and several Mexicans, who were found under most suspicious circumstances on the nearest rancho, had been made prisoners. This party examined several other ranchos: in one of them a Mexican uniform, American books and clothes, and a hidden Mexican, were found, which were also taken to our camp. They were examined there by some of the officers; and as only strong circumstantial evidence, but no direct proof, was found against them, they were acquitted. Some friends of the deceased, I understood afterwards, dissatisfied with the decision, followed the Mexicans on their way home, killed four or five of them, and burnt their ranchos.

San Francisco is a small village on the Rio Grande. No steamboat was in sight, but we were informed that there were several in Reynosa, 39 miles below. We left, therefore, San Francisco in the evening, and marching all night, we arrived next morning, on

June 2, in *Reynosa*, a small town on the Rio Grande. The river is here quite considerable, about 200 yards wide, and six or more feet deep. The banks are low, sandy, barren, and covered with chaparrál, like the surrounding plains. A barometrical observation which I made here, about 10 feet above the level of the water, gave an elevation above the sea of 184 feet, so that the fall of the river from here to the mouth, a distance by water of from 300 to 400 miles, would on an average be one foot in two miles.

The long wished for sight of steamboats at last greeted our eyes; two were lying in the river, and others were coming up. The *Roberts* and the *Aid* were engaged for our regiment, and everybody prepared for embarking. Our wagons had to be driven back to Camargo, and all our riding animals sent by land, through Texas, to Missouri; but as the latter was considered tantamount to a loss, most of us gave their horses away for a trifle, or made them run off. A great many of these animals, after a rest of some months, would have been better for service than imported ones, yet unused to the climate and country; but as there was no provision made for it, the men as well as the government suffered a loss.

On *June* 3, I went with the battalion of artillery on board the Roberts. As we had to cross a sand bar some miles below, the cannon and baggage had to be carried there by land, and then taken on board. This delayed us till evening, and we laid by for the night.

On *June* 4, we started with daylight, and, running all day, we made more than half way to Matamoros. The river was rather at a low stage, and it was not uncommon to hear and feel the boat strike on sand bars; but as the sandy river bed is clear of rocks and snags, there is no danger in such collisions. The course of the Rio Grande is certainly the most tortuous that I have seen; the Mississippi compared to it is a straight line. By observing only the direction, one will often be at a loss whether he ascends or descends the river. I remembered one place particularly, where it runs directly south; after having made some five miles, it returns due north so nearly to the same place from which it started, that it is only separated from it by a small strip of sand bank. The country around it was level and flat; near the river the soil seemed to be very good; but very few settlements or cultivated land were to be seen; the chaparrals seemed to grow thinner, and trees with long beards of Spanish moss (*Tillandsea asneoides*) made their appearance. Sundry wooding places provided the boat with wood, most of which was mezquite and black ebony. During the whole day we saw six steamboats; in the night we laid by again.

On *June* 5, about noon, we reached *Matamoros*. As the city is half a mile from the river, and we staid but half an hour, I could get only a glimpse of it. It is built on the plain, at a trifling elevation; the houses are either of stone or adobes; the plaza and the principal streets were occupied by Americans, and the rest of the city seemed rather deserted. As to beauty of situation or imposing buildings, it cannot compare with any of the larger cities we have met with on this route.

From Matamoros we passed by *Fort Brown*, where the star-spangled banner was flying, and the battle-fields of *Palo Alto* and *Resaca de la Palma* were pointed out to us in the distant chaparráls towards the north. The river was here in a very navigable state, but continued to be as crooked as ever. I saw many palm trees of small size; more settlements along the banks; sugar and cotton plantations among them, but chaparrál always in the back ground. We laid by in the night, but after midnight we started again with the rising of the moon, and arrived in the morning of

June 6 at the "*mouth of Rio Grande*," and encamped on the left bank of the river. About one mile from our camp was the high sea and the embouchure of the river. On the left side of the mouth were some commissaries' and private stores established, and the place is known as "*Mouth of Rio Grande.*" Opposite, on the right side, stands another small village, called "*Bagdad.*" In the river lay some smaller steamboats and schooners, but no larger crafts, which have a better anchorage nine miles from here, in Brazos Santiago. An express was sent there to engage vessels for our regiment as soon as possible: we staid here in the meanwhile, because it is a decidedly better camping ground.

We had to wait for three days, which I spent mostly on the seashore. The long-missed sight of the ocean, the salt plants and fine shells on the beach, and the refreshing sea bath, called many old recollections to my mind; and the fine oysters, sea-fish, crabs, and other delicacies, to be got in the modern Bagdad, left the body not without its share of "creature comforts."

During our stay here I tried, too, for the last time in Mexico, my faithful barometer, which I had brought with me from St. Louis, Missouri, and after daily use upon this long trip, had carried safely to the seashore. Often had I taken this delicate instrument on my back, and treated it like a spoiled child; but my paternal cares should be repaid. These last observations on the seashore proved it, to my gratification, to be yet in good order, and a further comparison in St. Louis showed that during the whole time it had changed but a trifle. I was in hopes to find on the seashore some meteorological tables for comparison and calculation of my barometrical observations, but in that I was disappointed. In the quartermaster's office, at Mouth of Rio Grande, was indeed a very good barometer hanging up, but no regular observations were made; it was used only for the "northers." On the 8th we were informed that ships were ready for us in Brazos. We left, therefore, on

June 9, our camp on the Rio Grande, and travelled by land to *Brazos Santiago*, (nine miles.) The cannon were carried there by water, the baggage in wagons, and the men went on foot. The road goes over deep sand, and for the greater part along the beach. A wooden bridge leads over the arm of the sea that forms the small island known as Brazos San-

6

tiago. We soon reached the harbor, where many vessels were anchored; and a number of frame houses, with commissaries' stores, groceries, etc., formed a village around it. This was the last place we saw on this side of the gulf, and no doubt the meanest which I have seen during the whole trip. The whole island is but one wide sheet of sand; never a tree or blade of grass has grown here; no other water is found but a brackish, half fresh, half salty liquid, from holes dug into the sand; no other faces are seen but those of stern officials, or of sly speculators, who would as soon go to Kamtschatka if they could make money there. In short, it is an awful place, where nobody would live, but from necessity or for money. Fortunately, our stay was not long. We slept but one night on the sand of the island, and went next day,

On *June* 10, on board of our ships, the *Republic* and the *Morillo*, both sailing vessels, for New Orleans. I embarked with the artillery on board the latter, and we cleared in the afternoon of the same day. After a voyage of seven days, not interrupted by any unusual accident, we arrived safely in New Orleans.

The noise and bustle of a large city confused me, as it were, for a short time; but those impressions from the lonesome prairie and desolate chaparrals were soon overpowered by the enjoyments and luxuries of cultivated life.

Our regiment was discharged and paid in New Orleans; and from a ragged set of boys, they turned at once into "gentlemen." Having finished my own business in New Orleans, I started for St. Louis, my home, and arrived there early in July, to rest awhile from the hardships of the expedition.

After an absence of 14 months, I had travelled from Independence to Reynosa, on the Rio Grande, about 2,200 miles by land, and about 3,100 by water, and had been exposed to many privations, hardships, and dangers; but all of them I underwent, for the scientific purpose of my expedition, with pleasure, except the unjust and arbitrary treatment from the government of the State of Chihuahua, which deprived me for six months of what I always valued the highest, my individual liberty, and prevented me in this way from extending my excursion as far as I at first intended, and of making its results more general and useful.

———

At the conclusion of my journal, it may not be amiss to add some *general remarks in relation to Northern Mexico.*

New Mexico and Chihuahua, which I consider here principally, because they fell under my immediate observation, are neither the richest nor the poorest States of Mexico; but both of them have resources that never have been fully developed.

Agriculture, as we have seen, is the least promising branch of industry. The want of more water-courses, and the necessity of irrigation, are the principal causes; but nevertheless, they raise every year more than sufficient for their own consumption; and failure of crops, with starvation of the people, is less common here than in many other countries, because the regular system of irrigation itself prevents it. Besides, there are large tracts of land in the country fit for agriculture, but allowing no isolated settlements on account of the Indians. Another reason, too, why farming settlements make slow progress, is, the large haciendas. That independent class of small farmers who occupy the greatest part of the land in the United States is here but poorly represented, and the large estates cultivate generally less ground than many smaller but independent farmers.

As a *grazing country*, both States are unsurpassed by any in the Union. Millions of stock can be raised every year in the prairies of the high table-land and in the mountains. Cattle, horses, mules, and sheep increase very fast; and if more attention were paid to the improvement of the stock, the wool of the sheep alone could be made the exchange for the greatest part of the present importation. But to accomplish that, the wild Indians, who chiefly in the last ten years have crippled all industry in stock raising, have first to be subdued.

Mining, another main resource of the country, needs to some degree, also, protection from the Indians, because valuable mines have sometimes been given up, from their incursions; and other districts, rich in minerals, cannot be even explored, for the same reason.

The silver mines of the State of Chihuahua, though worked for centuries, seem to be inexhaustible. The discovery of new mines is but a common occurrence; and attracted by them, the mining population moves generally from one place to another without exhausting the old ones. To make the mining more effectual, onerous duties and partial restrictions ought to be abolished, and sufficient capital to work them more thoroughly and extensively would soon flow to the State. New Mexico seems to be as rich in gold ore as Chihuahua is in silver; but yet, less capital and greater insecurity have prevented their being worked to a large extent.

To develop all those resources which nature has bestowed upon these two States, another condition of things is wanted than at present prevails there: a just, stable, and strong government is, before all, needed, that can put down the hostile Indians, give security of person and property to all, allow free competition in all branches of industry, and will not tax the people higher than the absolute wants of the government require. Under such a government, the population, as well as the produce of the country, would increase at a rapid rate; new outlets would be opened to commerce, and the people would not only become richer and more comfortable, but more enlightened, too, and more liberal.

Is there at present any prospect of such a favorable change?

The Mexicans, since their declaration of independence, have been involved in an incessant series of local and general revolutions throughout the country, which prove that republican institutions have not taken root amongst them, and that, although they have thrown off the foreign yoke, they have not learned yet to govern themselves. It could hardly be expected, too, that a people composed of two different races, who have mixed but not assimilated themselves, should, after an oppression of three centuries, at once be fit for a republic. Fanaticism alone may overthrow an old government, but it wants cool and clear heads to establish a new one adapted to the people, and a certain intellect of the whole people to maintain permanently a republic. But this wide-spread intellect does not exist yet in the mass of the Mexican populace, or they would not have been duped, as they have been for twenty years past, by the long succession of egotistical leaders, whose only aim and ambition was power and plunder; and during all these disgraceful internal revolutions, neither the general nor local governments have done anything to spread more intellect amongst the great mass of the people; they had neither time nor money for it, and it did partly not suit their ambitious plans to govern a more enlightened people.

Where shall the enlightening of the masses and the stability of government now come from? I cannot help thinking that if Mexico, debilitated by the present war, should afterwards be left to itself, the renewal of its internal strifes will hurry it to its entire dissolution; and what the United States may refuse at present to take as the spoils of the war, will be offered to them in later years as a boon.

The fate of Mexico is sealed. Unable to govern itself, it will be governed by some other power; and if it should not fall into worse hands than those of the United States, it may yet congratulate itself, because they would respect at least its nationality, and guaranty to it what it never had before, a republican government.

That the whole of Mexico would as well derive advantage from such a change as the whole civilized world, if this wonderful country should be opened to the industry of a more vigorous race, there is no doubt in my mind; but I doubt the policy on the part of the United States to keep the whole of Mexico in their possession, even if they could, because a heterogeneous mass of seven or eight millions of Mexicans, who have to be converted from enemies into friends, and raised from an ignorant and oppressed condition to the level of republican citizens, could not be as easily assimilated to the republic as a similar number of European immigrants, that arrive here in great intervals of time, with more knowledge, and with the fixed intention to live and die as Americans.

At the end of this war the United States will probably be bound to indemnify themselves for the large expenses of the war, by some Mexican provinces; but the more valuable the territory and the fewer Mexicans they acquire in this way, the more will the new acquisition be useful to the United States. In the northern provinces of Mexico both those conditions are united.

Let us suppose, for instance, that from the mouth of the Rio Grande a boundary line should be drawn up to Laredo, the headpoint of steam navigation on the Rio Grande, and in the latitude of Laredo a line from thence west to the gulf of California, that territory would embrace, besides the old province of Texas, a small portion of the States of Tamaulipas and Coahuila, the greatest part of the State of Chihuahua, the State of Sonora, New Mexico, and both Californias. The Mexican population of those States—if we except the highest probable estimates, and include, instead of the small slice of Tamaulipas and Coahuila, the whole population of the State of Chihuahua—is the following:

Chihuahua	-	-	-	-	-	160,000 inhabitants.
Sonora	-	-	-	-	-	130,000 "
New Mexico	-	-	-	-	-	70,000 "
Upper California	-	-	-	-	-	35,000 "
Lower California	-	-	-	-	-	5,000 "
						400,000 "

The whole population of those States amounts, therefore, only to about 400,000 souls, while this territory, according to the usual Mexican estimates, embraces an area of about 940,000, or, including the old province of Texas, already lost by Mexico, of about 1,200,000 English square miles.*

The greatest part of this territory has never been occupied or even explored by the Mexicans, and the thin population in the settled parts of it proves that they never had put great value upon it. The greater inducements which the South of Mexico offered on account of mines, climate, commerce, etc., have concentrated there the seven or eight millions of inhabitants that compose the Mexican nation, allowing but a small portion of them for the northern provinces. One half of this northern territory may in fact be a desert, and entirely worthless for agriculture; but to a great commercial nation like the United States, with new States springing up on the Pacific, it will nevertheless be valuable for the new connexions that it would open with the Pacific, for the great mineral resources of the country, and for its peculiar adaptation for stock-raising. Mexico itself would lose very little by the States composing this territory, as they always have been more a burden to it than a source of revenue. All the connexion which heretofore has existed between Mexico and those States, was, that the general government taxed them as highly as they would submit to, which never was very great, and dragged them as far as possible into the revolutionary vortex in which the South of Mexico was constantly whirling; but it never afforded them any protection against hostile Indians; never stopped their internal strifes, or ever promoted the spread of intellect or industry—in short, it heaped, instead of blessings, all the curses of the worst kind of government upon them.

Should the United States take possession of this country, the official leeches who consider themselves privileged to rule in those States will, of course, make some opposition—if not openly, at least by intrigue; but the mass of the people will soon perceive that they have *gained by the change;* and if to their national feelings some due regard is paid, they will after some years become reconciled to their new government, and, though Mexican still, they may nevertheless become good citizens of the Republic of the North.

Policy, as well as humanity, demands, in my humble opinion, such an extension of the "area of freedom" for mankind. If deserts and mountain chains are wanted as the best barriers between States, this line affords both these advantages by the Bolson de Mapimi in the east, and the extensive Sierra Madre in the west.

On the gulf of California, the important harbor of Guaymas would fall above that line. What sort of communication between Guaymas and the Rio Grande might be considered the best, a closer exploration of the country must decide; but a railroad would most likely in the course of years connect the Rio Grande with that harbor, and give a new thoroughfare from the Atlantic to the Pacific, for commerce as well as for the emigration to California and Oregon. The distance from Laredo to Guaymas, in a straight line, is about 770 miles. The plan of such a railroad, even if the height of the Sierra Madre in the west would not allow it to be carried in a straight line to the Pacific, but from Chihuahua in a northwestern direction to the Gila, would therefore be less chimerical than the much talked of

---

*The territory of the whole republic of Mexico, including the old province of Texas, is variously estimated at from 1,650,000 to 1,700,000 English square miles.

great western railroad from the Mississippi to the Columbia river; and if the above mentioned country should be attached to the United States, we may in less than ten years see such a project realized.

This boundary line would at the same time allow an easy defence; proper military stations at the Rio Grande and near the gulf of California, would secure the terminating points of that line; some fortifications erected in the mountain passes of the Sierra Madre, where but one main road connects the State of Chihuahua with the South of Mexico, would prevent invasions from that direction, and some smaller forts in the interior would be sufficient to check and control the wild Indians.

BOTANICAL APPENDIX.

Dr. Wislizenus has intrusted to me his very interesting botanical collections, with the desire that I should describe the numerous novelties included in them. Gladly would I have done so, had not leisure been wanting, and were I not here (in St. Louis) cut off from large collections and libraries. As it is, I can only give a general view of the flora of the regions traversed, and describe a few of the most interesting new plants collected; with the apprehension, however, that some of them may have been published already from other sources, without my being aware of it.

In examining the collections of Dr. Wislizenus, I have been materially aided by having it in my power to compare the plants which Dr. Josiah Gregg, the author of that interesting work "the Commerce of the Prairies," has gathered between Chihuahua and the mouth of the Rio Grande, but particularly about Monterey and Saltillo, and a share of which, with great liberality, he has communicated to me. His and Dr. W.'s collections together, form a very fine herbarium for those regions.

The tour of Dr. Wislizenus encompassed, as it were, the valley of the Rio Grande and the whole of Texas, as a glance at the map will show. His plants partake, therefore, of the character of the floras of the widely different countries which are separated by this valley. Indeed, the flora of the valley of the Rio Grande connects the United States, the Californian, the Mexican, and the Texan floras, including species or genera, or families, peculiar to each of these countries.

The northeastern portion of the route traverses the large western prairies, rising gradually from about 1,000 feet above the gulf of Mexico, near Independence, Missouri, to 4,000 feet west of the Cimarron river. The plants collected on the first part of this section, as far west as the crossings of the Arkansas river, are those well known as the inhabitants of our western plains. I mention among others, as peculiarly interesting to the botanist, or distinguished by giving a character to the landscape, in the order in which they were collected, *Tradescantia virginica, Phlox aristata, Oenothera missouriensis, serrulata, speciosa*, &c., *Pentstemon Cobaea, Astragalus caryocarpus,* (common as far west as Santa Fe,) *Delphinium azureum, Baptisia australis, Malva Papaver, Schrankia uncinata* and *angustata, Echinacea angustifolia, Aplopappus spinulosus, Gaura coccinea, Sida coccinea, Sophora sericea, Sesleria dactyloides, Hordeum pusillum, Engelmannia pinnatifida, Pyrrhopappus grandiflorus, Gaillardia pulchella,** *Argemone Mexicana*, (with very hispid stem and large white flowers.)

The plants collected between the Arkansas and Cimarron rivers are rarer, some of them known to us only through Dr. James, who accompanied Long's expedition to those regions in 1820. We find here *Cosmidium gracile*, Torr. and Gr., which has also been collected about Santa Fe and farther down the Rio Grande; *Cucumis? perennis*, James, found

---

*Abundant in the sands about the Arkansas river, with beautiful flowers, but only about 6 inches high; certainly annual.

also near Santa Fe and about Chihuahua, and by Mr. Lindheimer, in
Texas; the petals being united about two-thirds of their length, it cannot
be retained under the genus *Cucumis; Hoffmannseggia Jamesii*, T. and G.,
was also gathered on this part of the journey; several species of *Psoralea*,
Petalostemon and *Astragalus;* also Torrey's *Gaura villosa* and *Krameria
lanceolata; Erysimum asperum*, which before was not known to grow so
far south; *Polygala alba, Lygodesmia juncea*. Here we also, for the first
time, meet with *Rhus trilobata*, Nutt., which, farther west, becomes a
very common plant.* A new *Talinum*, which I have named *T. calycinum*,[1]
was found in sandy soil on the Cimarron. This plant has, like the nearly
allied *T. teretifolium* of the United States, a remarkable tenacity of life,
so much so that specimens collected, pressed and "dried," in June, 1846,
when they reached me in August, 1847, 14 months later, grew vigorously
after being planted.

Psoralea hypogæa, Nutt., was collected near Cold spring, and *Yucca angustifolia*, from here to Santa Fe.

From Cedar creek the mountainous region commences with an elevation of near 5,000 feet above the Gulf, and extends to Santa Fe to about
7,000 feet. With the mountains we get also to the region of the pines,
and of the cacti. Dr. Wislizenus has here collected two species of *Pinus*,
both of which appear to be undescribed, so that I venture to give now a
short account of them. The most interesting one, on account of its useful fruit, as well as its botanical associations, is the nut pine of New
Mexico, (Piñon,) *Pinus edulis*,[2] nearly related to the nut pine of north-

---

[1] *Talinum calycinum*, n. sp., rhizomate crasso, caulibus demum ramosis;
foliis subteretibus elongatis, basi triangulari productis; pedunculis elongatis nudis; cyma bracteosa; sepalis 2 ovato-orbiculatis, basi productis,
cuspidatis, persistentibus; petalis fugacibus calycembis superantibus; staminibus sub 30; stylo elongato, stigmatibus 3 abbreviatis.

In sandy soil on the Cimarron, fl. in June. Differs from *T. teretifolium*
by its larger leaves, larger flowers, much larger persistent sepals, larger
fruit and seed. Leaves 1½ to 2 inches long, flowers 10 to 11 lines in diameter; capsule and seeds twice as largé as in *T. teretifolium*.

[2] *Pinus edulis*, n. sp.—squamis turionum ovatis acutis adpressis; laciniis vaginarum abbreviatarum circinato—revolutis, demum deciduis; foliis
binis brevibus rigidis, curvis, tenuissime striatis, margine laevibus, supra
concavis glaucis, subtus convexis viridibus; strobilis sessilibus erectis,
subgloboso-conicis, squamis apice dilatato pyramidatis, inermibus; seminibus obovatis, apteris, magnis, testa tenuiore.

Not rare from the Cimarron to Santa Fe, and probably throughout New
Mexico. A small tree, 10 to 20, rarely 30 feet high; trunk 8 to 12 inches
in diameter; leaves 12 to 18 lines long, and, as is the case in all other pines,
concave on the inner or upper surface when in twos, and carinate when in
threes, which in our species is very seldom the case. Cones about 18
lines in diameter; seeds about 6 lines long, and 4 in diameter; shell
much thinner than a hazlenut's; kernel, when slightly baked, very pleasant.

*Like many other plants mentioned here, it has been collected in abundant and beautiful spe-
cimens by *Mr. A. Fendler*, a young German collector, who has investigated the regions about
Santa Fe during last season, (1847,) and has made most valuable and well preserved collections,
some sets of which he offers for sale. I shall repeatedly be obliged to refer to him when speaking of the flora of Santa Fe.

astern Mexico, *Pinus osteosperma*,[3] (specimens of which were sent to me by Dr. Gregg, as collected on the battlefield of Buena Vista,) and to the nut pine of California, *P. monophylla*, Torr. and Frem.—these three species being the western representatives of *Pinus Pinea* and *Cembra* of the eastern continent.

The second species, *Pinus brachyptera*,[4] is the most common pine of New Mexico, and the most useful for timber. A third species, *Pinus flexi-lis*, James, was overlooked by Dr. Wislizenus, but has been collected in fine specimens, by Mr. Fendler, about Santa Fe. Its leaves in fives and pendulous cylindrical squarrose cones assimilate it to *Pinus strobus*; but the seed is large and edible, as Dr. James has already remarked, and the leaves are not serrulate and much stouter. The Piñones, so much eaten in Santa Fe, appear principally to be the product of *Pinus edulis*. I shall have occasion to speak of three other *pines* when I come to the flora of the mountains of Chihuahua.

Linum perenne makes its first appearance here, and continues to Santa Fe, as well as the justly so called *Lathyrus ornatus*. Several species of *Potentilla, Œnothera, Artemisia,* and *Pentstemon,* were collected in this district.

Among the most remarkable plants met with were the *Cactaceæ.* After having observed on the Arkansas, and northeast of it, nothing but an *opuntia,* which probably is not different from *O vulgaris,* Dr. W. came at once, as soon as the mountain region and the pine woods commenced, on several beautiful and interesting members of this curious family, an evidence that he approached the favorite home of the cactus tribe, Mexico.

On Waggon-mound the first (flowerless) specimens of a strange *opuntia* were found, with an erect, ligneous stem, and cylindrical, horridly spi-

---

[3] *Pinus osteosperma*, n. sp.—squamis turionum elongato-acuminatis, fimbriatis, squarrosis; laciniis vaginarum abbreviatarum circinato-revolutis, demum deciduis; foliis ternis binisve brevibus, tenuioribus, rectiusculis, margine lævibus, utrumque tenuissime striatis, supra glaucis, subtus virescentibus; strobilis sessilibus, erectis, subglobosis, inermibus; seminibus obovatis apteris, magnis, testa dura.

Mountain borders, near Buena Vista, and about Saltillo. A small tree, 10 to 20 feet high; leaves in threes, more rarely in twos, 1 to 2 inches long, much more slender than in the foregoing species; nut of the same size, but much harder. *Pinus monophylla* has broadly ovate, obtuse, adpressed scales of the young shoots and mostly single, terete leaves; cone and seeds are similar to both others.

[4] *Pinus brachyptera*, n. sp.—squamis turionum longe acuminatis, fimbriatis, squarrosis, subpersistentibus; vaginis elongatis adpressis; foliis ternis (raro binis s. quaternis) utrumque viridibus et aspero striatis; strobilis erectis, ovatis s. elongato conicis, squamis recurvo aculeatis; seminibus obovatis breviter alatis.

Mountains of New Mexico, common. A large and fine tree, often 80 to 100 feet high, 2 and even 3 feet in diameter; sheaths 6 lines long, mostly black; leaves generally in threes, rough, $3\frac{1}{2}$ to 6 inches long, in the specimens before me, crowded towards the end of the branches; cones $2\frac{1}{2}$ to $3\frac{1}{2}$ inches long; seed larger than the wing, without this 3 to 4 lines long and 2 wide.

nous, horizontal branches. The plant was here only 5 feet high, but grows about Santa Fe to the height of 8 or 10 feet, and continues to be found as far as Chihuahua and Parras. In the latter more favorable climate it grows to be a tree of 20 or 30, and perhaps even 40 feet high, as Dr. W. informs me, and offers a most beautiful aspect when covered with its large red flowers. It is evidently the plant which Torrey and James doubtfully, though incorrectly, refer to *Cactus Bleo H. B. K.* It is nearly allied to *Opuntia furiosa*, Willd., but well distinguished from it; and as it appears to be undescribed, I can give it no more appropriate name than *O. arborescens*,[5] the *tree* cactus, or Foconoztle, as called by the Mexicans, according to Dr. Gregg. The stems of the dead plant present a most singular appearance; the soft parts having rotted away, a net work of woody fibres remains, forming a hollow tube, with very regular rhombic meshes, which correspond with the tubercles of the living plant.

The first *Mammillaria* was also met with on Waggon-mound, a species nearly related to *M. vivipara* of the Missouri, and also to the Texan *M. radiosa*, (Engelm. in Plant. Lindh. inedit.,) but probably distinct from either. Mr. Fendler has collected the same species near Santa Fe.

On Wolf creek the curious and beautiful *Fallugia paradoxa*, Endl., looking like a shrubby *Geum*, was found in flower and fruit; also a (new?) species of *Streptanthus*, and an interesting *Geranium*, which I named *G. pentagynum*,[6] because of its having its five styles only slightly united at

---

[5] *Opuntia arborescens*, n. sp., caule ligneo erecto, ramis horizontalibus, ramulis cylindricis, tuberculatis aculeatissimis; areolis oblongis, brevissime tomentosis, aculeos 12 to 30 corneos, stramineo-vaginatos teretes undique porrectos gerentibus; ramulis versus apicem floriferis; ovario tuberculato, tuberculis sub 20 apice sepala subulata et areolas tomentosas cum setis paucis albidis gerentibus; sepalis interioribus 10 to 13 obovatis; petalis obovatis, obtusis s. emarginatis; stigmatibus sub-8 partulis; bacca flava sicca, ovato globosa, tuberculata, profunde umbilicuta.

Mountains of New Mexico to Chihuahua, Parras, and Saltillo; flowers in May and June; fruit, at least about Santa Fe, ripening the second year (Fendler;) in the north 5 to 10, south 20 and more feet high, 5 to 10 inches in diameter, last branches 2 to 4 inches long; spines of the specimens on Waggon-mound 20 to 30 in each bunch; further south only 12 to 20, generally fewer on the under side of the branchlets; spines horn-colored, with straw-colored loose sheaths, from 3 to 10 lines, generally about 6 lines long. Flowers purple, 3 inches in diameter; stamens red; fruit about 1 inch long, yellow.

[6] *Geranium pentagynum*, n. sp., perenne, caule erecto ramoso cum petiolis retrorso-piloso; foliis strigoso-pubescentibus inferioribus 7-, superioribus 3-5-partitis, segmentis inciso-lobatis; pedicellis binis, glanduloso pubescentibus; sepalis glandulosis, longe aristatis; petalis basi villo brevi instructis, ad venas pilosiusculis, obovatis integris; filamentis ciliatis; ovario glanduloso; stylis ima parte solum connatis; capsula glanduloso-pubescente.

On Wolf creek, flowers in June. Several stems 1 foot high from a large ligneous rhizoma; similar to *G. maculatum*, but easily distinguished from this and most other species by the styles being united only for $\frac{1}{4}$ or $\frac{1}{3}$ of their length; flowers of the same size, but aristæ of sepals much larger; leaves only 2 or $2\frac{1}{2}$ inches wide.

base, while most other *Gerania* have them united for about two-thirds or more of their length.

In the prairies about Wolf creek, in an elevation of between 6,000 and 7,000 feet, the smallest of a tribe of cactaceæ was discovered, numerous species of which were found in the course of the journey south and southeast: several others have also been discovered in Texas. I mean those dwarfish *Cerei*, some of which have been described with the South American genus *Echinopsis*, or have been referred alternately to *Cereus* or *Echinocactus*, and which I propose to distinguish from all these under the name of *Echinocereus*,[7] indicating their intermediate position between *Cereus* and *Echinocactus:* they approach more closely to *Cereus*, in which genus they, as well as the genus *Echinopsis*, should perhaps be included as subgenera.

The species mentioned above is distinguished from all others known to me by its yellowish green flowers, the others having crimson or purple flowers. I have named it, therefore, *Echinocereus viridiflorus*.[8]

A careful examination of the seeds of numerous *cactaceae*, has indicated to me two principal divisions in that family: 1. Cotyledons, more or less distinct, directed with their edges to the edge, (or towards the umbilicus,) and with their faces to the flattened side of the seed; when curved, accumbent. 2. Cotyledons, mostly very distinct, foliaceous, direct with their edges to the faces, and with their faces to the edges of the seed, (or towards the umbilicus;) when curved, incumbent, and often circular or spiral.

The first class comprises *Mammillaria*, with a straight embryo; and

---

[7] *Echinocereus*, n. gen. Perigonii tubus ultra germen productus, abbreviatus. Sepala exteriora s. tubi subulata, in axillis tomentosis setas s. aculeos gerentes. Sepala interiora subpetaloidea et petala longiora pluriserialia corollam breviter infundibuliformem s. sub-campanulatam aemulantia. Stamina numerosissima tubo adnata, limbo breviora s. eum subaequantia. Stylus stamina vix superans. Stigma multiradiatum. Bacca pulvilligera setosa s. aculeata, perigonio coronata. Seminum testa dura tuberculata nigra. Embryo vix curvatus cotyledonibus brevibus contrariis.

Globose, or mostly ovate; simple, or mostly branching from the base or cespitose; tubercles, forming few or mostly a great many ribs; bunches of short or long spines, distant or approximate, often very crowded; vertex never woolly; flowers lateral, produced from last year's growth, opening only in sunshine, but for two or three days in succession; closed at night, or in dark weather.

[8] *Echinocereus viridiflorus*, n. sp. ovato-globusus, humilis, sub-13-costatus; areolis lanceolatis, approximatis, junioribus villosis; aculeis 16–18 rectis, radiantibus, lateralibus longioribus fuscis, reliquis albidis, centrali nullo s. elongato robusto, apice fusco; floribus lateralibus; tubo pulvillis 25–30 albo-tomentosis setas albas 5–10 gerentibus stipato; sepalis interioribus lineari-oblongis sub-10; petalis 12–15 lineari-oblongis, obtusis; baccis ellipticis virescentibus, seminibus parvis tuberculatis.

Prairies on Wolf creek, flowers in June; Santa Fe, flowers in May, (Fendler.) Body 1 to 1½ inch high, oval; spines 1 or 1½ to 3 lines long; central spine when present 6 to 7 lines long; flower 1 inch long and wide, outside green brown, inside yellowish green; petals only 2 lines wide, being about 5 lines long.

doubtless, also, *Melocactus*, seeds of which, however, have not been examined by me; and *Echinocactus*, mostly with a curved embryo. The second class includes *Echinocercus*, with a nearly straight embryo, and very short cotyledons; *Cereus*, with a curved embryo, and foliaceous incumbent cotyledons, (probably also *Echinopsis* and *Pilocereus*, and perhaps *Phyllocactus* and *Epiphyllum ;*) *Opuntia*, with a circular or spiral embryo, (circular and with a larger albumen in all *Opuntiae cylindraceae;* spiral and with a much smaller albumen in all *Opuntiae ellipticae*, examined by me,) and very large cotyledons. *Rhipsalis* and *Pereskia* may also belong here, but were out of my reach.

The flowers of all the species belonging to the first class, with the doubtful exception of some *Mammillariae*, make their appearance on the growth of the same year. Those of the second class produce the flowers always upon the growth of the next preceding or former years. The first class may, therefore, be distinguished by the name of *Cactaceae parallelae*, (from the direction of the cotyledons,) or *C. apiciflorae*, (from the position of the flowers.) The second class can be named, in a corresponding manner, *Cactaceae contrariae*, or *C. lateriflorae*.

Echinocereus is principally distinguished from *Cereus* proper by its low growth; its short, more or less oval stems, which are frequently branching at base, and thereby cespitose; by the diurnal flowers, with short tubes; by the nearly straight embryo, with short cotyledons. From *Echinopsis*, to which some species have been referred, it differs also by the short-tubed diurnal flowers, and by the numerous filaments being adnate to the lower part of the tube. For further particulars compare the note 7. The species of *Echinocereus* inhabit Texas and the northern parts of Mexico, where *Cerei* proper are very rare. They extend even farther north than the *Echinocacti*, but appear to be excluded from the old limits of the United States, where the cactus family is represented only by some *Opuntiae* and *Mammillariae*. The southern limits of the *Echinocerei* are unknown to me, but I doubt whether they extend far in that direction; the nearly-related *Echinopses*, on the contrary, appear to be exclusively inhabitants of South America, especially the La Plata countries.

As I am speaking of the geographical distribution of the *Cactaceae*, I may as well add here that *Mammillariae* were found throughout the whole extent of Dr. Wislizenus's tour, and that at least four species occur in Texas. *Echinocacti* were observed only south of Santa Fe, and from there to Matamoros, but none on the highest mountains, which were occupied by *Opuntiae, Mammillariae*, and *Echinocerei ;* two *Echinocacti* have been found in Texas. Only two species of true *Cerei* were seen; one of a peculiar type about Chihuahua, and another near the mouth of the Rio Grande, which does not appear to differ from the wide-spread *C. variabilis*, Pfeiff. *Opuntiae ellipticae*, as well as *cylindraceae*, were observed from New Mexico to Matamoros, and species of both are also found in Texas. *Melocacti, Phyllocacti*, and other genera of *Cactaceae*, not mentioned above, were not met with.

The notes and collections of Dr. Wislizenus confirm the opinion of that acute observer and successful cultivator of *Cactaceae*, Prince Salm Dyck, viz: that most species of this family have a very limited geographical range, the most striking exception being those belonging to the genus *Opuntia*.

On the same day two other species of *Echinocereus* were found in pine timber, both with beautiful deep red flowers.[9]

We shall have occasion to speak of others hereafter.

After leaving Santa Fe, Dr. Wislizenus directed his course southward along the Rio Grande. The country was partly mountainous and rocky; partly, and principally along the river, sandy; on an average between 4,000 and 5,000 feet above the ocean. Here we find again some of the plants of the plains and of Texas, as *Polanisia trachysperma*, T. and G.; *Hoffmanseggia Famesii*, T. and G. An interesting *Prosopis* with screw-shaped legumes nearly allied to *P. odorata*, Torr. and Frem., of California, was the first shrubby mimoseous plant observed during the journey, a tribe which hereafter becomes more and more abundant; *Mentzelia* sp. *Cosmidium gracile, Eustoma, Heliotropium currasavicum, Maurandia antirhiniflora*, a beautiful large flowered *Datura, Abronia, Hendecandra texensis*, and many others. Near Olla the first specimens appeared of a new species of *Larrea*,[10] the first and most northern form of the shrubby

---

[9] *Echinocereus triglochidiatus*, n. sp. ovato-cylindricus, 6–7 costatus, costis undulatis, acutis; areolis sparsis, orbiculatis, junioribus albo-lanatis; aculeis 3–6, plerumque 3, rectis compressis angulatis, cinereis, sub-deflexis; floribus lateralibus, tubo pulvillis 15–20 albo-tomentosis setas spinosas apice fuscas 2–5 gerentibus stipato; sepalis interioribus sub-12 oblongo-linearibus obtusis; petalis 12–15 obovatis obtusis; staminibus petala subaequantibus; stigmatibus 8–10 virescentibus.

On Wolf creek, in pine woods, flowers in June; Santa Fe (Fendler) 4 to 6 inches high, 2 to 2½ in diameter; spines in young specimens 4 to 6, in older ones generally 3, two lateral ones 8 to 14 lines long, one bent down only 6 to 8 lines long. Flowers 2 to 2½ inches long, 2 inches in diameter; setose spines of tube 3 to 6 or 7 lines long; petals deep crimson, 6 to 7 lines wide; filaments and anthers red. In specimens from Santa Fe, collected by Mr. Fendler, the flowers are near 3 inches long, the petals 8 to 9 lines wide, and the setae on the tube are spinous, with brownish points.

Echinocereus coccineus, n. sp. globoso ovatus, 9–11 costatus, costis tuberculosis subinterruptis; areolis ovatis junioribus albo-tomentosis; aculeis radialibus 9–10 albidis, rectis, oblique porrectis, superioribus brevioribus; centralibus 1–3 longioribus albidis s. corneis; floribus lateralibus; tubo pulvillis 18–25 albo tomentosis, setas tenues albidas 8-11 gerentibus stipato; sepalis interioribus 8–10 oblongo linearibus obtusis; petalis 10–12 obovatis obtusis; staminibus brevioribus; stigmatibus 6–8 virescentibus.

With the foregoing, also about Santa Fe.—Only 1½ to 2 inches high, 1¼ to 1½ inch in diameter; like most other species of this genus, either single or generally branching from the base and cespitose, sometimes forming clusters of 10 to 15 heads. Spines terete all more or less erect, none appressed as in many other species; radiating ones 3 to 6, central ones 8 to 10 lines long. Flowers 1½ to 1¾ inch long, and 1 to 1½ wide when fully expanded; bristles of tube 3 to 6 lines long; petals deep crimson 4 to 5 lines wide; filaments red, anthers red or yellow. The flowers resemble much those of the last species, but the plant is very different.

[10] *Larrea glutinosa*, n. sp. divaricato-ramosissima, ad nodos glutinosa; foliis breviter petiolatis, bifoliolatis, foliolis oblique ovatis mucronatis, ner-

Zygophyllaceae, more abundant farther south. In the same neighborhood the mezquite tree or shrub was first met with, probably *Algarobia glandulosa,* T. and G. From here the mezquite was abundantly found down to Matamoros, but the specimens collected appear to indicate that there are at least two different species.

On the next day, near Sabino, an interesting bignoniaceous shrub was collected for the first time, undoubtedly the *Chilopsis* of Don, which farther south appears more abundantly. Its slightly twining branches, willow-like slender glutinous leaves, and large paler or darker red flowers, render it a very remarkable shrub. Dr. Gregg mentions it under the name of "*Mimbre,*" as one of the most beautiful shrubs of northern Mexico. The character given by Don, and that of Decandolle, appear defective, though I cannot doubt that both had our plant in view. From the very complete specimens obtained both by Dr. Wislizenus and Dr. Gregg, I am enabled to correct those errors.[11]

Near Albuquerque a curious *Opuntia* was observed; it evidently belongs to *Opuntiae cylindraceae,* but has short clavate joints, which make the

---

vosis, coriaceis, adpresse pilosis glutinosis; floribus inter folia opposita solitariis; fructu 5-cocco villoso.

Common from Olla and Fray Cristobal, in New Mexico, to Chihuahua and Saltillo; also about Presidio, (Dr. Gregg;) flowers in March and April; fruit ripe in July. Shrub 5 to 8 feet high, very much branched, very glutinous; used as a sudorific and diuretic, and called *gobernadora,* or in the north *guamis,* according to Dr. Gregg. Leaflets 3 to 6 lines long and half as wide, cuspidate or mucronate; ovary 5 celled, each cell with 3 or 4 ovules; fruit 3 lines in diameter, globose, attenuated at base; seeds by abortion only one in each cell, falcate, smooth, shining.

[11] *Chilopsis* Don, char. emend. Calyx ovatus plus minusve bilobus, lobo altero breviter 3, altero 2 dentato; corolla basi tubulosa, curvata, fauce dilatata, companulata, limbo 5 lobo, crispato-crenato; stamina 4 fertilia didynama, antherarum nudarum lobis ovatis, obtusis; quintum sterile brevius nudum; ovarium ovatum; stylus filiformis, stigma bilamellatum; capsula siliquaeformis, elongata, bilocularis, septo contrario placentifero; semina transversa margine utroque comosa.

An erect Mexican shrub, 8 to 12 feet high, ends of branches often slightly twining; branches smooth, and glutinous or rarely woolly; lower leaves somewhat opposite, upper ones sparse, lanceolate-linear, long-acuminate, glabrous or glutinous; racemes compound, terminal, pubescent; pedicells bracted, corolls rose colored or deeper red or purple.

Along water-courses or in ravines, from Sabino, near Albuquerque to Chihuahua, Saltillo and Monterey. Leaves 2 to 4 inches long, 1 to 3 lines wide; flowers $1\frac{1}{4}$ to $1\frac{1}{2}$ inch long; fruit 6 to 10 inches long; seeds with the coma 6 lines long.

There are perhaps two species—one from the neighborhood of Saltillo, with larger, paler flowers, broader, not glutinous leaves, and woolly branchlets, perhaps the *Ch. saligna* Don; the other from New Mexico and Chihuahua, with longer, narrower glutinous leaves, perfectly glabrous, glutinous branchlets, and darker and smaller flowers; may be *Ch. linearis,* DC., or a new species, *Ch. glutinosa.* The Calyx is variable in both.

name of *O. clavata*[12] most appropriate. A singular plant, with the habit of a *Ranunculus*, but nearly related to *Saururus*, was also found in this neighborhood among grass on the banks of the Rio Grande. The genus has been described by Nuttall from specimens collected by him in California, but whether his *Anemopsis californica* is specifically identical with the new Mexican plant, remains to be seen, as this last has regularly 6 leaved involucres, about 6 stamens, and is perfectly glabrous.

While the last mentioned plants indicate that we approach another botanical region, we are surprised to meet here with *Polygonum amphibium*, common in the old and in the new world, and *Cephalanthus occidentalis*, so widely diffused in the United States.

The famous desert, the Jornada del Muerto, furnished, as was to be expected, its quota of interesting plants. A *Crucifera* near *Biscutella*, of Europe, but with very short styles and white flowers, was here met with abundantly. I had considered it as the type of a new genus, when I found in Hooker's London Journal of Botany of February, 1845, Harvey's description of his new Californian genus *Dithyrea*,[13] which probably must be made to embrace our plant as a second species.

---

[12] *Opuntia clavata*, n. sp. prostrata, ramulis ascendentibus, obovato-clavatis, tuberculatis; areolis orbiculatis albo-tomentosis, margine superiore setas albas spinescentes gerentibus; aculeis albis complanatis, radiantibus, 6–12 minoribus, centralibus 4–7 majoribus, longioribus deflexis; floribus terminalibus; areolis ovarii 30–45 albo-tomentosis, setas albas 10–15 gerentibus; sepalis interioribus ovato-lanceolatis acuminatis s. cuspidatis; petalis obtusis, erosis saepius mucronatis; stigmatibus 7–10 brevibus erectis; bacca elongato-clavata, profunde umbilicata, setaceo-spinosa.

About Albuquerque (W.,) about Santa Fe, on the high plains, never on the mountains, (Fendler.) Mr. Fendler informs me that the ascending joints sprout from or near their base, and that in this manner they finally form a large spreading mass, often 2 and even 4 feet in diameter, to which the white shining spines give a very pretty appearance. Joints or branchlets 1½ to 2 inches long, tubercles at their base smaller, with shorter spines, towards the upper and thicker end larger, with stouter and longer spines; radial spines 2 to 4, central ones from 4 to 9 or 10 lines long; ovary 15 lines long, flower yellow, 2 inches in diameter; stigmas only 1½ line long; fruit apparently dry and spiny, 1½ to 1¾ inch long; seeds smoother than those of most other opuntiae, rostrate, with a circular embryo. Apparently near *Opuntiae platyacanthae*, Salm.; but the tuberculated joints and the shape of the embryo approach it closely to *O. cylindraceae*.

[13] *Dithyrea*, Harv., char. emendat. Sepala 4 basi aequalia oblongo-linearia. Petala 4 spathulata, basi ampliata. Stamina 6 tetradynama, libera, edentula. Stylus brevissimus, stigma incrassatum. Silicula sessilis, biscutata, basi et apice emarginata, a latere plano-compressa. Semina in loculis solitaria, compressa, immarginata, horizontalia. Cotyledones planae radiculae descendenti septum spectanti accumbentes.

Annual (all?) plants of California and New Mexico, with stellate pubescence, repando-dentate leaves, yellow (?) or white flowers in simple terminal racemes.

Dithyrea Wislizeni, n. sp., erecta incano-pubescens ramosa, foliis brevi-

A new species of *Talinum,* with single axillary flowers, was found for the first time in the Jornada, but was again collected further south, towards Chihuahua. *Dalea lanata, Centaurea americana, Sapindus marginata,* and a *Bolivaria,* probably identical with a new Texan species, brought to mind the flora of Arkansas and Texas; while the gigantic *Echinocactus Wislizeni,*[14] reminds us again that we are approaching the

---

ter petiolatis repando-dentatis, racemo umbelliformi, demum laxo elongato; pedicellis eglandulosis, horizontalibus, flore longioribus, sepalis calycis aperti patulis; petalis (albis) obovatis, unguiculatis basi dilatata sub-cordatis; stigmate cordato conico; siliculis basi profundius emarginatis.

Common in sandy soil near Valverde and Fray Cristobal, north of the Jornada del Muerto; flowers in July. Plant about 1 foot high, annual or biennial; leaves ovate lanceolate, attenuate in the short petioles, closely resembling those of some species of *Gaura;* pedicells filiform, longer than the flower or fruit; flowers white, about 3 lines in diameter, open; petals obovate, with a long and distinct claw, which is widened at base; filaments also thickened at base; ovary tomentose; style hardly visible, more distinct in the fruit, which is 5 to 6 lines in transverse diameter, and about half as much from base to top; the valves appear to be closed at their attachment to the subulate solid dissepiment.

Dithyrea californica, Harv., pedicellis basi bi-glandulosis horizontalibus, flore multo brevioribus; sepalis calcycis cylindrici clausi erectis; petalis (aureis?) lineari-spathulatis; stigmate bilobo; siliculis apice profundius emarginatis.

Easily distinguished by the characters just enumerated from the New Mexican plant; though the difference in calyx and stigma will not permit a generic separation.

[14] *Echinocactus Wislizeni,* n. sp., giganteus, vertice villoso-tomentoso; costis .... acutis crenatis; areolis oblongis, approximatis, junioribus fulvo-tomentosis; aculeis radialibus flavis, demum cinereis, porrectis; lateralibus sub 15 setaceis elongatis laeviusculis, summis infimisque 5-6 brevioribus robustioribus, annulatis; centralibus rubellis annulatis, 3 rectis sursum versis, 1 inferiore robustissimo, supra plano, apice reflexo-hamato; floribus sub verticalibus, ovario et tubo brevi campanulato sepalis imbricatis, auriculato-cordatis 60-80 stipato; sepalis interioribus 25-30 ovatis obtusis; petalis lanceolatis mucronatis, crenulatis; stylo supra stamina numerosissima brevia longe exserto; stigmatibus filiformibus 18-20 erectis; bacca ovata, lignosa, imbricato-squamosa.

Near Doñana, collected in August with buds, open flowers, young and ripe fruits on the same specimen. It belongs therefore to those *Echinocacti* which flower through the whole season, like *E. setispinus,* Engelm., (in Plant. Lindh.) of Texas, while others are in flower only during a week or two in spring, e. g. *E. texensis,* Hpfr. In the latter, the young bunches of spines, together with the flower buds in their axills, come out at once in spring, and none more are formed during the season, while in the first they are gradually developed during the whole season. Plant 1½ to 4 feet high; oval, with a smaller diameter. Areolae 6 to 9 lines long, only 6 lines distant from one another; radial spines 1½ to 2 inches long; straight central ones 1¼ to 1½, and large hooked ones 2 to 2½ inches long;

Mexican plateau. This enormous cactus attained generally a height of 1½ to 2 feet; specimens 3 feet high were rare, but one specimen was found which measured 4 feet in height, and near 7 feet in circumference; its top was covered with buds, flowers, and fruits, in all stages of development. In size it ranges next to *Echinocactus ingens*, Zucc., specimens of which 5 to 6 feet high were collected near Zimapan, in Mexico. Another Mexican cactus, *E. platyceras*, Lem., is said to grow 6, and even 10 feet high, and proportionately thick. *E. Wislizeni* is therefore the third in size in this genus.

From the same neighborhood a beautiful *Mammillaria* was sent in dried, as well as living specimens. It appears to be one of the few *Mammillariae longimammae*, though it differs in having purple, not yellow flowers, and stiffer spines. By the name I have given it, *M. macromeris*,[15] I intended to indicate the unusually large size of different parts of the plant, the tubercles, the spines, and the flowers.

In the same region a strange plant was obtained for the first time, but then without flowers or fruit, and which, to the casual observer, appeared as curious as it is puzzling to the scientific botanist; single spiny sticks or stems having a soft and brittle wood, and a great deal of pith in the centre, one or more from the same root, but always without branches, 8 to 10 feet high, not more than half an inch thick, frequently overtopping the brush among which they were found, only towards the top with a few bunches of already yellow leaves. In the following spring the splendid crimson flowers of this plant were found by Dr. W. between Chihuahua and Parras, and to Dr. Gregg I am indebted for mature fruit, collected near Saltillo and Monterey. The plant proved to be a *Fouquiera*, two species of which had been found in Mexico by Humboldt; one of them, the *F. formosa*, a branching shrub, was only known in the flowering state; the other, *F. spinosa*, a spinous tree, only in fruit. The structure of the ovary of the first appeared to differ so much from that of the capsule of the second, that it was afterwards deemed necessary to distinguish both generically, and the second constituted then the genus *Bronnia*. Having both flowers and fruit of a third *Fouquiera*, I am enabled to solve the dif-

---

yellow flowers 2 to 2½ inches in length, campanulate; fruit 1¼ to 1½ inch long, topped with the remnants of the flower of the same length; seeds black, rough, obliquely oval, with considerable albumen, in which the curved cotyledons are partly buried.

[15] *Mammillaria macromeris*, n. sp. simplex, ovata, tuberculis laxis, e basi latiore elongatis cylindricis, incurvis, sulcatis; areolis junioribus albotomentosis; aculeis angulatis rectis, elongatis, omnibus porrectis; radialibus sub-12 tenuioribus, albidis; centralibus sub-3 robustioribus, longioribus, fuscis; floribus maximis, roseis; sepalis ovatis, acutis, fimbriatis; petalis mucronatis, fimbriatis; stylo supra stamina brevia longe exserto, stigmatibus 8.

Sandy soil near Doñana, in flower in August. All my specimens single; trunk oval, 1 to 2 inches high; tubercles in 8 rows, 12 to 15 lines long, incurved; groove at first tomentose down to the tomentose supra axillary areola; radial spines 1 to 1½, central 1½ to 2 inches long; flowers 2½ to 3 inches in length and diameter, probably larger than in any other species of this genus; petals rose-colored, darker red in the middle.

7

ficulty to some extent, and prove the necessity of reuniting *Bronnia* with *Fouquiera*.[16] The flower of *Fouquiera splendens*, as I have named the northern plant, is that of a true *Fouquiera*, while the fruit is nearly that of *Bronnia!*

Towards El Paso a curious capparidaceous plant was collected, which appears to be nearly allied to the Californian *Oxystylis* of Torrey and Frémont, and forms with it a distinct group in that family, approaching very closely to *Cruciferae*, as has been remarked by Professor Torrey.

I have named this new genus (in honor of its discoverer, who has, though unaided and often embarrassed in different ways, done so much towards the advancement of our knowledge of those northern provinces of

---

[16] *Fouquiera*, Humb. B. Kunth, charact. emendat. Calyx 5-sepalus, imbricatus, persistens. Corolla hypogyna, gamopetala, longe tubulosa, limbo brevi 5-partito, patente, aestivatione incomplete contorta. Stamina 10–15, hypogyna, exserta; filamenta inferne arcuata villosa, basi inter se cohaerentia; antherae biloculares, longitudinaliter dehiscentes, mucromatae, basi cordatae, imo dorso affixae, introrsae. Ovarium liberum sessile; placentae 3 parietales ad centrum productae neque connatae, ovarium inde incomplete triloculare; ovula sub-18 ascendentia, in quaque placenta 6 biseriata; stylus filiformis trifidus. Capsula coriacea trivalvis; valvae medio placentiferae; placentae demum margine centrali connatae et a valvis solutae placentam singulam centralem triangularem formantes. Semina 3–6 complanata, alata s. comosa; albumen tenuissimum membranaceum; embryo magnus rectus, cotyledonibus planis, radicula breviori infera.

Mexican shrubs or trees, with soft fragile wood, and tuberculated, angular branches, the tubercles bearing spines, and in their axills single or fasciculate obovate entire leaves; splendid crimson flowers in terminal or subterminal spikes or panicles. At present only the following species of this genus are known:

1. *F. formosa*, H. B. K. fruticosa, spinis brevissimis, foliis solitariis oblongis subcarnosis; floribus sessilibus arcte spicatis, staminibus 12; stylo apice tripartito.

2. *F. splendens*, n. sp. fruticosa, simplex, spinis longioribus, foliis fasciculatis, obovato-spathulatis, membranaceis; floribus breviter pedicellatis in paniculam thyrsoideam congestis, staminibus 15; stylo ultra medium tripartito, seminibus 3-6 comosis.

3. *F. spinosa*, H. B. K., arborea, ramosa, spinis longioribus, foliis plerumque fasciculatis, obovato-oblongis, membranaceis; floribus pedicellatis corymboso-paniculatis; staminibus 10; seminibus 3 membranaceo-alatis.

Fouquiera splendens is a common plant from the Jornada del Muerto, in New Mexico, to Chihuahua, Saltillo, and Monterey; flowers in April, fruit by the end of May.

A general description has already been given in the text. In New Mexico it was seen only 8 or 10 feet high, but farther south it was found from 10 to 20 feet high, and in favorable localities it is said to grow even 30 feet high, and rarely thicker than about one inch in diameter. Bark smooth and ashy gray; spines horizontal, slightly curved, 6 to 10 lines long, disappearing on old stems; leaves deciduous fascicled in the axills of the spines towards the top of the stem, short-petioled, spathulate, obtuse, membranaceous, glabrous, somewhat glaucous, 9 to 12 lines long, and 3

Mexico—the first naturalist, it is believed, who explored the regions between Santa Fe, Chihuahua, and Saltillo) *Wislizenia!*[17] From *Oxysty-*
lis it is principally distinguished by its long stipitate ovary and capsule,
which latter is reflexed, and by the elongated racemes; it may, however,
have to be united with that genus.

On the mountains about El Paso, another of those cylindraceous *Opun-*
tiae was found, but much thinner and more slender than both species,
mentioned previously. To judge from an imperfect description it must be
nearly related to the Mexican *O. virgata*, Hort. Vind. I have given it

to 4 lines wide; panicles from the upper fascicles of leaves, near the top,
one or several, erect, crowded, 4 to 6 inches long; pedicells bracted,
longer than the yellowish chartaceous calyx; sepals orbicular 2 lines long;
corolla scarlet 9 to 10 lines long; filaments at base slightly cohering with
one another, and with the base of the corolla, villous below and with a
small horizontal process, which forms an arch over the ovary. Placentae
in the ovary lateral, 3, bearing each 6 ascending acute ovula, at the inner
margin, where they appear to touch one another without being actually
united at that stage of the growth. Soon after they probably adhere in
the centre to each other, and towards the ripening of the capsule detach
themselves from the valves, presenting a free central triangular spongy
placenta, with about 6 (or by abortion less) seeds. Capsule coriaceous
oval, acutish, light brown, about 6 lines long. Seeds compressed, inte-
gument expanded in a wing, which is cordate at the upper end, and
finally resolves itself into a coma of silky fibres. If my view of the ovary
and fruit of this plant is correct, the ovary is 1-celled, with 3 lateral
placentae—that of a true *Fouquiera*, the ripe capsule is 1-celled, with one
central placenta—that of *Bronnia*, and the unripe fruit, must be 3-celled!

Fouquiera splendens grows readily from cuts, and is used about Chihuahua for hedges and fences.

[17] *Wislizenia*, n. gen., sepala 4; petala 4 oblonga, breviter unguiculata;
stamina 6 toro cylindrico inserta; filamenta filiformia longe exserta, aestivatione inflexa; ovarium longe stipitatum, globosedidymum, biloculare,
loculis 2-ovulatis; stylus subulatus, elongatus, stigma globosum. Capsula
siliculaeformis, didyma tuberculata cum stipite in pedicellum filiformem
refracta, bilocularis, loculis plerumque per abortum 1-spermis; valvae
urceolate a dissepimento pertuso solutis, semen includentibus; semen con-
duplicato-reniforme, laeve; cotyledones radiculae superae incumbentes.

A glabrous new Mexican annual, much branched, of the habit of *Cleo-*
mella, with ternate leaves, distinct laciniate-fimbriate stipules, and bracted
at last elongated racemes, small yellow flowers; fruit reflexed, stipe with
the equally long (not spinous) style, and the small dissepiment persistent
after the falling off of the valves.

W. refracta, n. sp. On the upper crossing of the Rio Grande, near El
Paso; flowers and fruit in August. An interesting and quite anomalous
plant, on account of its fruit with an almost complete dissepiment, and of
its stipules and bracts. Tuberculated valves of the capsule separating
from the placentae, and though open, retaining the only (rarely two) seed
placentae forming a complete dissepiment, which, in the perfectly ripe and
dry state, finally becomes perforated in the centre.

the name of *O. vaginata*,[18] as the straw-colored loose sheaths of the long spines are very remarkable. A new *Echinocereus* was also collected here, which, on account of its dense covering with small spines, I have named *E. dasyacanthus*.[19] I have in cultivation one of the largest specimens, seen by Dr. Wislizenus, which is one foot high. In this neighborhood *Opuntia Tuna*, Mill., was seen for the first time, and this is perhaps the most northern limit of that extensively diffused species, as well as of *Agave americana*, another common Mexican plant. Both were found in greater perfection near Chihuahua, and from there constantly down to Monterey and the mouth of the Rio Grande; the *Opuntia* appears to extend also high up in Texas.

Together with these a *Dasylirion*, perhaps the same as the Texan species, was found here, and afterwards again near Saltillo.

From El Paso to Chihuahua, the road lies in part through a dreadfully arid sandhill district, where a peculiar *Martynia*[20] was observed, and fur-

---

[18] *Opuntia vaginata*, n. sp. caule lignoso, erecto, ramulis teretibus vix tuberculatis; areolis orbiculatis, albo-tomentosis, margine superiore fasciculum setarum brevium fuscarum, inferiore aculeum elongatum corneum vagina laxa straminea involutum, deflexum gerentibus; floribus parvis, ovario obovato, areolis 13 tomentosis setigeris stipato; sepalis interioribus 8 et petalis 5 obovatis mucronatis; bacca obovata profunde umbilicata, carnosa, aurantiaca, seminibus paucis.

On the mountains near El Paso; in August in flower and fruit. Belongs to *Opuntiae cylindraceae graciliores*, (Salm-Dyck;) perhaps nearest to *O. virgata*, H. V., but distinguished by the longer deflexed spines. Apparently 3 or 4 feet high, ultimate branches $2\frac{1}{2}$ to 3 lines in diameter; spines single, $1\frac{1}{2}$ to 2 inches long, rarely with a second smaller one, straight, more or less deflexed; epidermical sheath yellow or brownish, very loose, at last coming off. Ovary 4 to 5 lines long; flower 6 to 9 lines in diameter, pale yellow, with a greenish tinge; stigma conic, with 5 adpressed segments; fruit 7 to 8 lines long.

[19] *Echinocereus dasyacanthus*, n. sp. ovato-oblongus, s. subcylindricus, 17–18 costatus, costis tuberculatis subinterruptis, areolis approximatis, ovato-lanceolatis, junioribus albo-villosis; aculeis albidis, junioribus apice rufidis, radialibus sub-18 porrectis, summis brevioribus tenuioribus, lateralibus inferioribusque longioribus; centralibus 4–6 pluribus deflexis.

El Paso del Norte. The specimen before me, one of the largest, is 12 inches high, and $3\frac{1}{2}$ inches below, and 2 inches above in diameter; wool on the young areolae unusually long, deciduous; upper spines 3 lines long, lower lateral ones slightly compressed 6 to 7 lines long, lowest 5 lines long; central spines nearly as long as the last, stouter than the others. From *E. pectinatus* and *E. caespitosus*,* which it resembles, it is distinguished by the longer, not appressed spines, the larger number and size of the central spines, &c.

[20] *Martynia arenaria*, n. sp. annua, glanduloso-pilosa foliis alternis, longe petiolatis, cordatis, 3–5–7 lobatis, lobis rotundatis, repando-denticulatis; bracteis lanceolatis calycem obliquum, infra fissum, dimidium aequantibus; staminibus 4; rostro pericarpium aequante.

· Sandhills below El Paso, flowers August. Leaves $1\frac{1}{2}$ to 2 inches wide

*See note 45.

ther on, through a lovely country, which, at that season, (August,) after the annual rains, was covered with a luxuriant vegetation. The elevation of the country is here between 4,000 and 5,000 feet above the gulf.

The rare *Cevallia sinuata*, which Dr. Gregg has also sent from Monterey, was found in this part of the journey. Here also occurred a perennial species of *Linum*, with yellow petals, so far, in America, the only perennial yellow flowering *Linum;* it is distinguished by its long aristate sepals, whence the name.[21] Several *Oenotherae*, not seen before, made now their appearance; different species of *Gilia*, a number of *Nyctagineae*, several *Asclepiadaceae, Malvaceae, Cucurbitaceae, Compositae*, and others, were here collected; including a number of new species, which only want of time and references have for the present prevented me from describing. Near lake Encinillas another *Martynia*[22] was found, which, in its foliage, comes nearer to *M. proboscidea*, but is readily distinguished by its purple flowers. A beautiful yellow-flowering bignoniaceous shrub, probably *Tecoma stans*, Juss., seen more frequently further south, was observed for the first time near Gallejo spring. Shrubby *Algarobiae* were seen more plentifully, as also some other *Mimoseae*.

Here would be the proper place to introduce a notice of the several species of *Yucca* found by Dr. Wislizenus. But, unfortunately, the labels of the specimens were partly lost, so that it is impossible at this time to arrange leaves, flowers, and fruits properly. Certain it is that several species besides *Yucca angustifolia*, mentioned above, were seen; that the leaves of all of them have filamentose edges, some with very fine, others with very coarse fibres on their margin; that the majority bear juiceless capsules with very thin, paperlike seeds, but that one species produces an edible succulent fruit with very thick seeds. Fortunately the seeds col-

---

and long; flowers spotted, "yellow," (Dr. W.,) a little smaller than in *M. proboscidea*.

[21] *Linum aristatum*, n. sp., caulibus e rhizomate ligneo pluribus, ramosissimis, angulatis; foliis sparis subulatis, aristatis, superioribus bracteisque denticulatis; sepalis lanceolato-linearibus trinerviis, aristatis, margine membranaceo glanduloso-denticulatis; petalis (flavis) calcycem sub-duplo superantibus; stylis coalitis; capsula ovata, acuta, sepalis persistentibus bis breviore.

In sandy soil near Carizal, south of El Paso; collected in August, in flower and fruit. The rhizoma in the specimen before me is 6 inches long and 3 to 4 lines in diameter, white; stems numerous, 1 to 3 feet high, divaricately branched; upper leaves (lower not seen) 3 to 4 lines long, sepals 4 lines long; flowers 10 lines in diameter; petals sulphur yellow; styles united for about three-fourths of their length; capsule 2 lines long.

[22] *Martynia violacea*, n. sp., annua, foliis alternis, cordatis, repando-sinuatis, acute denticulatis, glabriusculis; bracteis lanceolatis calyce obliquo, infra usque ad basin fisso dimidio brevioribus; staminibus 4; rostro pericarpium superante.

Near lake Encinillas, north of Chihuahua, flowers August; leaves 4 to 6 inches long, and nearly as wide, indistinctly sinuate-lobed, beset with small, sharp, distant teeth, flowers from pale red to deep violet purple, as large as in *M. proboscidea*.

lected by Dr. W. arrived here in the best condition, and some have already germinated, so that we may hope to raise some of these species. *Yucca aloëfolia*, of the southern United States and Mexico, is said also to bear an edible fruit, but has serrulate leaves; we have, therefore, different species of *Yucca* with edible fruits, which may constitute a peculiar section in this genus.

The soil appeared to be too fertile here for the production of *Cacti,*; and with the exception of some *Opuntiae*, the only species collected between Paso and Chihuahua, about 100 miles south of the former place, was *Cereus Greggii*[2 3], which was peculiarly interesting, as it is probably the most northern form of *Cereus* proper. The specimens sent for cultivation by Dr. W. were unfortunately dead when they arrived here, and neither flower nor fruit had been obtained; but Dr. Gregg has collected the same species near Cadena, south of Chihuahua, in flower, from which I completed the description. I could not have given it a more appropriate name than that of the zealous and intelligent explorer of those far off regions. I learn from Prince Salm-Dyck that a *Cereus*, probably the same species, was sent to England by Mr. Potts, of Chihuahua, but his specimens also did not live; they were very remarkable for having a thick turnip-shaped root. Neither Dr. W. nor Dr. G. having paid attention to the root, I am unable to say whether their specimens agreed with those of Mr. Potts in this particular.

Dr. Wislizenus was forced to go from Chihuahua westward to Cosihuiriachi. However prejudicial this involuntary interruption of his journey may have been to the primary objects of his expedition, it appears that he could not have selected a more favorable field for botanical researches. Amongst the porphyry mountains of Cosihuiriachi and Llanos, which vary from 6,000 to 8,000 feet in height, and their deep chasm-like valleys, a great many undescribed species of plants were found; in fact almost everything collected there appears to be new!

Among the trees, I mention three species of pines, entirely different from those found farther north, but perhaps identical with some species from the Pacific coast. The most magnificent of these three is a species nearly related to *Pinus strobus* and *Pinus flexilis*, which I name *P. strobiformis*.[2 4] Its size and growth, its foliage, as well as the shape of the

---

[2 3] *Cereus Greggii*, n. sp., erectus, ramosus, pentagonus; areolis distantibus oblongis, nigro-tomentosis; aculeis nigris, brevissimis, e basi incrassata subulatis, acutissimis, 6–9 radialibus subrecurvis, infimis longioribus, centrali singulo deflexo minuto; tubo floris elongato, areolis 60–80 cinereo-tomentosis setas 6–12 nigricantes s apice albidas gerentibus stipato; sepalis interioribus 15–20 et petalis 15–20 lanceolatis, acuminatis, integris.

North and south of Chihuahua; flowers April and May. Stem 1 to 2 feet high, about 6 lines in diameter; spines $\frac{1}{2}$ to 1 line long, extremely sharp; flower about 6 inches long and 2 inches in diameter, bristles of the tube $1\frac{1}{2}$ to 3 lines long; interior sepals reddish green, petals pale purple.

[2 4] *Pinus strobiformis*, n. sp., squamis turionum ovatis acuminatis; vaginis laxis, patulis, deciduis; foliis quinis filiformibus, supra albo-lineatis, acute carinatis, subtus convexis, margine tenuissime serrulatis; strobilis cylindricis, elongatis, squamis obtusis inermibus, demum recurvis.

Highest peaks about Cosihuiriachi. The largest pine in this region 100

cones, resemble the common white pine of the north, but the cones are two or three times as large, not to speak of the other differences. It only grows on the highest mountains of this region, of about 8,000 feet elevation, and attains the height of 100 to 130 feet.

Pinus macrophylla,[25] another inhabitant of the higher mountains of Chihuahua, is more common than the last; like it, it closely resembles a well-known species of the United States, *P. australis*, from which it differs by its short cones, which have on each scale a mammillary recurved tubercle, and by having the leaves not only in threes, but also in fours and even in fives. It may be near *P. occidentalis* of the interior of Mexico, but that has the regularly five leaves in each sheath.

Pinus Chihuahuana,[26] is the common pine of Cosihuiriachi and the mountains of Chihuahua, in general at an elevation of about 7,000 feet. It grows only 30 to 50 feet high, and resembles somewhat *P. variabilis*, though sufficiently distinct. Dr. Wislizenus was unable to obtain specimens of a fourth pine, which is said to grow on the still higher mountains to the west, near Jesus-Maria, bearing cones 15 or 18 inches in length.

On the highest peaks in this region a species of *Arbutus* was found, which the inhabitants call *Matronia*; it is a small tree with a smooth, red bark, bearing in November and December red edible berries. If it is at all distinct from *A. Menziesii*, Pursh, of the northwest coast, which it closely resembles, it ought, from the color of its bark, bear the name of

---

to 130 feet high. Sheaths 6 lines long, very deciduous, leaves 2 to $3\frac{1}{2}$, mostly 3 inches long; cone about 10 inches in length, very resinous. This species forms with *Pinus strobus* and *Pinus flexilis* a peculiar section, distinguished by their 5 leaves, and their cylindric pendulous squarrose cones; the leaves of *P. strobus* are the most slender, concave on the back, and strongly serrate; those of *P. strobiformis* are somewhat more rigid, convex on the back, and slightly serrate; those of *P. flexilis* are still more rigid, convex on the back, and entire.

[25] *Pinus macrophylla*, n. sp., squamis turionum longe acuminatis, fimbriato laceris, squarrosis, persistentibus; vaginis elongatis, adpressis, laceris; foliis ad apicem ramulorum congestis ternis, quaternis (rarius quinis) longissimis, margine carinaque serrulatis, utrumque aspero-striatis, subglaucis; strobilis ovato-conicis; sqamis tuberculo conico, apice spinifero, recurvo instructis; seminibus parvis, alatis.

Common on the higher mountains of Cosihuiriachi; 70 to 80 feet high; sheaths 15 to 20 lines long; leaves 13 to 15 inches long in the specimens before me; in fours as well as in threes; rarely in fives; cone $4\frac{1}{2}$ inches long. Evidently near *P. australis*, Mich., but well distinguished by the characters enumerated.

[26] *Pinus Chihuahuana*, n. sp., squamis turionum acuminatis, adpressis; vaginis adpressis, elongatis, laceris, deciduis; foliis ternis (rare quaternis) supra glaucis, subtus virescentibus, leviter striatis, margine tenuissime serrulatis; strobilis ovatis, abbreviatis; squamis transverse ovatis, inermibus.

The common pine of the mountains of Chihuahua, at an elevation of about 7,000 feet; a tree of only 30 to 50 feet in height; leaves 2 to $3\frac{1}{2}$ inches long; serrulate on the margin, but with nearly smooth striae; cone in the specimen before me $1\frac{1}{2}$ inch long.

A. sanguinea. These, together with a low scrubby oak tree, with small perennial leaves, were the only trees collected about Cosihuiriachi. A species of *Juniperus*, with red berries, a *Thuja*, and a small-leaved *Cowania* (?)[27] all of them in fruit, were also brought from there.

Between Chihuahua and Cosihuiriachi, but especially about the latter place, the porphyritic soil produced a number of *Cactaceae*, some strange *Echinocacti*, several *Mammillariae*, a few *Opuntiae*, and principally a great variety of *Echinocerei*. One of the latter is completely covered with stout and long spines;[28] another has short radiating spines, closely adpressed to the plant;[29] a third has short radiating spines, with single, stout black central ones, which project from the plant in all directions;[30] a fourth is distinguished by its longer and curved reddish radiating spines, with a stouter one projecting from their centre.[31]   I have all of these in

---

[27] *Cowania* sp. ?   Shrubby; leaves crowded, small, cuneate three-toothed at apex, revolute, tomentose below, glabrous and glandular above, sweetscented; turbinate tube of calyx, as well as the oblong lobes, 1 line long; 25 stamens, persistent; about 5 woolly ovaries.—Compare below note 51.

[28] *Echinocereus polyacanthus*, n. sp., elongato-ovatus, 10-costatus; areolis elevatis, ovatis, subapproximatis, junioribus albido 4-tomentosis; aculeis radialibus 10-12 flavidis, apice adustis, plus minus porrectis; lateralibus majoribus, demum subadpressis, superioribus minoribus; centralibus sub-4 corneis, apice fuscis, 3 superioribus sursum versis, inferiore singulo longiore porrecto, demum deflexo.
Cosihuiriachi.—Several oval stems, 4 to 5 inches high and 2½ to 3 in diameter, from one base; upper radial spines 4 to 5, lateral and inferior 8 to 10, upper central 9 to 12, lower one 15 to 20 lines long. Spines at last ashy-gray.

[29] *Echinocereus adustus*, n. sp., ovatus, 13–15-costatus; areolis elevatis, lanceolatis, approximatis, junioribus albo-tomentosis; aculeis radialibus 16–18 adpressis, albis, apice adustis; 4–5 superioribus brevibus, setaceis, lateralibus inferioribusque longioribus, robustioribus, centrali nullo.
Cosihuiriachi.—Plant 1½ to 4 inches high, 1 to 2 in diameter; upper spines 1, lower about 2, and lateral 4 to 5 lines long.

[30] *Echinocereus radians*, n. sp., ovatus 13–14-costatus, areolis elevatis, ovatis, subapproximatis, junioribus albo-villosis; aculeis radialibus 16-20 adpressis, junioribus apice adustis, superioribus brevibus setaceis, lateralibus inferioribusque longioribus robustioribus; centrali singulo porrecto, robusto, fusco.
Cosihuiriachi.--2½ inches high, 2 in diameter; upper radial spines 1 to 2, lower 3, lateral about 5 lines long; central spines brown or black, much stouter, 1 inch long.

[31] *Echinocereus rufispinus*, n. sp., elongato-ovatus, 11-costatus; areolis elevatis lanceolatis, approximatis, junioribus albido-villosis; aculeis radialibus 16–18, demum adpressis, intertextis; 3–5 superioribus setaceis, brevibus, albidis; lateralibus elongatis fuscis, recurvis, centrali singulo, robusto, fusco, porrecto.
Cosihuiriachi.—Stem 4 inches high, below 2½ in diameter; upper radial

cultivation, but have not seen as yet flowers or fruit from any of them; still they cannot but belong to my genus *Echinocereus*, to judge from analogy.

Some *Mammillariae* of Cosihuiriachi are distinguished by their compact shape; the tubercles are very short, globose, or even hemispherical, the spines strong, numerous, radiating, and adpressed, the fruits central from a woolly vertex: *Mammillaria compacta*.[32] Another, *M. gummifera*,[33] belongs together with two species from Texas, and from the mouth of the Rio Grande to the section *Angulares*, with pyramidal 4-angled tubercles, and milky juice, which, hardening, forms a gum. A third species belongs to *Crinitae*, and is a most elegant little plant with numerous hairlike radiating and one stout, hooked central spine; I have named it *M. barbata*.[34]

---

spines or bristles 1 to 2, lower about 4, and lateral 7 to 9 lines long; central spine much stouter, 1 inch long.

[32] *Mammillaria compacta*, n. sp., simplex, hemisphaerica, s. depresso-globosa; tuberculis abbreviatis, ovoideo-conicis, sulcatis; areolis ovato-lanceolatis, junioribus albo-tomentosis; aculeis omnibus radialibus, 13–16 subaequalibus, robastis, recurvatis, adpressis, intertextis, albidis, superioribus apice fuscis; sulcis tuberculorum axillisque junioribus et vertice tomentosis; floribus in vertice congestis; baccis ellipticis perigonio coronatis, viridibus; seminibus obovatis, laevibus, fulvis.

Cosihuiriachi.—Plant 2 to $3\frac{1}{2}$ inches in diameter and $1\frac{1}{4}$ to $2\frac{1}{2}$ inches high; tubercles in 13 rows, 4 lines high, 6 lines wide at base; spines interlocking, and thereby often deformed and twisted, stout, 7 to 10 lines long.

[33] *Mammillaria gummifera*, n. sp., lactiflua, simplex, hemisphaerica, tuberculis quadrangulato-pyramidatis; axillis areolisque junioribus albo-tomentosis; aculeis rectis, radialibus 10–12, inferioribus robustis, apice fuscis superiores setaceos albidos ter superantibus; centralibus 1–2 robustis, brevibus, fuscis, porrectis.

Cosihuiriachi.—From 3 to 5 inches in diameter, $2\frac{1}{2}$ to 4 inches high; when wounded it exudes a milky fluid, which, hardening, forms a transparent or whitish gum; tubercles mostly in 13 oblique rows, 6 to 7 lines long, and 5 to 6 lines wide at base; upper spines 2 to 3, lower 6 to 7, central about 2 lines long. Flowers and fruit not seen, but probably like those of two similar species, *M. applanata*, Engelm. ined., from the Pierdenales, in Texas, and *M. hemisphaerica*, Engelm. ined., from the mouth of the Rio Grande; both are also simple, lactescent, with pyramidal tubercles, and both have small reddish white flowers, and long clavate scarlet berries, without the remnants of the flower. It is a fact which I have repeatedly observed, and in a considerable number of species, that the red-globose, or clavate-berries of the mammillariae are always destitute of the remnants of the perigon, etc.; but the oval green fruits always are topped with it.

[34] *Mammillaria barbata*, n. sp., simplex, globoso-depressa; tuberculorum axillis nudis; aculeis radialibus numerosissimis pluriserialibus, exterioribus piliformibus albis sub-40; interioribus paulo robustioribus fulvis 10–15, centrali singulo robusto, uncinato, fusco, erecto; baccis oblongis, viridibus, apice floris rudimento coronatis.

The specimen communicated by Dr. Wislizenus, the only one found, was dead when it arrived here, but many fruits were adhering to the plant, and I was thus fortunate enough to cultivate it from the seeds.

Other remarkable cactaceae from the State of Chihuahua, which have been communicated to Dr. Wislizenus by Mr. Potts, of Chihuahua, are not described here, as it is believed that Mr. P. has sent them already to England, where, no doubt long before this, they have been published.

Amongst the other distinguished plants of Cosihuiriachi and Llanos, I cannot omit to mention a beautiful *Delphinium*,[35] which grew abundantly here; a *Silene*, which is perhaps new, but comes near to *S. multicaulis*, Nutt., of the Rocky mountains, and *S. Mociniana*, DC of Mexico; a new *Bouvardia*,[36] which is remarkably distinct from all the other Mexican species of this genus by its smoothness; an *Echeveria* perhaps identical with the Californian *E. caespitosa*, DC.; several *Gerania*, which appear to be undescribed, one of them with white flowers; an *Eryngium*,[37] with

---

Cosihuiriachi.—The only specimen seen was about 2 inches in diameter; tubercles 4 lines long; spines 3 to 4 lines in length; fruit 5 to 6 lines long, in a circle around the younger tubercles; seeds obovate scrobiculate, dark brown, minute.

[35] *Delphinium Wislizeni*, n. sp., perenne, erectum, simplex, glabrum; petiolis elongatis, infimis basi dilatatis; foliis pedatifide 5–7 partitis, laciniis incisis, segmentis linearibus, acutis, divaricatis; floribus laxe paniculato racemosis; bracteis subulatis; floribus longe pedicellatis; calcare subulato, curvato sepala paulo superante; sepalis 2 exterioribus acutis, 3 interioribus obtusissmis; petalis brevioribus acuminatis; ovariis glaberrimis.

On the Bufa, a porphyry rock near Cosihuiriachi, 8,000 feet high, in flower in September. Stem 2 to 2½ feet high, slender, glabrous, glaucous; flowers sparse, with the spur 1½ inch long, beautifully blue, on the outside slightly puberulent.

[36] *Bouvardia glaberrima*, n. sp., glaberrima, caule erecto terete; foliis ternatis, breviter petiolatis, ovatolanceolatis, utrinque acuminatis, patentibus s. reflexis; cyma composita, foliacea; calycis segmentis tubum bis superantibus; corolla calyce quintuplo s. sexuplo longiore, extus glabriuscula, intus parce barbata.

Cosihuiriachi, flowers September. Perennial; 2 feet high, leaves 3 to 3½ inches long, 8 to 10 lines wide; flowers bright crimson, 12 to 15 lines long. Apparently one of the largest species of the genus; leaves entirely glabrous, not revolute on the margin.

[37] *Eryngium heterophyllum*, n. sp., glaberrimum, caule erecto; foliis radicalibus oblanceolato-linearibus, acutis, penni-nerviis, serratis, serraturis cartilagineo-marginatis, aristatis; foliis caulinis inferioribus serrato-pinnatifidis, superioribus palmati-partitis, segmentis linearibus incisis; foliis involucralibus 10–13 linearibus acuminatis, spinoso-bidentatis, rarius integris, capitulum ovale longe superantibus; bracteis coeruleis subulatis flores superantibus, interioribus longioribus.

Common in valleys about Cosihuiriachi; flowers September. Biennial, 1½ to 2 feet high; radical leaves 2 inches long, 2 lines wide; involucral leaves 12 to 15 lines long, 1 line wide; heads about 4 lines in diameter.

the lowest leaves most elegantly pectinated, and the upper ones palmately divided; a *Zinnia*,[38] intermediate between *Zinnia multiflora* and *Z. elegans*, and which last season grew finely near St. Louis from seeds picked from these specimens. Many other *Compositae* have not yet been examined; a *Centaurea* may be found to be distinct from *C. Americana*, so far the only American species of that genus, which is so extensively diffused in the old world.

Leaving aside several *Dalcae*, *Lupini*, *Giliae*, a *Gentiana*, *Buchnera*, *Castilleia*, a number of *Labiatae*, *Gramineae*, and many others, I will only mention a few more, which I had time to study more closely. First of all, the beautiful and delicate *Heuchera sanguinea*,[39] probably the most southern, and certainly the most ornamental species of that genus. Next in beauty comes the bright-flowered *Pentstemon coccineus;*[40] *Lobe-*

Near two other Mexican species, *E. Carlinae*, Lar., and *E. Haenkei*, Presl., distinguished from the first by the larger number of linear, not ovate serrate involucral leaves; from the other also by the larger number of those leaves which are generally toothed, not entire.

[38] *Zinnia intermedia*, n. sp., caule erecto, ramoso, parce adpresse piloso; foliis scabris, inferioribus ovatis, basi obtusis, superioribus subsessilibus ovato-cordatis, acutis; pedunculo apice vix incrassato; involucri ovati squamis marginatis obtusis; paleis cristato-fimbriatis; radii ligulis oblanceolatis, extus scabriusculis, ciliatis; acheniis radii linearibus, disci 1-aristatis.

Common about Cosihuiriachi, flowers in September. Annual, 1 to 2 feet high; leaves 1 inch long, 6 to 8 lines wide; flowering heads 18 to 20 lines in diameter. The cultivated specimens grew 3 feet high; leaves 3 inches long and half as wide; heads hemispherical, larger, ligulae less acute. Differs from *Z. multiflora* by the less inflated peduncle, the broader and shorter leaves, the cristate paleae; from *Z. elegans*, to which the shape of the leaves and of the chaff much resembles, by the shape of the achenia. I may state here that in all the cultivated as well as native specimens of *Z. multiflora* the paleae are not entire, but fimbriate at the obtuse apex.

[39] *Heuchera sanguinea*, n. sp., petiolis patenti pilosis; foliis sinu latissimo cordatis, orbiculatis, 5-7-lobatis, lobis incisis duplicatim dentatis, ciliatis; junioribus pilosis; scapo nudo, infra parce piloso, supra cum pedicellis calycibusque colorato glanduloso; floribus laxe campanulatis; calycis lobis ovatis obtusis, subaequalibus; petalis lineari-spathulatis persistentibus, cum staminibus pistillisque inclusis.

Porphyry mountains of Llanos, flowers in September. Scape 8 to 12 inches high; upper part, together with the flowers, bright scarlet; enclosed petals inserted below the throat of the calyx; stamens still lower; filaments equal in length to the orbicular cordate red anthers.

[40] *Pentstemon coccineus*, n. sp., glaberrimus, glaucus, foliis infimis obovatis, caulinis inferioribus oblongo-linearibus, superioribus linearibus minutis; racemo laxo, pedicellis oppositis, elongatis, 2-bracteatis, 1-floris; calycis glandulosi segmentis ovatis; corollae tubo superne dilatato, limbo bilabiato, labio superiore ad medium bilobo; antheris divaricatis, filamento sterili glabro, apice dilatato; capsula acuminata.

Llanos, flowers in September and October. Stem 1 to 2 feet high, nearly *lia mucronata,*⁴¹ with fine red, and *L. pectinata,*⁴² with blue flowers Amongst the most curious plants collected here is also to be mentioned an *Eriogonum,*⁴³ with inflated clavate internodia, and dark red flowers. *Phaseolus bilobatus,*⁴⁴ is another interesting plant.

---

naked above, pedicels filiform, lower ones much longer than the flower, which is 15 to 18 lines in length; bright scarlet or crimson. Next to *P. imberbis,* Steud., but easily distinguished.

⁴¹ *Lobelia mucronata,* n. sp., perennis, caule simplici erecto, glabro, infra folioso, supra nudo; foliis lineari-lanceolatis, elongatis, acuminatis, argute denticulatis; floribus laxe spicatis; bracteis linearibus glanduloso-dentatis, inferioribus pedicellum superantibus, superioribus eum aequantibus; calycibus hemisphaericis et pedicellis hirtis; lobis calycis subulatis tubum duplo superantibus, tubum corollae dimidium aequantibus; lobis corollae superioribus lanceolatis, inferrioribus ovatis nuecronatis.

Cosihuiriachi along rivulets; flowers in September. Stem 1 to 2 feet high; racemes short, few (3 to 12) flowered; color of flower darker red than in *L. cardinalis,* more like *L. fulgens;* distinguished from all similar ones by the short lobes of the calyx, and the ovate mucronate lower segments of the corolla.

I insert here the description of a nearly related species from the country below Monterey.

Lobelia phyllostachya, n. sp., glabra, caule erecto, folioso; foliis lanceolatis, acuminatis, irregulariter dentatis s. inferioribus subintegris; spica infra foliosa, elongata, densiflora; bracteis serrulatis, inferioribus florem longe superantibus, superioribus pedicello longioribus; calycis glabri laciniis subulatis corollam vix aequantibus s. ea brevioribus; laciniis corollae superioribus linearibus, inferioribus lanceolato-linearibus, acuminatis.

Swamps between Monterey and Cerralbo; flowers in May. Near *L. texensis,* Raf., but distinguished by its entire smoothness by the long (6 to 12 inches,) thick and foliaceous spike, and by the shorter segments of the calyx.

⁴² *Lobelia pectinata,* n. sp., caule erecto, scabriusculo, folioso; foliis, bracteis et lobis calycinis pectinato-dentatis, scabris; foliis inferioribus oblongo-linearibus sessilibus, superioribus e basi lata cordata, decurrente angustatis; racemo elongato densifloro, bracteis florem subaequantibus; calycis tubo turbinato pedicellum aequante, lobis duplo breviore; tubo corollae brevi, lobis superioribus lanceolatis, inferioribus ovatis, ad medium coalitis; antheris styloque inclusis, 2 inferioribus apice barbatis.

Cosihuiriachi in moist places; flowers in September. Annual (?) 1 to 1½ foot high; leaves about 1 inch long; spike dense 4 to 6 inches long, blue flowers 6 lines long; tube with 3 slits about the middle.

⁴³ *Eriogonum atrorubens,* n. sp., perennis, foliis radicalibus petiolatis, lanceolatis, elongatis, villosis; caulis glabri glauci internodiis superne tumidis, clavatis; caule iteratim dichotomo, ad bifurcationes bracteis subulatis pilosis instructas involucrum alarem elongato-pedicellatum gerente; involucris campanulatis 5-dentatis, margine pilosis, multifloris.

Cosihuiriachi on the banks of streamlets, flowers in September. Perennial, 1½ to 2 feet high; leaves all radical, 5 to 6 inches long, 9 lines wide,

In the following spring Dr. Wislizenus accompanied the Missouri volunteers, under Colonel Doniphan, from Chihuahua to Parras, Saltillo, Monterey, and Matamoros.

Zealous as ever, he again made large collections on this tour, but his duties as a military surgeon occupied his time rather more than the naturalist should have desired. Nevertheless his collections are very full. Fortunately Dr. Gregg accompanied the same expedition, and also made rich collections in that almost unknown region, which we may consider as the southwestern limits of the valley of the Rio Grande.

Before going into detail I will only remark here, what a reference to the map and sections will more fully present, that the country between Chihuahua and Parras has a general elevation of from 4,000 to 5,000 feet; between Parras and Saltillo it rises from 5,000 to 6,000 feet, and thence it rapidly descends towards the lower Rio Grande.

South of Chihuahua, a curious leafless *Euphorbia* was collected, with tuberous roots and leafless stem, nevertheless apparently a near relative of *E. cyathophora*. Here, for the first time, *Berberis trifoliata*, Moric., was met with, which appears to inhabit the whole middle and lower valley of the Rio Grande, as we find it again in this collection from Monterey, and Mr. Lindheimer has sent beautiful specimens from the Guadaloupe, in Texas.

Echinocerei and *Echinocacti* appear in greater abundance. The rediscovery of the beautiful *Echinocereus pectinatus* (*Echinocactus pectinatus*, Scheidw., *E. pectiniferus*, Lem., *Echinopsis pectinata*, Salm, in part) is peculiarly interesting, as it furnishes the means of proving a Texan species, which has been confounded with it, to be entirely distinct. The description of the plant, (which died without producing flowers,) found in several works, as well as in the latest publication on *Cactaceae*, before me, of *Foerster, Leipzig*, 1846, was made, as Prince Salm informed me, from specimens sent from Chihuahua by Mr. Potts; it entirely agrees with my specimen from the same region. But the description in Foerster's work of the *flower* of a specimen in Cassel, flowering in 1843, (not

---

on shorter petioles; some of the lower joints about 6 lines in diameter, the upper ones much less tumid; pedicells 1 to 3, lowest even 4 inches long; involucrum about 1 line long and wide, always 5 toothed, including 25 to 30 deep red flowers; lobes about equal; nut olive green acuminate three winged. Singularly near *E. inflatum*, Torr. and Frem., perhaps too near to be specifically separated; but apparently distinct by the hairy leaves and bracts, the furcate division of the stem, the large number of flowers in each involucrum, and perhaps their purple color, (not mentioned by Torrey.)

⁴⁴ *Phaseolus bilobatus*, n. sp., caule prostrato, pilis retrosis hispido; foliolis adpresse pilosis reticulatis, lateralibus subsessilibus inaequaliter bilobatis, terminali petiolulato, lineari-oblongo; pedunculis folia longe superantibus multifloris; culycis hirsuti laciniis subulatis tubum aequantibus; leguminibus compressis, hirsutis, curvatis; seminibus laevibus.

Common about Cosihuiriachi, flowers in September. Resembles *Ph. leiospermus*, T. and Gr., but the brown-red flowers, and legumes much smaller; shape of the leaves very characteristic. Legume 9 lines long and 1 line wide, seed very small.

known from where obtained,) shows *that* to be identical with a Texan
species, common between the Brazos and Nueces rivers, which I have
described in Engelmann and Gray's Plantae Linheimerianae, Boston
Journal of Natural History, v, page 247, under the name of *Cereus caespitosus*, and which should now be named *Echinocereus caespitosus*. *Echinopsis pectinata*, β. *laevior*, Monv., and γ. *Reichenbachiana*, Salm, are
perhaps forms of this Texan plant, which varies considerably in its native
country. Dr. Wislizenus has sent me a living specimen and dried flowers of *E. pectinatus;* unfortunately the plant met with a similar fate to
those sent to England by Mr. Potts, and there is none now in cultivation,
if I am correctly informed; but I preserve the dried specimen in my herbarium, and have been enabled to draw up from it the description.[45]

---

[45] *Echinocereus pectinatus* mihi, (*Echinocactus pectinatus*, Scheidw.,
E. pectiniferus, Lem.,) simplex (an semper?), ovato-cylindricus, 23 costatus; areolis elevatis, linearibus, approximatis, junioribus albo-villosis;
aculeis radialibus 16–20 subrecurvis, adpressis, pectinatis, albis, apice
roseis, superioribus inferioribusque brevioribus, lateralibus longioribus;
centralibus 2–5 brevissimis, uniseriatis; tubo floris pulvillis 60–70 brevi-
tomentosis aculeos albos s. apice roseos 12–15 gerentibus stipato; sepalis
interioribus 18–20 oblanceolatis; petalis 16–18 oblongis, obtusis, eroso-
denticulatis, mucronatis.

Bachimpa, south of Chihuahua; flowers in April. Stem 7 inches high,
below 3½, above 2½ inches in diameter; upper and lower spines 2 lines,
lateral 4 lines long; central spines mostly 3, sometimes 2, and below as
much as 5, in one vertical row, ½ to 1 line in length. Flowers about 3
inches long and wide; red or purple, spiny bristles on the tube 2 to 3
lines long; the uppermost 3 to 5 lines long, only 3 to 5 together.

It will not be amiss to introduce here again a more complete and correct description of its Texan relative.

Echinocereus caespitosus mihi, (*Echinopsis pectinata*, authors in part;
Cereus caespitosus, Engelm, l. c.,) ovatus, caespitosus, 13–18-costatus,
areolis elevatis, linearibus, approximatis, junioribus albo-villosis; aculeis
radialibus 20–30 subrecurvis adpressis, pectinatis, albis (nonnunquam
roseis, Lindh.,) superioribus inferioribusque brevioribus, lateralibus longioribus, centralibus nullis; tubo floris pulvillis 80–100 longe cinereo-
villosis setas apice s. totas fuscas s. nigricantes 6–12 gerentibus, stipato;
sepalis interioribus 18–25 oblanceolatis integris s. denticulatis; petalis 30–
40 obovato-lanceolatis, obtusis, acutis, s. mucronatis, ciliato-denticulatis;
stigmate viridi infundibuliformi, 13–18-partito; bacca viridi ovata, perigonio coronata, villosa, setosa, demum nudata; seminibus obovatis tuberculatis, nigris.

From the Brazos to the Nueces, in Texas, Lindheimer; flowers in May
and June; generally 1 to 2 inches high, and of nearly the same diameter;
rarely as much as 5 or 6 inches high, and 2 to 3½ inches in diameter;
longer lateral spines in different specimens 2 to 4 lines long; flowers in
the northern specimens, from Industry, 2 inches long and wide, in those
from New Braunfels 2¼ to 3 inches in diameter and length; generally a
little wider than long when fully open. Brown or black bristles on the
tube 2 to 5 or 6 lines long, surrounded by wool, which is often 3 lines in
length.

Near San Pablo another *Echinocereus*⁴ ⁶ was found, and dried flowers as well as living specimens have safely arrived here. A large *Echinocactus*⁴ ⁷ was collected near Pelayo ; unfortunately no flowers were seen ; but the specimen brought to St. Louis is so far in fine condition. Of another smaller, but most elegant species of the same genus,⁴ ⁸ Dr. Wis-

---

⁴ ⁶ *Echinocereus enneacanthus*, n. sp., ovato-cylindricus 10 costatus ; areolis elevatis, orbiculatis, distantibus, junioribus breviter albo-tomentosis ; aculeis angulatis, compressis, rectis, albis ; radialibus 8 subaequalibus, centrali singulo longiore, demum deflexo ; floris tubo pulvillis 30–35 albo-tomentosis setas spinescentes albidas fuscatasque inferioribus 6, superioribus 2–3 gerentibus stipato ; sepalis interioribus 10–13 oblongo-linearibus, petalis 12–14 lineari-oblongis obtusis s. mucronatis, apice denticulatis ; stigmatibus supra stamina brevia exsertis, 8–10 linearibus elongatis.

Near San Pablo, south of Chihuahua ; flowers in April. Plant 5 to 6 inches high, 3 to 4 in diameter ; branching from the base ; areolae about 1 inch distant from one another, spines stout, angular, like those of *E. triglochidiatus*, lateral spines 9 to 16, central one 18 to 22 lines long. Flowers 2½ to 3 inches long, red ; spiny bristles in the axills of the lowest sepals (on the ovary) four brown 2 to 4 lines long, and two white 3 to 4 lines long ; higher up the number of the brown bristles diminishes, and on the upper part of the tube we find only two white bristles of 6 lines length in the axills.

⁴ ⁷ *Echinocactus flexispinus*, n. sp., globosus, vertice subnudo, costis 13 obliquis, tuberculato subinterruptis ; areolis ovatis, junioribus albo-tomentosis, distantibus ; aculeis junioribus rubellis, demum cinereis ; radialibus 9–11 rectis s. subflexuosis, superioribus tenuioribus, infimo breviori, curvato, lateralibus longioribus compressis annulatis, rectiusculis ; centralibus 4 angulatis compressis annulatis, 3 superioribus rectiusculis s. curvatis, inferiore longissimo flexuoso, plerumque paulo uncinato, deflexo.

Pelayo, between Chihuahua and Parras. The specimen before me is 10 inches high, and the same in diameter ; ribs thick but not rounded ; areolae (without the floriferous areolae, which are 3 to 4 lines long,) 6 lines long and 4 wide, 1 or 1½ inch distant ; upper spines the most slender, 1¼ to 1½ inch long ; lowest one 1 to 1¼ inch long, stouter ; lateral spines 1½ to 3 inches in length, slightly, and sometimes indistinctly annulated ; upper central spines 2½ to 4 inches long ; lower spine stoutest, 4 to 5 inches long, mostly deflexed, often flexuous and twisted, more curved or even hooked at the extremity, much compressed, 4-angled, sharply carinate above and below, slightly annulated.

⁴ ⁸ *Echinocactus unguispinus*, n. sp., depresso-globosus, costis 21 interruptis tuberculatis, areolis approximatis junioribus, albo-tomentosis ; aculeis radialibus sub 21 tenuioribus, albidis, recurvis, intertextis, centralibus 5 (rarius 6) robustioribus, longioribus, corneis, sursum versis, singulo robustissimo, fusco deorsum flexo ; floris ovario tuboque brevi sepalis membranaceis, auriculato-cordatis, fimbriatis stipato ; petalis oblongis obtusis ; stigmate brevissimo conico 10–15 sulcato, (s. partito ?)

About Pelayo, flowers in May. A very elegant plant ; the specimen lizenus collected the living plant and flowers, and Dr. Gregg the ripe fruit. It is distinct from the other *Echinocacti* found in those regions by the membranaceous very thin sepaloid scales on the tube of the flower and the juicy glabrous fruit, in which respect it resembles my *E. setispinus* from Texas; *E. texensis*, Hpfr., has a juicy fruit, covered with woolly and spiny scales; *E. Wislizeni* and others have a dry fruit, covered with hard scales.

My *Opuntia frutescens* (Plant. Lindh. l. c. p. 245) which had been collected by Mr. Lindheimer along the Colorado and Guadaloupe rivers, in Texas, was also found south of Chihuahua by Dr. Wislizenus, and again along the route near Parras, and below Monterey. The suggestion made in the Plant. Lindh., that it may be a southern variety of *O. fragilis* of the Upper Missouri, has proved to be erroneous, as they belong to quite distinct sections of the genus *Opuntia; O. frutescens*, together with *O. vaginata*, (vide note 18,) is one of the *Opuntiae cylindraceae graciliores*, and is apparently nearly related to *O. leptocaulis* DC., but is easily distinguished by its strong, white, single spines, while *O. lept.* has 3 short blackish bristles.

Agave Americana, with several relatives, was found in abundance on this part of the route; *Argemone Mexicana*, white, yellow, or rosecolored, was frequently met with; *Samolus ebracteatus* occurred in moist places so far inland, and on such elevations, while before it was only known as a litoral plant; *Malvaceae, Oenotherae, Asclepiadaceae, Giliae, Solaneae, Justiciae,* shrubby *Labiatae*, were collected of many different species; but the great characteristic of the country were the shrubs forming the often impenetrable thickets, called "chaparráls." They are mostly spinous,

---

before me 4 inches in diameter, 3 inches in height; the large recurved spines, especially the stoutest central one, which is of a bluish horncolor, with a brown point, and is curved and bent downward like a large fang, cover the whole surface of the plant, and give it a very pretty appearance. Lower radiating spines 6 to 10, upper 12 to 15 lines long; upper central spines 12 to 18 lines long, but lower stouter one only 10 to 12 lines in length. Flowers described from the shrivelled specimens found on the living plant; about 1 inch in length, and probably pale red. I have little doubt that some fruits collected in the same region (about San Lorenzo) by Dr. Gregg belong to this species; the fleshy oval berry is 10 or 12 lines long, covered with the same auriculate thin scales which we find on the flowers, and crowned with the remnants of the flower; seeds black, much compressed, somewhat rough, albumen considerable, embryo curved, cotyledons short obtuse. This is a very remarkable plant, and approaches in shape some *mammillariae;* the tubercles which form the interrupted ribs are sideways compressed, have a tomentose groove on their upper edge, which ends in a regular axillary depressed areola, like that of a true *mammillaria;* but the scaly ovary and the curved embryo prove it to be an *Echinocactus*. The specimen brought here by Dr. W. died soon after it arrived, as many of those collected in April and May during the flowering season, though only two months on the road, while those collected the year before, between August and November, which had been packed up for eight or ten months, mostly do very well now. Dr. Gregg's seeds, however, have germinated well.

very much branched, often with remarkably small leaves, and not rarely with edible fruits. Among them many rhamnaceous and celastraceous shrubs, and some *Euphorbiaceae*, were particularly conspicuous, as well as some *Mimoseae*, one of which I must not forget to mention, because it is perhaps the smallest shrub in this family; not more than one or two inches high, with diminutive leaflets, but large purple flowers; it was collected near Chihuahua.

One of the most offensive of these chaparrál-shrubs was the *Koeberlinia*, Zucc., called here *Junco*, (Gregg.;) a small tree rather than a shrub, about 10 feet high, stem 4 to 6 inches in diameter; wood hard, dark brown with white alburnum; terminal branches green, with a dark brown spinous termination, 1 to 2 inches long, and $1\frac{1}{2}$ to 2 lines in diameter; very small subulate leaves soon deciduous; small white flowers in short lateral racemes; fruit not seen; in flower in May. It was frequently seen from south of Chihuahua to Monterey, (and Matamoros, Gregg.)

We find here again the interesting *Chilopsis* mentioned above, (see note 11,) also *Larrea glutinosa*, (note 10,) and another zygophyllaceous shrub, a true *Guajacum*,[49] which appears to be an undescribed species; it belongs to those plants that connect the Mexican with the Texan flora, as we find it extending from Parras to Monterey, and from there to the Upper Colorado, in Texas. *Tecoma stans* reappeared here with smaller pubescent leaves and more alate petiole, though probably not distinct from the larger and smoother plant found below Paso.

The beautiful *Fouquiera splendens*, (see note 16,) with its panicles of long tubular crimson flowers, rose here above all other shrubs; in some instances it reached a height of from 20 to 30 feet, and perhaps more, always in single stems.

A few species of *Yucca*, together with *Opuntia arborescens*, (note **5**,) formed almost the only trees on the arid plains. But in the valley of the Nazas occur stately trees of a species of *Algarobia*, distinct from the *A. glandulosa* of the north, with broader legumes, larger seeds, and few or no glands on the leaves.

About Saltillo *Echinocactus texensis*, Hpfr., (*E. Lindheimeri*, Engelm., in Plant. Lindh. l. c.,) was found, which extends from here to Matamoros, and to the Guadaloupe and Colorado, in Texas. The pretty *Mammillaria strobiliformis*,[50] grows on rocks near Rinconada. *Hunne-*

---

[49] *Guajacum angustifolium*, n. sp., foliis sub-5 (4–8) jugis glaberrimis, foliolis oblongo-linearibus, reticulatis; pedicellis et basi calycis pubescentibus; ovario bilobo, pubescente; capsula bivalvi, seminibus 2 ovatis.

About Parras; collected also by Dr. Gregg, who has found the plant common from Monclova to Parras, Monterey, and Camargo; found by Mr. Lindheimer on the Pierdenales river in Texas; flowers in April and May. Shrub or small tree with very knotty branches; leaflets mostly in 5 or 6 pairs, only on young vigorous shoots 6 to 8 pairs, mostly only 4 lines long, $\frac{1}{2}$ to 1 line wide, reticulated on both sides. Purple flowers 6 lines in diameter; seeds yellow, of the size of small beans. The hard and heavy yellowish brown wood is called "*Guajacan*" about Saltillo, and used as a sudorific and in venereal diseases. (Dr. Gregg.)

[50] *Mammillaria strobiliformis*, n. sp, simplex ovato-conica, tuberculis imbricato-adpressis, conicis, applanatis, sulcatis; aculeis rectis radialibus

8

mannia fumariaefolia, Sweet, was collected near Saltillo, with smaller flowers, (1¼ inch in diameter,) and near Rinconada, with larger ones, (3 inches in diameter;) an interesting plant, the eastern representative of the Californian *Eschscholtzia*, but perennial, with a small torus, a different stigma, etc.

I cannot omit to introduce here a beautiful shrub discovered on the rocks about Agua Nueva and Buena Vista by Dr. Gregg. Depending upon Don's characters of *Cowania* as correct, I must consider this plant as the type of a new genus, which I have great pleasure to dedicate to its indefatigable discoverer, my friend Dr. Josiah Gregg, whose name has already been frequently mentioned in these pages.[5 1]   *Greggia rupestris* is a lovely, sweet-scented shrub, with flowers resembling roses in shape and color, so that Dr. Gregg was induced to name it the " Cliff rose."

North and northeast of Monterey we reach the lower country, and with it a different vegetation; here is the home of the shrubby *Cassieae* (*Parkinsonia, Casparea*, etc.,) and *Mimoseae; Sophora, Diospyros*, some species of *Rhus* and *Rhamnus* are common here, as well as a climbing yellow-flowered *Hiraea*, while another erect red-flowered species grows on the table-lands near Parras. One of the most beautiful shrubs of that district is *Leucophyllum texanum*, Benth., with its whitish tomentose leaves and sweetscented blue flowers. It is common from San Antonio, in Texas, to Monclova, and from Cerralbo to Camargo, but is not seen on the table-lands.

---

sub-10 albidis, centralibus 3 fusco-atris, 2 minoribus sursum versis, singulo longiore porrecto; floribus in vertice lanato centralibus, ovario lanoso; sepalis sub-10 lanceolatis, acutis, integris; petalis sub-24 ovato-lanceolatis, mucronatis, integris vel versus apicem erosis; stigmatibus 7 flavis erecto-patentibus exsertis.

Rinconada, on rocks; flowers in June. About 3 inches high, and 2 inches in diameter below; tubercles in 10 to 13 oblique rows closely adpressed, so as to give the whole plant the appearance of a pineapple or cone, tomentose in the groove and the axills, about 6 lines long; radial spines 3 to 5, central 5 to 8 lines long; flowers central, 3 to 5 in a cluster together imbedded in long and dense wool, about 15 lines long and wide; petals deep purple.

[5 1] *Greggia*, n. gen., (*Greggia*, Gaertn. = *Eugenia*, Mich., fide Endlicher,) calyx tubulosus, 5-lobus, imbricatus; petala 5 calycis fauci inserta; stamina numerosissima cum petalis inserta; ovaria plura fundo calycis inserta 1-rarius 2-ovulata; stylus villosus, deciduus, stigma nudum; ovulum supra basin ovarii placentae laterali insertum, anatropum; achenia villosa, ecaudata; semen unicum erectum, embryo radicula infera.

A Mexican shrub with small cuneate truncate dentate leaves with adnate stipules, and solitary rose-colored or purple sweetscented flowers.

Greggia rupestris, n. sp., cliffs about Saltillo, Buena Vista, and Agua Nueva, flowers January to March; several feet high, much branched, leaves about 6 lines long, and at the apex 3 lines wide, crowded; revolute on the margin, glabrous above, tomentose beneath; flowers terminal on short branchlets 15 to 18 inches in diameter. Nearly related to *Cowania*, but distinguished by the imbricate, not valvate calyx, the red, not yellow flowers, and the deciduous, not persistent style.

Vitis bipinnata and *V. incisa*, well known in the southwestern parts of the United States and Texas, were also found here. Remarkable herbaceous plants were a *Nicotiana*, an *Orobanche* (on the seacoast,) an *Eustoma*, several *Asclepiadaceae*, *Malvaceae*, *Cucurbitaceae*, *Labiatae*, and others. *Lobelia phyllostachya* has already been mentioned above. (See note 41.)

Hasty and imperfect as this notice of the collections of Dr. Wislizenus is, it cannot but impress the botanist with the richness and novelty of the flora of these countries, and invite the arduous explorer to further exertions.

GEORGE ENGELMANN, M. D.

St. Louis, *December,* 1847.

Upon the authority of Professor John Torrey, of New York, who has done me the favor to look over the botanical manuscript of Dr. Engelmann before its going to press, I add here the following two corrections:

Larrea glutinosa (n. sp., No. 10) seems to be *Larrea Mexicana* of Moricaud, described and figured in a work to which Dr. E. had not access.

Geranium pentagynum (n. sp., No. 6) seems to be *Geranium Frémontii* (Torr.) of Frémont's second report.

A. W.

THE METEOROLOGICAL TABLES

Are prepared from my meteorological journal, kept on the road. Some of the columns may require an explanation.

The column "*boiling point of water*," refers to my observations with two thermometers, constructed by my order, by J. W. Edmonds, of Boston, each varying from 85 to 100° Celsius, and every degree divided in tenths. I made many experiments with them on the road, to find the relative difference between the boiling point of water and the mercurial column of my barometer. From about 50 such observations, made within the range of from 23 to 29 inches of the barometer, I abstracted the general result, that 1 inch of my barometer at the temperature of 32° Fahr., was = $1°.04138$ boiling point Therm. Cels., and $1°$ Th. C. $= 0''.96026$ of the barometer. But, at the same time, I have come to the conclusion, as others before me, that the determination by the boiling point of water can never in correctness equal the barometrical measurement. A difference in fuel, in water, in the size of the vessel, in draught of air, &c., is apt to produce such a discrepancy in the relative boiling point, that this method will answer well enough as a correlative proof of the barometer, and for heights, where several hundred feet, more or less, is not a matter of consideration, but that it will never be capable of supplying the place of the barometer.

The *dew-point*, found by excess of temperature of the dry over the wet bulb, is calculated according to "tables for the determination of the dew-point," given in the Encyclopœdia Britanica, and republished in the "Report to the Navy Department of the United States on American coals, by Professor Walter R. Johnson: Washington, 1844." Observations beyond the reach of these tables, I calculated according to the rule given by Professor Espy : "The dew-point, when it is not very low, may be nearly obtained by multiplying the difference between dry and wet bulb temperature with 103, dividing the result by the wet-bulb temperature, and subtracting the quotient from the dry-bulb temperature; the remainder will be the dew-point."

In the column "*wind*," the force of the wind is designated, as recommended by Professor Espy, by numbers from 0 to 6; 0 being a calm, 1 a very gentle breeze, 2 a gentle breeze, 3 a fresh wind, 4 a strong wind, 5 a storm, and 6 a hurricane.

The *clearness of the sky* is also marked in numbers from 0 to 10; 0 representing entire cloudiness, and 10 entire clearness.

METEOROLOGICAL TABLES.

METEOROLOGICAL TABLE.

Date	Hour	Barometer	Attached	Detached	Wet bulb	Dew point	Boil'g point of water (Ther. C.)	Wind	Sky	Elevation above sea, in English feet	Camping places	From last camp	From Independence	Remarks
1846. May 9	5 A.	28.850	73.0	74.0	—	—	—	—	5	1,040	Independence, Mo., in Noland house.	—	—	
10	9 M.	28.955	67.0	69.0	—	—	—	—	5	—	Do. do.			
	12	28.960	70.0	75.0	—	—	—	—	6	—	Do. do.			
	3 A.	28.915	73.0	76.5	—	—	99.60	—	6	—	Do. do.			
11	9 M.	28.970	68.0	68.0	—	—	—	—	5	—	Do. do.			
	12	28.970	73.0	79.5	—	—	99.60	—	5	—	Do. do.			
12	3 A.	28.945	76.0	84.0	—	—	—	—	3	—	Do. do.			
	9 M.	28.880	70.0	72.0	—	—	99.45	—	3	—	Do. do.			
	12½ A.	28.845	77.0	79.0	—	—	—	—	1	—	Do. do.			
	3	28.775	77.5	79.0	—	—	—	—		—	Do. do.			On the night of 12th, and during 13th, constant rain.
15	Sunrise	—	—	44.5	44.0	42.7	—	SE. 3	5	1,020	Big blue camp, 3 miles west of Big Blue river.	—	20	
	9 M.	29.190	66.0	65.0	55.5	47.0	99.85	3	5	—	Do. do.			
	12	29.215	73.0	73.0	60.0	62.3	—	4	10	—	Do. do.			
	3	29.135	75.0	70.5	68.5	66.8	—	4	5	—	Do. do.			
16	Sunrise	—	—	52.0	51.0	49.8	—	—	8	—	Do. do.			
	9 M.	29.200	72.5	71.0	63.0	58.1	—	s. 4	5	—	Do. do.			
	12	29.175	82.0	80.0	68.0	62.4	99.80	4	5	—	Do. do.			
	4 A.	29.155	84.5	80.0	68.0	62.4	—	3	1	—	Do. do.			
18	Sunrise	29.245	71.0	67.0	63.0	60.5	99.85	NE. 4	0	—	Do. do.			
19	9 M.	—	—	52.5	51.0	48.1	—	4	1	—	Do. do.			
	12	29.265	68.0	64.0	56.0	49.0	—	E. 3	3	—	Do. do.			
	3 A.	29.250	77.5	73.0	62.0	55.1	—	3	5	—	Do. do.			
20	Sunrise	29.175	76.0	75.0	67.0	63.0	99.80	s. 2	0	—	Do. do.			

Date	Hour	Barom.	Ther.	Ther.	Ther.	Ther.	Barom.	Wind	a	b	Elev.	Station		Miles	Total	Remarks
21	9 M.	29.120	79.0	79.0	72.0	69.2		W.	2	2		Do.	do.			Thunder storm, with rain, about noon.
	12½ A.	29.030	75.0	69.5	68.5	67.2	99.65		1	2		Do.	do.			
	3½	28.990	74.0	72.5	69.5	67.3		E.	2	3		Do.	do.			Thunder storm and rain in the night.
22	Sunrise		62.0	61.5	60.0			SE.	1	2		Do.	do.			
	9 M	29.050	76.5	74.0					5	4		Do.	do.			
	12	28.985	84.0	82.0	70.0	64.9	99.70		4	4		Do.	do.			
	3 A.	28.925	84.0	83.0	68.0	61.1		S.	3	4		Do.	do.			
	9 M.	29.095	75.0	76.0	68.5	65.0			5	4		Do.	do.			Rain in the night.
	4 A.	28.985	82.0	80.0	70.0	65.7	99.65	W.	7	3		Do.	do.			
	3½ A.	28.915		62.0		77.4		SSW.	8	4	1,100	Night camp, in prairie	do.	5	25	
23	Sunrise		82.0	78.5					6	2		Do.	do.			
	1 A.	28.955	61.5	61.5		69.7		SSE.	1	3	1,190	Noon camp, in "Round Grove," (Lone Elm.)		10	35	
24	5 M.	28.925	85.0	84.0	73.5				5	2	1,138	Night camp in prairie, on a water pool.		5	40	
	6 A.	28.995	67.0	67.0	67.0			S.	0	3	1,245	Noon camp, at Black Jack point		12	52	
25	Sunrise	28.810	78.0	78.0	69.0	65.0	99.70		5	1	1,122	Night camp at Wackarussi point, past Hickory point.		12	64	
	1½ A.	28.865	63.4	64.0	63.0	62.3		SSW.	6	1	1,195	Night camp, on Rock creek		15	79	
26	5½ M.	28.940	83.0	82.5	69.0	62.2		NE.	10	3		Do.	do.			Wind storm from NE. in the night, a rain shower on next morning.
	2 A.	28.865	63.5	62.0	60.0	58.5	99.60	SSE.	0	1	1,043	Noon camp, on 110 Miles creek.		10	89	Thunder storm without rain, in night.
27	Sunrise	28.785	88.0	87.0	74.0	69.4			3	0	1,047	Night camp, on Bridge cr.		8	97	
	3¼ A.	28.560	59.0	55.0	55.0		99.10	NE.	2	0	1,158	Noon camp, on Switzler's cr.		6	103	Thunder storm, with light rain, from 3 to 7 o'clock, A.
28	6½	28.390	73.0	74.0	66.0	61.8			0	2	1,143	Night camp, on Fish creek		10	113	
	Sunrise	28.255	64.5	63.5	63.5			N.	1	0	1,343	Noon camp, on Pleasant Valley creek.		15	128	
29	12	28.290	51.5	50.5		59.1	99.30		8	2	1,420	Night camp in prairie, without water.		3	131	
	5 M.	28.585	79.0	76.0	65.0	47.7			5	0		Do.	do.			
30	5 A.	28.525	50.0	50.0	49.0	55.1	99.00	S.	0	3	1,170	Noon camp, on Bluff creek		6	137	
		28.290	75.0	57.0	55.5	54.1		S.	3	3	1,190	Night camp, in Council grove.		6	143	
									2	3	1,502	Noon camp, on Diamond spring.		15	158	
31	Sunrise											Night camp in prairie, without water.		7	165	

TABLE—Continued.

Date.	Hour.	Barometer.	Thermometer, Fahrenheit.				Ther. C. Boil'g point of water.	Wind.	Sky.	Elevation above sea, in English feet.	Camping places.	Supposed dist'ces in Eng. miles.		Remarks.
			Attached.	Detached.	Wet bulb.	Dew point.						From last camp.	From Independence.	
1846. May 31	4½ A.	28.240	58.0	54.5	–	–	–	NE. 4	0	1,526	Night camp, on Willow cr.	14	179	Thunder storms, with hail and rain, from noon till next morning.
June 1	7 M.	28.440	54.0	53.0	50.0	46.2	–	w. 3	10	–	Do. do.		185	
	4¾ A.	28.465	65.0	68.0	52.5	36.3	99.15	3	1	1,550	Noon camp, on Cottonwood creek.	6	191	
2	Sunrise	–	–	44.5	43.5	40.2	–	s. 1	7	–	Night camp in prairie, on a water pool.	6	203	
	2 A.	28.300	80.0	80.0	72.0	68.8	99.05	3	3	1,775	Noon camp, near Little Turkey creek.	12	213	
3	Sunrise	28.255	60.0	58.0	56.0	54.2	–	sw. 1	5	1,732	Night camp in prairie, without water.	10	223	
	2 A.	28.300	70.0	67.0	59.0	53.0	–	NE. 4	1	1,728	Noon camp, on Little Arkansas.	10	229	
4	Sunrise	28.340	49.0	48.0	46.0	42.9	–	2	1	1,603	Night camp in prairie, without water.	6	243	
5	3 A.	28.420	70.0	67.0	53.0	38.8	–	NW. 2	1	1,609	Noon camp, on Big Cow cr.	14	259	
	Sunrise	28.175	45.0	44.5	43.5	40.2	–	wsw. 1	1	1,750	Night camp at Camp Osage, near Arkansas river.	16	267	
6	10½ M.	28.130	73.0	75.0	68.0	64.6	98.80	wnw. 2	3	1,920	Noon camp, on Walnut cr.	8	286	
	5 M.	27.985	52.0	52.0	48.0	42.4	–	w. 1	5	1,970	Night camp, near Ash cr.	19	292	
	12¾ A.	27.980	83.0	79.0	61.0	49.6	98.60	sw. 1	0	2,109	Noon camp, on Pawnee fork.	6	308	
7	Sunrise	28.090	55.5	54.0	52.0	49.7	–	0	1	1,878	Night camp in prairie, without water.	16	314	
	12½ A.	27.875	80.0	80.0	65.0	57.1	98.60	wsw. 2	1	2,210	Noon camp, on Little Coon creek.	6		

No.	Hour	Barom.	Ther.	Ther.	Ther.	Ther.	Boiling point	Wind	Force	Clouds	Elevation	Locality	Miles	Aggr.	Remarks
8	9½ M.	27.875	74.0	73.0	63.0	57.0	—	SE.	2	5	2,180	Night camp in prairie, on a water pool.	17	331	The barometrical observations are made on both sides of the river, about 100 yds. distant from it, and about 10 feet above the level of the water.
9	5 A.	27.825	87.0	78.5	64.0	55.0	98.40	SE.	2	7	2,279	Noon camp, near Arkansas	10	341	
	Sunrise	27.700	55.0	52.0	51.0	49.8	—	SSE.	1	8	2,264	Night camp, on Caches of Arkansas.	12	353	
10	5½ A.	27.535	82.0	74.0	59.5	49.3	98.20	ESE.	2	5	2,703	Night and noon camp, at crossing of Arkansas.	20	373	
	10½ M.	27.445	74.0	75.0	61.5	53.0	98.10	SE.	3	3	—	Do. do. do.	—	—	
11	4 A.	27.295	83.0	77.0	49.5	46.3	—	s.	3	10	2,811	Do. do.	15	388	
	5¾ M.	27.160	54.0	52.0	59.0	44.1	—	s.	1	5	3,131	Night camp, on Battle ground.	18	406	
12	5½ A.	27.005	84.5	78.5	56.0	47.4	97.70	SSE.	4	10	2,923	Noon camp in prairie, without water.	17	423	
	7 M.	27.110	64.0	64.5	64.0	53.5	—	E.	3	10	3,120	Night camp, on Sand creek	8	431	
	4 A.	27.050	94.0	81.5	50.5	48.6	97.75	SE.	3	10	2,953	Noon camp, on Lower springs of Cimarron.	8	439	
13	5 M.	27.025	55.0	52.0	65.0	53.3	—	s.	0	8	3,455	Night camp, near Cimarron	18	457	
	5 A.	26.750	92.0	88.0	53.0	47.8	97.55	SE.	3	9	3,313	Noon camp, near Cimarron	8	465	
14	Sunrise	26.710	60.0	58.0	67.0	55.6	—		1	5	3,533	Night camp, on Middle springs of Cimarron.	3	468	
15	1½ A.	26.690	92.0	92.0	53.0	47.1	97.30	SW.	3	8	3,557	Noon camp, near Cimarron	12	480	
	Sunrise	26.475	59.0	57.5	66.5	57.3	—	SW.	1	8	3,749	Night camp in prairie, without water.	6	486	
16	12	26.450	85.5	84.0	60.0	52.4	97.10	W.	4	0	3,830	Noon camp, on Cimarron	8	494	About 1 A., light rain.
	7½ A.	26.290	73.0	71.0	59.0	56.9	—	S.	2	8	—	Night camp, at crossing of Cimarron.	17	511	Very foggy.
17	4½ M.	26.250	63.0	60.5	62.5	58.2	96.70	SW.	1	1	4,250	Noon camp, on Cimarron	6	517	
	5 A.	25.945	78.0	74.5	57.0	52.7	96.10	SW.	2	3	4,275	Do. do. on Cold Spring	8	525	
	4½ M.	25.800	57.0	57.0			—	SW.	1	0	—	Night camp in prairie, without water.	—	—	
18	12½ A.	25.465	83.0	85.0	64.0	55.3	95.75	NW.	1	9	4,848	Noon camp, on Cedar creek	12	537	In the evening thunder and lightning, without rain.
	Sunrise	25.370	59.5	59.0	57.0	49.9	—	E.	1	7	4,763	Night camp, on McNees' cr.	12	549	
	1 A.	25.135	85.0	80.5	62.0	48.6	—	E.	4	8	5,203	Noon camp, on Cottonwood branch.	—	—	
19	5 M.	24.735	53.0	52.0	50.5		—		0	10	5,422	Night camp, on Rabbit-ear creek.	12	561	

TABLE—Continued.

Date.	Hour.	Barometer.	Attached.	Detached.	Wet bulb.	Dew point.	Ther. C. Boil'g point of water.	Wind.	Sky.	Elevation above sea, in English feet.	Camping places.	From last camp.	From Independence.	Remarks.
1846. June 19	5½ A.	24.150	79.0	75.0	57.0	40.8	—	E. 3	5	6,202	Night camp, on Rock creek	20	581	In the afternoon thunder and lightning without rain, but with strong south wind.
20	4½ M.	24.140	55.0	54.0	53.0	51.9	—	s. 1	7	—	do. do.			
	12	24.105	76.0	77.0	63.0	54.8	94.70	s. 4	5	6,360	Noon camp, on Whetstone creek.	6	587	Very foggy, and drizzling.
21	5 M.	23.915	59.0	57.0	—	—	—	sw. 3	0	6,412	Night camp, on Point of Rocks.	14	601	In the afternoon thunder and lightning, with light rain.
	12	24.015	78.0	79.0	64.5	54.7	94.75	ssw. 3	6	6,486	Noon camp, in a cañon -	8	609	
22	Sunrise	24,520	50.0	49.0	49.0	—	—	0	10	5,642	Night camp, on Rio Colorado.	12	621	In the afternoon thunder and lightning without rain, in the evening a hail storm.
	12	24.405	80.0	76.0	66.0	62.5	95.00	w. 4	8	6,012	Noon camp, on Ocaté creek	6	627	
23	5¼ M.	23.965	60.0	57.0	56.5	56.0	—	2	2	6,356	Night camp in prairie, without water.	12	639	
	4¾ A.	23.995	80.0	78.5	63.0	53.0	94.50	sw. 4	8	6,511	Noon camp at Santa Clara, near Wagon mound.	12	651	
24	1 A.	23.900	78.0	78.0	63.0	54.2	94.40	s. 3	6	6,616	Noon camp, on Wolf creek.	13	664	
25	5 M.	23.755	58.0	54.5	—	—	—	N. 1	10	6,583	Night camp in prairie, (passed Rio Mora.)	14	678	
26	2½ A.	23.860	82.0	82.5	64.5	53.9	94.40	w. 4	4	6,705	Noon camp on Gallinas cr., east of Las Vegas.	12	690	Towards evening thunder and lightning, with rain and hail.
	5 M.	23.875	60.5	62.0	58.0	54.8	—	se. 1	0	6,357	Night camp, in a cañon -	6	696	
	1¾ A.	24.050	85.0	84.5	65.5	55.0	94.55	sw. 2	4	6,499	Noon camp on a creek, near Tocalote-abajo.	7	703	

Date	Hour	Barometer	Therm. att.	Therm. det.	Temp.	Temp.	Bar. 32°	Wind	Force	Clouds	Elevation	Localities	Miles	From Santa Fé	Remarks
27	5 M.	24.115	53.5	52.0	51.5	50.9	—		0	10	6,133	Night camp, east of San Miguel.	10	713	
	1 A.	24.140	89.0	91.0	62.0	42.9	—	w.	3	5	6,431	Noon camp, west of San Miguel.	4	717	
28	2¼ A.	23.590	88.0	89.5	58.0	33.6	94.10	nw.	3	7	7,098	Noon camp at Rio Pecos springs, opposite the old Pecos village.	20	737	
29	5 M.	23.135	50.0	47.5	45.8	40.8	—		0	8	7,250	Night camp, on Cottonwood branch.	6	743	
	1 A.	23.520	85.0	82.0	58.0	40.3	—	s.	2	3	7,176	Noon camp in a cañon, on a creek.	8	751	
30	3½ M.	23.440	56.0	—	—	—	93.80	nw.	1	10	—	Do. do. do.	6	756	
	5½ M.	23.205	51.0	49.5	45.5	37.5	94.40			6	7,184	Night camp in a cañon, near springs, (Armijo's camp.)			
July 1	11½ M.	23.835	83.0	80.0	—	—	—	s.	3	6	6,723	Noon camp, on a creek -	5	761	The barometrical observations in Santa Fé are made in a house on the "Plaza." The mean of all my barometrical and thermometrical observations made in Santa Fé, is:—Barometer, 23″.459; Thermometer attached, 77.9; Thermometer detached, 78.6: or, Barometer (with temperature of mercury reduced to 32° Fahrenheit) = 23″.447.
	5 A.	23.495	80.0	80.0	—	—	—	w.			7,047	Santa Fé -	4	765	
	9	23.505	75.0	75.0	—	—	—	w.							
	12	23.425	79.0	79.0	—	—	—	e.							
	3 A.	23.350	76.5	76.0	—	—	—								
2	9 M.	23.415	75.0	75.5	—	—	—	nw.							
	12	23.425	79.0	79.0	—	—	—								
3	3½ A.	23.355	80.0	80.0	54.0	33.1	—								
	6½ M.	23.445	73.0	73.0	60.5	45.7	—	sw.							
	9 A.	23.525	77.0	76.0	58.5	37.6	—								
4	12 M.	23.525	79.0	81.5	55.0	38.1	—	e.							
6	3 A.	23.430	83.0	86.0	58.0	37.3	—	n.							
	9 M.	23.570	75.0	74.0	59.0	43.6	—	w.							
7	12	23.525	80.0	84.5	57.0	36.0	—	s.							
	3 A.	23.440	79.5	81.0			94.26	sw.	4	0					
8	5 A.	23.755	83.5	83.0			—								
16	7 M.	25.285	69.0	67.5	64.5	61.9	—		0	0	6,732	Aqua Fria, 6 miles west of Santa Fé.	—	—	Drizzling rain.
17	5¾ M.	25.350	62.0	61.0	60.0	57.4	—	sw.	1	3	4,813	About 3 miles N. of Albuquerque, in a level plain near the Rio del Norte.	—	—	Do.
	4 A.	25.415	90.0	83.5	64.0	52.5	—	sw.	1	3	4,860	Do. do. do. Noon camp at Sandival's Hacienda, 2 miles N. of Albuquerque.	5	60	Do.
18	5 M.	25.085	63.0	62.0	59.0	56.7	—	ESE.	1	8	5,048	Night camp on hills, 2 miles SE. of Sandival's.		65	
	5 A.	25.410	95.0	85.5	63.5	50.3	—	ssw.	2	9	4,754	Night camp 3 miles S. of Sandival's, near R. del N.	3	68	

TABLE—Continued.

Date.	Hour.	Barometer.	Thermometer, Fahrenheit. Attached.	Detached.	Wet bulb.	Dew point.	Ther. C. Boil'g point of water.	Wind.		Sky.	Elevation above sea, in English feet.	Camping places.	Supposed dist'ces in Eng. miles. From last camp.	From Santa Fe.	Remarks.
1846. July 19	Sunrise	25.460	61.5	60.0	57.0	54.4	—		0	7	—	Night camp 3 miles S. of Sandival's, near Rio del Norte.			
20	3 A.	25.300	95.5	96.5	66.5	51.7	96.00	NW.	3	5	5,070	Noon camp 6 miles S. of Sandival's, near river.	3	71	
	Sunrise	25.290	66.0	64.5	57.0	50.8	—	N.	0	8	4,872	Night camp near river, opposite Isleta.	2	73	
21	3 A.	25.245	97.0	93.5	64.0	52.1	95.90	N.	3	8	5,122	Noon camp in Bosque or alamos de los Pinos.	5	78	
	5 M.	25.430	67.0	65.0	60.0	56.4	—		0	2	4,693	Night camp, at Mariano Chavez's Hacienda.	2	80	
22	3 A.	25.240	91.5	89.5	66.0	54.6	—	S.	3	3	5,091	Noon camp, near river	5	85	
	6½ M.	25.290	67.0	67.0	57.5	29.9	—	E.	1	9	4,861	Night camp, near Tomé	3	88	
23	3 A.	25.355	97.0	95.0	61.5	38.9	—	NW.	2	9	5,002	Noon camp, in plain	5	93	
	5 M.	25.290	61.5	58.0	51.0	42.9	—	E.	1	10	4,804	Night camp, at Casas coloradas.	6	99	
24	3 A.	25.265	96.0	96.5	63.0	41.8	—	S.	3	9	5,117	Noon camp, near river	4	103	
	5 M.	25.245	64.0	61.0	49.0	33.2	—	E.	1	6	4,875	Night camp, near river	3	106	
25	3 A.	25.385	93.0	91.5	61.5	41.3	—	S.	2	3	4,939	Noon camp, near river	5	109	
	5 M.	25.440	67.0	64.5	54.5	46.6	—		0	1	4,679	Night camp on river, two miles S. of Joyita.	4	113	
	2½ A.	25.475	90.0	90.0	—	—	—	S.	3	0	4,820	Noon camp, in Joya.	5	118	
26	5 M.	25.575	61.0	61.0	58.0	55.5	—	E.	1	6	4,497	Night camp, on river	3	121	Thunder and lightning, with drizzling rain.
	3 A.	25.555	82.0	83.0	—	—	—	NW.	2	0	4,674	Noon camp on river, 1 mile S. of Sabino.	10	131	
27	5½ M.	25.600	65.0	64.0	62.5	61.5	—		0	3	4,492	Night camp, near Parida	5	136	

Date	Hour	Bar.						Wind			Alt.	Locality		Dist.	Remarks
28	1 A.	25.610	87.0	87.5	65.0	53.5	96.20	NW.	1	5	4,644	Noon camp, near river	2	138	In the afternoon, thunder storm, with rain.
29	3½ A.	25.595	100.0	95.0	72.0	63.6	—	s.	1	7	4,733	Noon camp, near river	7	145	
	6 M.	25.560	67.5	64.0	60.0	57.1	—		0	10	4,545	Night camp, about 1 mile N. of Lopez.	2	147	
30	4½ M.	25.720	65.0	62.5	58.0	53.4	—	NW.	0	9	4,362	Night camp, near river	12	159	
	2½ A.	25.730	86.0	86.0	68.0	59.9	—		2	2	4,485	Noon camp, near river	6	165	
31	5 M.	25.840	63.0	62.0	54.0	46.2	—		0	9	4,212	Night camp, in a Cottonwood grove, (passed ruins of Valverde.)	6	171	
Aug. 1	2 A.	25.790	93.5	94.5	62.0	40.5	—	SE.	3	6	4,488	Noon camp, near river	4	175	
	7 M.	25.885	68.0	66.0	58.5	52.7	—	N.	1	10	4,295	Night camp, near river	7	182	
	1 A.	25.695	93.0	95.0	61.5	38.9	—	NE.	2	9	4,499	N. camp, near Fray Cristobal	5	187	
2	5 A.	25.385	92.0	87.5	62.0	45.8	—	SE.	2	6	5,019	Noon camp, near Ojo del Muerto, in Jornada del Muerto.	22	209	
3	12	25.575	89.5	88.5	61.5	44.0	—	NE.	2	2	4,799	Noon camp, on a hill without water, in Jornada del Muerto	20	229	
4	5 M.	25.730	65.5	64.5	58.5	52.8	—	E.	1	2	4,452	Night camp at Barilla, on a water pool, in Jornada del Muerto.	16	245	
5	12	25.945	78.0	77.0	67.0	62.1	—	E.	3	1	4,298	Noon camp on a waterpool, in Jornada del Muerto.	5	250	
	5 M.	25.830	64.0	62.0	59.0	56.7	—		0	5	4,328	Night camp, without water, in Jornada del Muerto.	18	268	
6	12	26.270	91.5	95.0	72.5	64.4	—	s.	1	5	4,044	Noon camp at Robledo, near river.	8	276	
	5 M.	26.240	66.0	64.0	—	—	—	—	—	—	3,891	Night camp, 2 miles south of Doñana.	12	288	
7	3½ A.	26.179	99.0	95.5	70.0	59.0	—	sw.	3	3	4,168	Noon camp, on a waterpool	5	293	
	5 M.	26.230	64.0	62.5	60.0	57.2	—	s.	0	6	3,890	Night camp, near river	3	296	
	3 A.	26.380	92.0	91.0	67.0	56.0	—		2	4	3,928	Noon camp, near riv., (Brazito.)	15	311	
8	9 M.	26.435	83.0	84.0	68.0	60.7	—	SE.	2	5	3,797	Upper crossing of Rio del Norte.	28	339	The observation is made on the low river bank.
9	9 M.	26.455	74.5	74.0	68.0	65.1	—	E.	1	0	3,814	El Paso del Norte.	6	345	The barom. obser. in el Paso are made in a house near the Plaza. The rainy season commenced. It rained almost every day, tho' more in evening than morning.
	12	26.435	74.5	25.0	72.0	70.7	—		1	1					
	3 A.	26.430	75.5	76.5	71.0	67.7	—		1	2					
10	5 M.	26.420	73.0	70.5	67.0	65.4	—		1	6					
	9 M.	26.465	77.0	80.5	71.5	67.0	—	NE.	2	8					
11	Sunrise	26.350	74.0	69.5	67.0	64.9	—		0						

TABLE—Continued.

Date	Hour	Barometer	Thermometer, Fahrenheit				Ther. C.	Wind	Sky	Elevation above sea, in English feet	Camping places	Supposed dist'ces in Eng. miles		Remarks
			Attached	Detached	Wet bulb	Dew point	Boil's point of water					From last camp	From El Paso	
1846. Aug. 11	11 M.	26.335	82.0	89.0	73.0	67.2	—	0 E.	7	—	El Paso del Norte	—	—	The mean of all my barometrical and thermometrical observations made in El Paso, is:—Barometer, 26″.372; Thermometer attached, 77.6; Thermometer detached, 73.5: or, Barometer, (with temper'ture of mercury reduced to 32° Fahrenheit,) 26″.360.
	4 A.	26.310	77.5	76.5	—	—	—	2	0					
	5½ M.	26.370	75.0	72.5	68.0	64.9	—	0	4					
12	9	26.375	79.0	84.0	69.5	63.3	—	2 W.	8					
	12	26.340	81.8	87.5	71.0	62.3	—	0	6					
	3 A.	26.315	82.0	81.0	71.0	64.7	—	—	5					
	5 M.	26.395	77.0	71.0	68.0	66.5	—	—	2					
	9	26.440	77.5	80.0	72.0	68.8	—	—	4					
13	12	26.375	80.0	84.5	72.5	67.2	—	—	4					
	3 A.	26.335	80.5	84.0	72.5	68.1	—	—	1					
	Sunrise	26.370	77.0	69.5	67.0	64.9	—	2 W.	5					
14	2 A.	26.265	81.0	92.0	71.5	62.9	97.00	2 NW.	2					
	6½ M.	26.295	76.0	74.0	67.5	64.3	—	3 sw.	9					
15 / 16	12	25.890	90.0	89.0	74.0	68.8	—	1	5	4,445	Noon camp, north of Sand hills.	—	32	From El Paso to Chihuahua we had every day about noon thunder and lightning, with more or less rain; it rained sometimes all night, but generally cleared up in the morning. We are amidst the rainy season.
17	6 M.	25.875	66.5	67.5	66.0	64.4	—	1 NE.	1	4,306	Night camp, at the southern end of Sand hills.	12	44	
	12	25.950	88.0	85.0	73.0	68.5	—	2 N.	3	4,355	Noon camp, south of Sand hills.	12	56	
18	6 M.	26.085	69.0	68.5	—	—	—	0	0	4,085	Night camp, in prairie	15	71	
	3 A.	26.120	83.0	80.5	—	—	—	0	2	4,133	Noon camp, in prairie, (passed Lake Patos.)	15	86	
19	6 M.	26.050	67.5	66.0	—	—	—	0	5	4,110	Night camp, in Carrizal	12	98	
20	5½ M.	25.960	68.5	67.5	—	—	—	0	0	4,219	Night camp, in prairie, beyond Rio Carmen.	15	113	
21	1½ A.	25.075	84.5	79.0	69.0	64.5	—	2 SE.	0	5,317	Noon camp, in prairie, (passed Gallejo spring.)	50	163	

Day	Hour	Bar.	Ther.	Ther.	Ther.	Ther.		Wind			Feet	Locality		No.	No.	Remarks
22	7 M.	25.215	62.0	61.0	—	—	—	—	0	0	5,004	Night camp, near north end of laguna de Encinillas.	—	8	171	
23	4 A.	25.275	70.0	70.5	—	—	—	NE.	2	0	5,004	Noon camp, in prairie, near south end of laguna de Encinillas.	—	20	191	
24	6½ M.	25.250	60.0	60.0	—	—	—	s.	2	0	4,953	Night camp, in el Pegnol	—	8	199	
24	1 A.	25,110	76.0	76.0	66.0	60.8	—	ssw.	2	2	5,237	Noon camp, in prairie	—	12	211	
24	6 M.	25.265	61.0	60.0	—	—	—	w.	1	7	4,940	Night camp, on Sacramento river.	—	10	221	
25	12	25.455	81.0	79.5	68.0	61.8	—	s.	1	5	4,873	Noon camp, 8 miles north of Chihuahua.	—	11	232	
26	9 M.	25.595	74.5	76.0	67.5	63.4	96 25	N.	1	8	4,640	Chihuahua	—	8	240	All barometrical observations in Chihuahua are made on the "Plaza."
26	12	25.530	75.0	81.0	68.0	62.0	—	E.	1	5			—	—	—	
26	3 A.	25.480	78.0	81.5	68.0	61.8	—	—	—	—			—	—	—	
27	6 M.	—	—	68.0	68.0	69.0	—	N.	1	6		Do.	—	—	—	
27	9	25.570	74.0	77.5	67.5	61.6	—	E.	2	7			—	—	—	Thunder and lightning and rain, in the evening.
27	12	25.550	77.5	80.0	68.5	61.0	—	N.	2	1			—	—	—	
27	3½ A.	25.475	80.0	81.5	65.0	61.1	—	—	2	—			—	—	—	
28	9 M.	25.570	73.0	72.0	66.0	59.4	—	NE.	1	0			—	—	—	
28	1 A.	25.595	80.0	79.0	65.0	58.1	—	—	1	1			—	—	—	
28	5	25.545	76.0	78.0	63.5	57.9	—	E.	1	3			—	—	—	
29	9 M.	25.555	73.0	73.0	62.5	53.8	—	NE.	1	8		Do.	—	—	—	
29	1	25.545	75.0	77.0	61.0	47.7	—	—	1	6			—	—	—	
29	4	25.510	75.5	77.5	63.0	56.4	—	N.	1	5			—	—	—	
30	9 M.	25.580	72.0	72.5	64.5	57.6	—	NE.	1	10			—	—	—	
30	12	25.563	74.0	77.0	—	—	—	sw.	1	6			—	—	—	Thunder storm, and rain.
30	3½ A.	25.495	72.0	74.0	—	—	—	—	1	0			—	—	—	
30	—	25.440	73.5	75.0	66.0	61.3	—	—	1	1			—	—	—	

TABLE—Continued.

Observations in Chihuahua—Continued.

Date.	Hour.	Barometer.	Attached.	Detached.	Wet bulb.	Dew point.	Wind.		Sky.	Remarks.
1846.										
Aug. 31	9 M.	25.480	73 0	75.0	65.0	59.5	NE.	1	2	
	12	25.455	75.0	78.0	65.0	58.1	N.	1	3	
	3 A.	25.385	76.5	78.0	–	–	N.	1	3	Rain in the evening.
Sep. 1	9 M.	25.505	74.0	75.5	66.5	60.1	SW.	1	9	
	12	25.470	79.0	81.0	66.5	59.4	NW.	1	4	
	3 A.	25.415	80.0	82.0	66.0	58.0	N.	1	4	
2	Sunrise	–	–	65.5			NE.	1	5	
	12	25.460	79.5	81.0	66.0	58.5	NE.	1	5	
	3 A.	25.430	80.0	81.0	65.0	56.6	SE.	2	4	Thunder and lightning, without rain.
3	9 M.	25.440	74.0	76.0	–	–	NE.	1	10	
	12	25.405	79.0	81.0	65.0	56.6	E.	1	5	
	3 A.	25.370	81.5	83.0	66.5	57.8	SW.	1	5	
4	9 M.	25.395	76.0	80.0	–	–	SW.	1	1	
	12	25.400	78.0	81.0	–	–	SE.	2	2	
	3 A.	25.315	77.0	79.0	–	–	NW.	1	0	Rain, with thunder & lightning, all night.
5	9 M.	25.385	73.5	73.0	63.0	57.0	NW.	1	3	
	12	25.355	77.0	78.0	–	–	N.	1	6	
Dec. 23	9 M.	25.765	53.0	53.0	–	–	E.	1	10	
	12	25.710	61.5	61.5	–	–	E.	1	9	
	3 A.	25.605	61.0	61 0	–	–	E.	1	8	
24	9 M.	25.730	49.5	49.5	–	–	NE.	1	10	
	12	25.660	61.0	61.0	–	–	NE.	1	8	
	3 A.	25.645	62.0	62.0	–	–	NE.	1	9	
25	9 M.	25.760	48.5	48.5	–	–	NE.	1	9	
	12	25.685	61.5	61.5	–	–	SW.	1	10	
	3 A.	26.655	65.0	65.0	–	–	E.	2	9	
26	9 M.	25.615	50.0	50.0	–	–	SE.	1	5	
	12	25.580	62.0	62.0	–	–	SE.	2	4	
	3 A.	25.550	67.0	67.0	–	–	S.	1	4	
27	9 M.	25.555	49.5	49.5	–	–	S.	1	8	
	12	25.520	67.0	67.0	–	–	S.	2	7	
	3 A.	25.420	69.0	69.0	–	–	SW.	2	5	
28	9 M.	25.410	59.0	59.0	–	–	SW.	2	7	
	12	25.400	70.0	70.0	–	–	SW.	2	7	
	3 A.	25.400	57.5	57.5	–	–	NE.	3	9	
29	7½ M.	25.525	32.0	32.0	–	–	NE.	1	10	
	9	25.520	42.0	42.0	–	–	NE.	1	10	
	12	25.465	59.0	59.0	–	–	E.	1	10	
	3½ A.	25.395	64.0	64.0	–	–	S.	2	5	
30	9 M.	25.460	60.0	60.0	–	–	S.	3	5	
	12	25.380	68.5	68.5	–	–	S.	4	5	
	3 A.	25.215	66.5	66.5	–	–	SSW.	4	5	
31	9 M.	25.395	37.0	37.0	–	–	NE.	4	9	
	12	25.345	43.5	43.5	–	–	NE.	3	8	
1847.										
Mar. 22	12	25.400	81.0	78.0	55.0	–	W.	2	3	
	3 A.	25.350	73.5	73.5	50.0	–	W.	2	3	
23	9 M.	25.655	50.0	47.5	34.0	–	NNW.	1	10	
	12	25.625	63.0	59.0	40.0	–	N.	1	10	

TABLE—Continued.

Observations in Chihuahua—Continued.

Date.	Hour.	Barome-ter.	Thermometer, Fahrenheit.				Wind.	Sky.	Remarks.
			Attached.	Detached.	Wet bulb.	Dew point.			
1847.									
Mar. 23	3 A.	25.520	69.5	67.0	44.0	–	NW. 1	10	
24	9 M.	25.415	57.5	56.0	40.0	–	S. 1	9	
	12	25.370	74.0	74.0	53.0	–	S. 1	7	
	3 A.	25.300	77.5	77.5	52.0	–	SW. 1	3	
25	9 M.	25.585	60.0	60.0	42.5	–	NNE. 1	10	
	12	25.595	67.0	67.0	46.0	–	NNE. 1	10	
	3½ A.	25.615	67.5	67.5	46.0	–	N. 2	10	
26	12	25.570	68.5	64.5	44.0	–	ESE. 2	8	
	3 A.	25.675	69.0	67.0	45.0	–	E. 2	9	
27	9 M.	25.690	53.5	53.5	39.5	–	E. 1	10	
	12	25.680	72.0	70.0	48.0	–	ESE. 1	10	
	3 A.	25.605	75.5	75.0	49.5	–	ESE. 1	10	
28	9 M.	25.640	61.5	62.5	47.0	–	SE. 1	9	
	12	25.625	80.0	78.5	54.5	–	E. 1	4	
	3 A.	25.560	80.0	79.0	–	–	NE. 1	5	
29	12	25.490	84.5	81.0	55.0	–	NE. 1	4	
	3 A.	25.385	85.5	84.0	56.0	–	E. 2	6	
30	9 M.	25.420	68.0	70.5	51.0	–	W. 1	5	
	12½ A.	25.410	82.5	82.5	55.0	–	SW. 1	6	
	3 A.	25.340	85.0	84.5	54.0	–	NW. 1	4	
31	9 M.	25.460	69.0	69.5	51.0	–	SW. 1	5	
	12	25.460	84.5	82.5	55.0	–	NE. 1	4	
	3 A.	25.375	84.0	85.0	58.0	–	NE. 1	4	
April 1	9 M.	25.570	72.0	72.0	53.0	–	W. 1	6	
	12	25.530	81.5	81.5	56.0	–	SW. 1	4	
	3 A.	25.490	88.0	86.0	55.0	–	SSW. 2	4	
15	12	25.685	54.5	49.5	47.5	–	NE. 1	0	Last night fell the first rain in Chihuahua since the rainy season of last year.
	3 A.	25.670	56.0	50.5	47.0	–	NW. 1	1	

The mean of all my barometrical and thermometrical observations made in Chihuahua, is:—Barometer, 25″.5097; Thermometer attached, 68.82; Thermometer detached, 69.93: or, Barometer, (with temperature of mercury reduced to 32° Fahrenheit,) 25″.42608.

Highest stand of Barometer, (reduced to 32° Fahrenheit,) 25″.717.
Lowest stand of Barometer, (reduced to 32° Fahrenheit,) 25″.137.

To the favor of Mr. J. Potts, in Chihuahua, I am indebted for the following table of the quantity (in inches) of rain that fell in the city of Chihuahua in the years 1843, 1844, and 1845:

January	-	-	0.17	0.09	0.00
February	-	-	0.00	2.61	1.90
March	-	-	0.02	0.00	0.76
April	-	-	0.00	0.00	0.00
May	-	-	0.07	0.00	0.00
June	-	-	0.83	2.05	1.28
July	-	-	7.73	8.37	9.45
August	-	-	6.33	5.73	6.02
September	-	-	3.66	6.10	5.93
October	-	-	0.00	2.00	1.14
November	-	-	3.35	0.00	0.07
December	-	-	0.00	0.00	0.00
			22.16	26.95	26.55

9

TABLE—Continued.

Date.	Hour.	Barometer.	Thermometer, Fah.			Wind.		Sky.	Remarks.
			Attached.	Detached.	Wet bulb.				
1847. Jan. 6	9 M.	23.840	48.0	49.0	34.0	N.	3	9	Observations made in Cosi-
	3 A.	23.805	50.0	56.0	38.0	N.	3	0	huiriachi, about ninety miles
7	9 M.	24.040	47.0	43.0	34.0	sw.	1	10	wsw. of Chihuahua, in the
	12½ A.	23.955	45.5	46.0	35.5	sw.	1	10	Sierra Madre.
	3	23.925	48.0	47.0	38.0	sw.	1	8	
8	10 M.	23.830	46.5	52.5	–	se.	3	5	
	12	23.745	50.0	57.0	39.5	nw.	2	6	
	3 A.	23.740	54.0	60.0	–	nw.	3	4	
9	9 M.	23.825	47.0	48.5	36.5	se.	2	8	
	12½	23.720	54.5	56.0	39.0	N.	3	1	
	3 A.	23.720	52.0	50.0	–	N.	1	0	The mean of all my baro-
10	10 M.	23.840	49.0	49.0	–		0	7	metrical and thermometri-
	3 A.	23.760	50.0	53.5	39.0	N.	2	10	cal observations made in Co-
11	9 M.	23.980	44.5	44.5	–	s.	2	10	sihuiriachi, is:—Barometer,
	12	23.875	49.0	50.0	40.0	NE.	3	10	23″.898 ; Thermo. attached,
12	Sunrise	–	–	34.0	–	N.	2	3	51.05 ; Thermo. detached,
	9 M.	23.960	46.0	44.0	38.5	s.	2	5	53.3 : or, Barometer, (with
	12½ A.	23.895	48.5	53.5	42.0	s.	2	5	temperature of mercury re-
	3 A.	23 885	48.5	52.0	41.0	s.	2	2	duced to 32° Fahrenheit,)
13	9 M.	24.010	46.0	49.0	40.0	N.	1	4	= 23″.857.
	12½	23.930	49.5	60.0	44.5	N.	2	2	
	3 A.	23.920	53.0	62.0	47.0	s.	2	5	
14	9½ M.	23.945	52.0	56.0	47.0	N.	2	5	
	12½ A.	23.870	57.5	64.5	49.0	s.	3	7	
	3	23.870	57.0	65.5	47.0	N.	3	5	
15	9 M.	23.880	53.5	56.0	47.0	se.	3	8	
	12	23.840	57.5	60.0	49.0	NE.	3	0	
	3 A.	23.810	57.5	59.0	–	NE.	3	3	In the afternoon, drizzling rain.
16	9 M.	23.985	51.5	53.5	46.0	s.	1	10	Observation in Cosihuiriachi.
	12	22.640	61.5	59.0	43.0	s.	3	9	Observation made on sum- mit of " Bufa," the highest mountain in the neighbor- hood.
	3 A.	23.910	58.5	64.0	45.5	s.	2	9	Observation in Cosihuiriachi.

TABLE—Continued.

Date	Hour	Barometer	Thermometer, Fahrenheit. Attached	Detached	Wind	Sky	Elevation above sea, in English feet	From last camp	From Chihuahua	Camping places	Remarks
1847. April 27	5½ M.	26.130	59.7	59.5	E. 1	5	3,956	-	32	Night camp, in Bachimba -	Observations made during the march of Col. Doniphan's regiment from Chihuahua to Monterey.
28	9 M.	26.240	74.0	73.5	sw. 1	7	3,915	20	52	Night camp, 1 mile S. of Santa Cruz.	
	12	26.195	89.0	86.5	NW. 1	7	-	-	-	Do. do.	
	3 A.	26.190	95.0	90.0	NE. 1	5	-	-	-	Do. do.	
29	3½ M.	26.180	90.0	88.5	sw. 2	2	3,955	23	75	Night camp, in El Saucillo.	
May 1	9¼ A.	26.145	89.5	83.0	NW. 2	5	4,019	30	105	Night camp, near Santa Rosalia.	
	1 A.	26.115	95.0	90.0	NW. 1	3	-	-	-	Do. do.	
2	3 A.	25.790	86.0	85.0	E. 2	5	4,318	24	129	Night camp, near La Ramada.	
3	4 A.	25.615	81.0	82.0	ESE. 2	5	4,490	33	162	Night camp, in Guajuquilla.	
4	Sunrise	25.680	56.0	56.0	0	7	-	-	-	Do. do.	
5	12	25.595	89.0	85.0	E. 2	5	4,607	3	165	Noon camp, at Hacienda de Dolores.	Observation made during the march, on a high table land, nearly in the middle between Guajuquilla and San Bernardo, which divides the waters of the Conchos and Rio Grande.
	9 M.	25.470	75.0	75.0	ESE. 2	5	4,706	-	-	Do. do. -	
6	Sunrise	25.615	63.0	65.0	sw. 1	8	4,577	60	225	Night camp, at San Bernardo springs.	
	4 A.	25.585	97.5	98.5	w. 2	5	4,643	10	235	Night camp at El Andabazo, or Cerro Gordo creek.	
7	4 A.	25.500	90.5	90.5	NE. 1	4	4,719	25	260	Night camp, at San José Pelayo.	
8	4 A.	25.220	95.5	94.0	sw. 1	6	5,056	18	278	Night camp, at Cadena.	
9	3 A.	25.725	96.5	98.0	w. 2	7	4,487	21	299	Night camp, in Mapimi.	
10	6 A.	26.325	87.5	81.0	SE. 1	5	3,785	35	334	Night camp in San Sebastian, on Nasas river.	
11	5 A.	26.310	91.5	93.0	NW. 1	8	3,815	24	358	Night camp in San Lorenzo, on Nasas river.	

TABLE—Continued.

Date.	Hour.	Barometer.	Thermometer, Fahrenheit. Attached.	Thermometer, Fahrenheit. Detached.	Wind.	Sky.	Elevation above sea, in English feet.	Supposed distances, in English miles. From last camp.	Supposed distances, in English miles. From Chihuahua.	Camping places.	Remarks.
1847. May 12	3 A.	26.365	100.0	99.0	NW. 1	5	3,770	15	373	Night camp at San Juan Bautista, on Nasas river.	
13	5 A.	26.150	92.0	93.0	W. 2	7	3,990	25	398	Night camp, at El Pozo.	
15	12 A.	25.220	83.0	84.0	NW. 2	5	4,987	26	424	Night camp, in Parras.	
16	12 A.	25.275	83.5	83.0	NW. 1	6	-	-	-	Do. do.	
	3 A.	25.210	82.0	83.0	W. 2	6	-	-	-	Do. do.	
17	6 A.	25.910	84.5	85.0	NW. 1	4	4,209	25	449	Night camp, in Cienega Grande.	
18	3½ A.	25.485	72.0	71.0	E. 3	8	4,717	18	467	Night camp, near Rancho Nuevo -	Thunder-storm and rain, on 19th, from 4 to 6 A.
20	5½ M.	25.285	84.0	84.5	W. 1	3	4,880	25	492	Night camp, at Vequeria.	
21	3½ A.	24.435	63.5	64.0	E. 2	1	5,920	22	514	Night camp, at San Juan.	
22	12 M.	24.260	81.0	82.5	N. 2	5	6,104	10	524	Night camp, at Encantada.	
	9 M.	24.270	77.0	75.5	N. 3	5	-	-	-	Do. do.	
23	9 M.	24.255	70.5	72.5	SE. 2	2	-	-	-	Do. do.	
	9 M.	25.010	79.0	79.0	NW. 3	9	5,242	12	536	Saltillo -	The observation is made near the Plaza, in the hotel of the "Great Western."
24	6 A.	25.215	76.5	76.5	SW. 1	6	4,955	6	542	Night camp, NE. of Saltillo.	
25	5½ M.	25.265	67.0	66.5	N. 1	6	-	-	-	Do. do.	
	5½ ·	26.665	68.5	68.0		3	3,381	30	572	Night camp, at Rinconada -	Thunder-storm and rain, in the evening of the 25th.
26	9½ M.	28.425	74.5	74.5		0	1,626	28	600	Monterey, near Plaza.	
	4 A.	28.440	77.0	77.0	S. 1	1	1,658	4	604	Night camp at Walnut springs, Gen. Taylor's camp.	
27	5½ M.	28.450	62.0	62.0		10	-	-	-	Do. do.	
28	5½ M.	28.795	63.0	63.0	E. 2	0	1,354	20	624	Night camp, in Marin.	

Date	Time	Barometer			Wind						Location	Remarks
29	6 M.	29.015	72.0	72.0	sw	0	7	1,107	33	657	Night camp, at Carrizitos.	The observation is made about 10 feet above the level of the river.
	1½ A.	29.205	94.0	94.0	SE.	2	10	1,006	7	664	Noon camp, in Cerralvo.	The observations on mouth of Rio Grande are made on the flat river bank, about 1 mile from the sea, and about .5 feet above the level of the sea. The mean of these observations is:—Barometer, 30″.170; Thermometer, attached and detached, 85.9 Fahrenheit: or, Barometer, (temperature of mercury reduced to 32° Fahrenheit,) 30″.025.
30	6 M.	29.365	73.0	73.0	SE.	2	9	708	15	679	Night camp, in Puntiagudo.	
31	4½ M.	29.695	77.5	77.5	s.	2	8	417	30	709	Night camp, at Mier.	
	6 A.	29.740	90.0	90.0	E.	3	7	422	25	734	Night camp, at Camargo.	
June 1	8½ M.	30.000	86.5	86.5	ESE.	2	4	184	48	782	Reynosa, on Rio Grande -	-
6	6 M.	30.255	82.0	82.0	ESE.	2	8	-	-	-	Mouth of Rio Grande -	-
7	9 M.	30.110	87.0	87.0	ESE.	3	8	-	-	-	Do. do.	-
	9 M.	30.075	86.0	86.0	ESE.	4	7	-	-	-	Do. do.	-
8	3 A.	30.070	88.5	88.5	ESE.	3	9	-	-	-	Do. do.	-

THE GEOLOGICAL SKETCH,

Which I have drawn, does not make any pretensions to a geological map, which even a more able geologist than I am could not give in the short time and haste, in which I travelled through that country, but it may elucidate and concentrate at least what little information I have acquired in relation to that object. To make it more intelligible, I will add yet a short summary of the various geological observations spread over the whole extent of the journal.

Independence, near the western frontier of the State of Missouri, is situated in the great Missouri coal basin, which occupies more than one-third of that State.

The first rock in situ which I saw in the prairie, after leaving Independence, was on Rock creek, (about 79 miles from Independence.) It was a yellow-brownish compact limestone, with encrinites, and similar fossils of the carboniferous limestone, as found in Missouri.

On Pleasant Valley creek (125 miles) the bluffs are formed by two different limestones: the one is white and compact; the other grayish, soft, and argillaceous. The first contained some indistinct fossils, but in too imperfect a state to determine what formation they indicate.

In Council grove (143 miles) a horizontal, grayish, argillaceous limestone prevails, without fossils.

Leaving Cottonwood creek (185 miles,) irregular heaps of bog-ore are seen in the prairie, and a ferruginous sandstone of yellow, brown, and blue color, extends from here to Pawnee fork, (a distance of about 100 miles.)

The bluffs of the Little Arkansas consisted of a spotted, yellow, calcareous sandstone, and isolated pieces of ferruginous sandstone.

Between Camp Osage (the first camp near the Arkansas river) and Walnut creek, (263 miles,) I met with a very porous and scoriaceous rock in situ, apparently the product of action of subterranean fires upon the ferruginous sandstone. Most likely a large coal-field lying beneath here has become ignited, and produced this change of the rock. The so-called Pawnee rock (between Walnut creek and Ash creek) consists of the same ferruginous sandstone, changed by fire. On Pawnee fork (292 miles) I saw the last of it; the ferruginous sandstone there was more compact, and deep red.

On a branch of Big Coon creek (332 miles) I found the bluffs to consist of common standstone below, and a white, fine-grained marl above it. This marl resembles very much some from the cretaceous formation of the Upper Missouri; but finding no fossils, I could not ascertain it.

Two miles beyond that place (341 from Independence,) I had the first chance to examine the bluffs on the Arkansas; it was a grayish, conglomerated limestone, with a few small fossils, that were rather imperfect, but seemed to belong to the cretaceous formation. The neighborhood of the above mentioned marl raises this presumption nearly to certainty. I have, therefore, not hesitated to lay it down as cretaceous formation. About 20 miles higher up on the Arkansas, I saw, upon a second examination, but a coarse conglomerate of sand and limestone. At the usual fording place (373 miles,) where I left the Arkansas for the Cimarron, no rocks were in situ.

Having crossed the Arkansas, I met with the first rocks again, on the "middle springs of Cimarron," (468 miles;) it was a sandy limestone above common sandstone.

Six miles west of the Crossing of Cimarron (500 miles from Independence,) light bluffs rise in the prairie, of a yellow, reddish, and spotted sandstone, combined with lime and argile.

A few miles beyond them a large, isolated mountain of boulders stands in the plains, composed of heavy blocks of quartz and quartzose sandstone, and many erratic rocks were afterwards found on our road.

On Cedar creek, McNees' creek, and Cottonwood branch, a yellow sandstone prevailed.

On Rabbit-ear creek I met for the first time with amygdaloidal basalt, a black, heavy, basaltic rock, with a great many irregular, vesicular cavities, that are generally hollow—sometimes, too, filled with lime; in rare instances, with olivin. This rock is most common throughout the high mountains of Mexico. It occurs in most irregular masses, in whole mountains, as well as in millions of pieces strewn over the surface of the country. Here it rose in high perpendicular walls, as bluffs of the creek, and a very compact quartzose sandstone was below in horizontal layer.

The Round mound, a mountain in the prairie about three miles further west, which I ascended, is formed of a brown, decomposed basaltic rock.

On Rock creek, and Whetstone creek, the amygdaloidal basalt with underlaying sandstone was found.

In going from there to "Point of Rocks," (600 miles,) extensive strata of a yellow, compact quartzose sandstone are passed, dipping gently towards the east. Point of Rocks itself, a spur of the western mountains, is a mass of sienite.

Some 12 miles beyond it, rises a hill in the plains, composed of very compact, black basalt, with underlaying white sandstone.

The bed and bluffs of the Rio Colorado and Ocaté creek (627 miles,) are formed by quartzose sandstone.

The Wagon mound, an isolated mountain in the high plain, consists of a compact, black, and spotted basalt, rising in columnar shape.

On Wolf creek (664 miles) the amygdaloidal basalt and quartzose sandstone reappeared, both in horizontal layers.

Reaching the Gallinas creek, near las Vegas, (690 miles,) I met, after a long interval, with limestone again. It was a dark blue, with casts of Inoceramus of the cretaceous series.

From here we penetrated into the very heart of the mountains. At first we met but with sandstone, common and quartzose, and of most different colors.

Near San Miguel (707 miles,) a coarse conglomerate was found of decomposed granite, sandstone, and lime, and large blocks of decomposed granite lined the Pecos river, opposite the old Pecos village, (737 miles.)

In the cañon leading from here to Santa Fe, at first sandstone is found, common, quartzose, and calcareous, of various colors and granulations, till about 15 miles from Santa Fe, granite in situ appears, and continues all the way to Santa Fe. Near where I met for the first time with granite in situ, the sandstone, if I may judge from a very limited examination, was suddenly uplifted and thrown back in an angle of nearly 100 degrees.

West of Santa Fe, granite seems also to prevail. In my excursion to the Placers, southwest of Santa Fe, I found sandstone below, and on the height of the mountains granite and trap rocks.

In the mountains of that neighborhood common limestone and sulphate of lime are said to exist; but on the road over which I travelled I had no chance to see any.

Granitic and trap formations seem to predominate, too, in the valley of the Rio del Norte below Santa Fe; but as the road leads always along the river, and the mountains on either side are generally about 10 miles distant, I could not examine them as I wished to do, and had often to depend alone upon the external form of the mountain chain, apparently indicating unstratified and igneous rocks. Whenever the mountains approached the river, I gained more information. So, for instance, I found between Joyita and Joya (about 115 miles from Santa Fe) quartzose sandstone and quartz in a spur of the eastern mountain chain; and in Joyita itself, bluffs near the river of amygdaloidal basalt.

Some miles west of Socorro, (140 miles,) on the right bank of the river, I examined the western mountains, and found porphyritic and trachitic rocks.

Near the ruins of Valverde (165 miles) I met with bluffs of a dark-brown, nodular sandstone; and about eight miles beyond, with amygdaloidal basalt again.

In the Jornada del Muerto granitic and basaltic formation, to judge from their shape, exists in the distant mountain chains; part of them in the eastern chains is called, for their basaltic appearance, Organ mountains.

Below Doñana I perceived some primitive rocks again, near the river, resembling a decomposed porphyry.

The mountains above el Paso belong mainly to the trap formation.

During my short stay in el Paso I made an excursion to the southwestern mountains of the valley, and was rather astonished to find mountains of limestone. The foot of the mountains was formed by a horizontal quartzose standstone, similar to that underlaying the amygdaloidal basalt. The very compact and gray limestone, intersected with many white veins of calcspar, rose upon it to the crest of the mountains; but on several places, granite and greenstone seemed to have burst through it and formed partial eruptions. After a long search I discovered some fossils, and though much injured and imperfect, they are nevertheless sufficient to determine the age of this formation. The fossils are a coral: *Calamopora*, and a bivalve shell of the genus *Pterinea*. This limestone is therefore a Silurian rock. Several mines have formerly been worked in it.

On the road from el Paso to Chihuahua I met in the first day or two with the same limestone. The pieces lying on the road were generally surrounded with a white crust of carbonate of lime; pieces, too, of what appeared to be fresh-water limestone, occurred. It is rather probable that this is the same material as the white crust of the blue limestone, and that both are the result of calcareous springs.

About 50 miles south of el Paso the limestone seems to cease, and porphyritic rocks of the most varied colors and combinations continued from here as far as Chihuahua, interrupted sometimes only by granitic rocks. The base of the porphyry is generally felspar.

Around Chihuahua and some distance to the south and west of it, in the Sierra Madre, porphyritic rocks predominate, and valuable mines are found in them.

Near Chihuahua, I understood, about 12 miles northeast of it, mountains of limestone appear; and through the favor of Mr. Potts, in Chihuahua, I received a piece of limestone from there, containing some casts of the chambers of an Orthoceras, proving that this limestone belongs also to the Silurian system. Mines are also found in it.

Another fossil I received in Chihuahua, said to come from the limestone near Corralitas, a mining place about 250 miles northwest of Chihuahua. It is a Pecten quinquecostatus (Sowerby,) of the cretaceous series; but not having travelled through that part of the State, I am not able to give any comment upon it.

From Chihuahua to Matamoros, travelling with the army as a surgeon, my time was so occupied that I could not make any distant excursions from the road; but generally, too, the geology of the country seemed to be very uniform and uninteresting.

From Chihuahua some distance south, the porphyritic rocks continued. In Saucillo (70 miles from Chihuahua) I perceived the first limestone again. From there to Santa Rosalia I passed some hills of amygdaloidal basalt, but the main chain of the mountains was all limestone, and continued to be so throughout the whole eastern ramification of the Sierra Madre, over which we travelled from here down to Saltillo and Monterey, where the low country begins. This limestone forms steep, often rugged mountains, rising on an average 2,000 feet above the plain; it is metalliferous, and has all the appearance of the Silurian limestone, found at el Paso and Chihuahua, but I was never able to discover any fossils on this route. Silver and lead mines are of various occurrence in it; in the limestone surrounding Cadena, coal has been found, I was informed, but I had no time to verify it.

From Monterey to the seashore I made but one interesting discovery; near Mier. On the bank of the Alamo river, about four miles above its mouth into the Rio Grande, I found an extensive bed of large fossil shells of Ostrea, belonging to the cretaceous formation. As the same formation has lately been discovered by Dr. Roehmer, of Berlin, as extending in Texas from the San Antonio to the Brazos, this cretaceous bed near Mier is in all probability a continuation of it. In looking over the recent publication of " Notes of the upper Rio Grande, by Bryan Tilden," I found, in a description of the river bank of the Rio Grande below Laredo, that "entire hills are to be seen, composed almost wholly of what appears to be a collection of large sea oyster-shells." I presume, therefore, that the same cretaceous formation extends in this direction higher up on the Rio Grande.

THE MAP.

The map which accompanies this work is based, as far as my own route is concerned, upon astronomical observations made at the principal places, upon daily observations of the compass, and in regard to localities which I have not visited, upon the best authorities in existence. The latitude and longitude of many places in Mexico will be found to differ often widely from their positions on Mexican maps, which lay the latitudes generally too far north ; the longitudes too far east.

Being rather poorly provided with astronomical instruments; occupied, besides that, in the most various pursuits, and having no scientific assistance whatever, I had to confine my astronomical observations only to the principal stations. But as on the northern part of my route many points had been already determined by former explorers, and in the southern part I enjoyed the valuable aid of Dr. J. Gregg, (as mentioned in the preface,) sufficient points have been ascertained for the practical purposes of a map, whose principal object is to enable the reader to follow my route and to correct the many gross errors, not only in minutes but even in degrees, that are commonly found in Mexican maps. In connecting my daily sketches, I have laid down the country only as far as it fell under my own observation, leaving to future explorers to ascertain the regions beyond that.

Taken as a whole, therefore, I believe that this map, though by no means as perfect as I wish it to be, will at least be found more correct than any other published at present of the northeastern part of Mexico; and although, on the two end points of my route, that have been explored also by the engineer corps of Generals Wool and Kearny, it will not be able to compete with their more elaborate maps, it may nevertheless deserve some credit for filling up a large intermediate space of nearly 1,000 miles between Santa Fe and Parras, where no engineer of the army has prepared a map of the country, and for connecting, in this way, the scientific labors of the two engineer corps attached to General Wool's and General Kearny's expeditions.

As my own route embraces in substance the long, celebrated march of Colonel Doniphan's regiment, it will afford for that reason additional interest to the public. Besides that, I have laid down the march of General Wool from Corpus Christi to Parras, and General Kearny's from Bent's Fort to Santa Fe, according to the unofficial memoranda of several officers of those corps, (I claim, therefore, no authenticity for them,) and have added all the rest of the most interesting routes that have ever been travelled from the United States and Texas, to New Mexico and Chihuahua.

THE BAROMETRICAL PROFILE.

If the elevation above the sea affords in other countries so probable a criterion for their climate and general character, that an elevation of 3,000 feet is considered equal in its effect upon the climate to nearly 10 degrees difference in latitude, an eminent proof of this rule is given in Mexico, where nature has combined, under the same degree of latitude, all variations of climate, from the tropical often to the coldest, by the mere difference in elevation above the sea.

Of the southern part of Mexico we possess already excellent profiles of the country, made by Alexander Von Humboldt, Burkhardt, and other scientific travellers; but of northern Mexico scarcely anything is known in that respect, and the series of elevations above the sea from Independence (Missouri) to Santa Fe, Chihuahua, Monterey, and the seashore, as represented in this profile, is the first one published, and will prove, as I am inclined to believe, highly interesting to every person that wishes to form for himself an opinion of the character of that country.

The calculations are based upon daily barometrical observations made by myself on the road, and cotemporaneous observations made by Dr. G. Engelmann in St. Louis, and by Mr. Lilly in New Orleans.

My barometer was a syphon barometer of 30 English inches. After having been filled with purified mercury, and boiled out several times, I compared it before my departure with Dr. Engelmann's, and found mine to be 0″.139 higher than the latter. After my return to St. Louis, another comparison proved it to be only 0″.123 higher: it had during the whole time changed but 0″.016—a most favorable result, if the long transportation of it by water and land, in carriages and on pack-mules, often over the roughest road, is considered.

The mean of my barometrical observations, made on the seashore, mouth of Rio Grande, was 30″.025, (the temperature of the mercury having been reduced to 32° Fahr.) By referring it to the cotemporaneous observations made in St. Louis, I calculated the elevation of St. Louis on the "city directrix," near the old market house, to be 420 feet above the sea. The city directrix is a well known and stable point, to which all the geometrical measurements in the city are at present reduced. It is supposed to be 38 feet 1 inch above the lowest water-mark of the river, and 7 feet 7 inches below the highest water-mark in 1844.

From Independence to Chihuahua I reduced my own observations to those made in St. Louis, by comparing my transient daily observations with the monthly mean of the St. Louis observations. From Chihuahua to Monterey I reduced them to the mean of my barometrical observations made in Chihuahua during summer, winter, and spring months, and containing, therefore, most likely the absolute mean of the whole year. From Monterey, where the low country begins, to the seashore, I reduced them to the observations of Mr. Lilly in New Orleans, to whom I am under obligations for a copy of his meteorological journal.

All the reductions and calculations have been made according to the known formula of Gauss.

MEXICAN COINS, MEASURES, AND WEIGHTS.

1 onza (gold)	= 16 dollars.
1 peso (silver)	= 1 dollar.
1 real (silver)	= $12\frac{1}{2}$ cents.
$\frac{1}{2}$ real (silver)	= $6\frac{1}{4}$ cents.
1 quartillo (copper)	= $3\frac{1}{8}$ cents.
1 tlaco (copper)	= $1\frac{9}{16}$ cent.

1 foot Mexican	= 0.928 foot English.
1 vara (3 feet Mexican)	= 2.784 ft. Eng. = 2 ft. 9.3141 inches Engl.
1 legua (26.63 to 1 meridian)	= 5,000 varas = 2.636 miles English.

1 onza (8 ochavos)	= 1 ounce.
1 marco (8 onzas)	= $\frac{1}{2}$ pound.
1 libra (2 marcos)	= 1 pound.
1 arroba (25 libras)	= 25 pounds.
1 quintal (4 arrobas)	= 100 pounds.
1 carga (3 quintals)	= 300 pounds.
1 fanega (140 pounds)	= about 2 bushels.
1 almuer (almuerza)	= $\frac{1}{12}$ of a fanega.
1 frasco	= about 5 pints.

ERRATA.

Page 4, line 26 from top,	for I. Gregg,	read J. Gregg.
" 8, " 10 "	" Willowgreen,	" Willow creek.
" 12, " 20 "	" mirage,	" *the* mirage.
" 14, " 7 from bottom,	" Salvador,	" Salvator.
" 17, " 6 "	" Armija,	" Armijo.
" 18, " 6 from top,	" or the Rio,	" on the Rio.
" 21, last line,	" 27 miles,	" 27 leagues.
" 36, " 15 from top,	" mimmoseae,	" mimoseae.
" 45, " 2 from bottom,	" Oj,	" Ojo.
" 46, " 23 "	" effervescence,	" efflorescence.
" 56, " 15 from top,	" feet more,	" feet, more.
" 66, " 12 from bottom,	" northeast,	" northwest.
" 69, " 22 "	" 24 miles to San Lorenzo,	" to San Lorenzo, (24 miles.)
" 70, " 11 "	" southern,	" northern.
" 71, " 22 & 43 from top,	" Captain Ried,	" Captain Reid.
" 76, " 11 from bottom,	" Moleno de Jusus,	" Molino de Jesus.
" 77, " 15 from top,	" stone,	" straw.
" 78, " 3 "	" tree ; a mimosea,	" tree, a mimosea.
" 78, " 5 "	" mineral,	" animal.

This book was indexed with the historian rather than the botanist in mind. Therefore, Dr. Engelmann's description of Dr. Wislizenus' botanical collection was indexed for personal names only. An index of the technical Latin terms for the local flora would have created a tail much longer than the dog, and would have been of little practical use to any reader.

Dr. Wislizenus, ordinarily a most meticulous note taker, frequently fell afoul of the Spanish language. His spelling is generally accurate, but his use of terms is not consistent. The reader is constantly confronted with rios and rivers; lagos, lagunas and lakes, sierras and mountains, often all referring to the same place. Cross references have been made in most cases, but the reader is exhorted to search under all variations if the desired reference is not found under the accepted form.

William H. Farrington

Santa Fe, N. M.

Index

Abiquiu, N. M.—24
Abo, N. M.—24
Acha Mountains—22
Agua de Leon spring—67
Agua Fria, N. M.—29,34
Agua Fria, N. L.—77
Agua Negra, N. L.—78
Aid, a steamboat—80
Alamito, Dur.—68,69
Alamo de Parras, Mex.—69
Alamo River—22,78,79.138
Alamos, N. M.—39
Alamos de Pinos—35
Albuquerque, N. M.—22,29,33,34,40
Alcontre River (see Alamos River)
Algodones, N. M.—24,29,34
Allende, Ignacio—60
Alvarez, Mr.   —29
American Hotel, Chi.—48,50
Ampudia, Gen. Pedro de—76
Andabago Creek—66,67
Andes Mountains—54
Angostura, Mex.—75
Apache Indians—53,57,59
Arkansas River—7,8,9,10,11,13,14,20,
   22,36,55,87,135,136
Arkansas troops—74
Armijo, Manuel—11,16,17,19,20,27,29,
   33,48,49
Arroyo Seco, Chi.—47
Ash Creek—7,9,10,135
Aztec Indians—60

Bachimba, Chi.—62,63
Bagdad, Tex.—81
Barilla, N. M.—39
Batopilas mines—57
Battle Ground—11
Benton, Sen. Thomas H.—2,4
Bent's Fort—8,10,11,139
Big Blue camp—5,7
Big Coon Creek—10,135
Big Cow Creek—8
Big John Creek—7
Big Turkey Creek—8
Bill, Mr.   (cook)—51
Black Jack Point—6
Bluff Creek—7
Bolson de Mapimi—2,67,68,69,70,71,72,
   85
Bonanza, N. M.—31
Bonillo, Francisco de Levya (see
   Levya, Bonillo Francisco de)
Boonville, Mo.—61
Bradbury, John—9n
Brazito, Battle of—53,54
Brazito, N. M.—39,41
Brazos River—138
Brazos Santiago—81
Bridge Creek—6
Buena Vista, Mex.—74
Buena Vista, battle of—55,61,75,77
Bufa Mountain—51,53
Bufa mine—52
Burkhardt, Mr.   —140

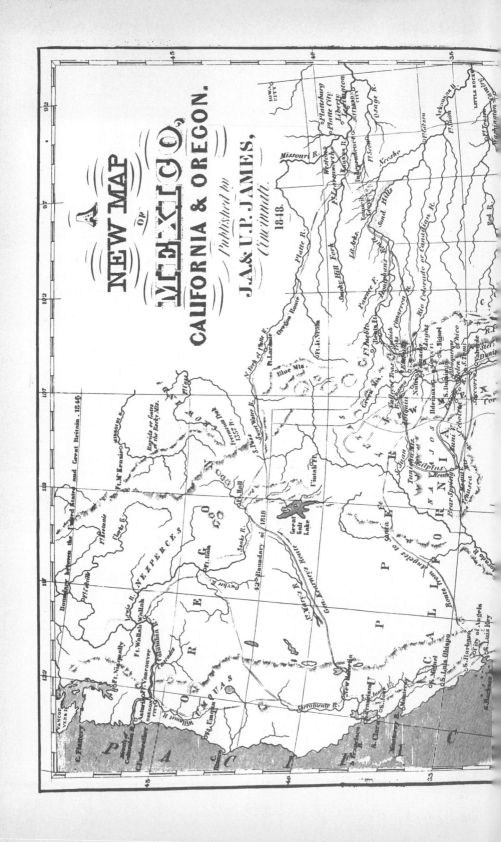